THE FAMILY
Handyman.

Our best
Storage &
Organizing
projects

THE FAMILY
Handyman

Our best Storage & Organizing projects

by The editors of *The Family Handyman* magazine and familyhandyman.com

The Family Handyman Our Best Storage & Organizing Projects

(See page 288 for complete staff listing.)
Editor in Chief: Ken Collier
Project Editor: Mary Flanagan
Designer: Barbara Pederson
Cover Design: Marcia Roepke
Contributing Copy Editors: Donna Bierbach, Peggy Parker
Indexing: Stephanie Reymann

Vice President, Integrated Solutions & Digital Development: Dan Meehan

The Reader's Digest Association, Inc.
President & Chief Executive Officer: Tom Williams
President, North America: Dan Lagani
Associate Publisher: Chris Dolan

Warning: All do-it-yourself activities involve a degree of risk. Skills, materials, tools, and site conditions vary widely. Although the editors have made every effort to ensure accuracy, the reader remains responsible for the selection and use of tools, materials, and methods. Always obey local codes and laws, follow manufacturer's operating instructions, and observe safety precautions.

ISBN 978-1-60652-426-8   1-60652-426-7

Address any comments about *Our Best Storage & Organizing Projects* to:
Editor, Storage & Organizing book 2011
2915 Commers Drive, Suite 700
Eagan, MN 55121

To order additional copies of *Our Best Storage & Organizing Projects*, call 1-800-344-2560.

For more Reader's Digest products and information, visit our Web site at rd.com.
For more about *The Family Handyman* magazine, visit familyhandyman.com.

Printed in the United States of America.
1 3 5 7 9 10 8 6 4 2

Introduction

> "Organizing is what you do before you do something, so that when you do it, it is not all mixed up."
>
> *A. A. Milne*

If your goal is to have a place for everything and everything in its place, you may never succeed. However, if your goal is to be able to stow the majority of your stuff and find it when you need it, congratulations! With the help of *Our Best Storage & Organizing Projects*, your goal is within reach. And you don't have to spend a lot of money. All the projects in this book are completely DIY. With just beginning to intermediate skills and basic tools, you can create your own storage solutions.

If your kitchen is the source of your biggest storage-space headaches, our cabinet rollouts are a sure cure. In an afternoon you can turn those long-lost areas in the way back of your cabinets into usable storage space! The garage is another common trouble spot, but with more than 60 pages of wall systems, racks, bins and cabinets, this book will help you corral the clutter so you can actually park your car in the garage.

Closets and entryways provide their own unique set of storage and organizing challenges. It's disheartening to come home to a mound of shoes inside the door and a closet overflowing with jackets, umbrellas, caps and backpacks. Choose from three different DIY closet organizer systems and dozens of tips to help you rein in the mess for less.

We haven't forgotten the two areas of your home where you go to get away—the bathroom and the workshop. Both are usually small and filled with lots of necessary items, so we've included plans for three workbenches and simple ways to get the most from any vanity cabinet.

And no book on storage and organizing would be complete without bookcase and shelving plans. We've included everything from a classic bookcase to shelves you can put up in minutes!

Our goal is to help you store and organize so that when you go to cook dinner, grab the camping gear or find your favorite wrench, as A. A. Milne puts it, "it's not all mixed up." If your goal is a less mixed-up home, you've come to the right place.

The editors of *The Family Handyman* magazine and familyhandyman.com

Contents

Chapter 4: Garage

Chapter 5: Outdoor

Kitchen

10

29

39

Kitchen cabinet rollout trays & bins

Rollout trays

Base cabinets have the least convenient storage space in the entire kitchen. Rollouts solve that problem. They make organizing and accessing your cabinet contents back-friendly and frustration free.

If you're stuck with cabinets without rollouts, don't despair. Here you'll learn how to retrofit nearly any base cabinet with rollouts that'll work as well as or better than any factory-built units.

It's really very easy. Once you take measurements, you can build the rollout tray (Photos 2–6), its "carrier" (Photos 7–9), and attach the drawer slides (Photos 6 and 7), all in your shop. Mounting the unit in the cabinet is simple (Photos 10–12). You'll also learn how to construct a special rollout for recycling or trash (Photos 14–15).

The project will go faster if you have a table saw and miter saw to cut out all the pieces. A circular saw and cutting guide will work too; it'll just take a little longer. You can build a pair of rollouts in a Saturday morning for about $20 per pair.

What wood products to buy

These rollout trays are made entirely of 1/2-in. Baltic birch plywood. Baltic birch is favored by cabinetmakers because it's "void free," meaning that the thin veneers of the plywood core are solid wood. Therefore sanded edges will look smooth and attractive. If your local home center doesn't stock Baltic birch, find it at any hardwood specialty store.

If you choose, you can make the sides of the rollout trays from any 1x4 solid wood that matches your cabinets and then finish to match (use plywood for the bases). But if you use 3/4-in. material for the sides, subtract 3 in. from the opening to size the rollout (not 2-1/2 in., as described in Photo 2 and Figure A).

The tray carriers (Figure A) are made from pine 1x4s for the sides (Photo 7) and 1/4-in. MDF (medium-density fiberboard) for the bottoms (Photo 9). The MDF keeps the tray bottom spaced properly while you shim and attach it to the cabinet sides. It can be removed and reused for other carriers after installation. If MDF isn't available, substitute any other 1/4-in. hardboard or plywood.

Side-mounted slides are the best choice among drawer slide options. Their ball-bearing mechanisms and precise fit make for smooth-operating trays that hold 90 lbs. or more. Shown here are 22-in. full-extension KV (800-253-1561; knapeandvogt.com) brand side-mount drawer slides that have a 90-lb. weight rating. That means they'll be sturdy enough even for a tray full of canned goods. Full-extension slides allow the rollout to extend completely past the cabinet front so you can access all the contents. Expect to pay about $20 per set of slides at any home center or well-stocked hardware store.

Measure carefully before you build

Nearly all standard base cabinets are 23-1/4 in. deep from the inside of the face frame (Photo 1) to the back of the cabinet. So in most cases, 22-in.-long rollout tray and carrier sides will clear with room to spare. Check your cabinets to make sure that 22-in. rollouts will work. If you have shallower cabinets, subtract whatever is necessary when you build your rollouts and their carriers (see Figure A).

Then measure the cabinet width. The tray has to clear the narrowest part of the opening (Photo 1). When taking this measurement, include hinges that

1 Open the cabinet doors to their widest point and measure the narrowest part of the cabinet opening (usually at the hinges).

Figure A:
Standard rollout tray

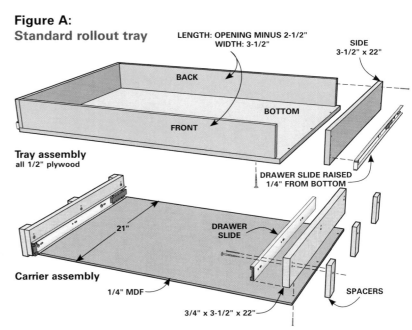

LENGTH: OPENING MINUS 2-1/2"
WIDTH: 3-1/2"

SIDE 3-1/2" x 22"

BACK

BOTTOM

FRONT

Tray assembly all 1/2" plywood

DRAWER SLIDE RAISED 1/4" FROM BOTTOM

21"

DRAWER SLIDE

Carrier assembly

1/4" MDF

3/4" x 3-1/2" x 22"

SPACERS

Figure B:
Wastebasket tray

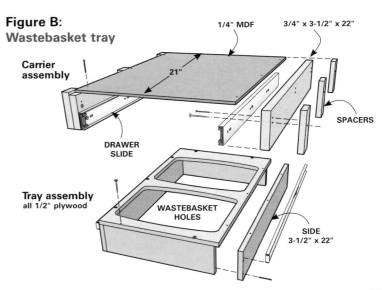

1/4" MDF

3/4" x 3-1/2" x 22"

Carrier assembly

21"

SPACERS

DRAWER SLIDE

Tray assembly all 1/2" plywood

WASTEBASKET HOLES

SIDE 3-1/2" x 22"

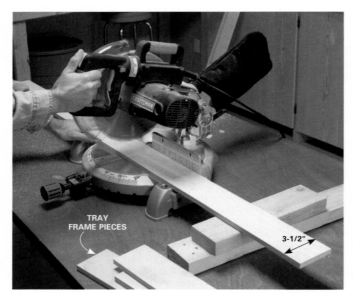

2 Rip 1/2-in. plywood down to 3-1/2 in. wide and cut two 22-in. lengths (tray sides) and two more to the measured width minus 2-1/2 in. (tray front and back; Figure A).

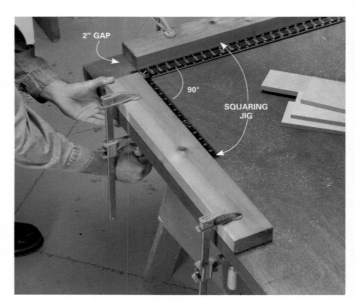

3 Clamp or screw two straight 24-in. 2x4s to the corner of a flat surface to use as a squaring jig. Use a carpenter's square to ensure squareness. Leave a 2-in. gap at the corner.

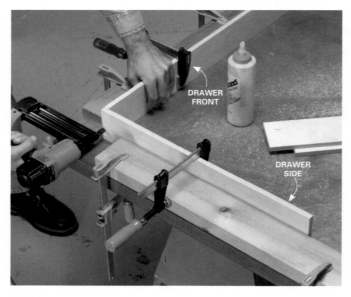

4 Spread wood glue on the ends and clamp a tray side and front in place, then pin the corner together with three 1-1/4-in. brads. Repeat for the other three corners.

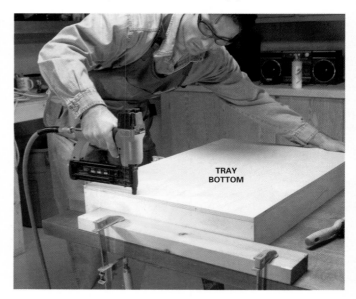

5 Cut a 1/2-in. plywood bottom to size. Apply a thin bead of glue to the bottom edges, and nail one edge of the plywood flush with a side, spacing nails every 4 in. Then push the frame against the jig to square it and nail the other three edges.

protrude into the opening, the edge of the door attached to the hinges, and even the doors that won't open completely because they hit nearby appliances or other cabinets. Plan on making the tray front and rear parts 2-1/2 in. shorter than the opening (Figure A).

Shown here are trays with 3-1/2-in.-high sides, but you can customize your own. Plan on higher sides for lightweight plastic storage containers or other tall or tippy items, and lower sides for stable, heavier items like small appliances.

Drawer slides aren't as confusing as they may seem

At first glance, drawer slides are pretty hard to figure out, but after you install one set, you'll be an expert. They're sold in pairs and each of the pairs has two parts. The "drawer part" attaches to the rollout while the "cabinet part" attaches to the carrier. To separate them for mounting, slide them out to full length and then push, pull or depress a plastic release to separate the two parts. The cabinet part, which always encloses the drawer part, is the larger of the two, and the mounting screw hole locations will be shown in the directions. (Screws are included with the drawer slides.) The oversized holes allow for some adjustment, but if you follow the instructions, you shouldn't have to fuss with fine-tuning later. When mounting the slides, you should make sure to hold them flush with the front of the rollout drawer and carrier sides (Photos 6 and 7). The front of the drawer part usually has a bent metal stop that faces the front of the drawer (or tray).

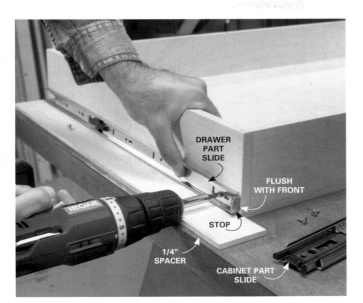

6 Separate the drawer slides and space the drawer part 1/4 in. up from the bottom. Hold it flush to the front and screw it to the tray side.

Labels: DRAWER PART SLIDE, FLUSH WITH FRONT, STOP, 1/4" SPACER, CABINET PART SLIDE

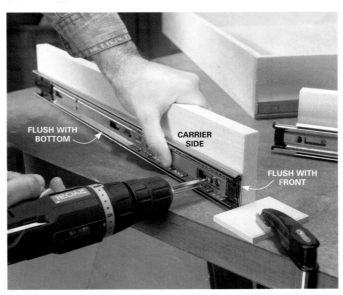

7 Mount the carrier part of the drawer slide flush with the bottom and front of the carrier sides.

Labels: FLUSH WITH BOTTOM, CARRIER SIDE, FLUSH WITH FRONT

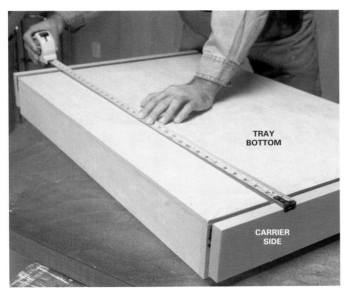

8 Slide the tray and carrier sides together and measure the carrier width. Cut 1/4-in. MDF to that width and 1 in. less than the carrier depth (usually 21 in.).

Labels: TRAY BOTTOM, CARRIER SIDE

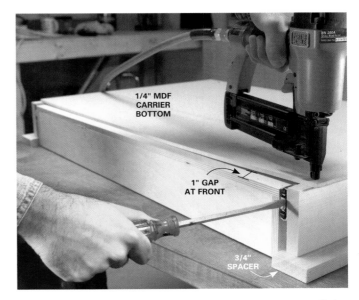

9 Rest the carrier assembly on 3/4-in.-thick spacers, pull the carrier sides slightly away from the tray, then nail on the carrier bottom (no glue).

Labels: 1/4" MDF CARRIER BOTTOM, 1" GAP AT FRONT, 3/4" SPACER

Assembling parts and finishing the trays

It's important to build the rollout trays perfectly square for them to operate properly. Photos 3 and 4 show a simple squaring jig that you can clamp to a corner of any workbench to help. Use the jig to nail the frame together, but even more important, to hold the frame square when you nail on the bottom panel. If it hangs over the sides even a little, the drawer slides won't work smoothly.

Use 1-1/4-in. brads for all of the assembly. Glue the tray parts together but not the bottom of the carrier. It only serves as a temporary spacer for mounting. (After mounting the carrier and tray, you can remove it if it catches items on underlying trays or even reuse it for other carriers.) If you'd like to finish the tray for a richer look and easier cleaning, sand the edges with 120-grit paper and apply a couple of coats of water-based polyurethane before mounting the slides.

To figure the spacer thickness, rest the lower carrier on the bottom of the shelf, push it against one side of the cabinet and measure the gap on the other (Photo 10). Rip spacers to half that measurement and cut six of them to 3-1/2 in. long. Slip the spacers between both sides of the carrier to check the fit. They should slide in snugly but not tightly. Recut new spacers if needed. In out-of-square cabinets, you may have to custom-cut spacers for each of the three pairs of spacers, so check each of the three spacer positions. It's easiest to tack the spacers to the trays to hold them in place before predrilling 1/8-in. holes and running the screws through the tray frames and spacers and into the cabinet sides (Photo 11).

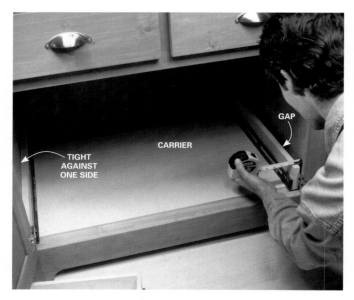

10 Remove the drawer, tip the carrier into the cabinet and push the carrier against one side. Measure the gap and rip six 3-1/2-in.-long spacers to half of the thickness.

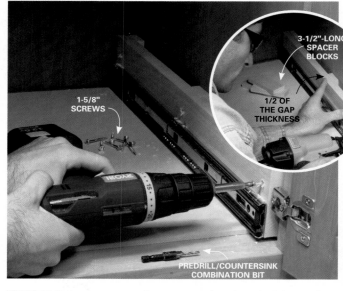

11 Nail the spacers to the center and each end of the carrier sides (not into the cabinet; see inset photo). Then predrill and screw the carrier sides to the cabinet in the center of each shim. Slide the tray back into place.

12 Cut plywood spacers to temporarily support the upper rollout and set them onto the carrier below. Rest the second carrier on the spacers and install it as shown in Photo 11.

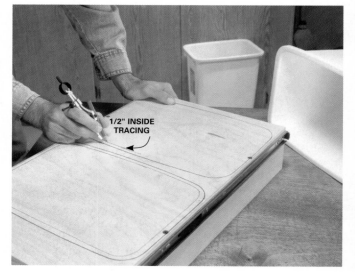

13 Build an upside-down version of the carrier and trays for the wastebasket tray (Figure B). Center and trace around the rim of the wastebasket(s). Use a compass to mark the opening 1/2 in. smaller.

Slip the tray into its carrier and check for smooth operation. If you followed the process, it should work perfectly. If it binds, it's probably because the spacers are too wide or narrow. Pull out the carrier, remove the spacers and start the spacer process all over again.

The best way to level and fasten the upper tray is to support it on temporary plywood spacers (Photo 12). The photo shows pieces of plywood cut 7 in. high. In reality, the exact height is up to you. If, for example, you want to store tall boxes of cereal on the bottom tray and shorter items on the top, space the top tray higher. You can even build and install three or more trays in one cabinet for mega storage of short items like cans, cutlery or beverages. (Those now-obsolete shelves you're replacing with trays are good stock to use for

your spacers.) Again, pin the spacers in place with a brad or two to hold them while you're predrilling and screwing the carriers to the cabinet sides. Be sure to select screw lengths that won't penetrate exposed cabinet sides! In most cases, 1-5/8-in. screws are the best choice. Strive for 1/2-in. penetration into the cabinet sides. Countersink the heads as far as necessary to get the proper penetration.

Building a wastebasket tray

A wastebasket tray is just an upside-down version of a standard tray. That is, the carrier is mounted on the top rather than the bottom of the tray and the slides are positioned at the bottom edge of the carrier sides. That lets the wastebasket lip clear the MDF. Follow Figure B on p. 18 for the details.

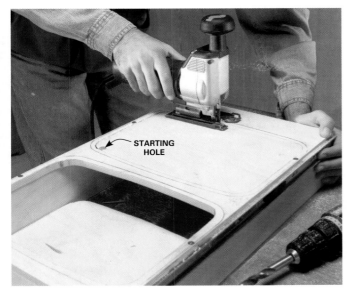

14 Drill 1/2-in. starting holes and cut the openings with a jigsaw.

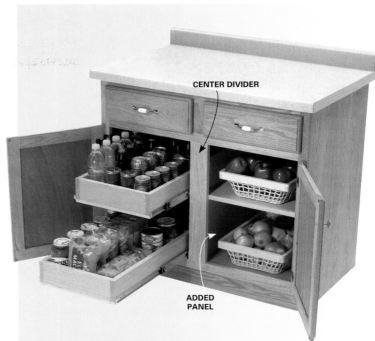

CENTER DIVIDER

ADDED PANEL

15 Mount the wastebasket carrier and tray as shown in Photos 10 and 11.

This wastebasket tray is built inside an 18-in.-wide cabinet, so it fits two plastic containers back to back. If you only have a 15-in. cabinet to work with, you may be limited to one container mounted sideways. Buy your containers ahead of time to fit your opening.

With some wastebasket trays, you may need to knock the MDF free from the carriers after mounting so the wastebasket lips will clear. That's OK; it won't affect operation.

It may not always work to center tray assemblies in all openings with equal spacers on each side. That's especially true with narrow single cabinets that only have one pair of hinges. It's best to test things before permanent mounting. But if you make a mistake, it's a simple matter to unscrew the assembly, adjust the shims and remount everything.

Building rollout trays in cabinets with center dividers

Many two-door cabinets have a center divider (photo above), which calls for a slightly different strategy. You can still build rollouts, but they'll be narrower versions on each side of the divider. (Check to be sure they won't be so narrow that they're impractical.)

The key is to install a 3/4-in. plywood, particleboard or MDF panel between the center divider and the cabinet back to support the carriers.

Cut the panel to fit loosely between the divider and the cabinet back and high enough to support the top rollout position. Center the panel on the back side and middle of the divider and screw it into place with 1-in. angle brackets (they're completely out of sight). Use a carpenter's square to position the panel perfectly centered and vertical on the cabinet back and anchor it there, again using angle brackets. Measure, build and install the rollout trays as shown here.

ROLLOUT TRAY

1" ANGLE BRACKET

ADDED PANEL

Rollout bins

If you're tired of digging through cans and boxes to find a jar of tomato sauce hidden at the back of the cabinet, these rollout bins are the perfect solution. You can size them to fit inside any lower cabinet and customize them to suit the items you want to store.

Here you'll learn exactly how to build them. The bins are simply plywood boxes with adjustable shelves—very easy to build. Sizing the boxes and mounting them on drawer slides can be tricky, but the techniques shown here make those steps nearly foolproof.

Money, time and tools

All the materials for these three rollouts cost just under $100. You could buy and install a manufactured system, but expect to spend about $80 per rollout.

You don't need advanced cabinet-building skills or tools to make your own rollouts—the joinery and assembly are simple. But a table saw is almost mandatory for fast, accurate, good-looking results. A pneumatic brad nailer will make the job faster and easier, although you can hand-nail or screw the parts together. Side-mount drawer slides can be tricky to install, but this project makes even that step foolproof, so don't let that part intimidate you. You'll be surprised how fast you can build yourself a few rollouts. Put in a full day and you'll be loading them with groceries that evening.

Sizing your rollout bins

Everything you need for this project is available at home centers (see the Materials list, p. 18). You'll have to guess at the quantity of bins at this point so you can buy the proper number of drawer slides. One sheet of plywood will provide enough material for at least four bins. You can roughly figure one bin for every foot of open base cabinet space you have. You can always return any uncut lumber or hardware you don't use.

To determine the width of your bins, gather the items you want to store. Then cut the 1x3 cleats to length and space them from each side of the cabinet with 3/4-in. blocks (Photo 1). That space allows the bins to clear the doors and hinges later. Arrange the items you want to store, separating them with the cleats. Leave at least 2-1/2 in. between your items and the cleats. This allows for the clearance of wood thicknesses and drawer slides and 1/2 in. extra to make it easy to load the items and take them out. It takes a bit of rearranging and thought to arrive at the best sizes. If your base cabinets have vertical dividers between the doors, give each opening its own bin.

You'll probably have some bins facing one way and some the other. That's because bin access may be blocked by neighboring cabinets at inside corners or because some cabinet doors don't swing all the way open. Determine the access direction while you assemble your bins. That's as simple as drilling the finger pull hole at the proper end. After the boxes are assembled, they'll work for either orientation.

Choosing the materials

Choose any 3/4-in. veneered interior plywood for your bins. Avoid construction plywood; it won't be as flat and may warp later. If you'd like your bins to match your cabinets, choose whatever type of wood does the job. The plywood end grain is sanded on these, but if you'd like a more polished look, buy iron-on edge banding to match the wood type and iron it on after assembling the boxes.

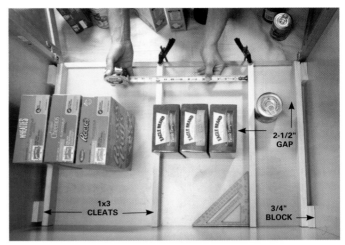

1 Plan rollout bin widths by laying out the cleats along with the items you want to store. Space the end cleats with 3/4-in. blocks.

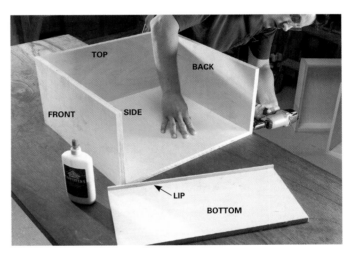

2 Assemble the boxes by gluing and nailing the front, top, back and bottom to the side panel and to each other. Nail the lip to the bottom shelf before assembling.

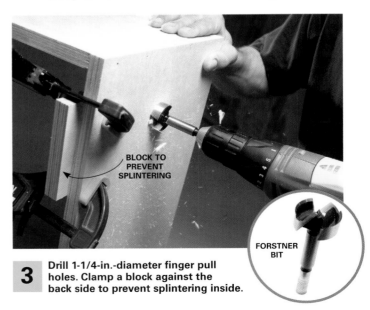

3 Drill 1-1/4-in.-diameter finger pull holes. Clamp a block against the back side to prevent splintering inside.

Figure A:
Standard rollout bin

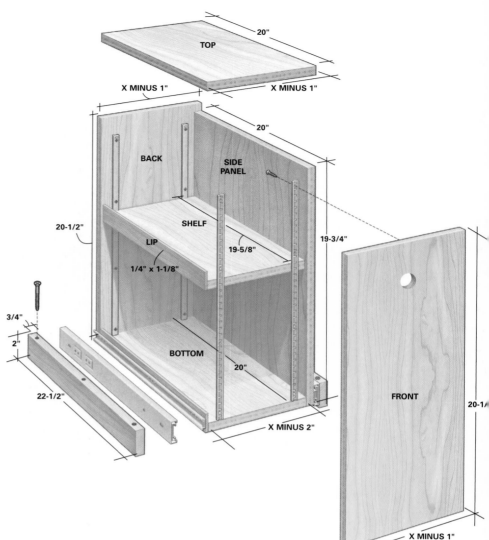

Materials list

ITEM	QTY.
1x3 the width of the cabinet (hold-down rail)	1
1x3 (drawer slide cleats)	2'
1/4-in. x 1-1/8-in. mullion (base and shelf front lips)	8'
2' shelf standards with clips	4
90-lb.-rated full-extension side-mount drawer slides	1 pair
1-1/2-in. pneumatic air nailer brads	
Wood glue	
Small box of 3-in. screws	
1-1/4-in. Forstner drill bit (for drilling finger pulls)	

Figure B:
Typical rollout bin grouping

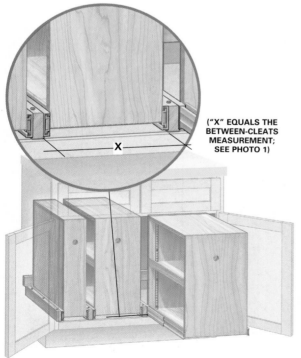

("X" EQUALS THE BETWEEN-CLEATS MEASUREMENT; SEE PHOTO 1)

Buy nice, straight, knot-free 1x3s for the cleats—the wood type doesn't matter. Select 22-in. European side-mount drawer slides rated to support 90 lbs. They'll come with their own screws and installation directions that show you how they work.

Cutting the parts

Most base cabinets are 22-1/2 in. deep and have a 21-in.-high opening (measured inside the face frame, not the cabinet interior). If your cabinets match these measurements, use the height and width dimensions shown in Figure A for all of the side panels. Also use Figure A for the lengths of each top, bottom, front and back panel and shelves. If your cabinets have shorter openings or are shallower, subtract those differences from the Figure A measurements to cut your parts. Calculate the bin widths based on your layout work inside the cabinet (Photo 7). Subtract 1 in. from the distances between the cleats to get the width for each bin's top, front and back panel. That'll leave the 1-in. clearance needed for the drawer slides. Subtract 2 in. to establish the width for each bottom panel and the adjustable shelves. That'll leave an additional 1-in. clearance for the thickness of the 3/4-in. side panel and the 1/4-in.-thick lip in the front.

Be especially careful when you lay out the cleats, measure openings and cut the bin parts. European side-mount drawer slides leave very little room for error. It's best to use a table saw for all of the cuts and to double-check widths and lengths so the boxes will fit together perfectly and engage and operate smoothly in the slides.

Assemble the rollout bin boxes

Glue and nail the lip on each bottom panel (and shelves) before assembling the bins. A thin bead of wood glue on each edge is all you need. Then hold the edges of each panel flush while you pin them together with 1-1/2-in. brads spaced about every 4 in. (Photo 2). Next, drill the 1-1/4-in.-diameter finger pull hole. A Forstner bit will make the neatest hole, but a sharp spade bit will work, provided you use a block on the back side to prevent splintering (Photo 3). The hole defines each bin's open side.

Cut the 24-in.-long shelf standards down to 18 in. with a hacksaw. Look at the embossed shelf numbers to determine which end is the top and cut from that end. Nail the standards in place with the brads provided (Photo 4).

This is the best time to apply the finish of your choice to the bins. Lightly sand everything with 220-grit sandpaper and add the finish. These boxes have two coats of water-based polyurethane to protect the wood against dirty fingers and marks from cans.

Get more storage space— without remodeling

Lower cabinets offer the biggest storage spaces in most kitchens. But according to kitchen designers, the back half of this space is usually wasted—it's packed with long-forgotten junk or left unused because stored items are out of view and hard to reach. Rollout bins let you see and use the whole space.

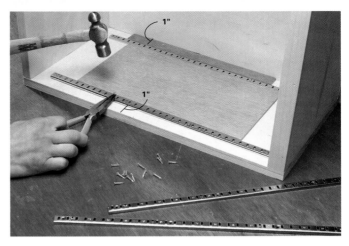

4 Nail shelf standards to the inside of the front and back of each box. Use spacers to position them.

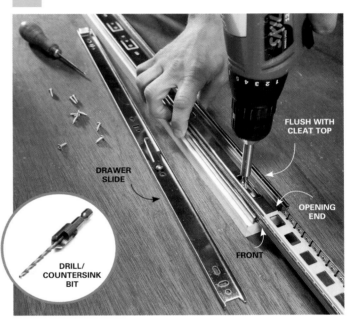

5 Screw the drawer slides to the cleats. Position each slide flush with the front and top of the cleat.

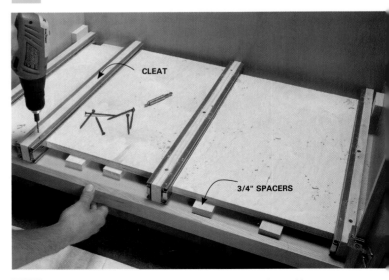

6 Predrill and screw the cleats to the cabinet. Use plywood scraps the same width as the boxes for perfect spacing.

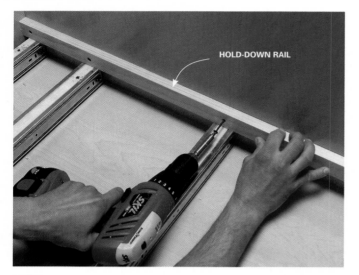

HOLD-DOWN RAIL

7 Screw the hold-down rail to the cabinet back directly above the cleats with 1-5/8-in. screws.

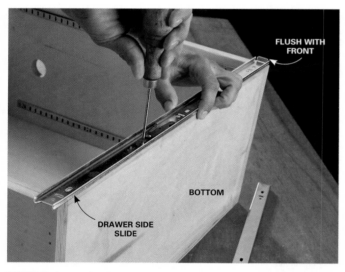

FLUSH WITH FRONT

BOTTOM

DRAWER SIDE SLIDE

8 Release the drawer slides from the cleat slides and screw them to the side of each box flush with the bottom and the front.

9 Slip the box-mounted slides into the cleat slides and push the box all the way in to fully engage the slides.

Install the drawer slides and cleats

Rip the 1x3s down to 2 in. and then screw on the drawer slides (Photo 5). It's easiest to remove the drawer part of the slide to access the anchor holes. Hold the slides flush with the top and front of each cleat while you punch little starter holes with a scratch awl, and then send in the screws. Drive just one screw at a time so you can adjust the placement as you add screws. You'll need right and left sides for the end cleats. Then remove the drawer side slides and lay the cleats in the cabinet.

Begin with one of the end cleats and press it against the temporary 3/4-in. blocks while you drill three 1/8-in. pilot holes. A combination drill/countersink bit works great for this. Then screw the cleat to the cabinet floor with 3-in. screws (Photo 6). Space the next cleat with a leftover scrap from the first bin top, front or back. That way the spacing between the drawer slides will be perfectly sized for smoothly operating bins. Hold the spacer up from the cabinet floor with 3/4-in. blocks so it'll be centered on the drawer slides. Hold the cleat snug, but not tight, against the spacer while you drill and then screw it to the cabinet floor. Repeat that step with the rest of the cleats. Skip the 3/4-in. blocks on the last cleat and just use the bin spacer. Screw a 1x3 "hold-down" rail to the back side of the cabinet (Photo 7). It'll help hold the rollout cleats in place when you pull out heavily loaded bins.

Finally, disengage the drawer side slides and screw them to the bottom of each bin flush with the bottom and front (Photo 8). Finish up by inserting each bin, then load them up!

Manufactured kitchen rollouts

Rollouts are one of the easiest and most satisfying upgrades you can make to your kitchen. They bring everything that's tucked out of sight in the back of cabinets right to your fingertips—you actually gain usable storage space.

If you don't want to pull out the tools to build your own rollouts, you can shop for moderately priced yet sturdy ones online or at Lowe's and Home Depot. You simply mount them to the existing shelves in your cabinets with four screws.

The biggest mistake is ordering the wrong size. When you measure the opening in the front of the cabinet, be sure to account for the door, hinges and other obstructions.

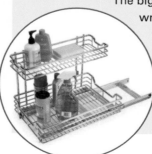

This two-level rollout fits around the drainpipes under a sink.

Kitchen cabinet & drawer upgrades

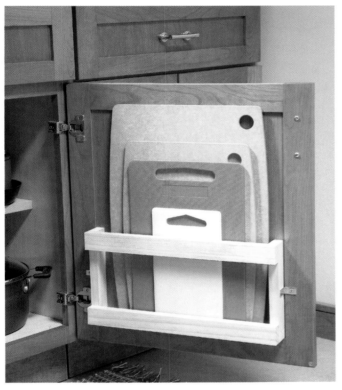

Cutting board rack

You can make this nifty rack for less than $10 and mount it inside a cabinet door to stash your cutting boards out of sight. It goes together in a snap since it only requires a 6-ft. 1x2 and two L-brackets.

Measure between the door stiles to get the maximum width of your rack. Make sure the rack will be wide enough for your cutting board (or spring for a new one). You'll also need to mount the rack low enough so it doesn't bump into a cabinet shelf when the door closes. Cut the bottom and face rails to match the space between the cabinet door stiles.

Cut the sides 7-1/4 in. long. Nail the sides to the base. Then nail the two face pieces at the top and bottom to complete the rack (Photo 1). The easiest way to mount the rack is to take the cabinet door off its hinges and lay it down. Predrill the screw holes for the L-brackets and mount the rack to the cabinet door using a 1-in. L-bracket centered on each side of the rack (Photo 2).

FACE RAIL

BOTTOM RAIL

1 Nail the base rail to the sides, then nail on the face rails. For a quick, clear finish, spray on two light coats of lacquer.

DOOR STILE

L-BRACKET

2 Mount the rack on the door with L-brackets. This is easiest if you remove the door. Be sure to predrill screw holes in the door stiles.

Blind-corner glide-out & swing-out shelves

Blind-corner cabinets—those with a blank face that allows another cabinet to butt into them—may be great for aging wine, but they're nearly impossible to see and reach into. This pair of accessories puts an end to this hidden wasteland. The hinged shelf swings out of the way, and the gliding shelf slides forward so you can access food items stored in the back. You can use the same hardware and techniques for making base cabinets more accessible too.

The key measurements and clearances:

Glide-out shelf dimensions. You can only make the unit as long as the door opening is wide (or else you can't fit it in!). Make the unit about 1/2 in. narrower than the inside width of the cabinet.

Swing-out tray dimensions. The corner-to-corner or diagonal measurement of the unit (Figure A) can't exceed the width of the door opening (or else that won't fit either!). Make the unit about 1 in. shorter than the opening height so it has room to swing freely when installed.

Piano hinges and bottom slides are available at rockler.com. The front moldings are manufactured by House of Fara, and these products are available at Menards and Home Depot.

GLIDE-OUT SHELF

HINGED SWING-OUT SHELF

Build the glide-out shelf

1 Glue and nail the 1x3s together using 4d finish nails, then secure the plywood bottom with 3d finish nails.

1x3

1/2" PLYWOOD BOTTOM

3d FINISH NAILS

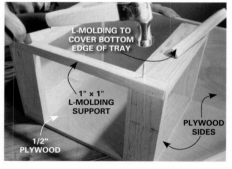

L-MOLDING TO COVER BOTTOM EDGE OF TRAY

1" x 1" L-MOLDING SUPPORT

1/2" PLYWOOD

PLYWOOD SIDES

2 Cut out the two plywood sides, then glue and nail the corners. Connect the trays to the two plywood sides using 1-in. drywall screws, then cut and nail L-molding to support the front corner. Cut and install L-moldings to support and cover the exposed plywood edges of the upper tray. Install 3/4-in. screen molding to cover the plywood edges of the bottom tray.

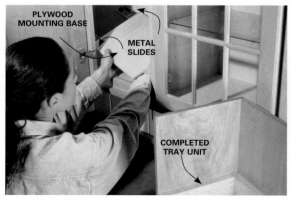

PLYWOOD MOUNTING BASE

METAL SLIDES

COMPLETED TRAY UNIT

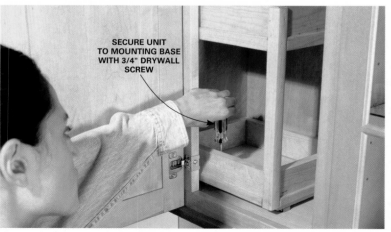

SECURE UNIT TO MOUNTING BASE WITH 3/4" DRYWALL SCREW

3 Cut the mounting base plywood slightly smaller than the other tray bottoms, then secure the two slides parallel to each other about 1 in. from each edge. Slip this mounting base into the opening, extend the slides, then screw them to the cabinet bottom at the rear of the cabinet. Install the slides parallel to the cabinet sides so the base slides back and forth freely.

4 Screw the tray unit to the mounting base using 3/4-in. screws. After installing the first screw, slide the unit forward and back, then adjust it until it runs parallel to the cabinet sides and install three more screws.

tips

- Beg, borrow or rent a compressor, finish nailer and brad gun, if you can. You'll work faster, eliminate hammer marks and split the wood less often than you would hand-nailing.

- Test-fit your shelf units in the cabinet as you work.

- Use a damp sponge to wipe up glue drips immediately. It'll save hours of sanding down the line.

Build the swing-out shelf

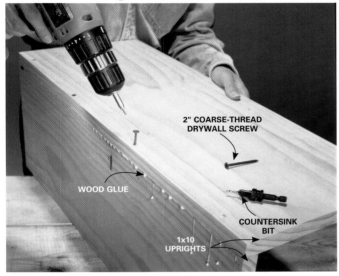

2" COARSE-THREAD DRYWALL SCREW

WOOD GLUE

COUNTERSINK BIT

1x10 UPRIGHTS

5 Cut the 1x10 swing-out uprights to length and width (one should be 3/4 in. narrower than the other). Use a countersink bit to predrill holes along one edge, then glue and screw the two edges together. The diagonal measurement (see Figure A) should be less than the cabinet opening.

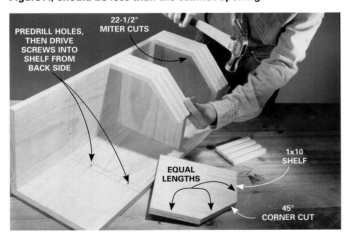

PREDRILL HOLES, THEN DRIVE SCREWS INTO SHELF FROM BACK SIDE

22-1/2° MITER CUTS

1x10 SHELF

EQUAL LENGTHS

45° CORNER CUT

6 Assemble the shelf unit. First mark the shelf positions on the uprights and predrill holes from the front side. Create the three shelves by cutting a 1x10 to length and width, then cutting the corner at 45 degrees. Hold the shelves in place and drive drywall screws through these holes from the back side into the shelves. Cut the 22-1/2-degree angles on the front moldings and secure them with 3d finish nails. You can use any type of wide decorative molding that's at least 1/2 x 3 in.

Figure A:
Glide-out & swing-out shelves
Shelf unit dimensions will vary according to cabinet size.

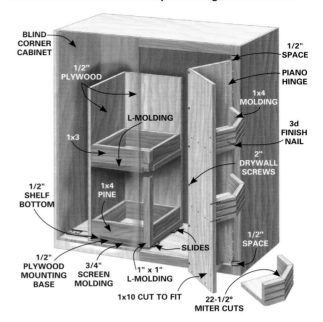

BLIND CORNER CABINET

1/2" PLYWOOD

L-MOLDING

1x3

1/2" SHELF BOTTOM

1/2" PLYWOOD MOUNTING BASE

3/4" SCREEN MOLDING

1x4 PINE

1" x 1" L-MOLDING

1x10 CUT TO FIT

1/2" SPACE

PIANO HINGE

1x4 MOLDING

3d FINISH NAIL

2" DRYWALL SCREWS

SLIDES

1/2" SPACE

22-1/2° MITER CUTS

These two measurements cannot exceed cabinet opening width.

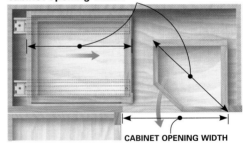

CABINET OPENING WIDTH

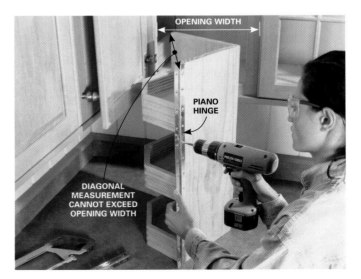

OPENING WIDTH

PIANO HINGE

DIAGONAL MEASUREMENT CANNOT EXCEED OPENING WIDTH

7 Screw the piano hinge to the front edge of the swing-out unit, then to the edge of the cabinet face frame. Make certain the swing-out has 1/2 in. of clearance top and bottom. Use an assistant to help you lift and hold the unit at the proper height while you're securing it to the cabinet.

Adjustable spice rack

This in-cabinet spice shelf puts small containers at eye level and still leaves room in the cabinet for tall items. The materials will cost you less than $10. You'll need a 4-ft. 1x3 for the top shelf and a 4-ft. 1x2 for the bottom ledger. You can find shelf pegs at home centers in two sizes, 1/4 in. and 3/16 in., so measure the holes in your cabinet before you shop. The secret is to assemble the shelf outside the cabinet and then set it on the shelf pegs.

Measure the sides and back of your cabinet and cut your shelf and ledger pieces. Subtract 1/8 in. from all sides so you can fit the unit into the cabinet. Attach the sides to the back of the bottom ledger and put two nails into each butt joint. Then nail the top shelf sides into place and pin the shelf back at the corners to hold it flush (Photo 1).

To install the shelf unit, carefully fit one end of the "U" into the cabinet, holding it higher at one end, and shimmy it down until it sits firmly on top of the shelf pegs (Photo 2). Shift the pegs up or down to adjust the shelf height. Spray a quick coat of lacquer on the shelf before installing it.

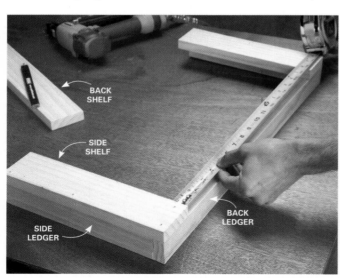

1 Nail the back and side ledgers together, then nail on the side shelves. Measure between the side shelves and cut the back shelf to fit.

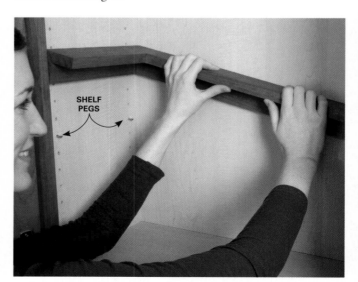

2 Set the spice shelf on adjustable shelf pegs. You may have to remove an existing shelf so you can tilt the spice shelf into place.

Cabinet door message board

A sheet of metal and a whiteboard can turn any cabinet door into a convenient message center. You'll find 2 x 2-ft. lengths of plastic-coated hardboard (sometimes called "dry-erase board") and sheet metal at a hardware store or home center. Larger hardware stores will cut the sheet metal to your specifications. Be sure to get steel instead of aluminum so magnets will stick. Including a can of spray adhesive, this project will cost you less than $20.

If you cut the metal yourself, wear gloves to protect your hands and use tin snips carefully. Use a metal file to smooth any ragged edges. If you don't have a table saw to cut the whiteboard, flip it over, mark your measurements and use a jigsaw to cut it from the back to prevent chipping or splintering. To get a straight cut, use a framing square as a guide (Photo 1).

To mount the metal sheet and whiteboard to the inside of the door, take the door off its hinges, lay it flat and carefully mask off the area where you want to spray the adhesive. Follow the directions on the can to apply the adhesive to the door, metal and whiteboard (Photo 2). Mount the pieces, press firmly and let dry.

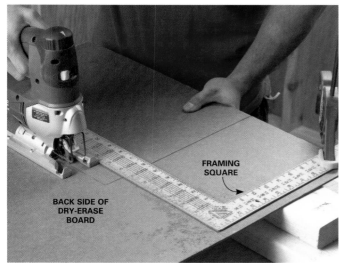

1 Cut the dry-erase board from the back to avoid chipping the plastic-coated face. Use a framing square as a guide to get a straight cut.

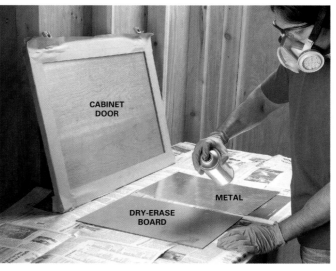

2 Spray adhesive onto the door, metal and dry-erase board. Carefully position the metal and board as you stick them to the door—once they're in place, you can't move them.

Sink cabinet shelf

All that wide open space under the sink is a black hole for cleaning products, shoe polish, trash bags—you name it. If you're tired of exploring its depths every time you need something, build this handy door-mounted shelf. Better than store-bought wire racks, it mounts securely, has the same wood finish as your cabinet and maximizes space because you custom-fit it for your cabinet.

The shelf is made from standard 1x4 lumber (which is 3/4 in. x 3-1/2 in.). If you have access to a table saw and have a drill, screwdriver, some wood glue and a tape measure, you can build this project. It takes only a few hours. You can also modify this design to work in other cabinets for holding spices, canned goods or craft supplies.

The shelf has a unique built-in system (Photos 6 and 7) to make mounting it to the back side of a cabinet door a snap. The shelf gets screwed into the solid wood stiles of the door (not into the panel).

Sizing tips

Because there's no standard size for sink base cabinets, here are a few tips to help you size your door-mounted shelf. Measure the height and width of the cabinet opening (Photo 1). The shelf unit must be 1/2 in. less in height and 2 in. less in width (not including the mounting ears shown in Photo 6). These measurements ensure that the shelf unit will clear the frame by 1/4 in. on all sides as you close the cabinet door. Here's how to size each part:

■ The height of the 3-1/2-in.-deep sides (A) must be 1/2 in. shorter than the height of the opening.

■ The 3-1/4-in.-deep shelves (B) are cut 3 in. shorter than the width of the opening. These pieces are ripped 1/4 in. thinner than the side to allow space for gluing the mounting strips (C) to the back side of the shelves (Photo 4).

■ The 1/4-in. x 3/4-in. mounting strips must be 2-1/2 in. longer than B or 1/2 in. shorter than the width of the door opening.

Preparing the sides

After measuring the opening's height and width, cut the sides (A) to length. Then cut a 45-degree taper on the tops of each piece, leaving 3/4 in. at the top as shown in Photo 2. Label the inside of each side so you don't cut the dado (groove) for each shelf on the wrong side. Notice that there are two 1/4-in. notches on the back edge of each side (Photo 2) to accept the mounting strips (C).

To cut the dadoes, set your table saw blade so it's 1/4 in. high. Mark the locations of each dado. The lower dado is on the bottom of the sides, and the top of the upper shelf is 13-1/2 in. from the bottom of the sides.

Cut the dadoes in the inner sides of A using your miter gauge as a guide to push the workpiece through the saw. The table saw shown has an extra-wide miter gauge for stability. If your table saw has a small miter gauge, screw a piece of wood to its front edge to extend it to within 1/4 in. of the saw blade. You could make the dado cut in one pass with a special dado blade, but if you don't have one, just make repeated cuts (Photo 2) with a standard blade.

Making the shelves

Cut the shelves (B) to length from 1x4, then rip them to a width of 3-1/4 in. Make the 1/4-in. x 3/4-in. mounting strips (C) and front rails (D) by ripping them from a wider piece as shown in Photo 3.

Before you glue these pieces to the backs of the shelves (Photo 4), drill a 3/16-in. hole 3/8 in. from each end. You'll use these holes later to mount the shelf to the door stiles.

You could make the dado cut in one pass with a special dado blade, but repeated cuts with a standard blade are just as easy for a small project.

Assembly

Lay out the sides face down as shown in Photo 5. Now, slip the shelves with the mounting strips attached into the dadoes and make sure they fit snugly. Drill pilot holes for the screws (3/4 in. from the front and back of A) through the sides into the shelves. Use 1-1/4-in. wood screws with finish washers to secure the shelves to the sides.

To finish the assembly, flip the shelves and sides face-up. Cut the 1/4-in. x 3/4-in. front rails (D) to length, drill pilot

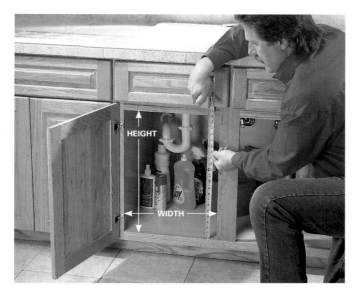

1 Measure the cabinet opening (height and width) to size the shelf system.

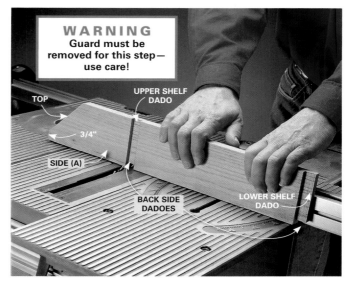

2 Cut the sides (A) to length, then cut the dadoes in the sides and back of each side. See text for dimensions.

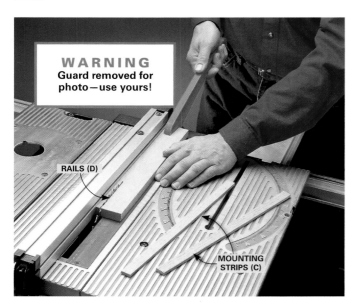

3 Rip the mounting strips (C) and the rails (D) from 1x4 lumber.

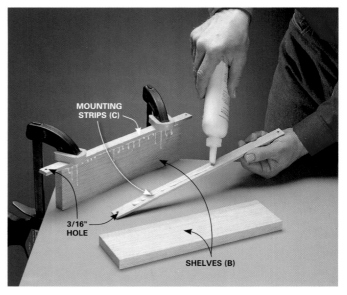

4 Glue the mounting strips (C) to the back side of the shelves. Drill holes in the mounting strips before assembling.

holes and fasten them (Photo 6) to the front of the sides. For the shelf shown, the lower rail is 2 in. up from the bottom shelf and the upper rail is 1-1/2 in. up from the upper shelf. These heights work fine for most products and allow you to pull things out instead of lifting them each time. You can always add a second rail just above, if needed.

tip

You can also modify this design to work in other cabinets for holding spices, canned goods or craft supplies.

Mounting to the door

Before mounting the unit to the door, apply masking tape to the inside of the door as shown in Photo 7. Close the door and mark the cabinet opening on the tape with a pencil from the inside. This will guide you when you're mounting the shelf to the door. Mount the shelf 1/4 in. from the top mark you made on the tape, and align the ear of the mounting strip 1/4 in. from the opening mark on the door. Mark the holes from the mounting strips onto the door and drill pilot holes for the screws. Be careful not to drill through the door! Screw the assembly to the door (Photo 7) using No. 8 x 1-in. screws and finish washers.

Because of the added weight of the shelf and the products, some doors with self-closing hinges may not snap closed as easily as before. To remedy this, you may need to install an extra hinge centered between the other two, or add a magnetic catch at the top of the door.

Remove the shelf from the door, sand it with 150-grit sandpaper, then apply varnish. Shown here are several coats of a clear lacquer spray available at hardware stores. Always apply lacquer in a well-ventilated area away from any pilot flames. **Note:** If you have small children, be sure that cabinets containing cleaning products have child-proof latches attached.

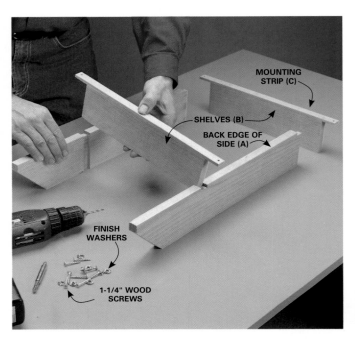

MOUNTING STRIP (C)

SHELVES (B)

BACK EDGE OF SIDE (A)

FINISH WASHERS

1-1/4" WOOD SCREWS

5 Slip the shelves into the dado cuts. Then drill pilot holes into the sides of A and screw the shelves in place with 1-1/4-in. wood screws and finish washers.

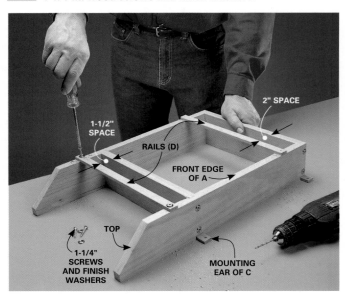

2" SPACE

1-1/2" SPACE

RAILS (D)

FRONT EDGE OF A

TOP

1-1/4" SCREWS AND FINISH WASHERS

MOUNTING EAR OF C

6 Fasten the rails (D) to the front of the shelf assembly. Drill pilot holes and use 1-1/4-in. wood screws and finish washers.

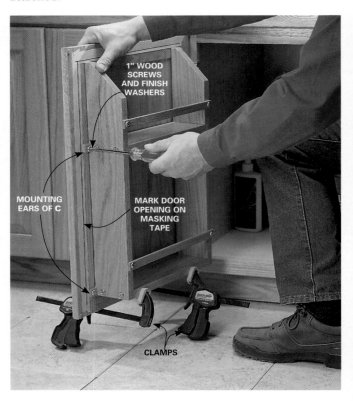

1" WOOD SCREWS AND FINISH WASHERS

MOUNTING EARS OF C

MARK DOOR OPENING ON MASKING TAPE

CLAMPS

7 Clamp and screw the assembly to the door stiles using 1-in. wood screws and finish washers.

Undersink storage

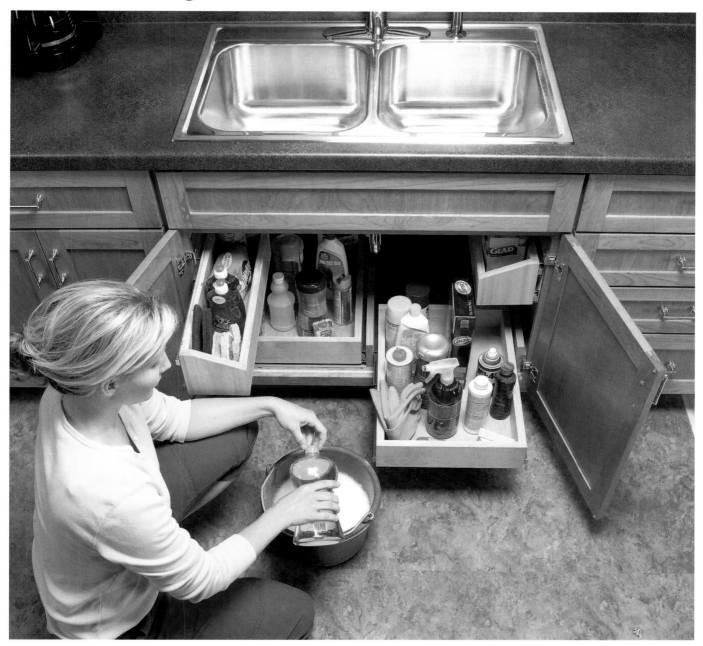

These two types of rollout trays, which ride on smooth-action ball-bearing drawer slides, will get everything under the sink out in the open.

This project isn't difficult. In fact, there aren't even any miter joints. All the parts are glued together and then nailed or screwed. The building products are readily available at home centers or hardware stores for as little as $75.

Simple carpentry tools and some careful measuring are all that's needed, although a table saw will help zero in on more exact measurements, especially for the lower tray bases where accuracy is important for the ball-bearing drawer slides.

The nail gun shown in the photos is also optional, but it makes assembly a lot faster and less tedious. It shoots thin 18-gauge nails.

Adapt the project dimensions to fit a particular sink space. For example, a bulky garbage disposer may not allow both upper slide-out trays. In that case, just make one tray instead. If plumbing comes up through the floor of the sink cabinet, shorten the lower trays to fit in front of the plumbing. In any case, add as many parts of this project as space permits to organize this black hole once and for all.

1 Measure the width of the kitchen base cabinet inside the frame. Cut the base (A) 1/4 in. narrower than the opening.

2 Find the center of the base (A) and mark it for the center partition. Cut the 20-in.-long partitions (B) from 1x4 stock.

Materials list

ITEM	QTY.
(This list applies to the rollout trays shown; quantities may vary.)	
3/4" x 4' x 8' hardwood plywood	1
1x4 x16' maple	1
1/2" x 2' x 2' hardwood plywood	1
1x6 x 2' maple	1
20" ball-bearing drawer slides	4 prs.
Woodworker's glue	1 pt.
Construction adhesive	1 pt.
6d finish nails, small box	1
1-5/8" wood screws, small box	1

Getting the right stuff

At a home center or lumberyard, look for hardwood plywood. Buy 2 x 4-ft. pieces instead of a whole sheet, if possible. The hardwood plywood has two good sides and is smoother and flatter than exterior-grade softwood plywood. It costs more too.

In the hardware department, look for ball-bearing side-mount drawer slides. The pairs of the brand shown here are exactly the same—there's no specific right or left, which makes things easier if parts get misplaced. The project shown has 20-in.-long side-mount slides to fit the 20-in.-long trays. This gives some wiggle room in the back and a bit of extra space to get the pieces into place. If plumbing comes up through the bottom of the cabinet, shorten the trays and buy shorter drawer slides if needed.

Sink cabinet tray detail

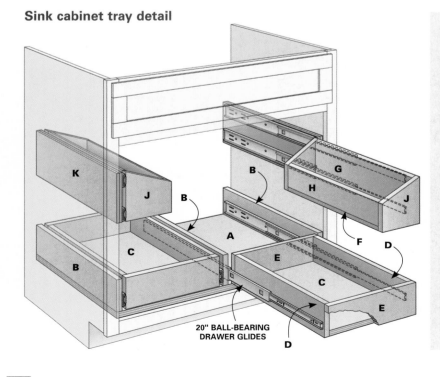

20" BALL-BEARING DRAWER GLIDES

Cutting list

(This list applies to the rollout trays shown; dimensions may vary.)

KEY	PCS.	SIZE & DESCRIPTION
A	1	3/4" x 32-3/4" x 20" plywood base
B	3	3/4" x 3-1/2" x 20" base partitions
C	2	3/4" x 12-3/4" x 18-1/2" plywood tray bottom
D	4	3/4" x 3-1/2" x 18-1/2" tray sides
E	4	3/4" x 3-1/2" x 14-1/4" tray fronts and backs
F	2	1/2" x 5-1/2" x 18-1/2" upper tray bottoms
G	2	3/4" x 5" x 18-1/2" upper tray (high side)
H	2	3/4" x 3" x 18-1/2" upper tray (low side)
J	4	3/4" x 5-1/2" x 5-1/2" upper tray front and back
K	4	1/2" x 5-1/2" x 20" side cleats (double layer)

Then follow the photos for the step-by-step measuring and assembly instructions. Here are a few specifics to consider:

■ If the opening between the open doors is narrower than the opening between the sides of the frame, use the shorter dimension when making the base.

■ If there's a center stile or partition between the doors, make two separate bases for each side and a tray for each to get them to fit.

■ Make sure the base and the tray parts are cut square and accurately so the trays slide smoothly.

A word about drawer slides

The ball-bearing slides are designed to mount on the sides of the trays (Photos 6 and 7). The slides require exactly 1/2 in. of space between the partition and the drawer on each side to work properly, so make sure the trays are exactly 1 in.

narrower than the distance between the partitions. If the trays are too wide, they'll bind and be tough to open. If that happens, take them apart and recut the tray bottom. If the trays are too narrow, the slides will not engage. Fixing this is a bit easier. Just shim behind the slides with thin washers.

Watch for protruding hinges and other obstructions when mounting the lower or upper trays. Adjust the height or placement of the trays to accommodate them.

Seal the trays with polyurethane

Spills or leaks are inevitable under the sink, so it's best to seal the wood. Once the project is finished, remove the trays and slides, sand them with 150-grit sandpaper and brush on two coats of polyurethane. Let the trays dry thoroughly, then look through all that stuff stored under the sink. Toss out the old and combine duplicate products—and enjoy the reclaimed and now easily accessible space.

RELEASE LEVER

BALL-BEARING DRAWER SLIDE

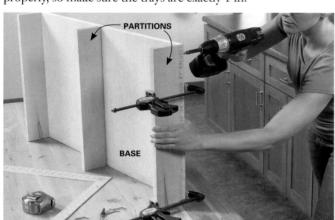

3 Clamp the partitions to the base, drill pilot holes, and glue and screw them to the base with No. 8 x 2-in. screws.

4 Measure the exact distance between the partitions. Make the outer dimension of the tray 1 in. narrower than this measurement to allow for the slides.

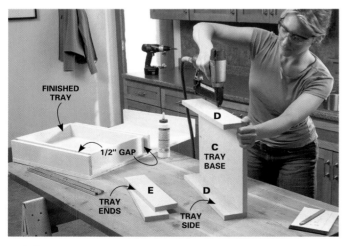

5 Cut the parts for the trays and glue and nail them together. Cut the bases perfectly square to keep the trays square.

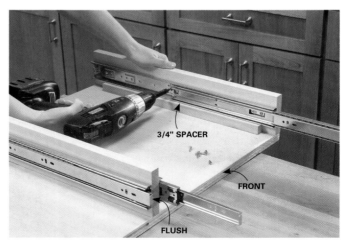

6 Set the drawer slides on 3/4-in. spacers, holding them flush with the front. Open them to expose the mounting holes and screw them to the partitions.

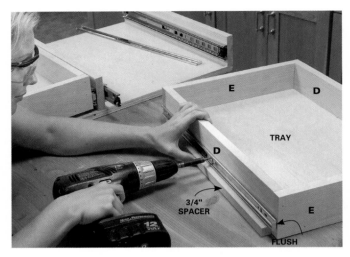

7 Remove the inner sections of the slides and screw them to the sides of the trays. Reassemble the slides and make sure they glide smoothly.

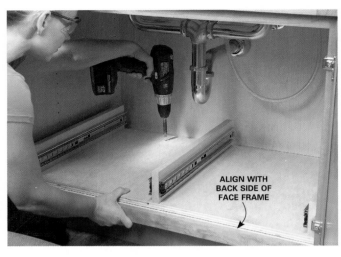

8 Insert the base assembly into the floor of the cabinet. Align the front of the base flush with the back side of the face frame. Screw the base to the floor of the cabinet.

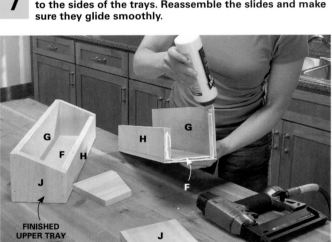

9 Cut the parts for the upper trays, drill pilot holes, and glue and screw them together. Cut two thicknesses of plywood and glue them together to make the 1-in.-thick side cleats (K).

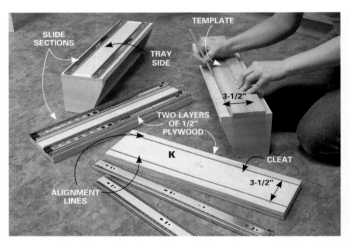

10 Cut a 3-1/2-in.-wide template, center it on the cleats and tall side of each tray and trace the edges. Center the mounting holes of the slides on these lines and screw them to the cleats (outer sections) and tray sides (inner sections).

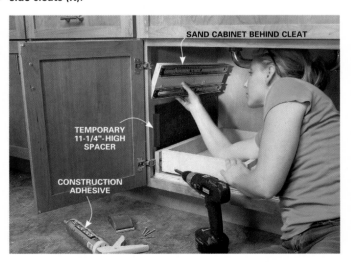

11 Sand the side of the cabinet to increase the adhesion, then glue and screw the cleats to the sides of the cabinet. Cut a plywood spacer to hold the cleat even.

12 Slide the upper trays into position and test the fit. Seal the trays with two coats of polyurethane to make cleaning easier.

Door-mounted spice & lid racks

These simple racks will help organize those chaotic gangs of spice bottles and pan lids. Here you'll learn how to build only the spice rack; the lid rack uses the same steps but without the shelves. Each spice rack can hold 20 to 30 bottles, and each lid rack two to six lids, depending on the height and width of your cabinet doors. Before building, measure your spice bottles and lids to determine the spacing of your shelves and dowels.

The key measurements and clearances:

Existing shelf depth. If the existing cabinet shelves are full depth, narrow them by about 2 in. to accommodate each door-mounted rack. Shelves that are permanently affixed in grooves in the cabinet sides will need to be cut in place with a jigsaw. Adjustable shelves can be removed, cut along the back side with a circular saw or table saw, then replaced. You may need to move brackets or add holes to remount narrowed shelves.

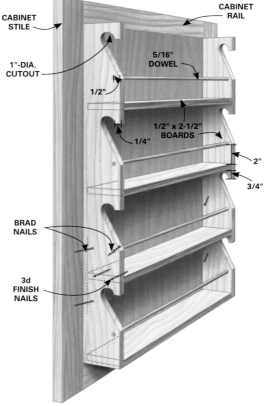

Spice rack depth and positioning.
Make certain the new rack won't hit the cabinet frame when the door swings. In this case, fitting the rack between the two 2-in.-wide vertical stiles (Photo 1) provided adequate room. If your doors are solid wood or laminate, hold in place a scrap of wood the same depth as the spice rack 2-1/2 in. was the depth used here) and swing the door. Move it away from the door edge until it no longer makes contact with the cabinet frame, then mark the door. This will determine the overall width of your spice rack.

Use high-gloss polyurethane for natural wood and high-gloss enamel for painted wood. These finishes are more scrubbable.

Use soft, easy-to-nail pine and basswood for both the spice and the lid racks. If you're using a harder wood, like maple or oak, position the pieces, then predrill holes through the side pieces and into the shelf ends. This will prevent splitting and make nailing easier. Install your shelves one at a time so you don't have to balance and juggle multiple pieces as you work. Always nail on a flat, solid surface.

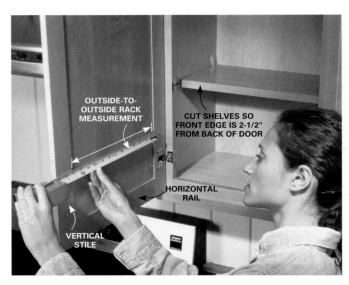

1 Measure the distance between the two vertical stiles and the two horizontal rails to determine the outside dimensions of your spice rack. Cut existing shelves back 2 in. so they don't interfere with the rack when the door is closed.

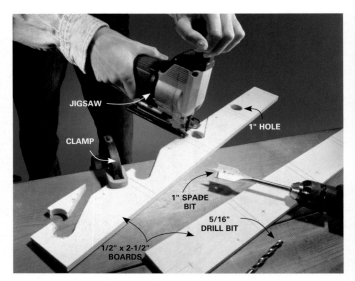

2 Transfer dimensions from the illustration on p. 33 onto 1/2 x 2-1/2-in. side boards. Cut out the sides of the spice rack. Drill 1-in. holes to create the circular shape, then finish the cutout with a jigsaw. Drill 5/16-in. holes for the dowels. Sand parts smooth.

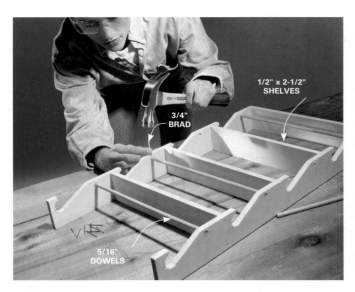

3 Glue and nail the shelves in place one at a time, using 3d finish nails. Then use 3/4-in. brads to pin the dowels in place. Sink all nail heads using a nail set. Apply polyurethane or other finish to match the cabinets.

4 Clamp the finished rack to the door, then drill angled pilot holes through the rack and into the door every 8 inches. Secure with brad nails (remove the door for this step if you find you need a more solid surface for hammering). Use wood glue for a more permanent installation.

Under-cabinet drawers

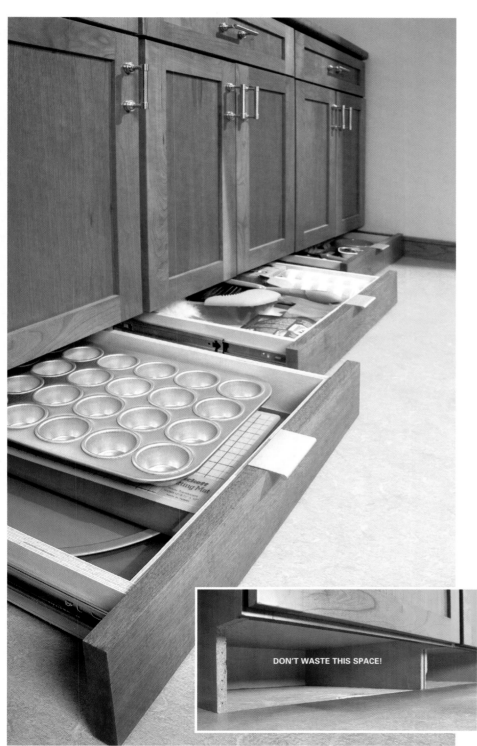

DON'T WASTE THIS SPACE!

Installing drawers under cabinets sounds like a tough job, requiring fussy planning, the skills of a cabinet-maker and child-size hands to work in that cramped space. But this project is amazingly easy. To simplify the whole process, you can assemble these drawer units in your shop and then slip them into place. To simplify planning, you'll need three basic measurements that let you size these drawers to fit under any cabinet. Even if you've never built or installed a drawer before, you can do it. This project is economical, too. The total materials cost for these three drawers was about $100. A cabinetmaker would have charged at least $350 to build and install them. The number of drawers is up to you; install them under all your cabinets or just one.

Will it work with my cabinets?

The vast majority of kitchen cabinets are similar to the ones shown here, with sides that extend to the floor (see Photo 1). But there are a few rare exceptions. Some cabinets, for example, stand on legs rather than the cabinet sides. Open the cabinet doors and take a look at the bottom of the cabinet

To gain storage space, you usually have to give up space somewhere else. Not in this case. Hidden under almost every kitchen cabinet, there's a cavity containing nothing but air. This low, shallow cavity isn't prime storage space for everyday items, but it's perfect for bakeware, cleaning supplies, pet dishes and more.

1 Break out the toe-kick backing to open up the spaces under the cabinets. Just drill a hole near the center, cut the backing in half and pull it out.

2 Build super-simple drawer boxes. Just glue and nail the sides, front and back together, then glue and nail on the plywood bottom.

Materials list

Here's what was used to build drawers to fit under three 24-in.-wide cabinets. Your quantities may differ.

ITEM	QTY.
4' x 8' sheet 1/4" birch plywood	1
2' x 4' sheet 1/2" birch plywood	1
1x4 pine	12'
1x6 maple	6'
Drawer slides	3 pair

Drawer pulls, wood glue, stain, polyurethane, 1-1/4" brads or nails, 1" and 1-5/8" screws

Figure A:
Drawer unit

The drawer, carrier and slides form a complete unit that's simple to build and easy to install under a cabinet.

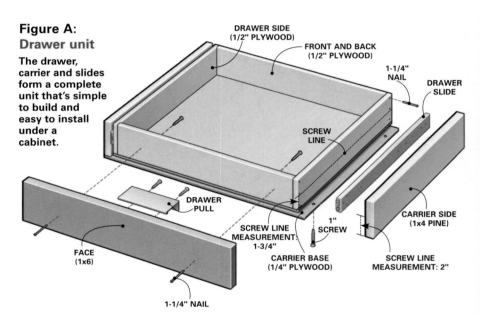

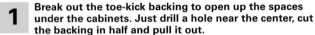

box. If you see screw heads or holes near the corners, your cabinets probably stand on legs rather than the cabinet sides (the screws or holes allow for height adjustment). In that case, installing drawers will require different steps than those shown here.

If your cabinets are constructed like the ones shown here, you can install drawers. There are just a few things to keep in mind:

■ If the cabinet is more than 30 in. wide, consider installing two drawers rather than one. Wider drawers tend to bind as you slide them in or out.

■ Your drawers will be shallow; don't expect to store kettles in them. A 4-in.-high toe space will give you storage space that's about 3 in. deep.

■ You can install drawers under a sink cabinet (or a bathroom vanity). But if the sink's plumbing runs through the bottom of the cabinet, the drawers will have to be shorter.

Tools and materials

You could build the drawers with nothing but hand tools and a circular saw, but a table saw and miter saw will give you faster, better results. A nail gun is another big time-saver, though you can hammer everything together with 1-1/4-in. finish nails instead.

All the materials are available at most home centers. In the hardware aisle, choose "full-extension" side-mount drawer slides (Photo 3). That way, only 3 to 5 in. of the opened drawer will be covered by the overhanging cabinet front. With cheaper "3/4-extension" slides, only about half the drawer will be accessible. If you can't find full-extension slides, or if you want "overtravel" slides that extend even farther, shop online. Search for "drawer slides" to find online suppliers. Slides are available in 2-in.-length increments. Most cabinets accept 18- or 20-in. slides.

Choose hardwood plywood like birch or oak for the

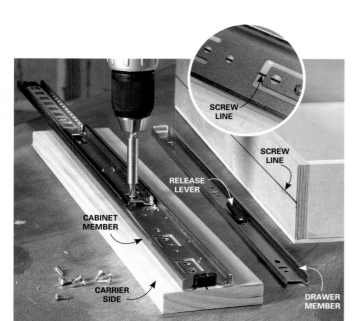

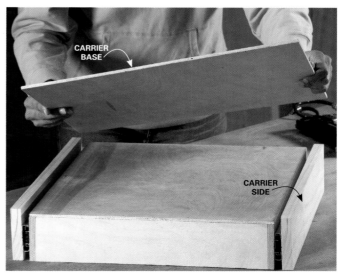

3 Mount the slides, centering the screw holes on the screw lines. Press the release lever to separate the drawer member from the cabinet member.

4 Add the carrier base to create a self-contained drawer unit. Fasten the base with screws only; glue could drip down and gum up the slides.

drawers. Construction-grade tends to warp. Most home centers carry plywood in 2 x 4-ft. and/or 4 x 4-ft. sheets, so you don't have to buy a full 4 x 8 sheet. Pick out straight pine 1x4s for the carrier sides. For the drawer faces, you'll need hardwood that matches your cabinets. If your toe-space height is 4 in. or less, a 1x4 board will do. For a taller toe space, you'll need a 1x6. Most home centers carry only a few types of wood such as oak, cherry, and birch or maple. If your cabinets are made from a less common species, look for a lumberyard that carries a wider selection. Or improvise—with the right stain, you can make birch or maple approximately match the color of just about any wood. The grain may look different, but that difference usually isn't noticeable in the dark toe space. Shown are maple faces, even though the cabinets are made from cherry.

Remove the toe-kick and measure

Before you buy materials, open up the cavity under the cabinets so you can take measurements. First, pull off the "toe-kick," the strip of plywood or particleboard in the toe space. Usually, the toe-kick is held by just a few small nails and is easy to pry off. If you don't plan to cover the entire toe space with drawers, be gentle so you can later cut the toe-kick to

length and reinstall a section. If layers of flooring have been added since the cabinets were installed, you'll have to pull the top edge of the toe-kick outward first and then pry it up to clear the built-up floor.

Next, remove the toe-kick backing under the cabinets (Photo 1). Simply drill a 1-in. hole and cut the backing with a drywall saw. Then grab a flashlight and check for obstructions. Break out any blocking with a chisel or pry bar. Pull out or cut off any nails. Now you're ready to take the three measurements to determine the sizes of the drawers. There's no need for complex calculations—it's all reduced to simple subtraction in Figure B.

Build drawers and carriers

If you've ever installed drawer slides similar to the ones shown, you know you have to be precise. They require a 1/2-in. space on both sides of the drawer—build a drawer that's a hair too wide or narrow and you've got a drawer that won't budge. To sidestep that precision work, build each drawer first and then build a carrier around it. If you want to install two drawers under one wide cabinet, build a single carrier with both drawers sharing one of the carrier sides and the carrier base.

Figure B:
Drawer sizing simplified

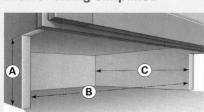

MEASUREMENT "A"

- Subtract 1-1/2 in. from "A" to determine the width of drawer sides, front and back.
- Subtract 1/2 in. from "A" to determine the width of drawer faces. The length of each face depends on the width of the cabinet.

MEASUREMENT "B"

- Subtract 3-3/4 in. from "B" to determine the length of the drawer front and back. This will make the entire drawer/carrier assembly 1/4 in. smaller than the width of the cavity.

MEASUREMENT "C"

- Subtract 1/4 in. from "C" to determine the length of the carrier and drawer sides.
- This is also the *maximum* length of the drawer slides you can use.

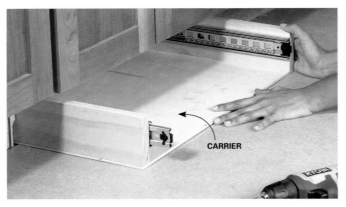

CARRIER

DRAWER
FACE

SPACER

5 Slip the carrier under the cabinet and drive screws through the cradle sides just below the slides. Small hands and a small drill make this part easier.

6 Rest the drawer faces on 1/4-in. spacers. Tack the face in place with two nails, then open the drawer and drive screws into the face from the inside of the drawer box.

These drawers are as easy as they get: Just nail them together (Photo 2). If you're using finish nails rather than a nail gun, predrill so you don't split the plywood parts. Remember to place the front and back between the sides. Then measure and cut the drawer bottoms. As you install each bottom, be sure the drawer box is square using a large carpenter's square or by using the plywood bottom as a guide (this only works if you've cut the bottoms perfectly square). Cut the 1x4 carrier sides to the same length as the drawer sides. In most cases, you can use 1x4s at full width (3-1/2 in.). But if your toe-space height (measurement "A" in Figure B) is less than 4 in., cut the carrier sides to a width 1/2 in. less than the toe-space height.

Next, mark screw lines on the drawer and carrier sides (see Figure A for measurements). Pull each slide apart to separate the drawer member from the cabinet member. Then screw them on (Photo 3). These drawer and carrier sides were the same length as the drawer slides—yours may not be. So be sure to position the *front* ends of each drawer member and cabinet member flush with the *fronts* of the drawer and carrier sides. Slip the slides back together, lay the drawer upside down and screw on the carrier base (Photo 4). Then flip the whole unit over and inspect your work. Make sure the drawer opens smoothly. When the drawer is closed, the front of it should be flush with the carrier sides, give or take 1/16 in. Any problems are easy to fix by removing screws and repositioning the slides. **Note:** With the drawer units assembled, the carrier sides are exactly the same height as the drawers. Your drawers may come out a bit higher or lower.

Install the drawers

Before you remove the drawers from their carriers, number them to avoid mix-ups later. Each drawer will slide smoothest in the carrier that was built for it. Slip each carrier into place and fasten it to the cabinet with four 1-5/8-in. screws. If you have flooring that's more than 1/4 in. thick, first set scraps of 1/4- or 1/2-in. plywood under the cabinet to support the carrier. The carrier base can be higher than or flush with the flooring, but not lower than the flooring. Position the carrier sides flush with the cabinet sides and tight against one side

(Photo 5). Screw the carrier to the cabinet, starting with the tight side. On the other side, don't drive in the screws so hard that you distort the carrier. If the drawer doesn't glide smoothly, slightly loosen those screws. Also be sure the drawer doesn't drag on the floor when opened. Load a few heavy objects into the drawer and open it. If it drags, remove the front screws from the carrier and slip washers under it. That will give the drawer a slight upward tilt to clear the floor.

Next, cut the drawer faces to width. When you cut them to length, avoid measuring mistakes by marking them while they're in place. Leave a 1/8- to 1/4-in. gap between neighboring faces. At the end of a row of cabinets, make the face flush with the outer side of the cabinet. The method we used to attach the faces works best with a nail gun (Photo 6). Driving nails with a hammer can knock the drawer or carrier out of position. If you don't have a nail gun, stick the faces in place with double-face carpet tape. Then pull out each drawer and attach the face by driving two 1-in. screws from inside the drawer. With the faces attached, be sure they don't drag on the floor. If necessary, raise them with washers as described above.

Finishing up

Remove the drawers from their carriers for finishing. Unscrew the slides from the drawers and sand the drawer faces with 120-grit sandpaper. Also prepare a few stain-testing blocks, using leftover scraps from the faces and sanding them. You could remove one cabinet door and take it to a paint store to have matching stain custom-mixed. If you have the patience to experiment, you could buy a couple of cans of stain and mix them to create your own. Either way, apply the stain to your test blocks before you stain the faces. The match doesn't have to be perfect, since the faces will be shaded by the overhanging cabinet fronts. After staining the faces, finish the drawers—faces and boxes—with two coats of water-based polyurethane. Before reinstalling the drawers, add the drawer pulls or knobs. If you can't find pulls that closely match your existing cabinet hardware, you can use pulls that fit over the tops of the drawer faces and are hidden under the cabinets ($3 to $8 each; see photo, p. 35).

Kitchen storage & organizing
hints & tips

VERTICAL PLYWOOD PANEL

CUT SHELF TO NEW LENGTH

DRILL HOLES FOR SHELF PINS

Measuring cup hang-up

Free up drawer space by hanging measuring cups inside a kitchen cabinet. Position and mount a wood strip so that the cups will hang between the shelves and allow the door to close completely. Mount a second strip for your measuring spoons, then screw in cup hooks on both strips.

Cookware organizer

Most kitchen base cabinets lack vertical storage space for big, flat cookware like cookie sheets and pizza pans. To provide it, just remove the lower shelf, cut a vertical panel of plywood and fasten it at the cabinet bottom with furniture braces and at the top with a strip of wood. Drill holes for the adjusting pins to match the original locations and trim the shelf to length.

Thyme saver

If your spices are jammed into a drawer with only the tops visible, this nifty rack that slips neatly into the drawer will solve the problem. And it only takes an hour to build. Make it with scraps of 1/4-in. and 1/2-in. plywood.

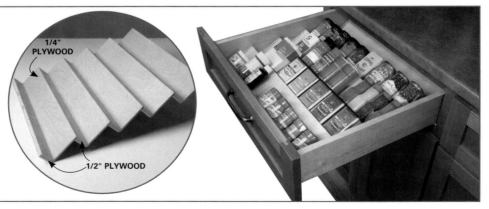

1/4" PLYWOOD

1/2" PLYWOOD

Racks for canned goods

Use those leftover closet racks as cabinet organizers. Trim the racks to length with a hacksaw and then mount screws to the back side of the face frame to hold the racks in place. The back side of the rack simply rests against the back of the cabinet. Now you can easily find your soup and check the rest of your inventory at a glance.

CLOSET ORGANIZER RACKS

ATTACH SCREWS TO BACK SIDE OF FACE FRAME

Spice storage

Small spice containers use shelf space inefficiently and are difficult to find when surrounded by taller bottles and items. Use a small spring-tension curtain rod ($3) as a simple shelf. It's easy to install and strong enough to support the spices.

T-MOLDING

FINISH WASHER

Wine glass molding

T-molding designed for wood floor transitions makes a perfect rack for stemware. Just cut it to length, pre-drill screw holes and screw it to the underside of a shelf. For a neater look, use brass screws and finish washers. Prefinished T-molding is available wherever wood flooring is sold. A 4-ft. section costs about $28.

Plastic bag dispenser I

An empty rectangular tissue box makes a convenient holder for small garbage bags, plastic grocery bags and small rags. Simply thumbtack it to the inside of a cabinet door.

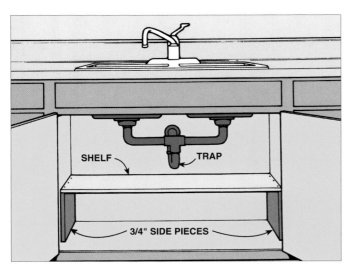

Easy cabinet shelf

Here's a fast and easy way to add a shelf to a kitchen cabinet under the sink, or to a bathroom vanity. Cut side supports from 3/4-in. plywood to the height you want, allowing the shelf to fit under the sink trap. Cut the shelf from either 1/2-in. or 3/4-in. plywood, about 1/4 in. shorter than the inside cabinet width. Nail the shelf to the side supports with 6d finishing nails, prime and paint the shelf and sides, and slide the unit in place.

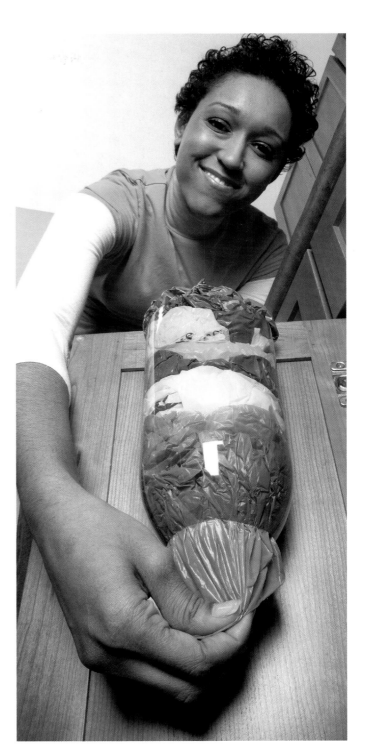

Plastic bag dispenser II

Make it easy to stow and reuse plastic bags with a dispenser made from a discarded 2-liter soda bottle. Cut off the top and bottom with a razor knife. Trim any jagged edges so you don't tear the bags when you pull them out, then screw the dispenser to a cabinet door or closet wall (or attach with hook-and-loop tape).

Charger hideaway

Nothing clutters up a space more than the spaghetti heap of cords and plugs needed to recharge all those cell phones and other electronic toys. Create a discreet charging station with a small bread box and place a power strip inside. Drill a hole in the back to run the cord to the receptacle. Plug in your power-hungry devices and close the door for an orderly desktop or kitchen counter.

Free drawer liner

Window shades make an excellent wipe-clean drawer and shelf liner. Recycle an old shade or ask the shade department staff at a local home center to go through their box of scraps. Heavy 12-mil shades make the best liners.

Unpeel peel-and-stick

Putting new contact paper in kitchen drawers can be really frustrating. To easily separate the paper from the backing, put a piece of tape on one corner of the paper, and another piece on the same corner of the backing. Fold down the top of each piece of tape about 1/2 in. to get a better grip, and then pull the pieces of tape apart. The paper and backing separate easily. This also works great on labels, stickers and the like.

Easy-to-build knife block

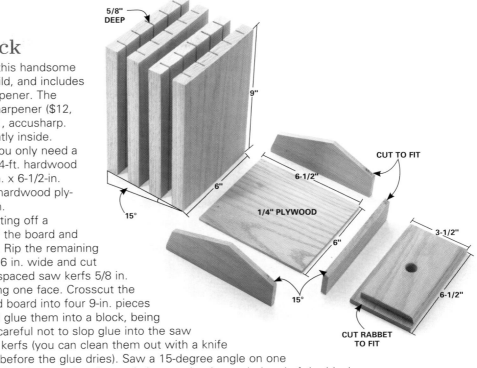

Store your kitchen cutlery in style with this handsome knife block. It's fast, easy and fun to build, and includes a 6-in.-wide storage box for a knife sharpener. The AccuSharp knife sharpener ($12, product No. 001, accusharp. com) tucks neatly inside.

To build one, you only need a 3/4-in. x 8-in. x 4-ft. hardwood board and a 6-in. x 6-1/2-in. piece of 1/4-in. hardwood plywood to match.

Begin by cutting off a 10-in. length of the board and setting it aside. Rip the remaining 38-in. board to 6 in. wide and cut five evenly spaced saw kerfs 5/8 in. deep along one face. Crosscut the slotted board into four 9-in. pieces and glue them into a block, being careful not to slop glue into the saw kerfs (you can clean them out with a knife before the glue dries). Saw a 15-degree angle on one end and screw the plywood piece under the angled end of the block.

Cut the 6-1/2-in. x 3-in. lid from the leftover board, and slice the remaining piece into 1/4-in.-thick pieces for the sides and end of the box. Glue them around the plywood floor. Cut a rabbet on three sides of the lid so it fits snugly on the box and drill a 5/8-in. hole for a finger pull. Then just add a finish and you're set for years of happy carving!

Concealed message center

Don't let shopping lists, phone messages and to-do notes clutter up counter space. Mount a dry-erase board and a plastic bin on the inside of a cabinet door with double-sided foam mounting tape. The bin will protrude into the cabinet, so be sure to position it where it won't collide with shelves or the stuff inside. Get the board, bin and tape at a discount or office supply store for about $15 altogether.

Tidy file organizer

Countertops are a landing pad for paper—mail, news clippings and other assorted notes. Get that mess off the counter with folders and a file holder. The one shown here ($8 at an office supply store) mounts with screws or double-sided foam tape. If there's not a suitable vertical surface, get a file holder that sits on the countertop. It will take up less space (and look neater) than a stack of loose papers.

Bathroom

46

65

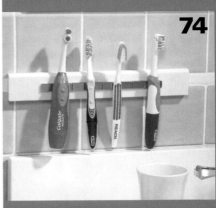

74

Simple bathroom cabinet

In most bathrooms, a picture or small shelf hangs above the toilet. But you can make better use of that space with an attractive cabinet that offers about three times as much storage as a typical medicine cabinet.

The simple joinery and store-bought doors make this a great project for a woodworking novice. Assembling the crown and base can be a bit tricky, but all the steps are explained here.

The total materials bill for this cabinet was $140. You'll need a miter saw to cut the trim. A table saw and a brad nailer will save time, but you can make all the cuts with a circular saw and drive the nails by hand if you prefer.

The height and width of your cabinet may differ slightly from this one, depending on the bifold doors available at your home center. So choose your doors first and then alter the lengths of the sides, top, bottom and middle shelves if necessary. Bifold closet doors are sold as a pair, usually joined by hinges. Each of the doors shown here measured 11-15/16 in. wide, and were cut to length as shown in the photo in the sidebar on p. 49.

Figure A:
Bathroom cabinet

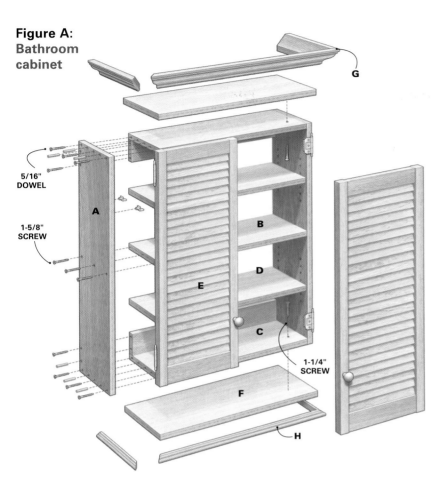

5/16" DOWEL

1-5/8" SCREW

A

B

D

E

C

F

G

H

1-1/4" SCREW

Materials list

ITEM	QTY.
4' x 8' x 3/4" birch plywood	1
2-1/4"-wide crown molding	5'
3/4"-tall base cap molding	5'
1-1/4" screws	1 box
1-5/8" screws	1 box
5/16" or 3/8" dowels	16
1-1/2" finish nails	1 box
Hinges*	4
Shelf supports	8
Spray primer	1 can
Spray paint	2 cans
Wood glue, wood filler	

*These hinges go by a number of different names. Look for hinges that look like the one in photo 4.

Cutting list

KEY	PCS.	SIZE & DESCRIPTION
A	2	8" x 32-5/8" sides
B	3	8" x 22-1/2" top, bottom and middle shelf
C	2	3" x 22-1/2" top and bottom cleats
D	2	8" x 22-1/4" adjustable shelves
E	2	11-15/16" x 32-3/8" doors
F	2	9" x 24" crown and base frames
G	3	2-1/4"-wide crown molding (cut to fit)
H	3	3/4"-tall base molding (cut to fit)

Except for moldings, all parts are 3/4-in. plywood.

The easy-to-install hinges used here are available online (see Materials list, right). All the other tools and materials, including the cabinet doors, are available at home centers. You may not find the exact same crown and base moldings used here, but most home centers carry a similar profile. Any 2-1/4-in. crown molding is appropriate for this project. For a more contemporary look, you can skip the crown and base altogether since they're purely decorative.

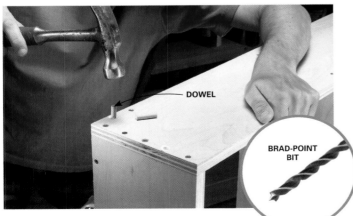

DOWEL

BRAD-POINT BIT

1 Assemble the cabinet box quickly with glue and wood screws. Then add glued dowels for rock-solid joints. Drill splinter-free dowel holes with a brad-point bit.

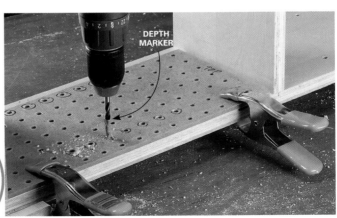

DEPTH MARKER

2 Drill shelf support holes using a scrap of pegboard to position the holes. Wrap masking tape around the drill bit so you don't drill all the way through.

3 Cut the doors using a homemade saw guide to ensure a straight cut. Lay the door face down so any splintering takes place on the back of the door.

4 Mount the hinges on the doors. A self-centering drill bit positions the screw holes for perfectly placed hinges.

5 Position the doors carefully and clamp them to the cabinet. Then screw the hinges to the cabinet from inside for a foolproof, exact fit.

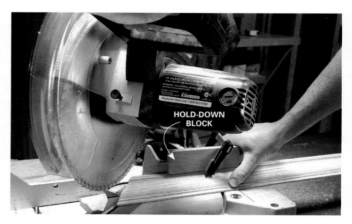

6 Cut the crown molding upside down and leaning against the fence. Clamp a block to the saw's fence so you can hold the molding firmly against the fence.

Build a basic box

Cut the plywood parts to size. The dimensions used here are given in the Cutting list, p. 47. To make the short end cuts, use the homemade guide shown in Photo 3.

Assemble the cabinet box with glue and screws, followed by wood dowels for extra strength (Photo 1). You can buy long dowels and cut them into short pieces, but dowels precut and fluted for woodworking are easier to work with. This assembly method is quick, easy and strong. But because it requires lots of wood filler to hide the fasteners, it's for painted work only. If you want to use stain and a clear finish, biscuits or pocket screws are a better choice.

Drill 1/8-in. pilot and countersink holes for the screws using a drill bit that does both at once ($6 at home centers). Attach the top, bottom and cleats to one side, then add the other side. Mark the middle shelf position on the sides, slip the shelf into place and fasten it (there's no need for glue).

Before you drill the dowel holes, make sure the box is square by taking diagonal measurements; equal measurements mean the box is square. If necessary, screw a strip of plywood diagonally across the back of the box to hold

it square. For clean, splinter-free holes, drill the dowel holes with a 3/8-in. brad-point bit ($5), making the holes 1/8 in. deeper than the length of the dowels. That way, you can sink the dowels below the surface of the plywood and fill the holes with wood filler. With the box completed, drill holes for the adjustable shelf supports (Photo 2) using a brad-point drill bit. Most shelf supports require a 1/4-in. hole.

Cut and hang the doors

Cut the doors using a saw guide (Photo 3). To make a guide, screw a straight 1x3 to a 14 x 18-in. scrap of 3/4-in. plywood. Then run your saw along the 1x3 to cut off the excess plywood and create a guide that steers your saw perfectly straight and indicates the exact path of the cut. Simply mark the doors, align the guide with the marks, clamp it in place and cut.

Screw the hinges to the doors 3 in. from the ends (Photo 4). The fronts and backs of louvered doors look similar, so check twice before you drill. Stand the doors against the cabinet, setting them on spacers to create a 1/8-in. gap at the bottom. The gap between the doors should also be about 1/8

7 Assemble the cabinet box quickly with glue and wood screws. Then add glued dowels for rock-solid joints. Drill splinter-free dowel holes with a brad-point bit.

CROWN

BASE

8 Center the crown on the cabinet and fasten it with screws driven from inside. Then center the cabinet on the base and attach it the same way.

in. Clamp each door in position and screw the hinges in place (Photo 5). If the doors don't align perfectly because the box is slightly out-of-square, don't worry. You can square the box when you hang it. The hinges also adjust up or down 1/16 in.

Add the crown and base

Measure the top of the cabinet (including the doors) and cut the plywood crown and base frames to that size. Set your miter saw to 45 degrees and cut the crown molding upside down, leaning against the fence (Photo 6). Also miter a "tester" section of molding to help you position the sidepieces when you nail them in place. To avoid splitting, be sure to predrill nail holes. With the sides in place, add the front piece

of crown molding. Cut it slightly long and then "shave" one end with your miter saw until it fits perfectly. Add the molding to the base frame the same way. Screw both the crown and the base to the cabinet (Photo 8).

A quick finish

Brushing paint onto louvered doors is slow, fussy work, but you can avoid that hassle by using aerosol-can primer and paint. First, remove the doors and hinges. Cover the dowels, nails and screw heads with wood filler and sand the filler smooth. Also fill any voids in the plywood's edges. Sand the cabinet box, crown, base and doors with 120-grit paper. Spray all the parts with a white stain-blocking primer (such as BIN, Cover Stain or KILZ). When the primer dries, sand it lightly with a fine sanding sponge. Finally, spray on at least two coats of spray paint. High-gloss paint will accentuate every tiny surface flaw, so consider using satin or matte.

To hang the cabinet, locate studs and drive two 3-in. screws through the top cleat. Then rehang the doors. Close the doors to check their fit. Nudge the bottom of the cabinet left or right to square it and align the doors. Then drive screws through the bottom cleat.

Store-bought closet doors keep it fast and simple

Building cabinet doors is a tricky, time-consuming job. But you can avoid all that fussy work by buying closet doors and cutting them to fit the cabinet. Shown here is a fast, foolproof way to hang the doors using special hinges.

tip

Painting supports
Here's how to paint both sides of a project without waiting for the first side to dry. Drive screws through small plywood blocks. Paint the back side first, then set the project on the screws and paint the other side. The tiny marks left in the paint by the screw tips will be barely visible.

Vanity sanity

Three sensible solutions for bathroom vanity disorder

Most vanities are poor storage spaces because they're designed for the convenience of plumbers, not yours. While that big, open box is nice for installing pipes, it leaves you with jumbled storage and wasted space.

But you can convert that box into useful space by installing any or all of these three upgrades. You'll expand the real estate under your sink and make it easy to find anything in seconds. Even a beginning DIYer can build all three projects in a weekend, at a total cost of about $75.

Swing-out shelf

Here's the answer to all that inaccessible clutter on the floor of your vanity. With one pull, you can bring stored items out of the dark recesses and into easy reach.

Chances are, the measurements shown in the illustration below won't be best for your vanity. The surest way to determine the right size for your shelf is to cut a quarter circle from cardboard and test the fit. If your vanity has double doors, you can still build this shelf, but you may need to open both doors to swing it out. Here are some tips for building your swing-out shelf:

NAIL AS A PIVOT **3/16" HOLE WITH PENCIL INSERTED** 11-3/4"

A homemade trammel is perfect for marking out the curved shelves.

- To make the curved shelves, just mark a half circle and then cut it into two equal quarter circles.
- A pneumatic brad nailer makes assembly a cinch. If you don't have a brad nailer, use trim screws. The awkward shape of the shelves makes hand nailing difficult. Whether you use nails or screws, also use glue.
- The shelf shown is finished with a couple of coats of polyurethane. A can of spray lacquer is also a good option.
- Piano hinges come in various lengths, but you probably won't find exactly what you need for your shelf. That's OK; you can cut it to length with a hacksaw.

Swing-out shelf parts and materials

Part A 1/2" x 11-3/4" x 12"
Part B 1/2" x 13" x 12"
Part C 1/2" x 11-3/4" radius
Part D 1/8" x 1-3/4" x 24"

Materials

1/2" plywood (A–C)

1/8" hardboard (D)

No. 4 screws and No. 6 finish washers

Piano hinge

Cabinet pull

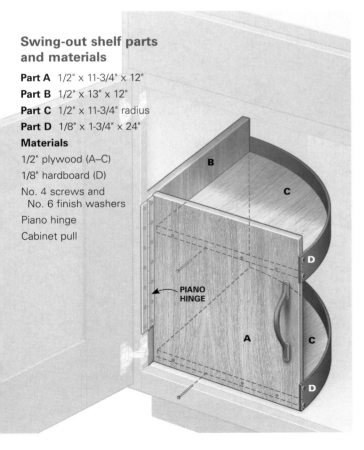

PIANO HINGE

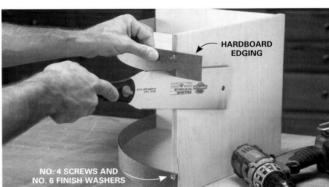

HARDBOARD EDGING

NO. 4 SCREWS AND NO. 6 FINISH WASHERS

1 **Install the edging, then trim it.** Cut the hardboard edging a few inches too long, fasten it with screws and slice off the excess with a fine-tooth saw. Finish washers give the screws a neater look.

PIANO HINGE

3/8" SPACERS

2 **Hang it on a hinge.** Raise the shelf with spacers and align the shelf back with the inside edge of the face frame. Screw the piano hinge to the shelf back, then to the cabinet. You may have to notch the shelf back to clear the door hinge.

Mini rollout

This handy little rollout has tall sides, fronts and backs to keep bottles and cleaners in place as you open it. The dimensions given in the illustration below are for the rollout shown, but you can alter the size to suit your needs. Here are some building tips:

■ Assemble the drawer boxes with glue plus trim screws, finish nails or brad nails.

■ Shown is a 14-in. "full-extension" drawer slide. This type of slide is typically mounted on the side of a drawer, but it works well as a light-duty undermount slide, too. If your home center doesn't carry full-extension slides in the length you need, go to any online cabinet hardware supplier. You can use a standard undermount slide, but your tray won't extend fully.

■ Finish the rollout with two coats of polyurethane or spray lacquer.

■ If you add a cabinet pull as shown here, be sure to set the base back a bit so the vanity door can close.

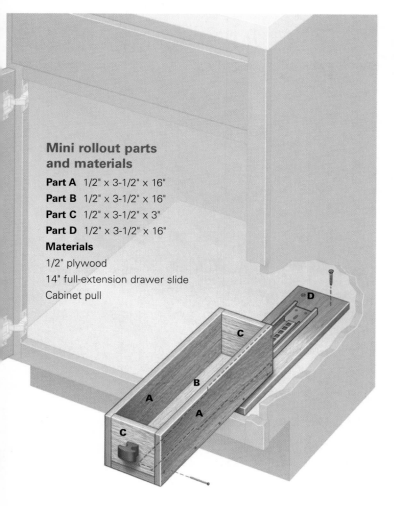

Mini rollout parts and materials

Part A 1/2" x 3-1/2" x 16"
Part B 1/2" x 3-1/2" x 16"
Part C 1/2" x 3-1/2" x 3"
Part D 1/2" x 3-1/2" x 16"

Materials
1/2" plywood
14" full-extension drawer slide
Cabinet pull

1 Mount the drawer slides. Separate the two parts of the drawer slide. Screw them to the tray and the base, aligned flush at the fronts.

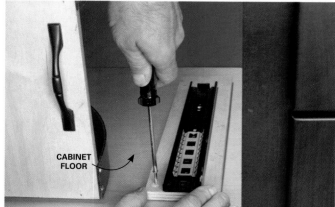

2 Elevate the drawer slide with a separate base. Fasten the tray base to the cabinet floor with No. 6 x 1-in. screws, then slide on the drawer.

Drawer-top trays

Drawers are often too deep for small bathroom stuff like razors, medicine and cosmetics. That means wasted space. These handy sliding trays reduce that waste and increase drawer real estate by 50 percent.

■ To size the tray, measure the drawer: Subtract 1/16 in. from the width of the drawer space and divide the length in half. Cut a piece of 1/8-in. hardboard this size.

■ You can make the tray any depth you like. If the opening in the vanity is taller than the height of the drawer, your tray can protrude above the drawer sides.

■ Finish the tray with a couple of coats of polyurethane or spray lacquer.

■ Stored items tend to slide around in the trays, so it helps to add shelf liner (available at home centers and discount stores).

Drawer-top trays materials

1/2" plywood
1/8" hardboard
Shelf liner

1/2" PLYWOOD TRAY SUPPORT

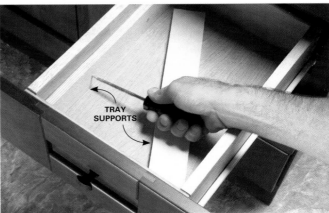

TRAY SUPPORTS

1 **Add tray supports.** Fasten strips of plywood to the drawer to support the tray. You only need two screws per support.

SHELF LINER

2 **Line the trays.** Cut shelf liner to fit the trays. Liner helps stored items stay put when you slide the tray.

Built-in bath cabinet

If you're short on bathroom storage space, this built-in cabinet could be just the ticket. It's large and spacious, yet the shallow depth allows easy viewing and access to all of the contents. No more digging around in drawers or the dark corners of linen closets to find what you need. And since it's recessed into the wall, you won't lose any valuable floor space.

This project is a great introduction to basic cabinet-building skills. It's a simple box with a face frame attached to the front. You buy the doors in the style that best fits your bathroom décor and mount them to the face frame. The doors shown here came complete with 35mm holes to accept the concealed Euro-style hinges. These hinges are great for novice cabinetmakers because they allow you to adjust the doors for a perfect fit.

Here you'll learn the entire cabinet assembly process. Then you'll see how to cut a hole in your wall and safely remove a stud to create a recessed space for the cabinet. Even with little woodworking experience, you should be able to complete the cabinet in a day. Applying the finish and installing the cabinet will take another five or six hours.

You could cut the cabinet sides and face frame parts with a circular saw and saw guide, but you'll get tighter-fitting joints if you use a power miter saw or a table saw with a miter gauge. For the cabinet shown, a pocket hole jig and pocket screws were used to assemble the face frame pieces and attach it to the box. If you don't own a pocket hole jig, glue and nail the face frame to the cabinet box with finish nails.

Including the doors, door glass and glass shelves, this cabinet cost about $400. If you use oak instead of cherry, you could build it for about $100 less. Patterned glass and glass shelves for the doors can be ordered from a local glass company or an online retailer. Euro-style mounting plates are available by mail order and online.

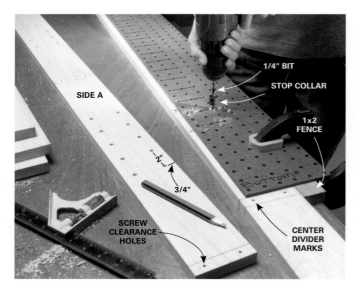

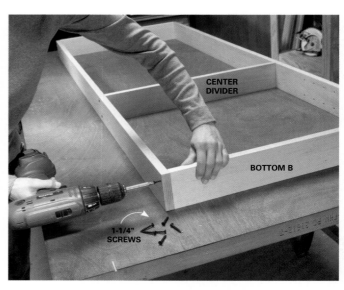

1 Cut the cabinet box pieces (A and B) to length. Mark the location of the center divider on the side pieces and drill screw-clearance holes. Also drill holes for the adjustable shelf supports using a pegboard jig.

2 Screw the sides to the top and bottom through the pre-drilled clearance holes. Then line up the middle horizontal divider with the marks and screw it in.

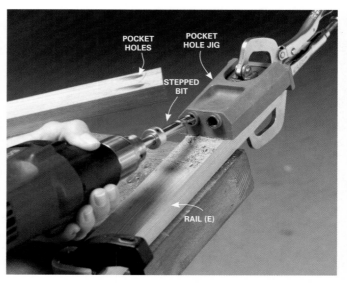

3 Align one edge of the 1/4-in. plywood back with the side of the cabinet. Predrill the screw holes and screw it into place with 1-in. screws. Then square the cabinet and screw the other three edges and center divider.

4 Cut the face frame parts to length (D and E; Illustration on p. 57). Drill pocket screw holes on the back side of the rails (E) with a special stepped bit and pocket hole jig.

Choose the cabinet location carefully

Before you order doors or start building the cabinet, make sure you have a good spot to install the cabinet. Exterior walls are out. There's likely to be insulation in them, and there may be structural issues to deal with as well. Look for a space that's about 26 in. wide and 68 in. high. After you've found a potential location, use a stud finder to locate the studs, then mark them with masking tape. Position the cabinet so that you only have to remove one stud. You can put your cabinet at any height. The top of this cabinet lines up with the door, 80 in. above the floor.

Then make sure the spot you chose doesn't have any

hidden obstructions. The easiest method is to cut two 6-in. square inspection holes in the drywall, one on each side of the stud you'll be removing. Then look in with a flashlight to make sure there aren't any electrical wires, plumbing pipes or heat ducts in the way. A less invasive but also less thorough method is to poke a bent clothes hanger through a hole in the wall and probe around. You'll have to do this in several places, though. If space is tight, you may have to adjust the cabinet dimensions to fit it in. When you've found a location, order the doors and hinges. If the door sizes are different from those shown here, adjust the cabinet sizes to fit them. The doors overlap the face frame 3/4 in. on all sides.

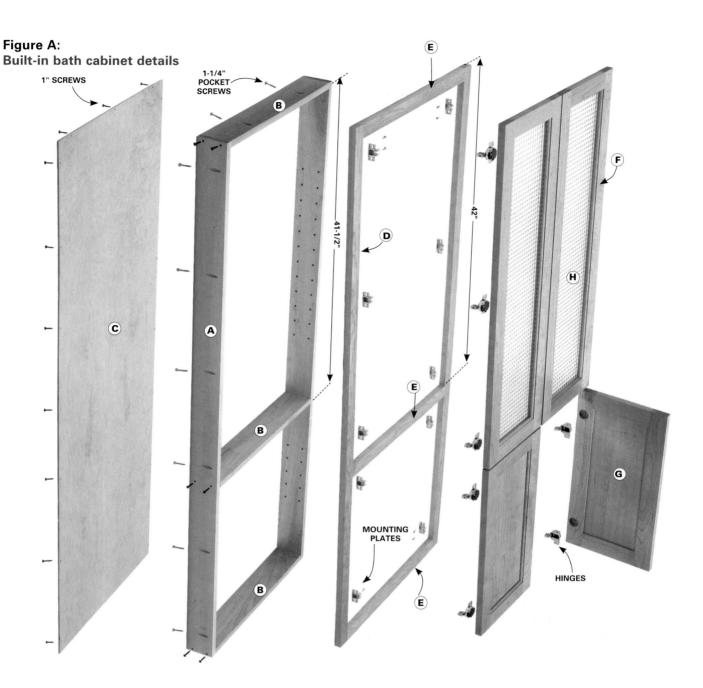

Figure A:
Built-in bath cabinet details

1" SCREWS

1-1/4" POCKET SCREWS

41-1/2"

42"

MOUNTING PLATES

HINGES

A · B · C · D · E · E · E · E · E · B · B · B · F · G · H

Wall opening Shopping list

ITEM	QTY.
2x4 x 8' studs	3
Metal angle brackets	2
Small container of Simpson No. 8 x 1-1/4" screws	1
2-1/2" drywall or cabinet screws	12
Joint compound for patching	
1/2" plywood scrap	
1-1/4" drywall screws	

Cutting list

KEY	PCS.	SIZE & DESCRIPTION
A	2	3/4" x 3-1/2" x 66-3/8" maple (sides)
B	3	3/4" x 3-1/2" x 22-7/8" maple (top, bottom, middle)
C	1	1/4" x 24-3/8" x 66-3/8" birch plywood (back)
D	2	3/4" x 1-1/2" x 67-5/8" cherry (face frame stiles)
E	3	3/4" x 1-1/2" x 22-5/8" cherry (face frame rails)

KEY	PCS.	SIZE & DESCRIPTION
F	2	3/4" x 12" x 42" cherry doors
G	2	3/4" x 12" x 24" cherry doors
H	2	patterned glass inserts to fit doors
J	5	polished-edge glass shelves

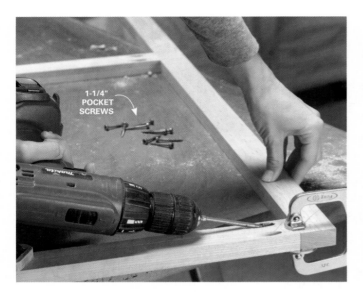

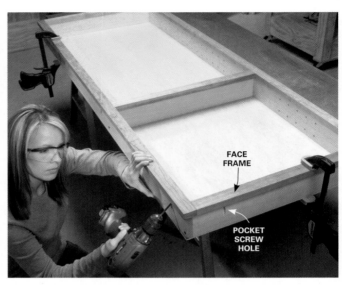

5 Align the face frame parts (D and E). Clamp them and join them with pocket screws.

6 Drill pocket screw holes on the outside of the cabinet box (parts A and B). Center the frame on the cabinet box (it should overlap the inside 1/8 in.), clamp it and attach it with pocket screws.

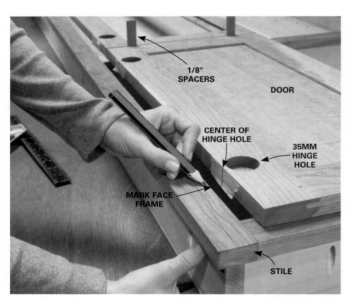

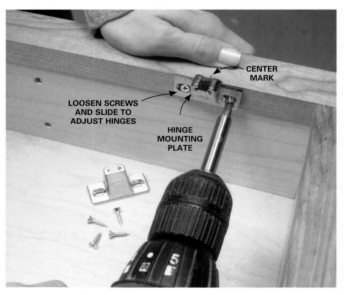

7 Mark the hinge hole centers on the edge of the doors with a combination square. Set two doors in place and transfer the hinge center locations to the face frame stile. For the other set of doors, transfer these marks to the opposite stile by measuring from the bottom of the face frame.

8 Center the hinge mounting plates on these marks, predrill and screw them to the face frame. Center the screws in the slots to allow adjustments up and down.

Build the box first

Start by cutting the 1x4 cabinet sides (A), and top, center and bottom (B) to length. Then use a square to mark the location of the center divider on the sides (Photo 1). Drill 5/32-in. screw-clearance holes through the sides at these marks and at the top and bottom. Complete the side pieces by drilling the shelf pin holes. Make a drilling jig by screwing a 1x2 fence to a strip of pegboard (make sure the pegboard has 1/4-in. holes). Position the edge of the 1x2 fence 3/4 in. from the center of the first row of holes. Use a 1/4-in. brad point bit to

drill the holes. Tighten a drill stop collar onto the bit to limit the depth of the holes to the thickness of the pegboard plus 1/2 in. Skip every other set of holes to create holes that are 2 in. apart. Be careful to mark the bottom of the jig and align it the same for both sides to ensure that the holes line up.

Screw the sides to the top, bottom and middle piece with 1-1/4 in. screws (Photo 2). Then cut 1/4-in. plywood for the back and attach it with 1-in. screws (Photo 3). Make sure the plywood back is perfectly square. Then align the cabinet edges with it to square the cabinet.

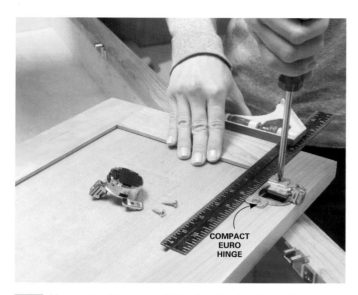

9 Line up the hinge parallel to the door's edge and screw the hinges to the doors.

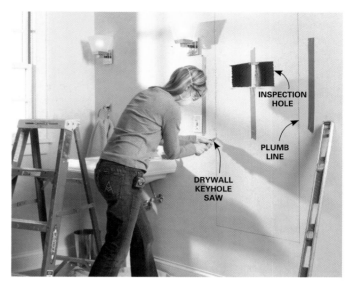

INSPECTION HOLE

PLUMB LINE

DRYWALL KEYHOLE SAW

10 Mark the cutout dimensions on the wall. Cut along the lines with a drywall keyhole saw.

Assemble the face frame and attach it to the cabinet box

Start with 1x2s that are milled accurately with square edges. Home centers and lumberyards usually stock a few species of hardwood 1x2s, but cherry may be a little harder to find. Check hardwood lumber suppliers or call a local cabinetmaker to find a source. Sight down the boards to make sure they're perfectly straight. Then use a miter saw or table saw to cut the pieces to length, making sure the end cuts are perfectly square. Arrange the face frame parts with the best-looking face down and make a pencil mark on the back of each piece. Using a pocket hole jig with a stepped drill bit, drill a pair of holes in both ends of the rails (Photo 4). Drill on the back, or marked, side. Complete the face frame by clamping the joints one at a time and joining them with 1-1/4 in. pocket screws (Photo 5). If you haven't used a pocket hole jig before, practice on scrap wood. You'll quickly get the hang of it.

Drill pocket holes around the outside of the cabinet box and attach the face frame with pocket screws (Photo 6). The face frame is sized to overlap the interior of the cabinet box by 1/8 in. Make sure this overlap is even all the way around, then clamp it before you attach the face frame. If you don't own a pocket hole jig, you can nail the face frame to the box with 6d finish nails and fill the holes later with putty in a matching color.

Attach the hinge mounting plates accurately

The hinges fit into the round holes bored in the doors and mount to a separate mounting plate that you'll screw to the face frame. Positioning them is a bit tricky. The first step is to attach the mounting plates to the edge of the face frame. Start by marking the center of each hole on a piece of masking tape stuck to the door's edge (Photo 7). Use a square to

mark the center of the hinge hole on the edge of the door. Then set one upper and one lower door in place, making sure they overlap the face frame on the top and bottom by 3/4 in. Leave a 1/8-in. gap between them (use a 1/8-in. spacer). Then mark the hinge centers on the face frame (Photo 7). After marking one side, use exact measurements to duplicate the hinge center positions on the other side. Finally, center the mounting plates on these marks and screw them to the edge of the face frame (Photo 8).

Mount the hinges next. Press the hinges into the holes and use a square to make sure the screw holes are parallel to the edge of the door (Photo 9). Then drive the mounting screws.

Cut the hole for the cabinet

In most cases, you'll have to remove a stud to make a wide enough opening (Photos 10–12). Photos 13 and 14 show how to add a header to support the cutoff stud. The metal angle brackets support the new header. The sill and side pieces aren't structural but provide backing for the drywall and a place to attach the cabinet.

Use a level and pencil to mark the cutout dimensions on the wall (Photo 10). Mark the outline 1/4 in. taller and wider than the cabinet box dimensions. Cut the drywall along the lines with a drywall saw and break it out.

The next step is to cut out the stud to make room for the header (Photos 11 and 12). Make a short level line 3-3/4 in. above the top of the cutout opening and centered over the stud. This is where you'll cut the stud to allow room for the header to fit under it. Make a similar line 1-1/2 in. below the bottom of the cutout. Cut through the stud at each spot (Photo 11). If you're careful to control the depth of the blade, you may be able to cut through the stud without cutting through the drywall on the opposite side. But don't worry.

11 Draw horizontal lines 3-3/4 in. above and 1-1/2 in. below the opening at the stud location. Cut through the stud at these lines with a reciprocating saw or handsaw. Also cut the stud in the middle to simplify removal.

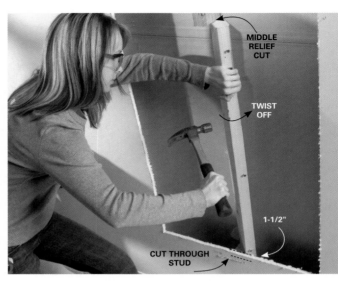

12 Pound on the corner of the cutoff stud to twist it away from the drywall. Pull it out of the opening.

13 Nail together the double 2x4 header and screw a metal angle bracket to one end. Slide it into position against the cutoff stud, and level the header.

14 Screw the metal angle bracket to the stud. Screw another special angle bracket to the opposite end of the header and to the stud.

Shopping list

ITEM	QTY.	ITEM	QTY.
1x4 x 6' birch or maple (A, B)	3	3-3/8" x 22-3/4" x 3/8" polished-edge glass shelves	5
1x2 x 6' cherry (D, E)	3	Shelf supports	20
4x8 x 1/4" birch plywood (C)	1	1-1/4" drywall or cabinet screws	12
12" x 42" cabinet doors (F)	2	1" drywall or cabinet screws	24
12" x 24" cabinet doors (G)	2	1-1/4" pocket screws	30
Pieces of patterned glass for doors	2	1-1/4" trim head screws (mount cabinet)	4
Compact Euro face frame hinges (such as Blum Compact 33)	10	Cabinet handles	4
3/4" overlay mounting plates	10	Polyurethane finish	1 qt.

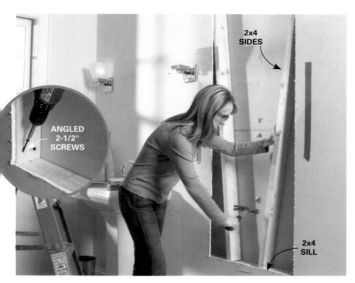

15 Nail a 2x4 sill to the cutoff stud. Level it and drive angled screws into the studs at each end. Cut 2x4s to fit between the header and the sill and fasten them even with the drywall edges with angled screws.

16 Slide the cabinet into the opening and level it. Secure it with trim screws driven through the sides into the framing. Conceal the screws by driving them into shelf pin holes.

If you do cut through, the thin slot will be easy to patch.

Remove the cutout section of stud by hitting it hard with a hammer on the edge nearest you to twist the nails or screws loose from the drywall on the opposite side (Photo 12). Measure the distance between the remaining wall studs and cut two 2x4s 3/16 in. shorter than the measurement. Build the 2x4 header by sandwiching scraps of 1/2-in. plywood or 1/2-in. strips of wood between the 2x4s and nailing them together with 12d nails. Slide the header up against the cutoff stud (Photo 13) and hold it temporarily in place with a screw through the drywall. Level the header and support it by screwing metal angle brackets to the studs with 1-1/4-in. screws (Photos 13 and 14). Cut a 2x4 the same length as the header for the sill, level it and attach it to the studs with 2-1/2 in. screws driven at an angle. Complete the framing by cutting 2x4s to fit between the header and sill on each side of the cabinet and securing them with angled 2-1/2-in. screws (Photo 15). Predrill to keep the sides from slipping back too far (Photo 15 inset).

Finish up by mounting the cabinet

It's easiest to sand and finish the cabinet before mounting it to the wall. Apply stain if you desire and three coats of polyurethane varnish. Then just slip the cabinet into the opening, level it, and screw it into the framing on each side (Photo 16). Don't overtighten or you'll pull the frame out of square. Remount the doors and adjust the hinges so the space between the doors is even (Photo 17). The top doors shown here were ordered to accommodate 1/8-in. glass. They came with a clear plastic strip that slid into a slot to hold the glass in place. Make sure to get recommendations from your door supplier for securing the glass in the door you order.

17 Reinstall the doors and adjust them until the space between the doors is even. Loosen the base plate screws to move a door up and down. Loosen the hinge screw to adjust the doors sideways.

Three bathroom storage upgrades

Bathrooms never have enough storage or shelf space. There's hardly enough room to store essential items like extra toilet paper, blow dryers, curling irons, cans, soaps and bottles, let alone display knickknacks. Once the vanity is filled, there's really no more storage in a small bathroom.

Three solutions:

1. Bigger medicine cabinet

Replace that tiny medicine cabinet or mirror with a larger, surface-mounted cabinet.

2. Glass shelves

Add glass shelving to the unused space over the toilet.

3. Built-in pantry cabinets

Steal space from an adjoining room or closet by insetting kitchen pantry cabinets (or tall utility cabinets) into the wall.

Installing a new medicine cabinet and shelving is easy and fast. Each project takes less than an hour. For these simple projects, a screw gun and a 2-ft. level are all you need. This project features a foolproof way to solidly support the cabinets, regardless of the type of wall behind them.

The flush-mounted pantry cabinets are more challenging because they require cutting into the wall and stealing space from a neighboring room or closet. But don't worry. The following step-by-step photos show the cutting and fitting. A drywall saw, a few 8-ft. 2x4s and a table and miter saw for trimming out the pantry cabinets are needed to complete the project. It takes one day to install the cabinets, but allow another day for walling in the cabinet backs in the room or closet behind the bathroom.

2 Glass shelves

1 Bigger medicine cabinet

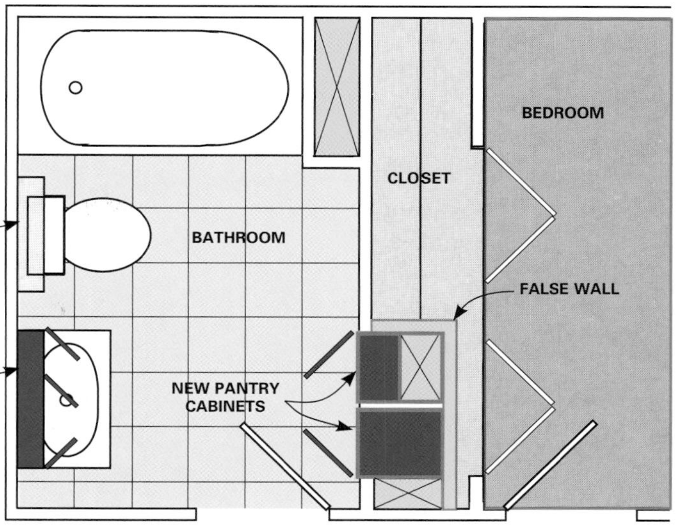

GLASS SHELVES

BEDROOM

CLOSET

BATHROOM

FALSE WALL

BIGGER MEDICINE CABINET

NEW PANTRY CABINETS

3
Built-in pantry cabinets

BEFORE

Buying the cabinets

A wide variety of medicine cabinets and shelves is available at home centers and kitchen and bath specialty stores. When sizing a medicine cabinet, measure the space available behind the sink, both height and width. Keep a few inches away from existing light fixtures (unless the plan is to move them). Buy a cabinet that fits within those dimensions.

When sizing the larger kitchen pantry cabinet(s) to recess into the wall, look for 7-ft.-tall, 15-in.-wide cabinets to fit between the wall studs. If they're not in stock, special-order them. Special-ordering allows a wider style selection. Expect to pay a minimum of $200 for a bare-bones, 7-ft.-tall pantry cabinet, or up to $1,500 for an upscale cherry unit with fluted glass doors.

For storing linens, towels or larger items, go with 24-in.-deep cabinets, but if the closet they project into is less than 24 in. deep, go with the 12-in. units or cut down the 24-in. ones. When ordering pantry cabinets, also order three matching, prefinished 8-ft.-long, 1/4-in. x 2-in. mullion strips for trim around the outside (Photo 12, p. 68). Also order an 8-ft.-long, 3/4-in. x 2-in. filler strip to join the cabinets in the center (Photos 9 and 10, p. 68). If buying unfinished cabinets, get unfinished boards of the same wood type in the millwork area at the store.

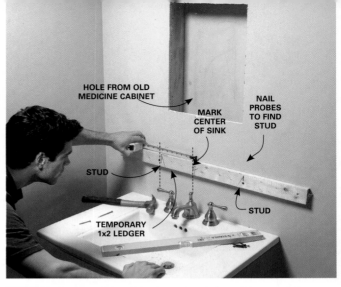

1 Mark the height of the bottom of the cabinet and draw a line with a 2-ft. level. Find the studs by probing with a nail and mark the stud positions above the level line. Screw a temporary 1x2 ledger board through the drywall into the studs. Mark the center of the sink on the ledger, and then measure over from the center mark to the left and right studs.

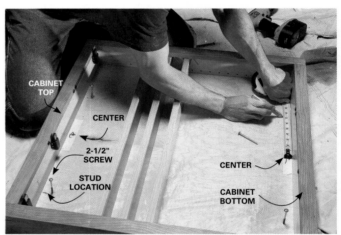

2 Mark the center of the cabinet at the top and bottom and transfer the center-to-stud locations inside the cabinet. Start 2-1/2-in. screws at those marks.

3 Set the cabinet on the ledger and line up the center of the cabinet with the center mark on the ledger. Drive the screws into the studs, then remove the ledger. Fill the screw holes with spackling compound and touch up the paint.

Bigger medicine cabinet

Surface-mounting a large medicine cabinet is simply a matter of centering it, leveling it and screwing it to the wall studs.

An old cabinet may be surface-mounted or recessed into the wall cavity between the framing. Remove a recessed unit simply by opening the door, backing out the screws in the side of the cabinet and pulling it out of the recess. Cut around it with a utility knife if it's caulked or painted in around the edges. Have a helper support surface-mounted cabinets, then back out the screws; or if working alone, hold the cabinet by screwing a temporary 1x2 support ledger under the cabinet as shown in Photo 1. Move or replace the lighting beside or above the old cabinet, if needed.

Hold the new medicine cabinet against the wall and adjust it up and down to find the perfect height, then mark the bottom and set the cabinet aside. Use the mark to draw a level line for positioning the 1x2 ledger (Photo 1). Then follow Photos 2 and 3 for installation details.

The larger mirror on the medicine cabinet will make your bathroom feel more roomy.

② Glass shelves

Most bathrooms have one space for additional storage, and that's over the toilet. Open glass shelving is a great way to display decorative bathroom bottles or knickknacks. There are many glass shelving systems on the market. Follow the directions that come with the system for the installation details, but read on for help anchoring them to the wall because studs probably aren't exactly where they're needed. Use masking tape to avoid marking the walls.

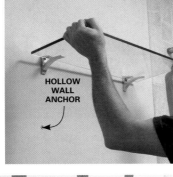

HOLLOW WALL ANCHOR

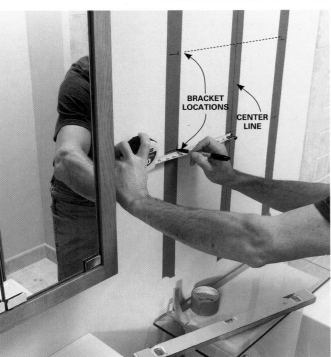

BRACKET LOCATIONS

CENTER LINE

1 Apply a strip of 2-in.-wide masking tape above the center of the toilet and on both sides where the shelf brackets will be mounted. Draw a center line with a level and mark the shelf heights on the center tape. Transfer the heights to the bracket tape with a 2-ft. level. Measure from the center line to mark the exact left and right locations for the brackets.

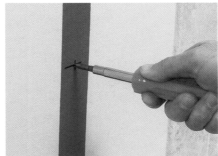

2 Indent the drywall at the marks with a Phillips head screwdriver and then remove the tape.

90-LB.-RATED WALL ANCHOR

3 Drive hollow wall anchors through the drywall.

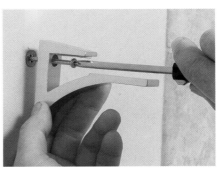

4 Screw the brackets to the wall using the screws included with the anchors.

1 Remove the closet rod and shelf from the closet behind the bathroom wall. Cut a rough inspection hole, then check for electrical cables by peering down into the stud spaces with a flashlight. Cut horizontally between the studs 2 to 3 in. from the ceiling and the baseboard. Then cut out drywall using the studs as a guide.

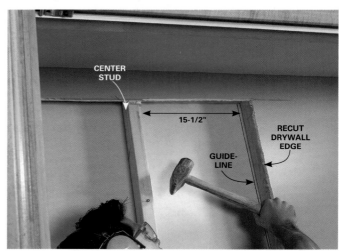

CENTER
STUD

15-1/2"

RECUT
DRYWALL
EDGE

GUIDE-
LINE

2 Draw a line along the studs on the back side of the drywall, and then use a 2-lb. maul to pound the side studs over until each opening is 15-1/2 in. wide. Use the line as a guide to tell when the stud has moved about 1 in. Pound mostly at the very top and bottom of the stud to slide it along the plates. Smaller taps between the top and the bottom will loosen the grip of drywall screws or nails. Toe-screw the studs to the plates with 3-in. screws and cut off the overhanging drywall edge.

③

Built-in pantry cabinets

Most small bathrooms have all of the plumbing on one wall, and the door usually swings against a blank wall. Often, there's a closet on the other side of the blank wall to steal space from. If there's not a closet, it's possible to take 1 or 2 ft. of floor space from the other room, but that requires going to the trouble of framing, drywalling, taping, painting and trimming a false wall to conceal the unsightly cabinet backs.

Add either one or two cabinets to a wall using the method shown here. To add more, it's better to reframe the entire wall. A full 14-1/2-in.-wide stud space is needed for each cabinet in the blank wall (that space will be expanded to 15-1/2 in. wide). It's easiest to go into the bathroom and find the studs with a stud finder to see how many 14-1/2-in. stud spaces are available.

When a bathroom backs against a closet, there are rarely electrical cables inside the wall. Photo 1 shows an inspection hole needed to check for cables or other obstructions. Reroute an electrical cable if there is one.

 tip

Sometimes a stud will bow in the center. If it bows toward the opening, push it into position and hold it there by running drywall screws through the drywall into the stud.

If there's carpeting, unhook it from the tack strips and pull it and the padding back a couple of feet. Cut them both around the cabinets (or false wall), then staple down the padding and push the carpet onto new tack strips when the project is finished. Chop off the tack strip in front of the wall openings with a chisel and reuse it at the back of the cabinets.

Crib up the cabinets with overlapping 2x4s to establish

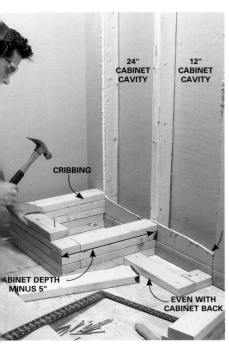

24" CABINET CAVITY

12" CABINET CAVITY

CRIBBING

CABINET DEPTH MINUS 5"

EVEN WITH CABINET BACK

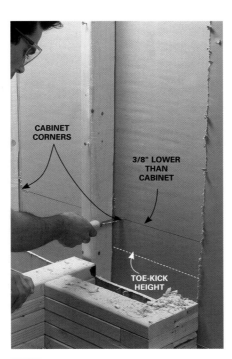

CABINET CORNERS

3/8" LOWER THAN CABINET

TOE-KICK HEIGHT

3 Subtract 5 in. from the depth of the cabinets and draw lines on the floor to mark the cabinet backs. Use the lines to position the bottom row of 2x4 cribbing. Center the middle 2x4 over the center stud so it supports both cabinets. Position the outside 2x4s even with the side studs. Overlap the rows at the corners and nail them together with 10d nails.

4 Draw level lines on the back side of the bathroom drywall to mark the top and bottom of the cabinet face. (Base the layout on the cabinet face frame. The recessed toe-kick does not protrude into the bathroom.) Poke a drywall saw through the drywall to mark the corners of each cabinet.

5 Use the corner cuts from inside the bathroom to redraw the top and bottom cuts, adding 1/4 in. to the top and bottom for wiggle room. Cut out the bathroom drywall from the bathroom side. Remove the thin strip of drywall that covers the center stud (Photo 6).

DRYWALL STRIP REMOVED

1x2 STOP BLOCK

1/2" BLOCK

24"-DEEP CABINET

1x2 STOP BLOCK

12"-DEEP CABINET

1x2 STOP BLOCK

NEW SCREWS

TRIM BLOCKING

STANDARD RECESS TOE-KICK

6 Tack four 1/2-in.-thick spacer blocks about 6 in. in from the top and bottom edges of the opening, then screw 1x2 stop blocks across both bays with 3-in. screws.

7 Remove the doors, drawers and shelving from the cabinets and slip them into the stud spaces to make sure they'll fit.

8 Screw the bathroom-side drywall into the shifted studs. Push back the cabinets a few inches and screw 2x4 blocking to the drywall at the top and bottom for trim backing.

9 Rip the 3/4-in. filler strip to 1-3/4 in. wide and cut it the exact length of the cabinet face frames. Slip the filler into the opening, then place it between the cabinets. Pull the cabinets against the stop blocks.

1-3/4" FILLER STRIP

STOP BLOCK

10 Clamp the filler strip flush with the face of the cabinet frames and with the top and bottom. Shim under the cabinet bases to get the tops and bottoms aligned, if needed. Then drill pilot, clearance and screw-head countersink holes and screw both cabinets to the filler strip with 2-1/2-in. screws spaced about every 12 in.

FLUSH EDGES

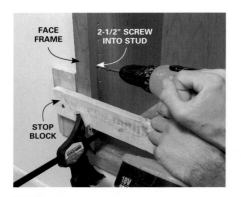

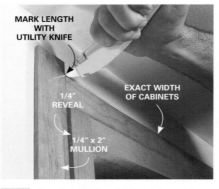

11 Hold the face frames tight against the stop blocks with clamps and screw the cabinets to the studs with 2-1/2-in. screws spaced about every 12 in. Be careful not to overtighten the screws and pull them through the cabinet sides.

FACE FRAME

2-1/2" SCREW INTO STUD

STOP BLOCK

12 Cut the 1/4-in.-thick x 2-in.-wide mullion strips the exact width of the top and bottom of the cabinets and nail them on with 1-1/2-in. brad nails. Then mark the side trim for length and cut and nail it to the side studs.

MARK LENGTH WITH UTILITY KNIFE

1/4" REVEAL

EXACT WIDTH OF CABINETS

1/4" x 2" MULLION

13 Frame 2x4 stud walls directly behind the cabinets. Nail the bottom plates into the subflooring and the top plates into the ceiling framing with 10d nails. Use construction adhesive to glue any plates and studs that join surfaces that don't have underlying framing. Hang and tape the drywall and corner bead, then paint.

the cabinet height (Photos 3 and 4). At a minimum, keep the bottom of the face frame 2-1/2 in. above the bathroom base trim. This eliminates any trim or tilework to hassle with inside the bathroom. If using shorter cabinets, adjust the height for convenience and the best appearance.

Finishing around the cabinet backs is optional if they're in a closet. Build a separate wall (Photo 13) or put drywall directly against the cabinet backs if desired. Lay drywall

Check the existing doorstop to make sure the knob doesn't hit the new cabinets. If a standard stop isn't adequate, use hinge- or floor-mounted stops.

against the cabinets; don't use screws or nails because they'll penetrate the cabinet backs. Instead, glue the drywall to the cabinet backs with construction adhesive and use paper-flanged corner beads that you tape on instead of nail. To minimize taping, stand the drywall sheets upright to eliminate seams to tape. Cut the drywall to fit tightly into existing drywall at walls and the ceiling, and caulk those seams with paintable caulk.

Space-saving wall niche

If you need to carve out more storage space in your bathroom, this is the project for you. Bathrooms are notoriously cramped, so this cabinet is designed to fit inside a wall where it won't take up valuable space. The width is slightly narrower than the 14-1/2-in. stud space, so the cabinet will fit even if the studs are a little off center or bowed. You can complete the project in just one weekend: Build and stain (or paint) it on Saturday, then stick it in the wall on Sunday!

Tools and materials

Everything you need for this project is available at home centers. It's made out of oak, which kept the cost to about $48. You'd pay $135 to more than $500 to buy a cabinet like this in a store.

To complete the project, you'll need a miter saw, a circular saw or table saw, and a drywall saw. A brad nailer will make nailing fast and easy, but it's not absolutely necessary (you can hand-nail instead). You'll also need a router with a 1/4-in. round-over bit and a 1/4-in. Roman ogee bit to rout the shelves and sill nose.

Where to put the cabinet

This cabinet is installed next to a shower, but it'll also fit nicely behind the bathroom door if there's no other available space. In most cases, it won't work over the toilet because there's a vent pipe in the wall. Also avoid exterior walls because they're filled with insulation.

Figure A:
Wall niche details

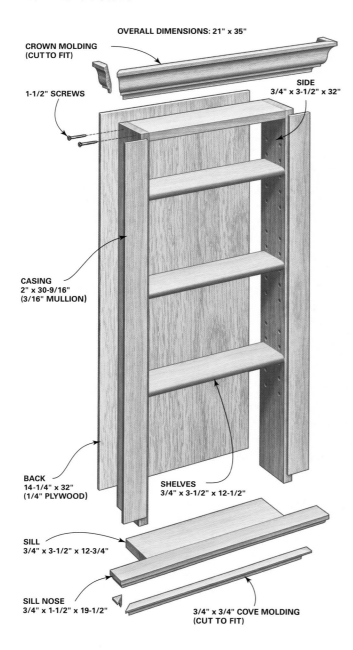

OVERALL DIMENSIONS: 21" x 35"

**CROWN MOLDING
(CUT TO FIT)**

1-1/2" SCREWS

**SIDE
3/4" x 3-1/2" x 32"**

**CASING
2" x 30-9/16"
(3/16" MULLION)**

**BACK
14-1/4" x 32"
(1/4" PLYWOOD)**

**SHELVES
3/4" x 3-1/2" x 12-1/2"**

**SILL
3/4" x 3-1/2" x 12-3/4"**

**SILL NOSE
3/4" x 1-1/2" x 19-1/2"**

**3/4" x 3/4" COVE MOLDING
(CUT TO FIT)**

Materials list

ITEM	QTY.
1x4 x 96" oak	2
1x2 x 24" oak	1
1/4" x 24" x 48" oak plywood	1
3/16" x 2" x 72" mullion	1
11/16" x 3-1/4" x 36" crown molding	1
3/4" x 3/4" x 36" cove molding	1
Shelf brackets	12

**SHELF
BRACKET
HOLES**

**ROMAN
OGEE ROUT**

SILL

**SILL
NOSE**

1 Tack the cabinet box together quickly with a brad nailer.
Then add screws for rock-solid corners. Glue the sill nose
to the sill before assembling the cabinet.

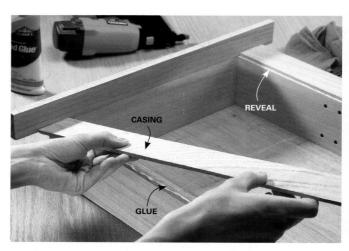

REVEAL

CASING

GLUE

2 Add casing to the box using as few nails as possible.
Three nails will hold the casing tight while the glue dries.

When choosing a location, check both sides of the wall for obstructions. A light switch or showerhead on the other side of the wall means the wall contains electrical cable or plumbing pipes.

You could also choose a different room. The cabinet can store—or display—anything you like in a hallway, bedroom or family room.

Cut, rout and drill the pieces

Get started by cutting all the pieces to size (see Figure A, left). Then run a router with a Roman ogee bit along the bottom front and both bottom sides of the sill nose. Use a round-over bit to rout the top and bottom front of the shelves.

Apply wood glue along the front edge of the sill, center the sill nose over it, then clamp the pieces together until the glue dries. Use a damp cloth to wipe away any glue that oozes out.

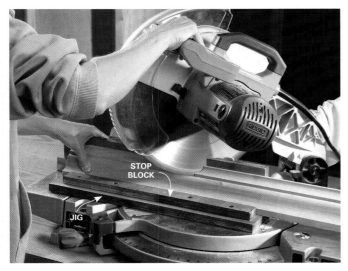

3 Cut the crown molding using a simple homemade jig. The jig holds the crown upside down as you make the cuts.

4 Glue the crown corners together without nails or clamps. Just hold each return tightly in place for about 60 seconds. Set the completed crown aside for 20 minutes, then attach it to the cabinet.

If the sill and sill nose surfaces aren't flush, sand the pieces flat with 80-grit sandpaper.

Lay out the sides for the shelf bracket holes, following the illustration. Drill the holes 3/4 in. from the edges and spaced 1 in. apart. Use a 1/4-in. drill bit (or whatever bit size is required for your brackets). You only need to drill the holes 3/8 in. deep (wrap tape 3/8 in. from the end of the drill bit to mark the depth), although it's OK to drill all the way through the sides since the other side will be hidden inside the wall.

After drilling the holes, sand off the pencil lines remaining on the sides with 120-grit sandpaper.

Assemble the cabinet

Use wood glue and 1-1/4-in. brad nails to assemble the cabinet frame (Photo 1), following Figure A. Then drill two 1/8-in. pilot holes in each corner and drive 1-1/2-in. screws to hold the corners together.

Run a thin bead of glue along the back of the entire frame, then set the back panel over it. Use the back panel to square the frame, then tack the panel into place with 5/8-in. brad nails.

Lay the cabinet on its back and fasten the casing (Photo 2). Three 5/8-in. nails will hold the casing until the glue dries.

Precision cuts are required for the molding corners to fit tightly. Measure along the bottom edge of the molding when you make the cuts (the top measurements will vary depending on the type of molding).

To get accurate cuts, build a simple jig to hold the molding in place during cuts. Screw or nail wood scraps together at a 90-degree angle. Set the crown molding upside down in the jig so the flat part on the back (the part that sits against the cabinet after installation) is flush against the vertical part of the jig. Fasten a stop block to the horizontal part of the jig

along the top of the molding. Screw or hot-glue the jig to the fence on your miter saw so it won't move.

Set the crown molding upside down in the jig and cut it (Photo 3). If the molding moves in the jig even a tiny bit during the cut, recut the molding or the corners won't fit tightly together. To cut the molding returns (sides), use the jig to make the angle cuts, then cut the 90-degree angles.

Nailing the mitered corners together won't work—the molding will crack or move as you nail it. Instead, simply glue the corners (Photo 4). Cut the cove molding for the bottom of the cabinet in the miter saw (without using the jig). Glue the cove molding pieces together.

Glue and tack the assembled crown and cove moldings to the cabinet with 5/8-in. brad nails.

Apply a finish and install the cabinet in the wall

Sand the entire cabinet with 120-grit sandpaper and wipe away the dust with a clean cloth. Then brush on a finish. This cabinet has Minwax Golden Oak stain followed by two coats of Minwax Fast-Drying Polyurethane.

Then get the wall ready. Using a drywall saw, cut a small inspection hole in the wall where the cabinet will go. Shine a light in the opening and use a small mirror to look for obstructions in the wall. If you find electrical cable or plumbing pipe, patch the hole and move over a stud space.

Make an outline on the wall (between two studs) 1/4 in. larger than the cabinet back (so it'll fit easily) and cut out the drywall with a drywall saw. Be careful not to cut into the drywall on the other side of the wall.

Finally, put the cabinet into the wall, level it, then nail through the stiles into the studs with 2-1/2-in. finish nails.

Bathroom storage & organizing

hints & tips

Bathroom shelving unit

In a small bathroom, every single square inch counts. These shelves make the most of wall space by going vertical. The version shown here, made of cherry, cost about $100. But you can build one for $50 or less if you choose a more economical wood like oak or pine. All you need is a 6-ft. 1x4, a 6-ft. 1x6 and a 6-ft. 1x8.

Cut the middle spacers and the shelves 12 in. long. Cut the bottom spacer 11 in. long to allow for a decorative 1-in. reveal. Cut the top spacer to fit (the one shown was 7-1/4 in.). Measure 1 in. from one edge of the backboard and draw a guideline for the shelves and spacers along its length. Nail the bottom spacer in place, leaving a 1-in. reveal at the bottom edge. Center the first shelf by measuring 3-1/4 in. in from the edge of the backboard and nail it in place. Work your way up the backboard, alternating between spacers and shelves (Photo 1).

On the back side, use a 1/8-in. countersink bit to drill two holes, one at the top and one at the bottom of each spacer. Drill two holes spaced 1 in. from each side of the backboard into each shelf ledge. Drive 1-1/4-in. drywall screws into each hole (Photo 2). Paint or stain the assembled unit. If you'd like to clearcoat it, use a wipe-on poly or spray lacquer—using a brush would be really tough. Mount the unit on the wall with two 2-1/2-in. screws and screw-in drywall anchors (E-Z Ancor is one brand). Drive the screws where they won't be seen: right below the bottom shelf and right above the top shelf.

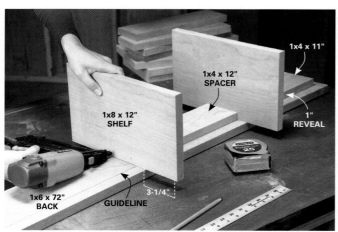

1 Nail the spacers and shelves in place, starting at the bottom and working your way up. Place the bottom spacer 1 in. from the lower edge of the backboard.

2 Strengthen the shelves by driving screws through the backboard into the shelves and spacers. Drill screw holes with a countersink bit.

Behind-the-door medicine cabinet

The biggest challenge in installing a recessed cabinet is finding unobstructed stud cavities in an open wall. The wall behind the door is usually open, but make sure that pipes, ducts and wiring don't get in the way. To choose the location for the cabinet, begin by finding the studs with a stud finder. Hold the cabinet to the wall at the best height and mark the cabinet near one side of a stud. Find the exact location of that stud by sawing through the drywall until the blade is stopped (Photo 1). Use the cuts to define one cabinet side, and draw the cabinet outline.

Cut out the drywall and then cut off the exposed stud (Photo 2). Add the framing, then screw the cabinet to the framing (Photo 5). Add trim around the edges if necessary to conceal the rough drywall edges.

tip

Before you cut a full-size hole in the wall, cut a 6 x 6-in. hole and shine a flashlight inside to check for obstructions.

STUD EDGE

CABINET OUTLINE

SAW CUT

1 Outline the inset medicine chest to fall against a stud on one side and cut out the opening with a drywall saw.

2 Cut the intermediate stud flush with the drywall on the back side. Push it sideways to release the drywall screws on the back side and remove the stud.

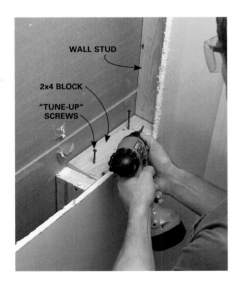

WALL STUD

2x4 BLOCK

"TUNE-UP" SCREWS

3 Screw blocking to adjacent studs at the top and bottom of the opening. Drive temporary "tune-up" screws into the block to help position it.

DRYWALL EDGE

4 Cut and tap in vertical backing flush with the drywall edge, then toe-screw it to the blocking.

2" SCREW

ADD TRIM

5 Slip the cabinet into the opening and anchor it with pairs of 2-in. screws. Add trim if needed.

Magic toothbrush holder

The problem: Battery-powered toothbrushes don't fit in toothbrush holders and end up lying on a wet, messy countertop.

The solution: Mount neodymium ("rare earth") magnets on a Corian mounting strip with Super Glue. Glue the strip to the wall with Super Glue or silicone caulk.

Tools and materials: To make the mounting strip, cut a Corian threshold ($12 at tile stores) with a miter saw or jigsaw. Neodymium magnets are available from several online retailers. Shown here are 1/2-in. x 2-in. x 1/8-in. magnets, grade N42. You can double them up if you need more holding power.

Note: Neodymium magnets are incredibly strong but break if handled roughly. Order several more than you need—shipping is expensive. Also, don't handle neodymium magnets if you wear a pacemaker, and never leave them next to your computer.

1 Mark the position of the magnets and glue them on the mounting strip, orienting the magnets so they attract each other.

GEL-TYPE SUPER GLUE

NO. 4 x 3/8" SCREW

2 Glue the mounting strip to the wall with Super Glue, hot-melt glue or silicone caulk.

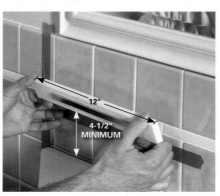

12"

4-1/2" MINIMUM

Make any toothbrush stick

Battery-powered toothbrushes have hidden steel parts that stick to magnets. Mount standard toothbrushes by adding a tiny screw or metal washer to the back.

His-and-hers shower shelves

If you need more than shampoo and a bar of soap in the shower, here's how to provide space for all your vital beauty potions: Get a couple of those shelves that are designed to hang from a shower arm and hang them on cabinet knobs. Use No. 8-32 hanger screws ($1) to screw the knobs into studs or drywall anchors.

Razor holder

Keep your razor from falling into the tub with this simple holder. Cut a 3-in. length of 1-in. PVC pipe with a handsaw. Cut two 1/8-in. wide notches in the pipe. Strap the pipe to your wire shower caddy with two plastic tie straps hooked in the notches. Drop the razor into the pipe; the blade will catch on the edges of the pipe, keeping the razor off the floor.

Two recessed medicine cabinets

Most bathrooms have a spot—usually next to the door—that's perfect for an extra medicine cabinet. If you install a recessed cabinet that fits inside the wall between the studs, you won't lose an inch of space in the bathroom. If wall space allows, you can even install two cabinets this way, side-by-side or over-under. Medicine cabinets are available at home centers and kitchen and bath showrooms starting at about $30.

PVC curling iron holsters

Solve the problem of unruly curling irons with PVC pipe. Use hook-and-loop tape to attach 5-in. lengths of 2-in.-diameter pipe to a vanity door to hold the curling irons. You can do the same thing with 3-in. pieces of 1-1/2-in.-diameter pipe to hold the cords. Just measure your curling irons to see how long your "holsters" need to be. Let your curling irons cool before you stow them away.

Laundry room ironing center

To keep your ironing gear handy but out from underfoot, make this simple ironing center (about $25). All you need is a 10-ft. 1x8, a 2-ft. piece of 1x6 for the shelves and a pair of hooks to hang your ironing board.

Cut the back, sides, shelves and top. Align the sides and measure from the bottom 2 in., 14-3/4 in. and 27-1/2 in. to mark the bottom of the shelves (Photo 1). Before assembling the unit, use a jigsaw to cut a 1 x 1-in. dog-ear at the bottom of the sides for a decorative touch.

Working on one side at a time, glue and nail the side to the back. Apply glue and drive three nails into each shelf, attach the other side and nail those shelves into place to secure them. Clamps are helpful to hold the unit together while you're driving nails. Center the top piece, leaving a 2-in. overhang on both sides, and glue and nail it into place (Photo 2). Paint or stain the unit and then drill pilot holes into the top face of each side of the unit and screw in the hooks to hold your ironing board. Mount the shelf on drywall using screw-in wall anchors.

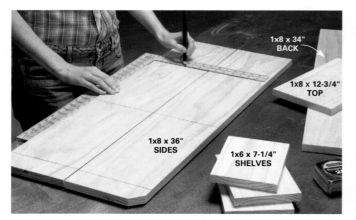

1 Place the sides next to each other and mark the shelf positions. For easier finishing, sand all the parts before marking and assembly.

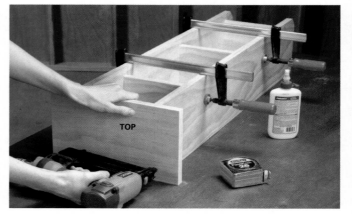

2 Glue and nail the back and shelves between the sides, then add the top. After painting or staining, screw on hooks for the ironing board.

Fold-away folding table

This 2 x 5-ft. table is a handy option for any laundry room. Located right across from the washer and dryer, it's the perfect place for sorting colors before washing, and folding the clothes as soon as they're dry. This project uses heavy-duty brackets that'll hold more than 100 lbs. and neatly fold the top down (preventing future clutter).

Buy the countertop (and end cap) at a home center or salvage one from a friend who's getting new countertops. Also buy three 8-ft. pine boards— a 1x2, a 1x3 and a 1x4—as well as some wood screws. Buy 1-1/4-in. and 2-1/2-in. wood screws for mounting the wall cleats and the countertop stiffeners. Follow Photos 1–6 for clear step-by-step instructions.

You'll need to order the clever fold-away brackets for this project. Get them from Rockler Hardware, (800) 279-4441, rockler.com, part No. 29819 ($23).

UNDERSIDE OF COUNTERTOP BLANK

1 Buy a 6-ft. plastic laminate countertop blank from a home center. Measure in 1-1/2 in. from the back side, and draw a straight line. Cut this section away with a circular saw equipped with a sharp blade. Trim the countertop to length, cutting from the back side. Longer tables will sag without an additional bracket. Space the brackets no farther than 32 in. apart.

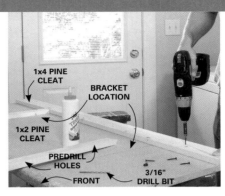

1x4 PINE CLEAT
BRACKET LOCATION
1x2 PINE CLEAT
PREDRILL HOLES
FRONT
3/16" DRILL BIT

2 Glue and screw 3/4-in.-thick pine supports to the underside of the countertop. Use a 1x4 along the back and 1x2s at the bracket locations. The supports will stiffen the countertop and provide better backing for the bracket screws.

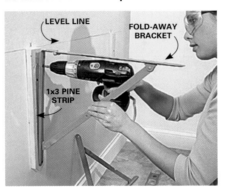

LEVEL LINE
FOLD-AWAY BRACKET
1x3 PINE STRIP

3 Draw a level line 1-1/2 in. below the finished height of the laundry table. This one is 33 in. high including the thickness of the top. Screw 1x3 pine strips to the wall into the studs behind. For concrete walls, predrill holes for anchors and then screw the steel laundry table brackets to the strips and wall with 2-1/2-in. screws.

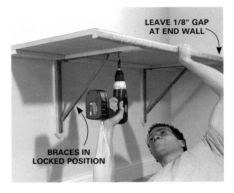

LEAVE 1/8" GAP AT END WALL
BRACES IN LOCKED POSITION

4 Set the top onto the brackets and screw them into the pine cleats (use 1-1/4-in. screws) under the table. Remember to keep about 1/8-in. clearance between the wall and the end so you lift and close the table. This will keep the wall from scarring each time the tabletop is lifted and closed.

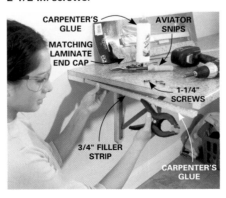

CARPENTER'S GLUE
AVIATOR SNIPS
MATCHING LAMINATE END CAP
1-1/4" SCREWS
3/4" FILLER STRIP
CARPENTER'S GLUE

5 Glue and screw the 3/4-in.-thick filler strips to the exposed bottom edge of the counter. Align the filler strip so it's flush with the edge of the top.

6 Trim the laminate end cap with aviator snips to fit the size of the end panel. Set the iron on medium heat and slide it across the whole end panel until the glue bonds. Ease any sharp edges with a smooth-cutting metal file.

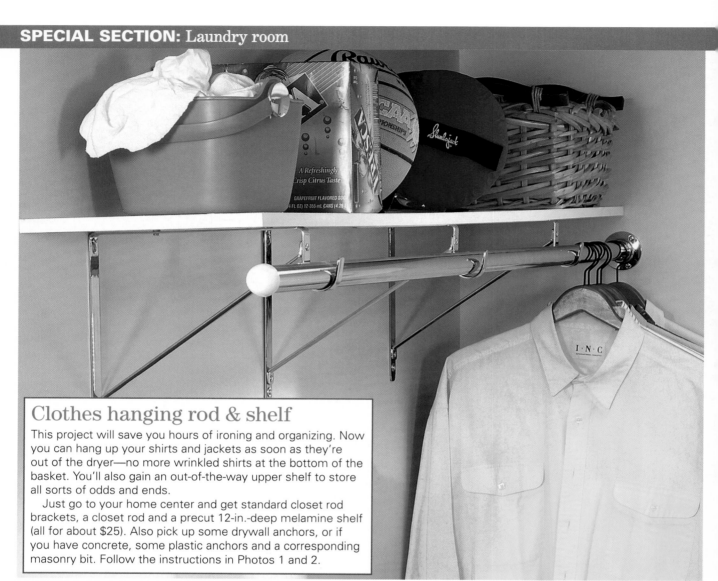

Clothes hanging rod & shelf

This project will save you hours of ironing and organizing. Now you can hang up your shirts and jackets as soon as they're out of the dryer—no more wrinkled shirts at the bottom of the basket. You'll also gain an out-of-the-way upper shelf to store all sorts of odds and ends.

Just go to your home center and get standard closet rod brackets, a closet rod and a precut 12-in.-deep melamine shelf (all for about $25). Also pick up some drywall anchors, or if you have concrete, some plastic anchors and a corresponding masonry bit. Follow the instructions in Photos 1 and 2.

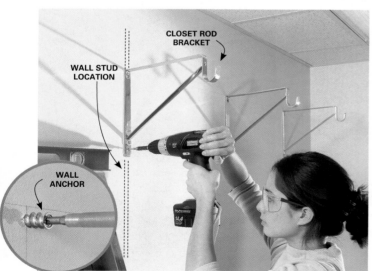

WALL STUD LOCATION

CLOSET ROD BRACKET

WALL ANCHOR

1 Draw a level line about 78 in. above the floor and locate the studs behind the drywall. Fasten at least two of your closet rod brackets into wall studs (4 ft. apart) and then center the middle bracket with two 2-in.-long screws into wall anchors (inset).

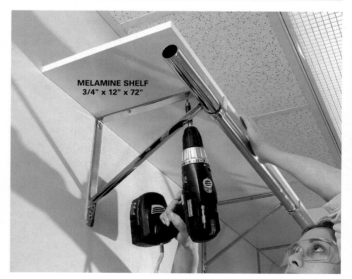

MELAMINE SHELF 3/4" x 12" x 72"

2 Fasten your 12-in.-deep melamine shelf onto the tops of the brackets with 1/2-in. screws. Next, insert your closet rod, drill 1/8-in. holes into the rod, and secure it to the brackets with No. 6 x 1/2-in. sheet metal screws.

Behind-the-door shelves

The space behind a door is a storage spot that's often overlooked. Build a set of shallow shelves and mount it to the wall. The materials cost about $40. Measure the distance between the door hinge and the wall and subtract an inch. This is the maximum depth of the shelves. Use 1x4s for the sides, top and shelves. Screw the sides to the top. Then screw three 1x2 hanging strips to the sides: one top and bottom and one centered. Nail metal shelf standards to the sides. Complete the shelves by nailing a 1x2 trim piece to the sides and top. The 1x2 dresses up the shelf unit and keeps the shelves from falling off the shelf clips.

Locate the studs. Drill clearance holes and screw the shelves to the studs with 2-1/2-in. wood screws. Put a rubber bumper on the frame to protect the door.

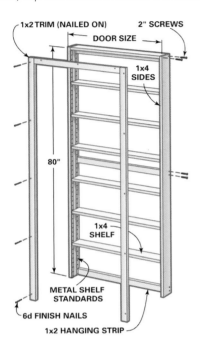

1x2 TRIM (NAILED ON)   2" SCREWS
DOOR SIZE
1x4 SIDES
80"
1x4 SHELF
METAL SHELF STANDARDS
6d FINISH NAILS
1x2 HANGING STRIP

Basement laundry rods

If you need a clothes rod in the laundry room and you have exposed joists, check out this simple, solid and fast way to get it. Attach some 3/4-in. J-hooks (these are used for hanging pipe) to the joists and snap a 7/8-in. dowel rod in the curve.

Another option for additoinal clothes-hanging space in your basement laundry area, is to make this rod from 3/4-in. copper or steel pipe and pipe hangers.

3/4" J-HOOK   7/8" DOWEL ROD

PIPE HANGER

tip

Looking for a basic towel bar like this one? Find one at any hardware store. Expect to pay about $8.

Utility sink towel bar

Get those messy rags out of the sink and onto a towel bar so they can actually dry. Shop for an easy-mounting towel bar that can be shortened if needed. Pick one up at the hardware store or home center that has easy mounting holes right on the face of the mounting plate and a removable bar. Cut the bar to size with a hacksaw so it will fit nicely on the side of the sink. Also buy stainless steel mounting bolts, washers and acorn nuts to mount the bar. This project uses 7/8-in. No. 8-24 bolts.

ACORN NUTS

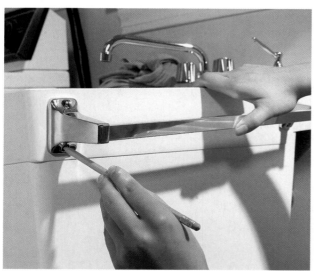

1 Mark the location of the towel bar on the thick rim near the top of the sink. Shorten the bar first by pulling the bar from the ends and trimming it to about 16 in., if needed.

ACRYLIC LAUNDRY TUB

2 Drill clearance holes at your marks and fasten the towel bar ends to the sink with bolts, washers and acorn nuts.

Undersink shelf

Tired of moving all that stuff under the sink to mop the floor? Just buy a melamine closet shelf ($5) from a home center and a length of suspended-ceiling wall angle (sorry, it only comes in 10-ft. lengths, but it's cheap and can be cut for transport). Also pick up four 1/2-in. No. 8-24 bolts, washers and nuts and then follow Photos 1–3.

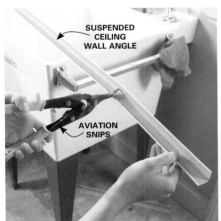

1 Using aviation snips, cut two lengths of suspended ceiling angle to support the undersink shelf.

SUSPENDED CEILING WALL ANGLE

AVIATION SNIPS

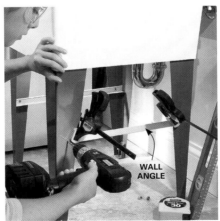

2 Clamp pieces of ceiling angle to your sink legs (about 11 in. from the floor) and drill through with a 3/16-in. bit. Insert 1/2-in.-long No. 8-24 bolts from the inside and thread on acorn nuts to cover sharp bolt edges.

WALL ANGLE

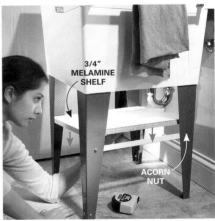

3 Cut a shelf from the 3/4-in. melamine board and drop it onto the angle braces. Notch the shelf if the sink trap is in the way. Paint the raw edges of the board to protect them from moisture.

3/4" MELAMINE SHELF

ACORN NUT

Laundry room wall cabinet

Turn that wall space above the washer and dryer into a valuable dust-free storage space by adding a utility wall cabinet. This project shows a 54-in.-wide, 24-in.-high and 12-in.-deep cabinet that's available at home centers. It's prefinished inside and out, so it'll be easy to clean.

Chances are, a dryer vent or some other obstruction exists right where you'll want to put the new cabinet. To solve this problem, simply cut away the back and insert a 4-in. galvanized duct as a liner to give the cabinet a 1-in. clearance from the dryer vent, preventing heat from building up inside the cabinet. With the liner in place, the vent is isolated behind the cabinet, keeping everything inside cool and clean. Follow the step-by-step how-to in Photos 1–5.

Buy an easy-to-clean melamine wall cabinet from a local home center—no painting required. Expect to pay about $100.

CABINET POSITION

DRYER VENT

BACK SIDE

6"-DIA. SEMICIRCLE

2" FROM BACK SIDE

BACK SIDE OF CABINET

1 Draw a 6-in.-diameter circle 2 in. in from the back edge of the cabinet to correspond with the location of the dryer vent. Flip the cabinet upside down and draw the same circle to correspond with the top.

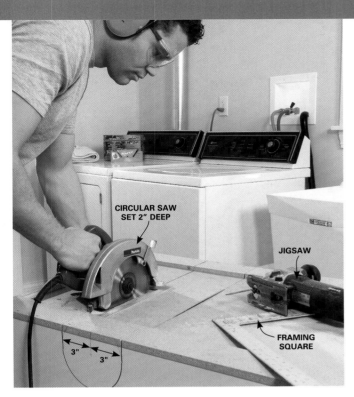

2 Cut slots 6 in. apart on the back side of the cabinet that align with the edges of the semicircles. Set the circular saw for a 2-in. depth of cut. Once the back is cut, use a jigsaw to cut along the circles at the top and bottom of the cabinet.

3 Nail a 4-in. steel vent pipe to the cabinet to act as a liner for the dryer vent. Use 3/4-in.-long, No. 17 wire nails. This liner will prevent heat buildup inside the cabinet and allow the contents of the cabinet to stay cool.

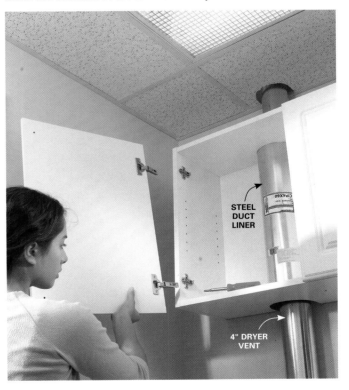

4 Level and screw a temporary 1x4 cleat to the wall studs with 2-1/2-in. drywall screws. The cabinet will rest on the cleat and a partner will be able to slide the cabinet left or right to align it. Once the cabinet is in place, screw it to the studs with the cabinet screws provided.

5 Reattach the cabinet doors and drill holes for the door pulls. Cut the shelves for the cabinet with a jigsaw to fit around the new vent shield.

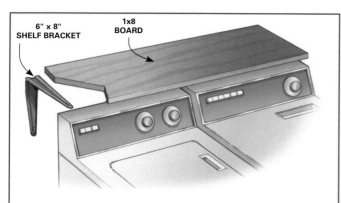

6" x 8" SHELF BRACKET

1x8 BOARD

Quick washer/dryer shelf

Clean up the clutter of detergent boxes, bleach bottles and other laundry room stuff. Install a shelf that fits just above the washer and dryer. Screw ordinary shelf brackets to the wall and mount a board that just clears the tops.

Ironing board hooks

Ordinary coat hooks on the back of a closet door keep your ironing board out of the way but close at hand when you need it.

Hanger shelf

Sometimes you just need another place to hang clothes, like on the shelf over your washer and dryer. Turn the edge of that shelf into a hanger rack by predrilling some 3/4-in. plastic pipe and screwing it to the top of the shelf along the edge.

Simple laundry organizer

Make laundry day easier with this shelf for all your detergents, stain removers and other supplies. Build this simple organizer from 1x10 and 1x3 boards. If you have a basement laundry room, you may need to cut an access through the shelves for your dryer exhaust.

Stop losing socks

Stuff a strip of foam pipe insulation into the space between your washer and your dryer or along the wall. That way, socks can't slip into the abyss. Use the size for 3/4-in. or 1-in. pipe.

PIPE INSULATION

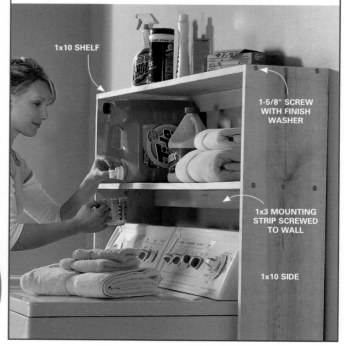

1x10 SHELF

1-5/8" SCREW WITH FINISH WASHER

1x3 MOUNTING STRIP SCREWED TO WALL

1x10 SIDE

Washer-dryer pedestal

Set your washer and/or dryer on a box and save your back. And save a lot of money by making the pedestal yourself.

The key is to make the pedestal sturdy, especially for front-loading washers, since they have a tendency to move around if they're not on a solid, level surface.

To start, measure the length and width of your washer and/or dryer. That's your minimum size for the pedestals. You can make them longer and wider if you want the extra space to stand on to reach overhead shelving or to set laundry baskets on. Or you can make one long pedestal to fit under both the washer and the dryer (see illustration).

Build the pedestal out of 2x10 or 2x12 lumber. Feel free to add an attractive finish. Use shims to level the pedestal before you set the appliances on it.

Fasten the frame together with 3-in. screws. Attach a joist in the middle. Apply construction adhesive to eliminate squeaks, then fasten 1/2-in. plywood over the top with 1-5/8-in. screws.

1-5/8" SCREWS

1/2" PLYWOOD

CONSTRUCTION ADHESIVE

JOIST

3" SCREWS

2x10 OR 2x12

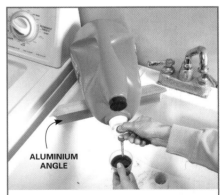

ALUMINIUM ANGLE

Minimize liquid detergent mess

Dripless liquid detergent containers always drip just a little. Keep it under control with a special shelf on the corner of the laundry tub. Just cut a 1-1/2-in. aluminum angle long enough to support the front edge of the container, then glue it to the tub with silicone caulk. Rest the container on the ledge and drips will just fall into the laundry tub instead of creating a gooey mess somewhere else.

Closet & Entryway

94

115

134

Small-closet organizer

Most standard bedroom closets suffer from lack of organization—stuff on the floor; a long, overloaded closet rod; and a precariously stacked, sagging shelf. The simple shelving system shown here cleans up some of that clutter. It provides a home for shoes; several cubbies for loose clothing, folded shirts, sweaters or small items; and a deeper (16-in.-wide) top shelf to house the stuff that keeps falling off the narrow shelf. Besides the storage space it provides, the center tower stiffens the shelf above it as well as the clothes rod, since it uses two shorter rods rather than a long one.

Here you'll learn how to cut and assemble this shelving system from a single sheet of plywood (for a 6-ft.-long closet), including how to mount drawer slides for the shoe trays. Birch plywood is used because it's relatively inexpensive ($35 to $40 per 4 x 8-ft. sheet) yet takes a nice finish. The edges are faced with 1x2 maple ($40) for strength and a more attractive appearance. The materials for this project cost $125 at a home center.

The key tool for this project is a circular saw with a cutting guide for cutting the plywood into nice straight pieces (Photo 1). An air-powered brad nailer or finish nailer makes the assembly go much faster, and a miter saw helps produce clean cuts. But neither is absolutely necessary.

BEFORE

AFTER

Cut the birch plywood to size

First, rip the plywood into three 15-3/4-in. by 8-ft. pieces (Photo 1), then cut the sides and shelves from these with a shorter cutting guide. For an average-size closet—6 ft. wide with a 5-1/2-ft.-high top shelf—cut all the sides and shelves from one piece of 3/4-in. plywood. Making the shelving wider means settling for fewer shelves/trays or buying additional plywood. Be sure to support the plywood so the pieces won't fall after completing a cut, and use a guide to keep the cuts perfectly straight.

1/2" PARTICLE-BOARD GUIDE

A A

B E

E

C

D E

D

2x4 SUPPORTS

1 Cut the sheet of plywood into three equal widths using a saw guide. Then crosscut the sections into the pieces shown in Figure A, p. 90, using a shorter guide.

BEST SIDE FACING DOWN

Figure A:
Small-closet organizer

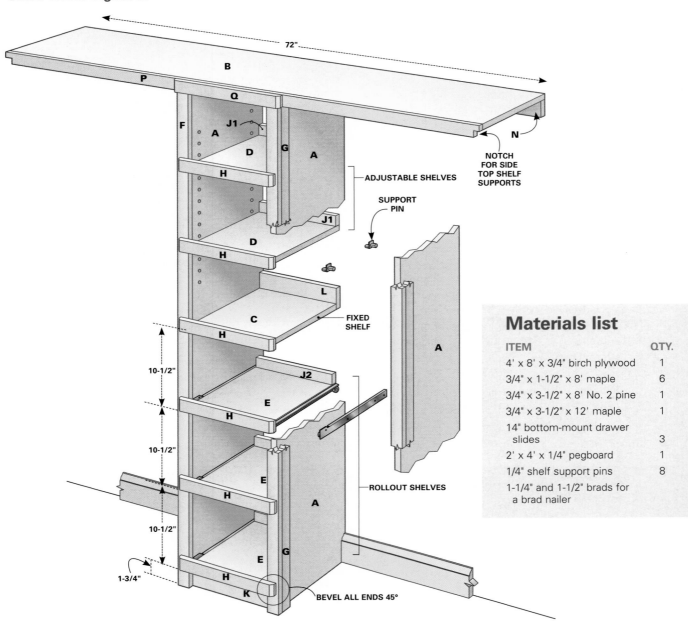

72"

B

P

Q

J1

F

A

D

G

A

H

D

H

NOTCH
FOR SIDE
TOP SHELF
SUPPORTS

N

ADJUSTABLE SHELVES

SUPPORT
PIN

J1

L

C

FIXED
SHELF

H

A

10-1/2"

J2

E

H

ROLLOUT SHELVES

10-1/2"

E

A

H

10-1/2"

E

G

1-3/4"

H

K

BEVEL ALL ENDS 45°

Materials list

ITEM	QTY.
4' x 8' x 3/4" birch plywood	1
3/4" x 1-1/2" x 8' maple	6
3/4" x 3-1/2" x 8' No. 2 pine	1
3/4" x 3-1/2" x 12' maple	1
14" bottom-mount drawer slides	3
2' x 4' x 1/4" pegboard	1
1/4" shelf support pins	8
1-1/4" and 1-1/2" brads for a brad nailer	

Cutting list

KEY	PCS.	SIZE & DESCRIPTION
A	2	15-3/4" x 65-1/4" plywood (sides)
B	1	15-3/4" x 72" plywood (top shelf)
C	1	15-3/4" x 12" plywood (fixed shelf)
D	2	15-3/4" x 11-7/8" plywood (adjustable shelves)
E	3	15-3/4" x 11" plywood (rollout shelves)
F	2	3/4" x 1-1/2" x 64-1/2" maple (vertical front trim)
G	2	3/4" x 1-1/2" x 65-1/4" maple (vertical side trim)
H	6	3/4" x 1-1/2" x 14-1/2" maple (shelf fronts)
J1	2	3/4" x 1-1/2" x 11-7/8" maple (shelf backs)

KEY	PCS.	SIZE & DESCRIPTION
J2	3	3/4" x 1-1/2" x 11" maple (rollout shelf backs)
K	1	3/4" x 1-1/2" x 12" maple (base)
L	5	3/4" x 3-1/2" x 12" pine (bracing)
M	2	3/4" x 3-1/2" x 24" maple (side top shelf supports—not shown)
N	2	3/4" x 3-1/2" x 29-1/4" maple (rear top shelf supports)
P	1	3/4" x 1-1/2" x 72" maple (top shelf edge)
Q	1	3/4" x 1-1/2" x 15-3/4" maple (top trim)

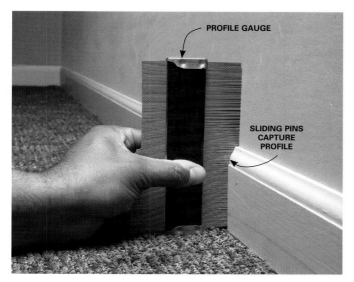

2 Make an outline of the baseboard with a profile gauge and, using a jigsaw, cut out the pattern on the lower back side of the two shelving sides. (See Figure A and Photo 4.)

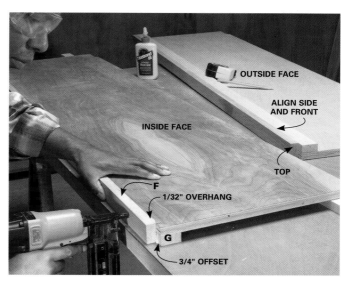

3 Cut the 1x2s to length. Then glue and nail them to the plywood sides (Figure A) with 1-1/4-in. brads. Note the slight (1/32-in.) overhang along the inside.

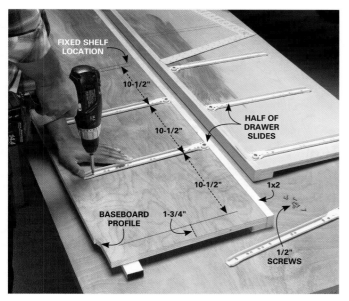

4 Mark the center and rollout shelf locations using a framing square. Then mount half of each of the two-piece drawer slides even with the 1x2 on each side.

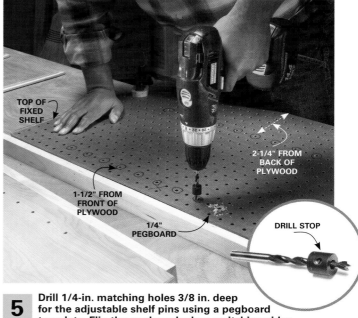

5 Drill 1/4-in. matching holes 3/8 in. deep for the adjustable shelf pins using a pegboard template. Flip the pegboard when switching sides.

Use a plywood blade in a circular saw to minimize splintering. Cut slowly on the crosscuts, and make sure the good side of the plywood is down—the plywood blade makes a big difference, but the thin veneer will splinter if you rush the cut.

Mark and cut the baseboard profile on the plywood sides, using a profile gauge ($8; Photo 2) or a trim scrap to transfer the shape, or

> **tip**
>
> Hold the brad nailer perpendicular to the grain whenever possible so the rectangular nail heads will run with the grain instead of cutting across it. This makes them less prominent.

remove the baseboard rather than cutting the plywood and reinstalling it later. Either method works fine.

Attach the maple edges

Glue and nail the side 1x2s (G) to the best-looking side of the plywood (so it faces out), holding them flush with the front edge (Photo 3). Be sure to use 1-1/4-in. brads here so the nails don't go completely through the side. Use 1-1/2-in. brads everywhere else.

Then attach the front 1x2s (F). These 1x2s should be flush with the bottom of the sides, but 3/4 in. short of the top. The 1x2s will overlap the edge slightly because 3/4-in. plywood is

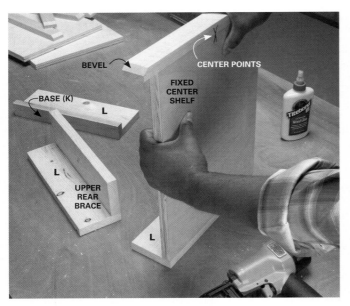

BEVEL — CENTER POINTS

FIXED CENTER SHELF

BASE (K)

L

L

UPPER REAR BRACE

L

6 Assemble the shelves and shelving braces using glue and 1-1/2-in. brads. Align the centers of each piece for accurate positioning.

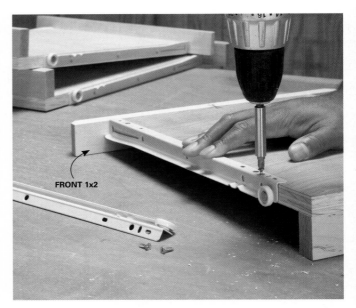

FRONT 1x2

7 Attach the other halves of the slides to the rollout shelves with 1/2-in. screws. Butt them against the front 1x2.

slightly less than a full 3/4 in. thick. Keep the overlap to the inside.

Lay out the locations for the drawer slides and the fixed center shelf before assembling the cabinet—the 12-in. width is a tight fit for a drill. Use the dimensions in Photo 4 and Figure A for spacing. Vary any of these measurements to better fit shoes or other items. Then take the drawer slides apart and mount them on the tower sides (Photo 4). Remember that one side of each pair is a mirror image of the other.

Make sure the pegboard has square sides.

To position the shelf support pins for the two adjustable shelves, align the bottom of the 1/4-in. pegboard with the fixed shelf location, then drill mirror-image holes on the two sides (Photo 5). Mark the holes to be used on the pegboard—it's all too easy to lose track when flipping the pegboard over to the second side. Use a brad point drill bit to prevent splintering, and place a bit stop or a piece of tape for a 5/8-in. hole depth (1/4-in. pegboard plus 3/8 in. deep in the plywood). Most support pins require a 1/4-in.-diameter hole, but measure to make sure.

Cut the bevels and assemble the shelves

Cut the bevels in all the 1x2 shelf fronts, then glue and nail them to the plywood shelves, keeping the bottoms flush (Photo 6). Nail 1x2 backs (J1 and J2) onto the adjustable and rollout shelves. Next, nail together the bracing (L) and the base piece (K), which join the cabinet. And add the slides to the rollout shelves (Photo 7).

Assembling the shelving tower is straightforward (Photo 8). Position the L-shaped bracing at the top and braces at the bottom, add glue to the joints, then clamp and nail. Because of the slight lip where the 1x2 front trim (F) overlaps the ply-

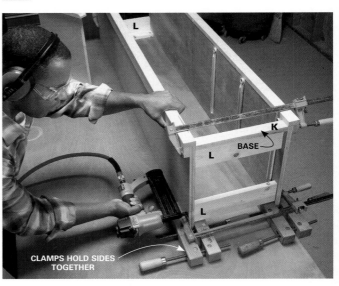

L

K

BASE

L

L

CLAMPS HOLD SIDES TOGETHER

8 Set the sides on edge, glue and clamp the braces (L) in place and nail the assembly together with 1-1/2-in. brads. Make sure the braces are square to the sides.

wood, it requires chiseling out a 1/32-in.-deep x 3/4-in.-wide notch so the fixed shelf will fit tightly (Photo 9).

Set the cabinet in the closet

Remove the old closet shelving and position the new cabinet. If there's carpeting, it's best to cut it out under the cabinet for easier carpet replacement in the future (Photo 10). For the cleanest look, pull the carpet back from the closet wall, cut out the padding and tack strip that fall under the cabinet, and nail new tack strips around the cabinet position. Then reposition the cabinet, push the carpet back against it and cut the carpet. Or, simply cut out the carpet

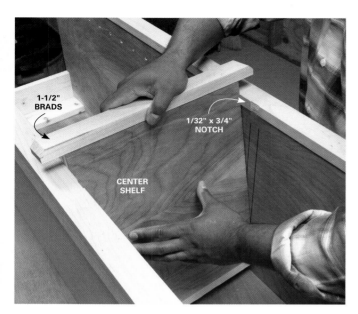

9 Chisel shallow slots in the 1x2 overhang, then slide the center shelf into place. Nail at the front, back and sides.

1-1/2" BRADS

1/32" x 3/4" NOTCH

CENTER SHELF

10 Center the cabinet in the closet against the back wall, mark its position and cut the carpet out around it. Tack the loose edges of carpet to the floor.

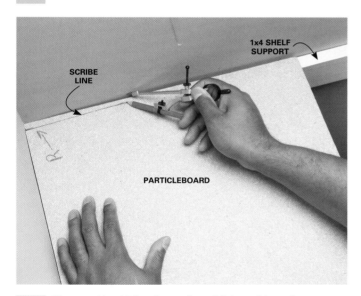

1x4 SHELF SUPPORT

SCRIBE LINE

PARTICLEBOARD

11 Shove a 16 x 24-in. sheet of particleboard into the shelf corners and scribe a line. Cut along the scribe line and use the particleboard as a pattern. Nail the shelf to the supports and cabinet top.

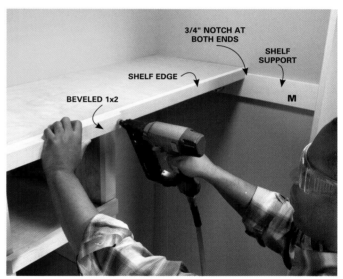

3/4" NOTCH AT BOTH ENDS

SHELF SUPPORT

SHELF EDGE

BEVELED 1x2

M

12 Notch the 1x2 shelf edge over the end supports and nail it into place. Then trim the top of the cabinet with a beveled 1x2.

and tack strip under the cabinet and tack the loose carpet edges to the floor (but it won't look as nice).

Plumb and level the cabinet, then screw it to the wall. Use hollow wall anchors if the studs are hard to find. The cabinet will be firmly anchored by the upper shelf anyway.

Scribe the top shelf for a tight fit

Closet shelves are tough to fit because the corners of the walls are rarely square. To cut the shelf accurately, scribe a leftover 16-in.-wide piece of particleboard or plywood in both corners (Photo 11) and use it for a template for cutting the ends of the shelf. Then the shelf will drop right into place

and rest on 1x4 supports nailed to the side walls and back wall. Make sure the front of the shelf is flush with the front of the tower and nail it to the top. If the back wall is wavy, scribe the back of the shelf to the wall and trim it to make the front flush. Then cut and notch the front 1x2 and nail it to the shelf (Photo 12).

Lightly sand all the wood and apply a clear finish. When it's dry, mix several shades of putty to get an exact match to your wood and fill the nail holes. Add another coat of finish and let it dry. Screw on the clothes rod brackets, aligning them with the bottom of the 1x4. Then pile on the clothes.

His & hers closet organizer

Annoyed by an overstuffed closet packed so tightly that you can't find your favorite shirt or shoes? Where the closet rod bends under the weight of all of "his" and "her" clothing?

If so, the simple closet organizing system shown here is a great solution. It utilizes the closet space much more efficiently by dividing your closet into zones that give your slacks, dresses, shirts, shoes and other items their own home. As a result, your clothing is better organized and you can find your party shirt or power skirt quickly and easily. It also prevents "closet creep," where "her" clothing tends to infringe on "his"

zone. (Or vice versa!) Overall, you'll get double the useful space of a traditional single pole and shelf closet.

Here you'll learn how to build this simple organizer, step-by-step, and how to customize it to fit closets of different sizes. It's designed for simplicity; you can build it in one weekend, even if you're a novice. However, to do a nice job, you should have experience using two basic power tools: a circular saw and a drill. A power miter box and an air-powered brad nailer make the job go a bit faster, but they aren't necessary.

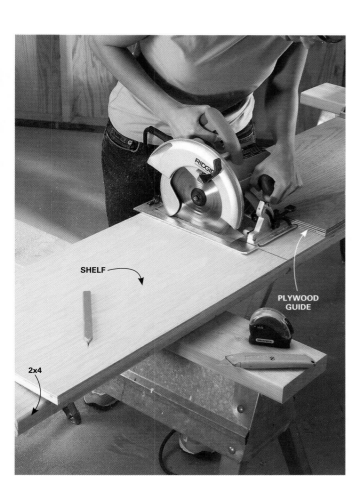

1 Measure your closet dimensions and cut the plywood vertical dividers and shelves to size (Figure A). Use a guide to make crosscuts perfectly square.

2 Measure the baseboard height and thickness and cut notches with a jigsaw on the vertical dividers to fit over it.

Don't buy it—build it!

While you may be tempted to buy a prefabricated organizer, it'll be surprisingly expensive when you tally up the cost of all the pieces. The materials for this organizer cost only $150. It uses 1-1/2 sheets of oak veneer plywood, plus several types of standard oak trim that you'll find at most home centers and lumberyards. (See the Materials list on p. 96.) Keep in mind that if you use other wood species, you may have trouble finding matching trim, and you'll have to custom-cut it from solid boards on a table saw. If you choose to paint your organizer, you can use less expensive plywood and trim, and cut your expenses by about one-third.

Begin by measuring the width of your closet. The system shown here works best in a 6-ft. closet. If your closet only measures 5 ft., consider using a single vertical divider, rather than the two shown in Figure A.

Assemble the center unit

After referring to the Cutting list (p. 96) and your closet dimensions, cut the plywood into two 13-3/4-in. pieces for the vertical dividers. If you plan to cut plywood with a circular saw, be sure to use a straightedge to get perfectly straight

cuts. Shown here are hook strips, used to attach the center unit and shelves to the closet walls, as well as for spacing the uprights (Figure A). If you want to save a bit of cash, you can cut these strips from the leftover plywood (and enjoy the gratification that comes from using the entire sheet). Cut the plywood to length using a factory plywood edge as a guide (Photo 1). Fully support your project with 2x4s so the cutoff doesn't fall and splinter. Also, for smoother cuts, use a sharp blade with at least 40 teeth.

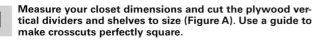

You don't have to cut out the baseboard in the closet or even trim the back side of the dividers to fit its exact profile. The back of the organizer will be mostly out of sight, so square notches will do (Photo 2).

You'll have to trim the tops of the dividers back to 10-3/4 in. to make it easier to slide stuff onto the top shelf (unless you have an extra-deep closet). You can angle this cut to the first shelf point (Figure A, detail, p. 96).

Figure A:
Closet organizer

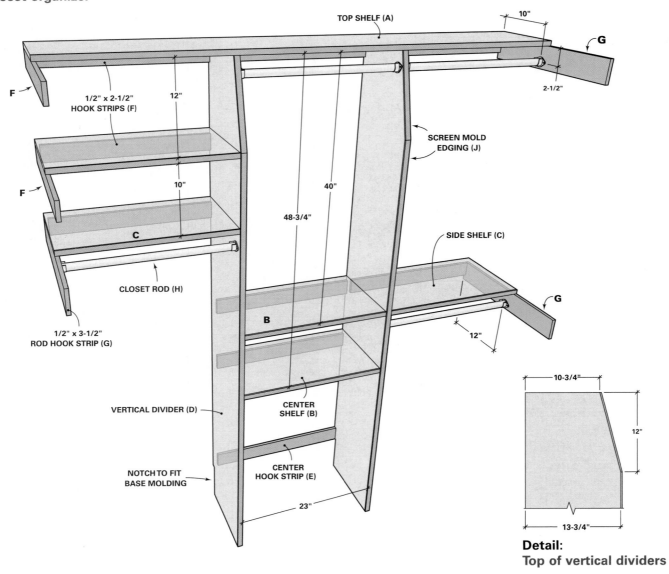

TOP SHELF (A)

10"

G

2-1/2"

F

1/2" x 2-1/2"
HOOK STRIPS (F)

12"

10"

F

C

CLOSET ROD (H)

SCREEN MOLD
EDGING (J)

40"

48-3/4"

SIDE SHELF (C)

G

12"

1/2" x 3-1/2"
ROD HOOK STRIP (G)

B

VERTICAL DIVIDER (D)

CENTER
SHELF (B)

NOTCH TO FIT
BASE MOLDING

CENTER
HOOK STRIP (E)

23"

10-3/4"

12"

13-3/4"

Detail:
Top of vertical dividers

Materials list

ITEM	QTY.
3/4" x 4' x 8' sheets of oak plywood	1-1/2
1/2" x 2-1/2" hook strip	24'
1/2" x 3-1/2" hook strip	9'
1/4" x 3/4" x 8' screen molding	4
1-1/16" closet rod	8'
Pairs of rod holders	4
6d finishing nails	1 lb.

Cutting list

KEY	PCS.	SIZE & DESCRIPTION
A	1	3/4" x 10-3/4" x closet length, plywood (top shelf)
B	2	3/4" x 13-1/2" x 23" plywood (center shelves)
C	3	3/4" x 13-1/2" x measured length plywood (side shelves)
D	2	3/4" x 13-3/4" x 82" plywood (vertical dividers)
E	4	1/2" x 2-1/2" x 23" (center hook strips)
F	7	1/2" x 2-1/2" x measured lengths (hook strips)
G	3	1/2" x 3-1/2" x closet depth (hook strips for rods)
H	4	1-1/16" x measured lengths (closet rods)
J		1/4" x 3/4" x measured lengths (screen molding)

SCREEN MOLDING

SHELF BRACKET CLAMPING SYSTEM

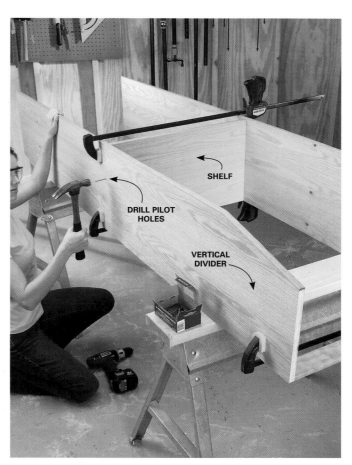

SHELF

DRILL PILOT HOLES

VERTICAL DIVIDER

3 Smooth the cut plywood edges with 80-grit sandpaper and a block, then glue and tack 3/4-in. screen molding onto the edges that will show. Apply a stain or finish and let it dry.

4 Lay out the intermediate shelf positions with a square, spread glue on the shelf edges and nail the shelf to the dividers with 6d finish nails. Nail the 1/2-in. hook strips to the dividers as well.

Apply the screen molding to hide the raw plywood edges on the dividers and shelves. You'll have to cut a 7-degree angle on the molding with a circular saw, jigsaw or miter saw to get a perfect fit on the dividers. Cut this angle first and when you get a nice fit, cut the other ends to length. You could also apply edge veneer (iron-on) or any other 3/4-in. wood strips to cover the edges.

Now sand all the parts to prepare them for finishing. A random orbital sander (starting at about $50) with 120-grit sandpaper will make quick work of this, but a few squares of sandpaper and a wood block will also do the trick. After sanding, wipe the surface of the wood with a clean cloth to remove dust.

It's easiest to apply your finish before assembly. Shown here is a warm fruitwood-tone Danish Finishing Oil. This type of finish brings out the natural grain of the wood, looks velvety smooth, and is easy to renew when you scratch or scuff it. Use a small cloth to rub a generous amount of oil

When you're gluing and nailing your screen molding (Photo 3), have a damp cloth handy to promptly wipe away any glue ooze.

into the surface until the plywood and hook strips have an even sheen, and allow it to dry overnight.

After the finish oil dries, assemble the center unit. Lightly mark the vertical dividers where the interior shelves and hook strips will be positioned and drill 1/8-in. pilot holes to simplify the nailing. Then spread a thin bead of wood glue onto the shelf ends and clamp the unit together. Use four 6d finish nails to pin the shelves securely (Photo 4), then countersink the nail heads with a nail set. Nails and glue are strong enough for holding garments and other light items, but if you plan to store items weighing more than about 50 lbs. on a closet shelf, put a cleat under the shelf to bear the weight.

Position one of the center unit's interior hook strips at the very top of the dividers and one above the bottom notches, and one under each shelf. The strips will shore up the unit and keep the plywood from bowing when you install it.

To make perfect crosscuts on plywood, score your pencil line with a utility knife. This will give you a finer cut with less splintering of the veneer.

CENTER OF UNIT

CENTER OF CLOSET

WALL STUD

5 Set the center unit in the closet, level it with shims, predrill and tack the hook strips to the wall studs with 6d finish nails.

HOOK STRIPS

6 Level the hook strips with the top of the dividers, then predrill and nail them to the studs. Continue the strip around the closet sides.

In the closet

If you have a thin carpet and pad, you can place the center unit directly on top of it. However, if you have a plush rug with a soft padding, stability is a concern. After determining the exact placement of your unit (by centering the unit on the midpoint of the closet; Photo 5), mark and cut out two 3/4-in.-wide slots in the carpet and pad so the dividers rest on the solid floor below.

Find the studs using a stud finder and mark them with masking tape. Also measure and mark the center of the wall on tape. This way you'll avoid marking up your walls. Set the unit in its position against the wall (Photo 5). Level and shim as necessary.

Predrill the hook strips with a 1/8-in. bit, then nail the unit to the studs. Level and nail on the remaining hook strips (Photo 6), starting with wider hook strips along the side walls to accommodate the hanging rod hardware (Figure A and Photo 8).

The inside walls of the closet will never be perfectly square because of joint compound and taping of the drywall

corners. Measure your closet width and cut your shelf to the widest dimension, then tilt the shelf into position. At the corners, mark a trim line along each end to achieve a snug fit (Photo 7).

Getting the top shelf over the central unit and onto the hook strips may take some finagling. Once you have the shelf resting squarely, drill pilot holes and nail it into the tops of the dividers and the hook strips (Photo 7).

Clothes rods and hardware

To avoid having to squeeze around shelves, install all your closet rod hardware before you put in the side shelves.

The hardware for the closet rods should be positioned about 1-1/2 to 2 in. down from the shelf above and about 10 to 12 in. from the back wall. These top rods were hung 10 in. from the back, which is good for pants, and the bottom rods, for shirts and blouses, were hung at 12 in. If you want your top rod 12 in. out, make the top shelf 12 in. wide and trim less off the top of the vertical dividers.

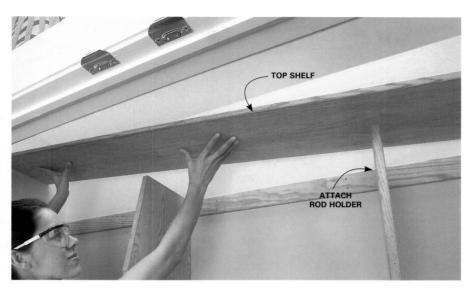

TOP SHELF

ATTACH
ROD HOLDER

7 Trim the top shelf ends to fit the side walls, drop the shelf into place, and nail it to the tops of the vertical dividers and to the hook strip with 6d nails.

8 Sand the cut edge of the side shelves to prepare them for glue. Determine the exact shelf placement and drill pilot holes. Spread glue on the shelf end and secure it with 6d nails.

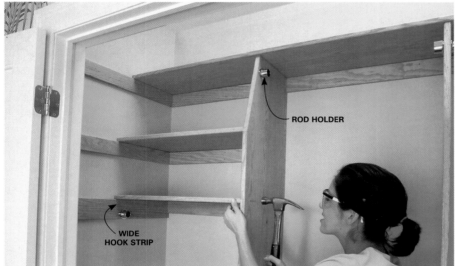

ROD HOLDER

WIDE
HOOK STRIP

Installing side shelves

To best secure the side shelves, sand the cut edge that will be in contact with the center unit with 100-grit paper. This will break up any finishing oil and provide a cleaner surface for the glue.

Lay out the remaining shelves on their side wall hook strips and use a level to determine their exact position on the center unit.

Mark and drill the pilot holes through the center unit, then lift out the shelf and apply a thin bead of glue. To prevent smearing, put the center unit side in first while tipping up the wall side of the shelf. Keep a cloth handy to wipe up the inevitable glue smudges.

Nail the shelves in place and you're done.

Protect prime space

Your bedroom closet is valuable real estate, and the only way to protect it is to store off-season or rare-occasion clothing elsewhere.

Many people use garment bags, plastic bins (stored off the floor in a humidity-controlled basement) or a freestanding wardrobe. However, many mid-century homes have closets on the main level that are 4-1/2 ft. deep or better, and they're perfect candidates for off-season use.

Deep closets can fit double rods mounted parallel to each other in the front and the back. It's an ideal setup for tightly stashing off-season outfits. Add a rolling bin on the closet floor to store accessories, beachwear or ski gloves in Ziploc Big Bags (about $2 each). This will keep your bedroom closet clear and your active gear at hand.

Every clothing item should be handled annually and those not worn in a given season can be donated. Passing along unused attire creates the luxury of space and ease in any closet.

Handsome closet organizer

Is your closet too small and overstuffed? Do your cluttered shelves, packed and sagging clothes rods, and jumbled shoes all cry out for more space? Of course, the coolest solution would be to expand the existing closet, but that's usually impossible. Instead, you can organize your existing closet with this attractive system, to make every cubic inch count and get more dresser space to boot.

It's surprisingly easy and economical to squeeze more storage out of limited space. Here you'll learn how to remodel a standard 8-ft.-long, 30-in.-deep closet, a size that's found in millions of homes. Here's what you can do to maximize storage.

Cabinet module: The 2-ft.-wide, 23-in.-deep, 78-in.- tall cabinet module is designed to provide extra drawer and shelving space. The unit is mounted 6 in. above the floor for easy cleaning. The mounting height also makes installation easier because you don't have to fool with removing and reinstalling carpeting or baseboards.

Clothes rods: Rod capacity is maximized because the rods are double-stacked at one end of the closet for shorter clothes like shirts and skirts. The single rod at the other end of the closet is for slacks and dresses.

Shoe shelves: To tame shoe scatter, we've designed a two-tier shoe shelf. Including the space under the shelves, you'll have nine luxurious feet of shoe storage—enough for even those beat-up, knockabout shoes you can't bear to throw out.

Custom-build your own closet system

It's easy to upgrade the typical single rod and shelf found in standard closets for more efficient "closetry." Home centers offer several lines of mix-and-match closet cabinets and organizers so you can design and install a custom closet system. Those systems look inexpensive—until you start adding up all the parts! A similar-size Melamine cabinet module alone will cost about $300. This is a more handsome, lower-cost alternative—custom-build your own. For that same $300, you'll have a closet full of cabinetry that's so doggone good-

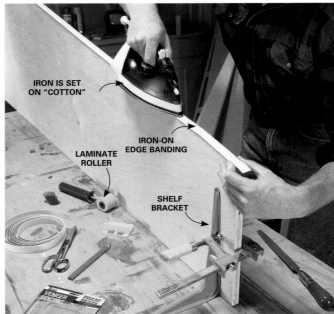

1 Cut the sides to length and width using a ripping jig. Rip the drawer dividers to width only. Cut the angles on the front edge of each cabinet side.

2 Clean off any sawdust on the edges and then iron the edge banding onto the outside edges of the sides and the two lengths of drawer divider stock.

looking that you'll want to leave the closet doors open.

This project doesn't call for any fancy woodworking joints. All the parts are end-cut and simply screwed together. While that makes for easy construction, it means you'll have to use plywood-core, veneered plywood because it'll hold screws and has a smooth, even surface ready for finishing. If you want to use particleboard-core sheets, plan on joining parts with biscuits, dowels or any other fastening system that is familiar to you. Birch plywood was used here to match the bedroom's existing woodwork. All of the materials shown are found at any well-stocked home center.

As for tools, you don't need much aside from a good circular saw, a screw gun, a carpenter's square and two 30-in. bar clamps. You'll also have to blow the dust off the clothes iron

NO. 8 FINISH WASHER

2" NO. 8 OVAL HEAD SCREW

and use it to apply the edge banding (Photo 2). But there are a few other optional tools you'll find useful. While it is possible to hand-nail the parts together, a brad nailer (Photo 8) will speed up construction. (Since you can now buy a brad nailer for less than $100, this project is a good excuse to add it to your tool collection.) Also pick up an edge-banding trimmer for quick, accurate edge trimming (less than $10; Photo 3).

Building the cabinet box

Start the project by cutting the cabinet box sides and two 23-in.-wide lengths for the drawer dividers; see Photos 1 and 5. Consult Figure A, p. 103, for all of the cutting dimensions. Before you cut the drawer dividers to length, edge-band one edge. That way the exposed edges will be finished before they're cut to length.

Materials list

ITEM	QTY.	ITEM	QTY.
3/4" plywood	3 sheets	Closet rod end brackets	3 sets
1/2" plywood (buy a 4x4 sheet if it's available)	1 sheet	No. 8 finish washers	50
1/4" plywood	1 sheet	No. 8 2" oval head screws	40
Iron-on edge banding	3 rolls	No. 8 3" oval head screws	12
Construction adhesive	1 tube	22" bottom-mount drawer slides	4 sets
Woodworking glue		Drawer pulls	4 (or 8)
8' chrome closet rods	1	Shelf brackets	12
6' chrome closet rods	1		

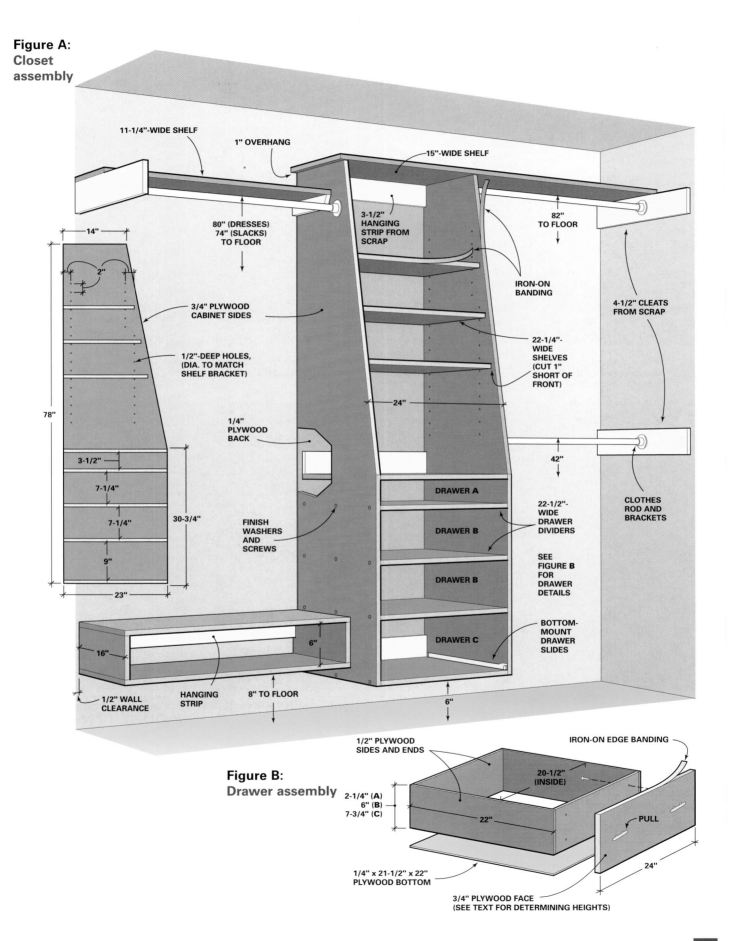

Figure A:
Closet assembly

11-1/4"-WIDE SHELF

1" OVERHANG

15"-WIDE SHELF

80" (DRESSES)
74" (SLACKS)
TO FLOOR

3-1/2"
HANGING
STRIP FROM
SCRAP

82"
TO FLOOR

IRON-ON
BANDING

4-1/2" CLEATS
FROM SCRAP

14"

2"

3/4" PLYWOOD
CABINET SIDES

1/2"-DEEP HOLES,
(DIA. TO MATCH
SHELF BRACKET)

22-1/4"-
WIDE
SHELVES
(CUT 1"
SHORT OF
FRONT)

78"

24"

1/4"
PLYWOOD
BACK

42"

CLOTHES
ROD AND
BRACKETS

3-1/2"

7-1/4"

DRAWER A

7-1/4"

30-3/4"

FINISH
WASHERS
AND
SCREWS

DRAWER B

22-1/2"-
WIDE
DRAWER
DIVIDERS

SEE
FIGURE **B**
FOR
DRAWER
DETAILS

9"

DRAWER B

23"

BOTTOM-
MOUNT
DRAWER
SLIDES

DRAWER C

6"

16"

1/2" WALL
CLEARANCE

HANGING
STRIP

8" TO FLOOR

6"

Figure B:
Drawer assembly

1/2" PLYWOOD
SIDES AND ENDS

IRON-ON EDGE BANDING

20-1/2"
(INSIDE)

2-1/4" (**A**)
6" (**B**)
7-3/4" (**C**)

22"

PULL

1/4" x 21-1/2" x 22"
PLYWOOD BOTTOM

3/4" PLYWOOD FACE
(SEE TEXT FOR DETERMINING HEIGHTS)

24"

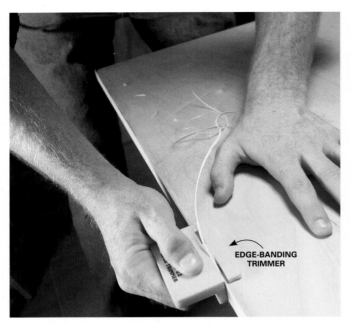

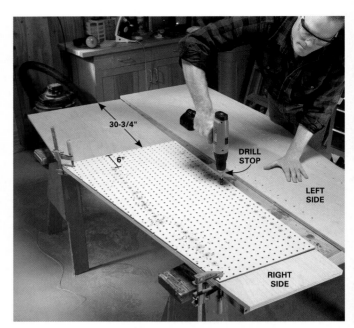

3 Trim the overhanging edges of the edge banding with a trimming tool, then file and sand the edges smooth and flush with the edge.

EDGE-BANDING TRIMMER

4 Mark the shelf bracket hole locations on pegboard and use it as a drilling template. Flip the pegboard to drill the other side.

30-3/4"
6"
DRILL STOP
LEFT SIDE
RIGHT SIDE

5 Cut the five edge-banded drawer dividers to length with the crosscutting jig, four from one length and one from the other.

5TH DRAWER DIVIDER
EDGE-BAND ONE EDGE
22-1/2"
DRAWER DIVIDERS
CROSSCUT JIG

6 Screw a scrap to the top of the cabinet, spacing the sides 22-1/2 in. apart, then clamp the bottom drawer divider between the sides. Predrill and fasten.

SCRAP
22-1/2"
BOTTOM DRAWER DIVIDER

Before you assemble the cabinet, drill the holes for the adjustable shelving. The old trick of using a pegboard jig for consistent hole spacing is used here (Photo 4). Because the sides taper, you'll have to shift over a row or two of holes to keep the narrower top shelf brackets within a few inches of the front. Try to keep the front and rear holes about 2 in. from the edge. Buy a drill bit that matches the shaft on the shelving brackets that you chose. It's best to use a "brad point" drill bit to prevent splintering the veneer. Either use

a depth stop or mark the drill bit with a piece of tape to keep from drilling through the plywood.

Begin assembling the cabinet on its back by attaching a spacer strip at the top and then screwing the bottom drawer divider into place (Photo 6). Predrill with a 1/8-in. bit and drive 2-in.-long No. 8 oval head screws with finish washers. Then stand the cabinet and, using spacer blocks ripped from scraps, position and hold the drawer dividers in place while you screw them to the sides. Keeping the dividers tight to the

7 Stand the cabinet upright and rip spacer blocks from scrap to space and support the other drawer dividers as you screw them into place.

SPACER BLOCK
SPACER BLOCK
CENTER
2"
2"

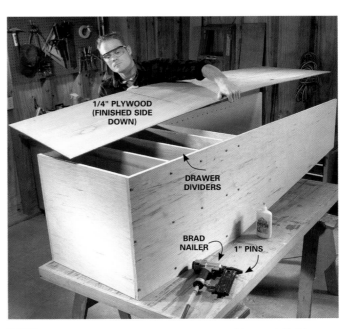

8 Glue and pin the cabinet back to the sides and dividers to square the cabinet. Then glue and pin the hanging strips to the back and sides.

1/4" PLYWOOD (FINISHED SIDE DOWN)
DRAWER DIVIDERS
BRAD NAILER
1" PINS

9 Glue and pin the drawer sides together with 1-in. brads. Before the glue sets, square each drawer by gluing and pinning the bottom in place.

1/4" PLYWOOD
SIDE
FRONT OR BACK
1-1/4" SHORT OF OPENING
1/2" PLYWOOD

10 Screw the drawer slides into the cabinet and bottom edges of the drawer boxes. Slide each drawer into place to check the fit.

OPENING HEIGHT MINUS 1-1/4"
OPENING HEIGHT
1/4" GAP (USE PLYWOOD SPACER)
FLUSH WITH FRONT
FLUSH WITH FRONT
DRAWER SLIDE

spacers as you screw them into place is important for the drawers to work properly.

Edge-banding basics

If you've never used iron-on edge banding, it'll only take a couple of attempts to achieve proficiency. Don't worry if you make a mistake; run the iron over it and the heat-sensitive glue will release so you can adjust the piece.

IRON-ON EDGE BANDING

You'll save a lot of time simply by edge-banding all the parts after ripping them to width and before cutting them to length. Then you won't have so many individual parts to edge-band, or those pesky short drawer front ends to deal with. Pay attention to the simple little clamping tip using a shelf bracket shown in Photo 2.

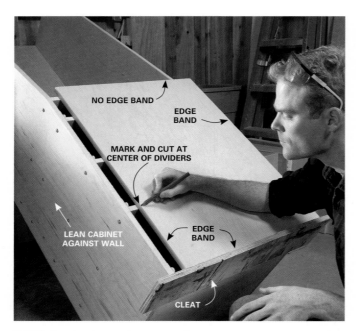

11 Set the drawer front panel (edge-banded on three sides) on a cleat screwed to the cabinet bottom. Mark and cut lowest drawer front. Edge-band raw edges.

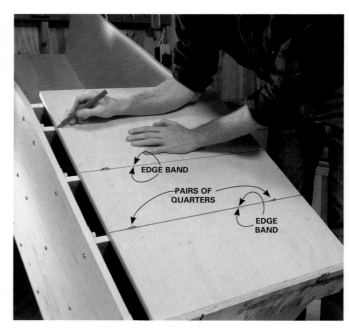

12 Space each panel two quarter coin thicknesses apart, then measure and cut the next. Edge-band the two raw edges that meet, then repeat the procedure.

13 Place crumpled newspaper behind each drawer and replace the drawers. They should stick out about 1/2 in. beyond the cabinet front.

14 Apply four beads of construction adhesive to the drawer boxes and restack the drawer fronts, spacing them with a pair of quarters.

Cut each strip of banding about 1 in. extra long with sharp scissors. Leave 1/2 in. or more of banding overhanging the starting corner because it tends to creep when you iron it. Move the iron (set on "cotton") along at about 1 in. per second all the way to the other end, guiding it with your other hand as you go. As you guide it, make sure the banding edges hang over each side of the plywood. Before it cools,

push a block or roller over it to embed the banding. Then let the edge banding cool for 30 seconds or so and check for voids. Re-iron and embed any loose spots.

Cut the ends as close to the plywood as possible with the scissors and then run the edge-band trimmer down both sides to trim off the overhang. You'll have to make multiple passes to get all of the spots flush. The trimmer works best if you

15 Lay a board across each edge of the fronts and clamp overnight. Then drive four 1-in. screws through each box into the fronts.

16 Set cabinet on blocks and center it in the closet. Plumb it, shimming as needed, and drill 1/8-in. pilot holes through the cleats into studs or drywall.

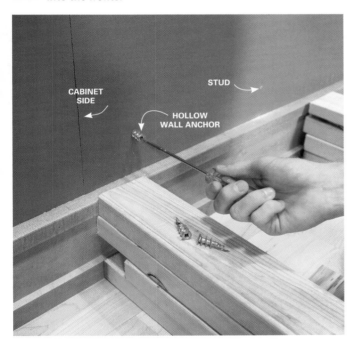

17 Remove the cabinet and screw drywall anchors into the holes without stud backing. Reposition the cabinet and screw it to the wall.

18 Build the shoebox about 1/2 in. short of the wall. Screw a cleat to the wall, then screw the box to the cabinet and nail it to the cleat.

trim with the grain. Sometimes that means reversing direction in the middle of trimming. Use a file held at a 45-degree angle to remove oozed-out glue and banding that's still a little proud, then sand all the joints smooth with a sanding block and 100-grit paper.

Drawer construction

Building drawers isn't all that hard. The key is to build the cabinet and the drawer boxes square. If you're using drawer slides other than the ones called for, read the directions before building the drawers. They'll tell you the necessary height and side-to-side clearances.

Building a square drawer is easy if you pin together the

19 Screw the closet rod brackets to the cleats and the cabinet, then install the clothes rods. Cut the top shelves and fasten them to cleats (Figure A).

20 Add the drawer pulls and adjustable shelves, then fill it up. *Still* not enough space? Donate whatever doesn't fit to charity!

sides and then square them up with the plywood bottom (Photo 9). Accurate side-to-side dimensions are crucial (Figure B, p. 103). You can shim out the drawer slides if the drawers are narrow, but if they're too wide, rebuild them.

Now is a good time to finish ripping and edge-banding your adjustable and fixed shelves. Don't cut them to final width until the cabinet is mounted so you can measure and cut exact widths to fit their selected positions. Stain and finish everything at the same time prior to installation. An oil-based honey maple stain and a topcoat of two coats of satin polyurethane were used here.

Making it fit in your closet

The cabinet unit is 78 in. tall, so it will fit in any closet with 8-ft. walls, even with the 6-in. gap at the floor. Alter the height if you have a lower ceiling.

You'll have to set the cabinet aside before mounting it to install drywall anchors unless you're lucky enough to have the cabinet fall in front of two studs. Position the cabinet in the closet, then plumb and mark the wall (Photo 17) so the pilot holes line up with the anchors after you reset it. Then measure to the wall to determine the final length for the top shelf—don't forget to add 1 in. for the left-side overhang. Place the cleats and shelves anywhere you wish.

Making it fit your space

Build the cabinet taller, wider or with more drawers. Drawer sizes can be easily altered too—make deeper ones for sweaters or shallower ones for socks. The how-to steps shown here will work for whatever configuration best suits your needs.

Closet storage & organizing
hints & tips

Accessory clip-up

Create the perfect hangers for soft items like hats and gloves using a length of metal or plastic chain and binder clips. Squeeze the metal handles to free them from the clips, slip them through the chain links, then reattach the clips. You'll have a neat hangout for all your winter gear.

SQUEEZE HANDLE

CHAIN · **1-1/2" DOWEL** · **SCREW HOOK**

SHOWER TENSION BAR

Temporary valet rod

If you often need temporary clothes-hanging space around the house, keep an extra shower tension bar handy. Put it between the jambs in the laundry room door on heavy laundry days. And other times, use it in your bedroom closet to pack for trips or stick it in the closet opening in the guest room/den so overnight guests can hang up their clothes. It's a quick and easy way to gain an extra closet!

Trapeze clothes hanger

Here's a quick way to add another clothes rod in a closet. It's especially useful in a child's closet, because you can easily adjust the height to accommodate the changing wardrobe of a growing child. Use lightweight chain attached to both the upper and the lower rods with screw hooks. Squeeze the screw hooks closed with pliers. Attach the chain to screw eyes directly or use S-hooks or carabiners. Carabiners make adjusting the height of the extra rod a snap.

Vacuum gear

It seems like the vacuum cleaner always ends up in one closet and the vacuum cleaner bags in another, and the attachments get shoved in a corner or spread all over the floor. Here's a simple tip that will keep everything together and out from underfoot. Screw a hook to the door of your storage closet and hang a mesh or cloth bag on it. You can store all your vacuum cleaner bags and attachments in one place, and the bag lets you carry everything you need from room to room or up and down the stairs in one trip.

Glove and cap rack

Make a simple rack for gloves and caps on the back of your closet door. Straighten a coat hanger and feed it through the middle screw eye mounted to the door. Put as many clip clothespins on the wire as you need, then bend a loop in the wire at each end, around the outer screw eyes.

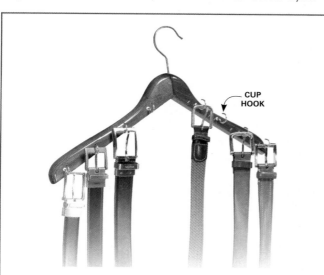

Belts and other hang-ups

Where do you store your belts? In many homes, the answer is: (a) on the floor, (b) over a chair, (c) stuffed in a drawer and (d) all of the above. All you need to get those belts organized is a wooden hanger and some cup hooks. If some of your belts have unusually thick buckles, just widen the cup hook slightly with needle-nose pliers. This is a great way to hang small handbags, too.

Wire shelving "corral"

If you store your gift wrap propped against the wall in the hall closet, some of the rolls can fall over and get lost behind other things or end up wrinkled or torn. Here's a better idea: Use plastic shelf clips and a small section of wire shelving to create a wrapping paper "corral." The rolls stay neatly organized and are easy to reach. You could corral other tall items too, like hockey sticks, bats and umbrellas.

Tie, scarf and belt organizer

Clean up a messy closet by hanging your ties, belts and scarves on this 3-in-1 closet organizer. All you need is a 2 x 2-ft. piece of 1/2-in. plywood ($10 to $15), a wooden hanger and a hook (the one shown was taken from a hanger).

This organizer is 12 in. wide and 16 in. tall, but yours can be taller or narrower. To get a nice curve at the top, use the wooden hanger as a guide. Center it, trace the edge and cut it out with a jigsaw. Make a pattern of holes, slots and notches on a piece of paper and transfer it to your board. Use a 2-in. hole saw to cut the holes, making sure the board is clamped down tightly to keep the veneer from chipping (Photo 1). Use a jigsaw to cut out the side notches. To cut the slots, punch out the ends with a 5/8-in. Forstner drill bit (or a sharp spade bit) to prevent chipping, and then use a jigsaw to finish cutting out the center of each slot (Photo 2).

Sand the wood and apply several coats of sealer or poly to smooth the edges so your scarves and ties don't snag (this is the most time-consuming step). Using a 1/4-in. round-over bit with a router makes the sanding go faster. Drill a small hole into the top of the organizer for your hook, squeeze in a bit of epoxy glue to hold it and then screw it in.

1 Drill scarf holes with a 2-in. hole saw. Clamp the plywood tightly against a piece of scrap wood to prevent chipping as the hole saw exits the plywood.

2 Use a 5/8-in. Forstner drill bit or a sharp spade bit to punch out the ends of the slots, and then finish cutting them out with a jigsaw.

Double-duty luggage

Put your luggage to use when it's not on vacation. Fill it with off-season clothes and stash it under the bed.

Closet nook shelves

Salvage the hidden space at the recessed ends of your closets by adding a set of shelves. Wire shelves are available in a variety of widths. Measure the width and depth of the space. Then choose the correct shelving and ask the salesperson to cut the shelves to length for you or cut them yourself with a hacksaw. Subtract 3/8 in. from the actual width to determine the shelf length. Buy a pair of end mounting brackets and a pair of plastic clips for each shelf.

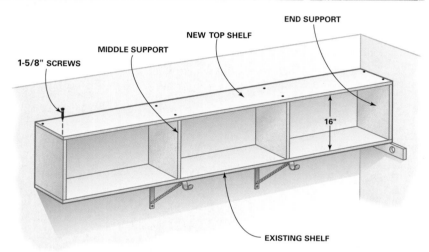

1-5/8" SCREWS

MIDDLE SUPPORT

NEW TOP SHELF

END SUPPORT

16"

EXISTING SHELF

Two-story closet shelves

There's a lot of space above the shelf in most closets. Even though it's a little hard to reach, it's a great place to store seldom-used items or off-season clothing. Make use of this wasted space by adding a second shelf above the existing one. Buy enough closet shelving material to match the length of the existing shelf plus enough for two end supports and middle supports over each bracket. Twelve-in.-wide shelving (about $9 for an 8-ft. length) is available in various lengths and finishes at home centers and lumberyards. Cut the supports 16 in. long, or place the second shelf at whatever height you like. Screw the end supports to the walls at each end. Use drywall anchors if you can't hit a stud. Then mark the position of the middle supports onto the top and bottom shelves with a square and drill 5/32-in. clearance holes through the shelves. Drive 1-5/8-in. screws through the shelf into the supports.

S-HOOK

S-hook hang-up

Turn any closet into a useful hang-up storage space by adding S-hooks to wire shelving. This provides tidy storage for mops, brooms and other cleaning tools.

Entry organizer

N eed a home for all the coats, toys, books, shoes and other stuff that accumulates next to your entry door? Adjustable shelves and hooks make this open locker the perfect catchall. Construction is simple—just cut the pieces to length and nail them together. The total cost is about $300, but you can build it for $200 if you substitute plywood for the 16-in.-wide laminated pine panels shown here.

First, sand the plywood back and both sides of the pine panels with 120- or 150-grit sandpaper. Check the ends of the panels to make sure they're square, and measure the widths to make sure they're all the same. If you want to paint the plywood back and pine panel sides and shelves different colors, as shown, paint or stain all the pieces separately before putting the locker together.

Cut all the panels and shelves to the lengths in the Cutting List on p. 114. Glue and nail the top, bottom and center nailers to the sides, nailing from inside with 1-1/4-in. brad nails so the nails are hidden. Set the sides upright on a large worktable or flat area of the floor, then nail the top, bottom and center fixed shelves to the nailers. Keep the best edges of the sides facing up. Check to be sure all the edges are aligned to each other in the front as you assemble the locker.

After the shelves are nailed into place, square the locker by measuring diagonally from corner to corner, first from one side and then the other, and then pushing the corners in or out until the measurements are equal. Set the two center dividers into place, square them against the front edge, and then nail them through the top and bottom fixed shelves, using four nails at each end.

Turn the locker over so the back is facing up. Measure the location of the center dividers and shelves from the sides, then mark these locations on the back of the plywood. Set the plywood on the back of the locker with the best side facing down. Predrill and screw the plywood down at one corner, then align the rest of the framework to the plywood as you screw it down to the sides. Finally, screw the plywood to the center dividers and shelves. Use four screws for each divider and shelf and eight for each side.

Turn the locker over again and glue and nail the back shelf supports to the plywood, tight up against each shelf. Fasten the nailers to the plywood with 1-1/4-in. nails, but drive them at about a 15-degree angle so they don't stick through the back of the plywood. You may also need to lower the air pressure on your compressor.

Nail the front trim to the front edge of the shelves and to the sides, then glue and nail the front support under the bottom shelf, into the back of the 1x4 base.

Materials list

ITEM	QTY.
16" x 3/4" x 8' laminated pine panel	6
4' x 8' x 1/2" finish-grade plywood	1
1x2 x 8' pine	3
1x3 x 10' clear pine	1
1x4 x 6' clear pine	1
Shelf standards (5' or 6')	12
1-1/4" screws	1 lb.
1-1/4" brad nails	1 lb.

Finally, attach the shelf standards and hooks. You can make one cubby all shelves or leave the shelves out entirely and just make space for hanging coats. Locate and mark the wall studs, then move the locker into position. For a permanent installation, remove the baseboard and recut it around the locker. Shim the base of the locker, if necessary, then screw the locker to the studs just above the center shelf to prevent it from ever tipping forward.

Figure A:
Organizer
details

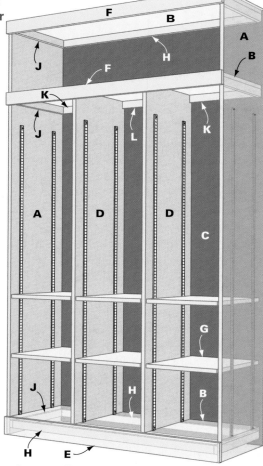

Overall dimensions: 84" H x 48" W x 17-1/4" D

Cutting list

KEY	PCS.	SIZE & DESCRIPTION
A	2	3/4" x 16" x 7' sides
B	3	3/4" x 16" x 46-1/2" fixed shelves
C	1	48" x 84" x 1/2" plywood back
D	2	3/4" x 16" x 65-1/4" center dividers
E	1	3/4" x 3-1/2" x 48" front trim
F	2	3/4" x 2-1/2" x 48" front trim
G	6	3/4" x 16" x 14-1/2" shelves
H	3	3/4" x 1-1/2" x 45" supports
J	6	3/4" x 1-1/2" x 16" nailers
K	2	3/4" x 1-1/2" x 14-1/4" shelf supports
L	1	3/4" x 1-1/2" x 15" center shelf support

Shoe-storage booster stool

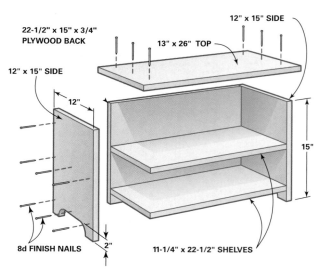

Build this handy stool in one hour and park it in your entryway. You can also use it as a step to reach the high shelf in a closet. All you need is a 4 x 4-ft. sheet of 3/4-in. plywood, wood glue and a handful of 8d finish nails. Cut the plywood pieces according to the illustration. Spread wood glue on the joints, then nail them together with 8d finish nails. First nail through the sides into the back. Then nail through the top into the sides and back. Finally, mark the location of the two shelves and nail through the sides into the shelves.

22-1/2" x 15" x 3/4"
PLYWOOD BACK

12" x 15" SIDE

13" x 26" TOP

12" x 15" SIDE

12"

15"

8d FINISH NAILS

2"

11-1/4" x 22-1/2" SHELVES

Entryway coat locker

This furniture-quality coat locker utilizes pocket screw joinery, so even a novice woodworker can achieve excellent results. Don't be intimidated!

Pocket screw joints are best described as a screw version of toenailing, where boards are joined by angling a fastener through the edge of one into the other. The concept is simple, but the precisely engineered drill guide (the jig), drill bit and pocket screws are what make the system so easy and foolproof.

Buy a good pocket screw jig

Purchase a Kreg pocket screw jig, the special clamp, the stepped drill bit with a stop collar and the square driver bit from the Kreg Tool Company (kreg-tool.com; amazon.com). The model shown in the photos on p. 118 is no longer available, but the newer models work just the same. Avoid the temptation to buy an inexpensive jig; you'll never experience the real benefits of pocket screws if you're frustrated by a poorly designed tool. Less-expensive jigs lack the self-aligning lip and built-in clamp found on this and other high-quality models. You can get higher-priced pocket hole jigs that have more elaborate clamping systems and built-in motors to speed up the operation, but the end result is essentially the same.

Materials list

ITEM	QTY.
3/4" x 4' x 8' birch plywood	2
1/4" x 4' x 8' birch plywood	1
1x2 x 12' birch or maple board	2
1x3 x 6' birch or maple board	2
1x4 x 6' birch or maple board	2
1x6 x 8' birch or maple board	1
1x6 x 5' birch or maple board	1
1x8 x 3' birch or maple board	1
11/16" x 1-3/8" x 6' birch base cap	1
9/16" x 2" x 6' birch cove molding	1
2x4 x 3' scrap for fillers	
1-1/4" pocket screws	130
1-1/4" drywall screws	8
No. 8 x 1-1/4" pan head screws	8
No. 10 finish washers	8
6d finish nails	1 lb.
1" x 17-gauge brads	1 pkg.
1" paneling nails	1 pkg.
Carpenter's glue	8 oz.
Blum B230M 12" drawer slides	2 pairs
Coat hooks	6
Drawer knobs	2
Benjamin Moore No. 241 Colonial Maple stain	1 qt.
Black stain	1 pt.
Sanding sealer	1 qt.
Satin finish varnish	1 qt.
Interior wood primer and paint	

Cutting list

KEY	PCS.	SIZE & DESCRIPTION
PLYWOOD BOX		
A	8	3/4" x 13-3/4" x 16-7/8" horizontals
B1	2	3/4" x 14" x 72" sides
B2	1	3/4" x 13-3/4" x 72" upright
C	1	3/4" x 14-7/8" x 36-1/4" top
D	1	1/4" x 35-1/2" x 72" back
FACE FRAME PARTS		
E	1	3/4" x 5-1/2" x 31" rail
F	1	3/4" x 3" x 31" top rail
G	4	3/4" x 1-1/2" x 14-3/4" intermediate rails
H	2	3/4" x 2-1/2" x 72" side rails
J	1	3/4" x 1-1/2" x 62-7/8" middle rail
TRIM AND EDGE BAND		
K1	2	3/4" x 1-1/2" x 17" edge band*
K2	1	3/4" x 1-1/2" x 40" edge band*
L1	2	3/4" x 3" x 16" base*
L2	1	3/4" x 3" x 40" base*
M1	2	11/16" x 1-3/8" x 16" base cap*
M2	1	11/16" x 1-3/8" x 40" base cap*
N1	2	9/16" x 2" x 17" cove molding*
N2	1	9/16" x 2" x 40" cove molding*
P	2	3/4" x 3-1/2" x 16-7/8" hook strips
*Miter-cut to finished lengths during assembly		
DRAWER PARTS		
Q	4	3/4" x 12-1/4" x 4-3/4" ends
R	4	3/4" x 13" x 4-3/4" sides
S	2	1/4" x 13-3/4" x 13" plywood bottom
T	2	3/4" x 5-13/16" x 14-9/16" fronts
U	4	1" x 2" x 6-3/4" fillers
V	2	3/4" x 6-3/4" x 13-3/4" filler panels
W	2	3/8" x 1-1/2" x 13-3/4" filler strips

The joinery system is incomplete without the specially designed pocket screws. These screws have a narrow shank with a thread-cutting tip to avoid splitting hardwoods, and a strong head with a square recess for slip-proof driving. The most common length is 1-1/4 in., the best size for joining 3/4-in.-thick material. Corrosion-resistant exterior screws, washer head screws for joining particleboard, and hi-lo thread screws for softwood are also available. To check out the various types, order an assortment for about $30 from the Kreg Tool Company (kregtool.com).

Building the coat locker

This coat locker is constructed of 3/4-in. birch plywood with 3/4-in. solid-birch boards for the face frame, drawer sides and front, baseboard and top edge. The back and drawer bottoms are 1/4-in. birch plywood. The plywood and boards shown here were purchased from a local hardwood lumber supplier. This is usually the best source for good-quality hardwood boards, and you can have them cut to the right width and planed smooth on all four edges. You can also get your materials at home centers and full-service lumberyards.

Even though this coat locker is built with simple pocket screw joints, many of the parts must be cut to precise dimensions. You can use a circular saw guided by a clamped straightedge to cut the plywood. You'll need a power miter box ($25 a day to rent) for cutting the face frame, edge band, drawer sides and moldings.

Cut out the plywood parts and drill pocket holes in the horizontal fixed shelves (A) and top and bottom pieces (also A). See Photo 1. For this project, the pocket holes will either be hidden from view or filled, so there's no need to precisely locate the holes.

Join all of the horizontal panels (A) to the sides and upright (B1 and B2) with pocket screws, making sure to face the screw holes to the hidden or least conspicuous side (Photo 2). Check the cabinet box for square by measuring

continued on p. 119

Figure A:
Coat locker

SECTION VIEW AT TOP RIGHT

C
A
K1
N1
1" BRAD
B1
1-1/4" DRYWALL SCREW
1-1/4" POCKET SCREWS

36" OVERALL
F
3"
J
11"
G
1-1/2"
1-1/2"
2-1/2"
14-3/4"
72"
H

1-1/4" POCKET SCREW (TYPICAL)

K1
K1
C
K2

A
A
45° MITER (TYPICAL)

F

N1

N2

1" BRAD

A

A

P

1/4" DEEP x 1/2" RABBET

G

G

J

B2

B1

D

1" PANEL NAIL

B1

M1

1-1/4" POCKET SCREWS
1-1/2"
G
G
6"
E
5-1/2"
5/8"

FACE FRAME
(REAR VIEW)

1/2" SPACING FOR DRAWER SLIDES (TYPICAL)

B1

R

V

U

5/16"-DIA. HOLE

Q

T

1-1/4" POCKET SCREW (TYP.)

H

U

V

A

W

G

U

E

M2

H

R

S

Q

R

Q

T

NO. 8 x 1-1/4" PAN HEAD SCREW AND NO. 10 WASHER (4 REQD.)

DRAWER KNOB

L1

45° MITERS (TYPICAL)

L2

6d FINISH NAIL

1" BRAD

DRAWER SLIDE

1" PANEL NAIL

1 Clamp the pocket hole jig to the horizontal panel (A) and workbench. Follow the manufacturer's instructions for setting the stop collar on the special bit to the correct depth. Insert the bit into the jig's metal sleeve before you turn on the drill. Start the drill so the bit is turning at full speed (2,000 rpm is recommended). Then bore the clearance and pilot hole in one step by pushing the bit into the workpiece until the stop collar contacts the metal sleeve. Bore three holes on both ends of the eight horizontal panels.

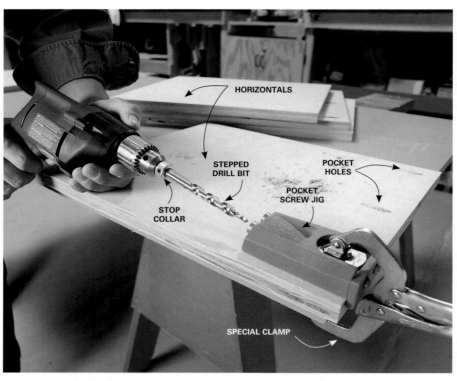

HORIZONTALS

STEPPED DRILL BIT

POCKET HOLES

POCKET SCREW JIG

STOP COLLAR

SPECIAL CLAMP

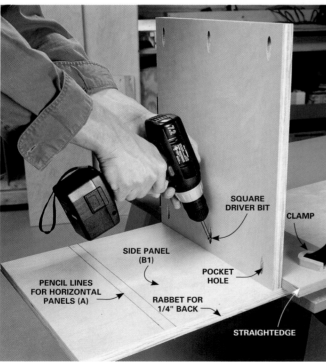

SQUARE DRIVER BIT

CLAMP

SIDE PANEL (B1)

POCKET HOLE

PENCIL LINES FOR HORIZONTAL PANELS (A)

RABBET FOR 1/4" BACK

STRAIGHTEDGE

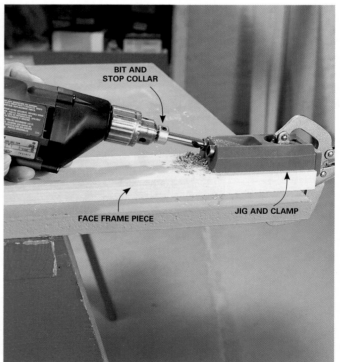

BIT AND STOP COLLAR

FACE FRAME PIECE

JIG AND CLAMP

2 Lay out the horizontal panel (A) locations with a framing square. Then clamp a straightedge along the line to hold the panels in position while you drive in the 1-1/4-in. pocket screws. Attach all eight panels (A) to the sides and upright (B1 and B2).

3 Clamp the jig to the end of a face frame board and bore holes for two pocket screws. Drill the opposite end, and all other face frame parts that need pocket screw holes. Remember that only one half of each joint needs pocket screw holes. Drill parallel to the grain, as shown.

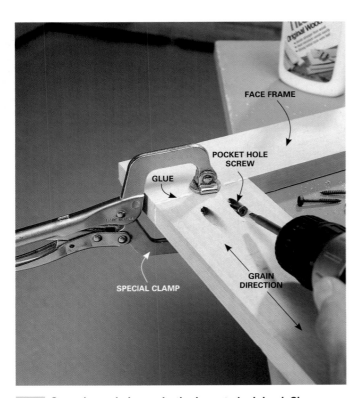

4 Spread wood glue on both pieces to be joined. Clamp the joint together to hold the faces flush, and drive in the 1-1/4-in. pocket screws. Shown is a special locking pliers–type clamp provided by the jig manufacturer.

Labels on image: FACE FRAME, POCKET HOLE SCREW, GLUE, SPECIAL CLAMP, GRAIN DIRECTION

continued from p. 116

diagonally across the corners. Now you can use the box as a pattern for cutting out and joining the face frame parts.

Cut the 3/4-in. solid-birch face frame parts to length using a power miter box. For tight-fitting joints, the edges of the boards must be square to the face and the end joints cut perfectly square. Bore the pocket screw holes (Photo 3). Now assemble the frame without glue and set it onto the box to check the fit. Take the frame apart, adjust the size if necessary, reassemble it using glue, and attach it to the box (Photos 4 and 5).

Photos 6 and 7 show how to assemble the drawer box and attach the slides. You can use the inexpensive epoxy-coated drawer slides, as shown, but for better access to the drawer interior, you could install full-extension slides instead. Use whatever shimming material you have around to build out the sides of the drawer compartments flush with the edge of the face frame. Then you can mount the slide as shown in Photo 7.

Attaching the drawer front (T) so it's perfectly aligned is a little tricky. Start by drilling four 5/16-in. holes in the front of the drawer box. Place the drawer in the opening. Use double-faced carpet tape or hot-melt glue to temporarily secure the drawer front to the drawer box. Gently open the drawer and clamp the front to the box. Attach it with four No. 8 x 1-1/4-in. pan head screws with No. 10 finish

Pros and cons of pocket screws

Pocket screw joints have many advantages over more traditional joinery:

■ You can assemble large frames without needing an arsenal of expensive clamps because the screws provide the clamping action while the glue dries.

■ No fancy cutting is required; joints are simply butted together, saving time and reducing tool costs.

■ The use of an alignment clamp during assembly ensures flush joints without any tricky measuring.

Pocket screw joints aren't perfect:

■ Every joint leaves behind a long, oblong hole that looks bad when it's prominent, like on cabinet doors. Luckily, you can order wood plugs in just about any species to fill these odd holes—you just glue them in and sand them flush. Dowels, biscuits or mortise-and-tenon joints would be a better choice if the back side of a joint will be highly visible.

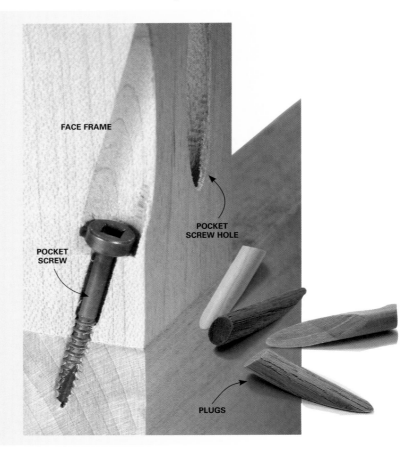

Labels on image: FACE FRAME, POCKET SCREW HOLE, POCKET SCREW, PLUGS

5 Attach the face frame to the box. First bore pocket screw holes every 16 in. along the inside front edge of the box, placing them in concealed locations when possible. After checking the alignment, spread an even layer of wood glue on the edge of the plywood and use a clamp to hold the frame in position while you attach it to the box with pocket screws. Remove excess glue with a damp rag. When the glue is dry, sand the outside edge of the face frame flush with the box, being careful not to sand through the thin veneer on the plywood.

Since screws enter the center upright panel from opposite sides, be sure to offset the pocket holes so the screws don't collide.

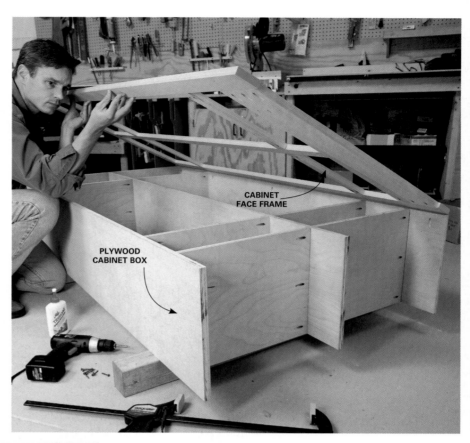

CABINET FACE FRAME

PLYWOOD CABINET BOX

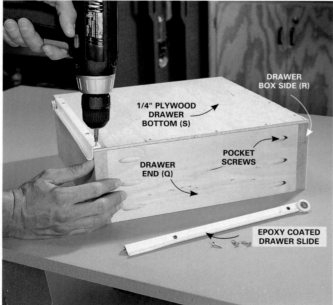

DRAWER BOX SIDE (R)

1/4" PLYWOOD DRAWER BOTTOM (S)

POCKET SCREWS

DRAWER END (Q)

EPOXY COATED DRAWER SLIDE

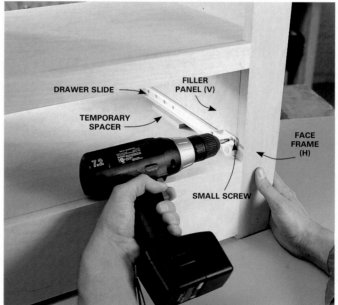

DRAWER SLIDE

FILLER PANEL (V)

TEMPORARY SPACER

FACE FRAME (H)

SMALL SCREW

6 Cut 1x6 boards to form a box that is 13 in. long and exactly 1 in. narrower than the drawer opening in the face frame. Bore pocket holes on the end drawer pieces (Q) as shown and screw the box together. Use a framing square to square up the drawer. Then nail on the 1/4-in. plywood bottom with 1-in. paneling nails. Attach the 12-in. epoxy-coated slides to the drawer with the screws provided, aligning the front (the end without the wheel) of the slide with the front of the drawer box.

7 Shim the sides of the drawer compartments flush to the face frame with scraps of plywood and shims ripped to the proper thickness. Then attach the other half of the drawer slides, holding the front edge of the slide even with the front edge of the face frame. (Check the manufacturer's specifications for exact placement.) Use a spacer to hold the drawer slide parallel to the cabinet bottom while you screw it in.

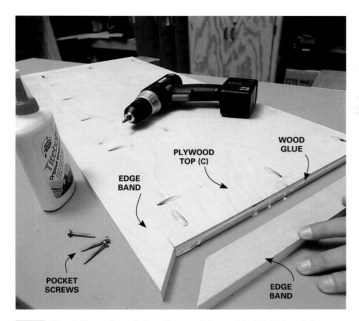

POCKET SCREWS
EDGE BAND
PLYWOOD TOP (C)
EDGE BAND
WOOD GLUE

8 Band the edge of the plywood top with 1-1/2-in. strips of birch (K1 and K2), mitered to fit. Spread wood glue on both edges and secure the 1x2 band to the plywood (C) with pocket screws as shown. Wipe off the excess glue with a damp rag. Use an orbital sander to sand the 1x2 flush with the plywood. Position the top on the cabinet so that an equal amount hangs over both sides and the front. Hold the top in place with a clamp while you attach it through the top of the cabinet box with 1-1/4-in. drywall screws.

COVE (N1)
EDGE-BANDED TOP
COAT HANGING STRIPS (P)
BASE (L2)
BASE CAP (M2)

9 Mark, miter and nail on the 2-in. cove (N1 and N2), the 3/4-in. x 3-in. base (L1 and L2) and the 1-5/8-in. base cap (M1 and M2). Use 6d finish nails for the base, and 1-in. brads to attach the moldings. Drill pilot holes for the nails to avoid splitting the moldings. Attach the hook strips with pocket screws. Then cut a piece of 1/4-in. plywood (D) to fit the back and attach it with 1-in. paneling nails. Draw lines to indicate dividers to help in placing the nails accurately.

Make sure you can get your project out the door!

Whether you're building a coat locker or a house for your favorite four-legged friend, be sure you can get your project out of your workshop! Don't laugh—this has happened to many novice and experienced DIYers alike.

As you're building, take measurements and make sure your project will fit through all of the doors it will need to get through to reach its final destination. DIYers have been known to remove the trim, door and door frame to get their project out of the workshop! A little planning will prevent you from the same fate.

washers under the heads. Snug the screws but don't tighten them. The extra-large holes will allow you to tap the drawer front into exact alignment before you fully tighten the screws.

Construct the cabinet top by attaching edging strips (K1 and K2) to the plywood (C) with pocket screws (Photo 8). Use this same procedure for edge-gluing boards for a tabletop or attaching wood nosing to a counter.

Complete the cabinet as shown in Photo 9. Glue wood plugs, available from the Kreg Tool Company (kregtool. com), into the exposed pocket holes on the cabinet interior and sand them flush.

Traditional coat & mitten rack

This coat rack is easy to build with butt joints connected by screws that get hidden with wooden screw-hole buttons and wood plugs. It mounts easily to the wall with screws driven through the hidden hanging strip on the back. The five large Shaker pegs are great for holding hats,

umbrellas and coats, and the hinged-hatch door at the top keeps the clutter of gloves and scarves from view.

Maple is an ideal wood for Shaker-style pieces, but any hardwood will do. Figure on spending about $60 for wood, hardware and varnish.

NOTE: Be sure this project is screwed to the wall studs. Drill two holes into the hanging strip at stud locations and use 2-1/2-in. or longer wood screws.

Figure A:
Coat & mitten details

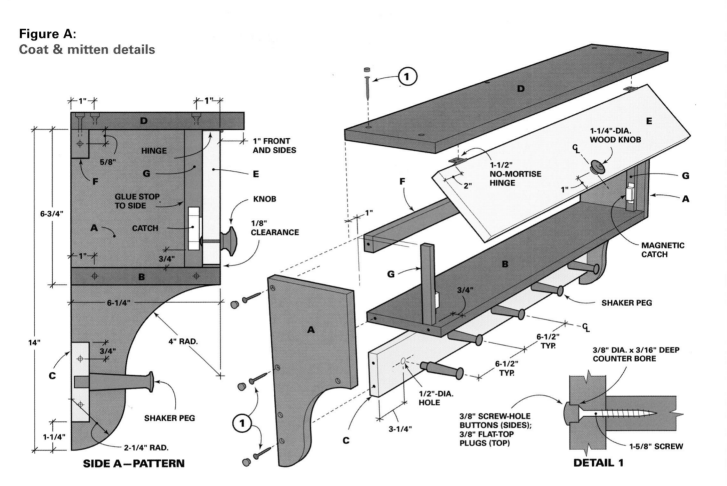

SIDE A—PATTERN

Labels in figure:
- 1"
- D
- HINGE
- 5/8"
- F
- G
- A
- 6-3/4"
- GLUE STOP TO SIDE
- CATCH
- B
- 6-1/4"
- 4" RAD.
- 14"
- C
- 3/4"
- SHAKER PEG
- 1-1/4"
- 2-1/4" RAD.
- 1" FRONT AND SIDES
- E
- KNOB
- 1/8" CLEARANCE
- 3/4"
- 1"

- 1
- F
- 1"
- G
- 3/4"
- B
- A
- C
- 3-1/4"
- 1/2"-DIA. HOLE
- 6-1/2" TYP.
- 6-1/2" TYP.
- 3/8" SCREW-HOLE BUTTONS (SIDES); 3/8" FLAT-TOP PLUGS (TOP)
- D
- E
- 1-1/4"-DIA. WOOD KNOB
- 1-1/2" NO-MORTISE HINGE
- 2"
- 1"
- G
- A
- MAGNETIC CATCH
- SHAKER PEG
- 3/8" DIA. x 3/16" DEEP COUNTER BORE
- 1-5/8" SCREW
- **DETAIL 1**

Cutting list

KEY	PCS.	SIZE & DESCRIPTION
A	2	3/4" x 6-1/4" x 14" maple sides
B	1	3/4" x 6-1/4" x 32-1/2" maple shelf
C	1	3/4" x 3-1/2" x 32-1/2" maple peg strip
D	1	3/" x 7-1/4" x 36" maple top
E	1	3/4" x 5-13/16" x 32-5/16" maple hatch
F	1	3/4" x 1-1/4" x 32-1/2" maple hanging strip
G	2	3/4" x 1/2" x 6" maple hatch stop

Materials list

ITEM	QTY.
1-1/2" no-mortise hinges	1 pair
1-1/4" beech knob	1
narrow magnetic catch	2
3-3/8" long Shaker pegs	5
3/8" screw-hole buttons	10
3/8" plugs	5
3/8" spade bit	1
1/2" spade bit	1
1-5/8" wood screws	15
Wood glue	1 pint
Danish oil	1 pint
150- and 220-grit sandpaper	

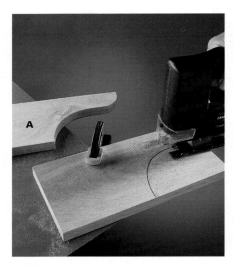

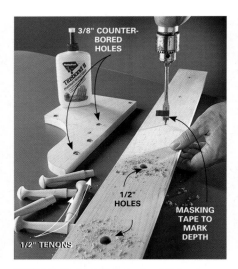

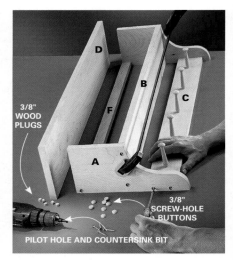

1 Cut the side pieces (A) using a jig-saw or band saw. Sand the curved edges smooth.

2 Drill the 1/2-in. holes 5/8 in. deep for the 3-3/8-in. Shaker pegs and the 3/8-in. counterbore holes 3/16 in. deep for the screw-hole buttons in parts A.

3 Assemble the shelf by clamping parts C, F and B to the sides. Drill pilot holes and screw the pieces together. The screws will be covered by the buttons and plugs.

Cutting the pieces

First transfer the pattern measurements in Figure A, p. 123 (using a compass) and then cut the sides (A) with a jigsaw. Next cut the top (D) to length and rip the shelf (B) to the width given in the Cutting list, p. 123. Cut the hanging strip (F) and the peg strip (C) to the same length as the shelf (B). Now drill the 3/8-in. counterbore holes for the screw-hole buttons (with your spade bit) 3/16 in. deep into the outsides of parts A (as shown in Figure A, and Photo 2). Also drill the 3/8-in. counterbore holes in the top. These holes must be 3/8 in. deep.

Mark and drill the 1/2-in. holes for the Shaker pegs in the peg strip. Drill the holes for the Shaker pegs perfectly perpendicular to the peg strip to ensure they all project evenly when glued in place.

Assembly

Lay the pieces on your workbench, as shown in Photo 3. Align the hanging strip (F), the shelf (B), and the peg strip (C) as shown and clamp the sides (A) to these parts. Predrill the holes with a combination pilot hole/countersink bit using the center of the counterbore holes as a guide. Next, screw the sides to B, C and F. Fasten the top (D) to the sides in the same manner.

Glue and clamp the hatch stops to the insides of parts A, as shown in Figure A. To finish the assembly, cut the hatch (E) to size and install the hinges to the underside of part D and the top of the hatch. Now glue the buttons and pegs into their corresponding holes. Use only a small drop of glue for the buttons but be sure to apply a thin layer of glue completely around the plugs. This will swell the plugs for a tight fit.

Finishing

Lightly sand the entire piece after assembly with 220-grit sandpaper. Apply two coats of clear Danish oil to all the surfaces (remove the hinges and knobs). Once the finish is dry, add two magnetic catches to the hatch-stop molding (G).

1 Clamp the 1x3 support to a piece of scrap wood as you drill the holes to prevent the wood from splintering.

6-3/4"
1-3/8"   3-1/2"
5-1/8"
3/4" HOLE
5/8"

Shoe ladder

Without constant vigilance, shoes tend to pile up into a mess next to entry doors. Untangle the mess with a simple, attractive shoe ladder that keeps everything from boots to slippers organized and off the floor.

Cut and drill the dowel supports (Photo 1), then screw them to 1x4s (Photo 2). Cut the 1x4s to fit your shoes and the available space—an average pair of adult shoes needs 10 in. of space. Nail or glue the dowels into the dowel supports, leaving 2 in. (or more) extending beyond the supports at the end to hang sandals or slippers.

Apply finish before you mount the shoe ladder to the wall. Screw the shoe ladder to studs or use heavy-duty toggle-bolt style anchors to hold it in place.

5/8" DOWEL

45° CUT

2"

1-5/8" SCREWS

2 Predrill through the back of the 1x4 into the 1x3 supports, then glue and screw the pieces together.

Coat rack & storage bench

If your entryway is littered with shoes and jackets, purses and book bags, this simple bench and matching shelf might be just what you need. With coat hooks and shelves, they provide an orderly home for all that clutter. Even if you already keep your entryway neat and tidy, these stylish pieces will dress it up and give you a convenient seat while you pull on your shoes.

This article will show you how to build both pieces from raw lumber to finishing. These projects were designed for fast, easy building; they're basically plywood boxes with decorative parts added. There's no tedious precision work, no intricate joinery. Even the curved parts are simple to make. If you're an intermediate woodworker, you can handle this project, and if you have only a little woodworking experience, this is a good "step-up" project.

Time, money and tools

Building this set will take you two or three days, plus a few hours of finishing work. These pieces were built from cherry boards and cherry plywood. Cherry is expensive: The total materials bill was $250 (see the Materials list for everything you'll need). Made from oak, this ensemble would cost about $125. A maple or birch set would cost $160. For a more rustic look, use construction-grade pine and plywood and spend less than $100.

This project requires two special tools: a table saw to rip solid wood to width and a pocket screw jig ($60) to make strong butt joints. If you don't own a pocket screw jig, buy one. It's a good investment and is easy to use. In addition, you'll need a drill, miter saw, random orbital sander and jigsaw. An air-powered 2-in. brad nailer isn't absolutely necessary, but it'll save lots of time and give you better results.

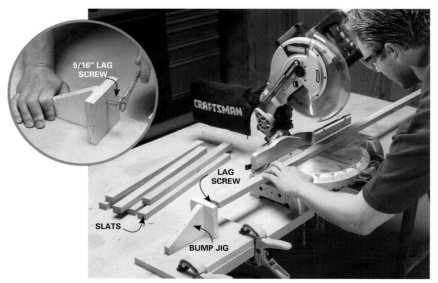

5/16" LAG SCREW

CRAFTSMAN

LAG SCREW

SLATS

BUMP JIG

1 Rip the parts for the grille. Cut all the slats to identical lengths using a bump jig. Make fine length adjustments by turning the lag screw in or out.

2 Drill pocket holes in the grille parts. To avoid confusion, lay out the grille with the best-looking side of each piece face down. Put each part back in place after drilling.

POCKET HOLE JIG

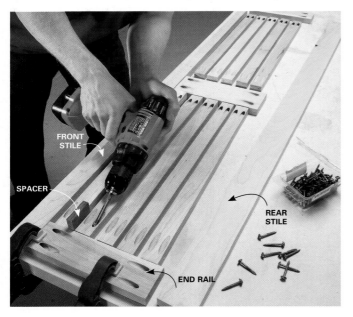

3 Assemble the grille with pocket screws. Screw the front stile to one end rail first, then position the slats using a 7/16-in. spacer. Attach the rear stile last.

FRONT STILE

SPACER

REAR STILE

END RAIL

Plywood cutting diagram

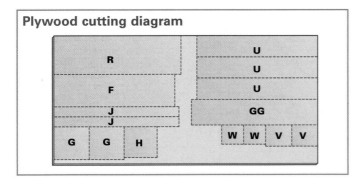

The bench begins as a box

The box that forms the core of the bench is made mostly from 3/4-in. plywood. For the floor of the box, a grille was made from solid wood slats. You could save a couple of hours by using a 12-in. x 44-in. piece of plywood instead, but a slatted grille looks better.

Rip the grille parts to the widths shown in the Cutting list (p. 131) and then cut them to length. All the slats (A) must be precisely the same length, so make a simple bump jig from plywood scraps and a lag screw (Photo 1). Clamp your miter saw and the bump jig to your workbench and make the repetitive cuts.

Pocket screws make assembling the grille fast and easy (Photos 2 and 3). For tips on using a pocket screw jig, visit familyhandyman.com and search "pocket screws." Use wood glue on your pocket screw joints later in this project, but skip the glue when you assemble the grille—removing excess glue from between the slats is nearly impossible. When the grille is complete, sand all the joints flush with a random orbital sander and a 100- or 120-grit disc. Then switch to a 150- or 180-grit disc and sand the entire surface. Use this same sanding sequence on all the solid-wood bench and shelf parts.

Cut the plywood box parts following the Cutting list. If you don't have a table saw, use a circular saw and straightedge. Lightly sand the plywood parts with 150-grit sandpaper before you assemble the box with glue and brads (Photo 4).

Add parts to the box

To complete the bench, you just make up the remaining parts and attach them to the box. Assemble the face frame with glue and pocket screws and sand the joints flush. Always make sure your parts fit the box correctly before you apply any glue. When you attach the face frame to the box (Photo 5), make sure the lower rail is flush with the top of the grille. It's OK if the upper rail isn't perfectly flush with the cleat, since that joint will be covered by the seat later.

Next, make a trammel to mark the arches (P) that fit under the bench sides (Photo 6). Use a 1-1/2-in. x 12-in. scrap for the trammel arm. Drill a 5/16-in. pencil hole near one end of the arm, then drill a 1/8-in. screw hole 8-1/2 in. from the center of the pencil hole. For the trammel base, use an 8-in. x 12-in. scrap of 3/4-in. plywood. Drill a screw hole 6-1/8 in. from the long edge of the base and screw the arm to the plywood. Mark and cut the arches from pieces of wood 3-1/4 x 14 in. long. Then cut rungs (N). Don't rely on the Cutting list when you cut the rungs and arches to length—instead, set them into place and mark them flush with the back of the bench. Glue and nail them into place and add the rear legs (Q; Photo 7). We nailed 3/4-in. plastic feet to our bench. Plastic can stain wood finishes. So if you plan to put your bench on a wood floor, use cloth or felt pads instead.

Figure A:
Bench details

SEAT

R

T

S

J

SEAT BOX

G

F

H

GRILLE

C

E

N

Q   D

A   B

P

FACE FRAME

K

L

M

L

K

**Overall dimensions: 47-3/4" long
x 15-1/4" deep x 17-3/4" tall**

Figure B:
Shelf details

TOP

GG

JJ

HH

SHELF BOX

V

U   V

Y
Z

W

X

DD

FACE
FRAME

EE

BB

12-7/8"

13"

12-7/8"

CC

AA

**Overall dimensions: 47-1/2" long x
10-3/8" deep x 19-3/4" tall**

FF

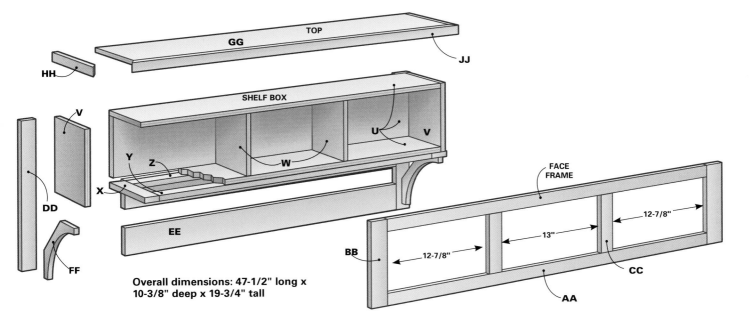

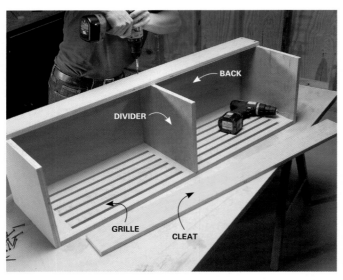

4 Cut the plywood parts and assemble the seat box, sides, back, partition and grille with 1-3/4-in. brads and glue. Predrill and screw the cleats to the top of the box.

BACK

DIVIDER

GRILLE

CLEAT

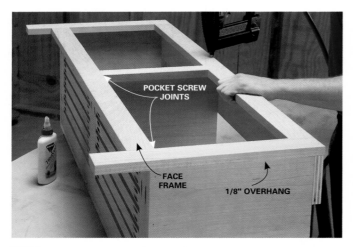

5 Assemble the face frame with glue and pocket screws and nail it to the seat box. Remember that the face frame overhangs the sides of the box by 1/8 in.

POCKET SCREW JOINTS

FACE FRAME

1/8" OVERHANG

The seat (R) is simply a slab of plywood banded on three sides with solid wood (S, T). Mitering the banding accurately can be difficult and frustrating. Make the joints tight by trial and error. Start by mitering parts about 1/8 in. too long. Hold them in place to check the fit, then readjust the angle on your miter saw and shave a hair off the parts again and again until they fit perfectly. Although mitered joints look best, you may prefer to band the seat with square-cut wood if you don't have experience with miters. Screw the seat to the bench without glue (Photo 8) so you can remove the seat while finishing the bench.

Furniture assembly with a brad nailer

The skinny nails driven by a brad nailer aren't strong enough to hold furniture together. With brad nails alone, this bench and shelf would eventually fall apart. So use wood glue wherever you shoot brad nails. Glue gives the joint its permanent strength; brads simply hold the parts together while the glue sets. You could do that with clamps, but brads are faster and more convenient. You'll have to fill every nail hole later (see "A no-curse strategy for invisible nail holes," p. 132), so drive only enough brads to force the parts tightly together. The number of brads you need depends on how well the parts fit together. Our bench face frame was perfectly straight and flat, so it required only six brads. Our shelf face frame had some warped areas and required a dozen brads to draw it tight against the box. You may even find spots where no amount of brads will force parts together. In that case, a well-placed clamp or two will hold parts tight until the glue sets.

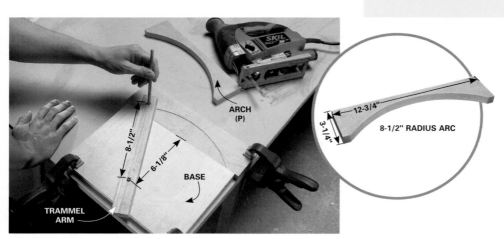

ARCH (P)

8-1/2"

6-1/8"

BASE

TRAMMEL ARM

12-3/4"

3-1/4"

8-1/2" RADIUS ARC

6 Draw an 8-1/2-in.-radius arc using an arc jig. Cut the arch with a jigsaw and sand it smooth. When you cut the arch to length, trim from both ends to center it.

Cutting list

KEY	PCS.	SIZE & DESCRIPTION
A	10	1-1/8" x 18-1/4" (slats)
B	1	1-1/8" x 44" (front stile)
C	1	2-1/4" x 44" (rear stile)
D	2	2-1/4" x 8-5/8" (end rails)
E	1	3" x 8-5/8" (middle rail)
F	1	12-1/4" x 44" (back panel)
G	2	12-1/4" x 12-3/4" (end panels)
H	1	11-1/2" x 12" (divider)
J	2	3-3/4" x 45-1/2" (cleats)
K	2	2" x 41-1/4" (upper and lower rails)
L	2	2-1/4" x 17" (front legs)
M	1	1-3/4" x 10-1/4" (middle stile)
N	2	1-1/2" x 12-3/4" (rungs)
P	2	3-1/4" x 12-3/4" (arches)
Q	2	2-1/4" x 17" (rear legs)
R	1	14-1/2" x 46-1/4" (seat panel)
S	2	1-1/2" x 15-1/4" (side bands)
T	1	1-1/2" x 47-3/4" (front band)
U	3	8" x 44" (top, bottom, back)
V	2	8" x 9-1/2" (end panels)
W	2	7-1/4" x 8" (dividers)
X	2	2" x 8" (stiles)
Y	1	1-1/4" x 41-3/4" (front rail)
Z	1	2" x 41-3/4" (rear rail)
AA	2	1-1/2" x 41-3/4" (upper and lower rails)
BB	2	2" x 10-1/4" (end stiles)
CC	2	1-1/2" x 7-1/4" (divider stiles)
DD	2	2" x 19" (rear stiles)
EE	2	3-1/2" x 41-3/4" (coat hook rails)
FF	2	3-1/2" x 11-1/2" (brackets)
GG	1	9-5/8" x 46" (top panel)
HH	2	1-1/4" x 10-3/8" (side bands)
JJ	1	1-1/4" x 47-1/2" (front band)

7 Nail the rungs to the underside of the box. Then add the arches and rear legs. Add plastic feet or felt pads after the glue sets.

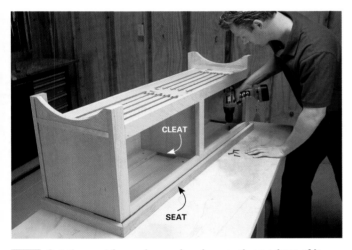

8 Cut the seat from plywood and cover three edges of it with solid wood. Fasten the seat to the bench with 1-1/4-in. screws driven through the cleats.

Materials list

ITEM	QTY.
4' x 8' sheet of 3/4" plywood	1
Solid wood (36 linear feet of 1x6)	18 board ft.
1-1/4" screws	
1-3/4" and 2" brads	
3/4" plastic or cloth feet	
Wood glue	
Wood filler	
Spray lacquer	
Coat hooks (3 large and 2 small)	
Pocket screw jig: woodworkershardware.com or kregtool.com.	

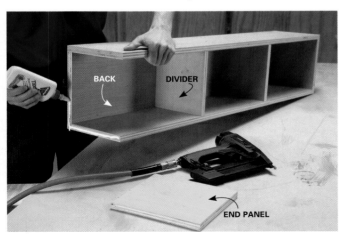

9 Cut out the shelf box parts. Glue and nail the bottom to the back first. Then add the dividers, the top and finally the end caps.

10 Nail rails and stiles directly to the underside of the shelf box. Assemble the face frame with pocket screws and nail it to the front. After the glue sets, sand all the joints smooth.

11 Assemble the back frame with pocket screws, sand the joints flush, and fasten it to the shelf box. Then assemble the shelf top and attach it with glue and brads.

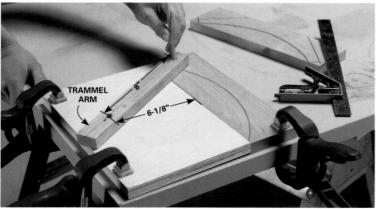

12 Draw an 8-in.-radius arc for the shelf brackets using the arc jig. Cut the arches using a jigsaw and the straight cuts with a miter saw set at 45 degrees.

A no-curse strategy for invisible nail holes

The wood fillers that fussy carpenters use to hide nail holes in trim aren't a good choice for furniture projects. They stay soft for years, so they're not sandable and they can rub off on clothing. Fussy furniture makers prefer fillers that dry hard. These sandable fillers are often labeled "stainable," but they usually absorb more or less than the surrounding wood, leaving light or dark dots at each nail hole.

If you want to avoid nail dots, try this technique that works every time. The key is to make the patches lighter than the surrounding finish and darken them later. These extra steps may sound like a lot of trouble, but they add only a few minutes to the process:

■ Buy the lightest color of filler available.

■ Before you fill the holes on your project, shoot a few nails into a wood scrap and fill those holes. When dry and sanded, the filler must be no darker than the wood.

■ Apply stain or clear finish to the test scrap first. In most cases, the nail patches remain lighter than the wood. If they turn darker, "pretreat" them so they absorb less finish. Mix two drops of wood glue with a drop of water and apply the thinned glue to the patches with a fine-tip artist's brush. Keep glue off the surrounding wood. After about 30 minutes, lightly sand each nail patch.

■ Stain and finish the wood as usual. But before you apply the final coat of clear finish, use a fine-tip marker to darken each nail patch. An art supply store is the best source for a wide variety of colors. With two or three different markers, you can match the differing wood tones in your project and the nail holes will be invisible to everyone but you.

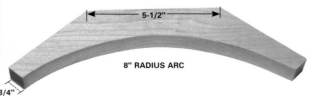

Build the shelf just like the bench

In terms of construction and techniques, the shelf is just a smaller variation of the bench. It starts with a plywood box (Photo 9). The top, bottom and back of the box are identical parts (U). Be sure to place the back between the top and the bottom pieces. Add rails and stiles to the underside of the box, then assemble and attach the face frame (Photo 10). The back frame (Photo 11) provides a mounting surface for coat hooks later. Make the shelf top just as you made the bench seat: Wrap a piece of plywood (GG) with solid wood banding (HH, JJ). When you nail the top to the shelf box, use plenty of glue—the top will support the entire weight of the shelf when you hang it on the wall (see Photo 14). Draw the arc for the shelf brackets using the same arc jig you used to make the bench arches—just be sure to reposition the screw 8 in. from the pencil hole (Photo 12). If you don't have a clamp that's long enough to hold the bracket against the shelf box (Photo 13), tack it into place with 2-in. brads.

A fast finish

If you remembered to sand all the parts before assembly, you won't have much prep work before finishing. Just fill the nail holes and inspect all the glued joints for glue smudges.

Cherry usually doesn't take stain evenly, so you can skip the stain and applied a clear finish only. With the bench and shelf's corners and cramped spaces, brushing a finish on them would be a nightmare. Choose a spray-on lacquer finish. Lacquer is one of the fastest, easiest finishes to apply. Here's how to use it:

- Wear an organic vapor respirator ($25) and spray the lacquer outdoors or in the garage with the door open. Lacquer contains nasty solvents.
- Spray on two very light coats, wait 30 minutes and lightly sand with 220-grit paper.
- Vacuum off the sanding residue and apply two or more light coats until you get the look you want. There's no need to sand between coats unless specks of dust settle on the finish.

Let the finish harden overnight before you add the coat hooks and hang the shelf (Photo 14).

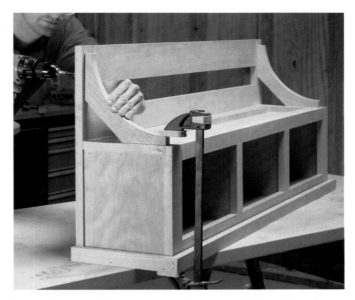

13 Glue, position and clamp the upper end of each bracket and fasten the other end with screws driven from behind. Predrill so you don't split the bracket.

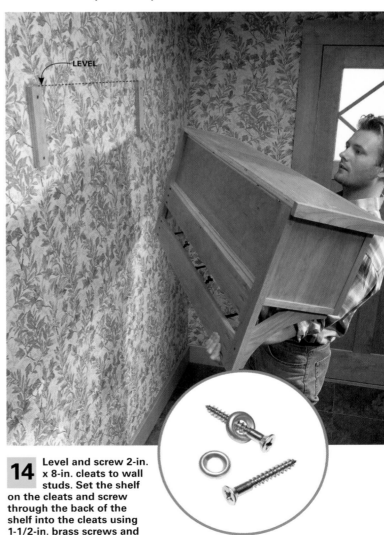

14 Level and screw 2-in. x 8-in. cleats to wall studs. Set the shelf on the cleats and screw through the back of the shelf into the cleats using 1-1/2-in. brass screws and finish washers.

Sleek coat & hat rack

Organize your hallway or mudroom with this simple, attractive coat and hat rack. You just cut the boards to fit your space, paint them, outfit them with different kinds of hooks to suit your needs and then screw them to the wall. Shown are 6-ft.-long 1x4s, but use whatever length works for you and the space available. Shown is poplar, which is the best choice if you want a painted finish. If you're after a natural wood look, choose any species you want.

Finish the boards first and then attach your hooks. Shown here are drawer pulls down the middle and a robe hook near the top to hold backpacks and larger items. You'll find hooks in a tremendous range of styles, colors and prices at hardware stores and online retailers.

Attach the boards to studs, or to the drywall with screw-in drywall anchors (E-Z Ancor is one brand). Drive three screws in each board: one at the top, one in the middle and one at the bottom.

MASKING TAPE FOR LAYOUT

FINISH WASHER

PROTRUDING TIP

2-1/2" SCREW

1 Drive your screws partway into each board so the screw tips poke out the back. Place the boards where you want them, and press hard to mark the spots for your drywall anchors.

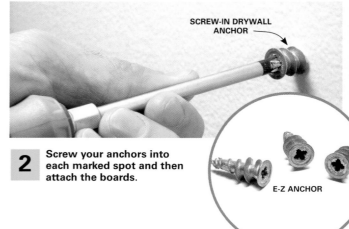

SCREW-IN DRYWALL ANCHOR

2 Screw your anchors into each marked spot and then attach the boards.

E-Z ANCHOR

Entryway storage & organizing
hints & tips

Mitten and shoe dryer

Drill pairs of 1/8-in. holes in a scrap of 2x4 and insert U-shaped pieces of galvanized 14-gauge wire (50 ft. sells for about $3 at home centers). If you have forced-air heat, drill 1-in. holes between the pairs of 1/8-in. holes using a spade bit, and set the rack on a register for fast drying.

STIFF WIRE

2x4

Entryway caddy

This easy-to-make egg crate-type shoe case solves the problem of entryway clutter. The inner partitions are 1/4-in. plywood, double-notched to slip together. The sides are 3/4 in., and the top and bottom are 1/2-in. plywood. Coat hooks above complete the package.

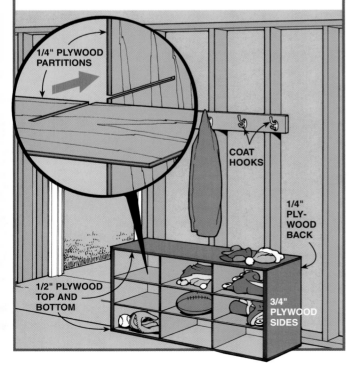

1/4" PLYWOOD PARTITIONS

COAT HOOKS

1/4" PLYWOOD BACK

1/2" PLYWOOD TOP AND BOTTOM

3/4" PLYWOOD SIDES

Wet boot tray

What do you get when you mix boots and winter weather? A dirty, slippery floor (and wet socks). Make life neater and safer for everyone in your house by building this simple boot tray. All you need is a plastic tray or a large metal baking sheet with a lip. Put a layer of medium-size stones in the tray so the boots can drain. To keep the stones in place and give the tray a handsome finished look, build a 1x2 frame around the tray and paint it the same color as the trim in your entryway.

Garage

148

153

170

Five easy options for five kinds of clutter

Garage entry storage center

If you have an attached garage, the door to the house is probably a dumping ground for shoes, sports gear, jackets and all kinds of other stuff that you don't have space for indoors. These five cabinets can eliminate that mess so you don't have to walk through an obstacle course to get in the house. Each cabinet is a simple box that has been customized to solve a different storage problem. Build one or all five.

You can build, install and load these cabinets in a weekend. The only power tools you'll need are a drill and a circular saw. But a table saw and a sliding miter saw are handy for ripping and crosscutting the plywood, and a brad nailer helps tack the cabinets and drawers together before you drive the screws.

Each cabinet requires one sheet of plywood or less and costs about $50, including the hardware and finish. Shown is birch plywood. You could use oak plywood (which is more expensive) or even MDF (medium-density fiberboad, which is less expensive). For the pantry cabinet, you'll need 1/4-in. plywood for the drawer bottoms. All the materials are available at home centers except the drawer slides for the pantry cabinet.

1 Get perfectly straight, accurate cuts with a circular saw using a homemade saw guide. Clamp the saw guide at your mark on the plywood.

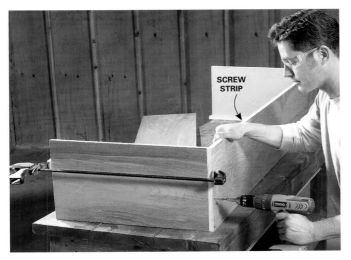

2 Clamp the frame parts together, including the screw strip. Drill pilot holes and drive screws.

SCREW STRIP

SAW GUIDE

STUD LOCATIONS

CLEAT

3 Set the cabinets on a cleat, then screw them to the wall at the studs (use tape to mark the stud locations). Drive screws through the cabinet bottoms into the cleat.

$50 and 3 hours per cabinet

These cabinets were designed with economy and speed in mind. Here are three tricks to cut costs and assembly time:

- Size all parts to use the plywood efficiently. The sides, for example, are just under 12 in. wide (11-7/8 in.), so you'll get four from a 4 x 8-ft. sheet.

- Eliminate the cabinet backs, saving time and materials. Just be sure to handle the cabinets gently—they're a bit flimsy until they're screwed to the wall.

- Apply the finish before assembly. After you cut the parts to size, sand everything with 120-grit sandpaper and apply a coat of Minwax Wipe-On Poly.

Box assembly tips

These cabinets are surprisingly easy to build. The illustrations tell you most of what you need to know. Here are some tips for smooth assembly:

- If you don't have a table saw to rip the plywood, use a saw guide and a circular saw (Photo 1).
- Use a shorter saw guide or a sliding miter saw to get straight, square crosscuts.
- Drill 1/8-in. pilot holes to prevent splitting. Keep screws 1 in. from edges.
- If you have a brad nailer, tack parts together to make drilling easier. But don't rely on brads alone—you still need screws. If you don't have a brad nailer, use clamps (Photo 2).
- If your cuts were slightly off and the top, bottom and sides aren't exactly the same width, don't worry. Just make sure the front edges of the box are flush.
- Attach the screw strip to the top before attaching the side pieces.
- Attach hardware (drawer slides, shelf standards) to the sides before building the box.
- Screw the top, bottom and any fixed shelves onto one side before attaching the other side.

Wet clothes cabinet

An airy hangout for damp or dirty coats and boots

The wire shelves in this cabinet allow boots to drip dry and air to circulate freely so clothes will dry. The extra-wide screw strip lets you attach coat hooks. To build the cabinet, you'll need 6 ft. of 12-in.-deep wire shelving and coat hooks.

Attach the back cleats flush with the sides. Inset the front cleats 1/4 in. Cut the wire shelves at 22-1/4 in. This gives you 1/8 in. of play on each side. Cut the shelves with bolt cutters or have the home center cut them for you. The metal in the shelves is very tough and hard to cut with a hacksaw.

Place plastic end caps over the shelf ends. Secure the shelves to the front cleats with C-clamps. Fasten two clamps per shelf. Hold the coat hooks in place in the cabinet, drill pilot holes and then drive the screws that came with the hooks to fasten them in place.

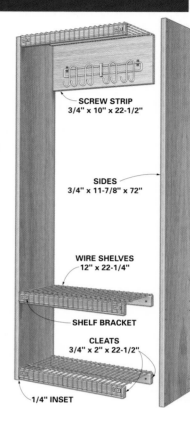

SCREW STRIP
3/4" x 10" x 22-1/2"

SIDES
3/4" x 11-7/8" x 72"

WIRE SHELVES
12" x 22-1/4"

SHELF BRACKET

CLEATS
3/4" x 2" x 22-1/2"

1/4" INSET

Open-shelf cabinet

Spacious, adjustable shelves that cut entryway clutter

This open-shelf cabinet needs a fixed shelf in the middle to keep the sides from bowing, but you can make the rest of the shelves adjustable. Install as many adjustable shelves as you want—this cabinet can hold a lot of stuff!

You'll need four 6-ft. shelf standards for this cabinet. Get started by marking the shelf standard locations and the fixed middle shelf location on the two cabinet sides. Cut the shelf standards to length with a hacksaw, then screw them to the sides above and below the fixed shelf marks.

Install the adjustable shelves after you hang the cabinet on the wall.

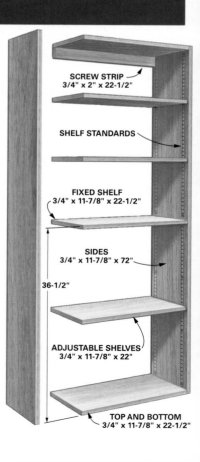

SCREW STRIP
3/4" x 2" x 22-1/2"

SHELF STANDARDS

FIXED SHELF
3/4" x 11-7/8" x 22-1/2"

SIDES
3/4" x 11-7/8" x 72"

36-1/2"

ADJUSTABLE SHELVES
3/4" x 11-7/8" x 22"

TOP AND BOTTOM
3/4" x 11-7/8" x 22-1/2"

Sports gear cabinet

A compact organizer for all kinds of equipment

The cabinet dividers let you store long-handled sports gear, like hockey sticks, bats and rackets. The lip on the top shelf keeps balls from falling off. Nail the lip to the shelf before installing the shelf at any height that suits your needs.

When installing the dividers, cut two 7-in. spacers and place them between the cabinet sides and the dividers to keep the dividers straight as you install the cabinet face.

Measure diagonally from box corner to corner to make sure the cabinet is square before attaching the face. Set the face on the cabinet, leaving a 1/8-in. reveal along both sides and the bottom. Drill pilot holes and screw the face to the sides and the dividers.

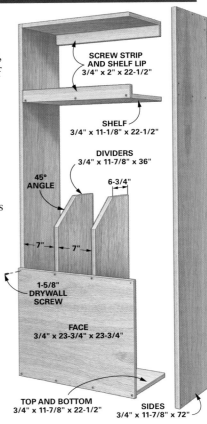

SCREW STRIP AND SHELF LIP 3/4" x 2" x 22-1/2"

SHELF 3/4" x 11-1/8" x 22-1/2"

DIVIDERS 3/4" x 11-7/8" x 36"

45° ANGLE

6-3/4"

7" 7"

1-5/8" DRYWALL SCREW

FACE 3/4" x 23-3/4" x 23-3/4"

TOP AND BOTTOM 3/4" x 11-7/8" x 22-1/2"

SIDES 3/4" x 11-7/8" x 72"

Shoe & boot cabinet

Eliminate the footwear pileup on the back steps

The lower shelves in this cabinet hold boots and shoes, while the cubbyholes at the top are for slippers and sandals. The screw strip is lower in this cabinet than it is in the rest, but it'll still hold the cabinet in place.

Install the lower shelf first, then add the divider and screw on the shelves that fit between the divider and the cabinet sides.

Build the cubbyholes on your work surface, then stick the assembled cubbies into the cabinet. Start by screwing two dividers onto a shelf. Make two shelves this way. Then install a center divider between these two shelves. Add a shelf to the bottom, over the two dividers. Then insert the cubbies inside the cabinet and screw through the sides into the shelves and through the top into the dividers.

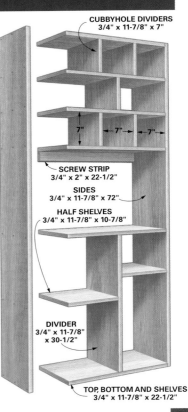

CUBBYHOLE DIVIDERS 3/4" x 11-7/8" x 7"

7" 7" 7"

SCREW STRIP 3/4" x 2" x 22-1/2"

SIDES 3/4" x 11-7/8" x 72"

HALF SHELVES 3/4" x 11-7/8" x 10-7/8"

DIVIDER 3/4" x 11-7/8" x 30-1/2"

TOP, BOTTOM AND SHELVES 3/4" x 11-7/8" x 22-1/2"

Hanging the cabinets

Install a 2x2 cleat on the wall for the cabinets to sit on. You'll need 24 in. of cleat for each cabinet. Keep the cleat at least 8 in. above the floor so you can sweep under the cabinets.

Snap a level chalk line on the wall for the cleat (measure down from the ceiling if your floor slopes!). Attach the cleat at the chalk line by driving a 3-in. drywall screw into each stud. Set the cabinets on the cleats. Place a level alongside the cabinet to make sure it's standing plumb and square. Then drill pilot holes through the screw strips and attach the cabinets to the wall with 3-in. drywall screws (Photo 3). Screw adjoining cabinets together by driving 1-1/4-in. drywall screws through the side near the top and the bottom.

NOTE: All cabinets are 11-7/8" deep x 24" wide x 72" tall.

Pantry cabinet

Bulk storage that frees up kitchen space

If you buy groceries in bulk, this is the storage solution for you. The bottom drawers in this cabinet are deep enough to hold two cases of soda. The top drawers are perfect for canned goods or bottled water. The upper shelves are adjustable for more bulk storage. The cabinet faces and door keep everything enclosed.

Inexpensive drawer slides let the drawers open and close easily. The ones shown are from Woodworker's Hardware No. B230M 12CM; wwhardware.com). You'll also need two 6-ft. shelf standards.

Lay the cabinet sides next to each other and mark the center for each drawer slide. Place a slide over each mark, drill pilot holes (a self-centering drill bit works best) and screw the slides into place. Cut the shelf standards with a hacksaw and screw them to the cabinet sides, above the fixed shelf.

Assemble the drawers with 1-5/8-in. screws. Place the drawer slides on the drawers, drill pilot holes and attach them with screws. Test-fit them in the cabinet. If the cabinet sides are bowed even slightly, attach a 2-in. rail in the back to hold the sides in place so the drawers slide smoothly.

Fasten the faces to the drawers with 1-1/4-in. screws driven from inside the drawers. Build the handles with leftover plywood and attach them with 2-in. screws (driven from the inside).

Attach the door to the cabinet with 1/2-in. overlay hinges, also called half-wrap hinges. They're available at home centers or wwhardware.com (No. A07550).

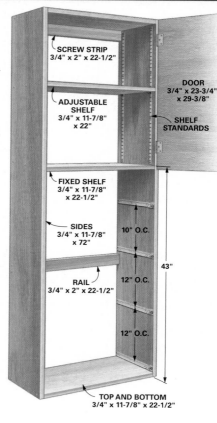

SCREW STRIP
3/4" x 2" x 22-1/2"

DOOR
3/4" x 23-3/4"
x 29-3/8"

ADJUSTABLE
SHELF
3/4" x 11-7/8"
x 22"

SHELF
STANDARDS

FIXED SHELF
3/4" x 11-7/8"
x 22-1/2"

SIDES
3/4" x 11-7/8"
x 72"

10" O.C.

RAIL
3/4" x 2" x 22-1/2"

12" O.C.

43"

12" O.C.

TOP AND BOTTOM
3/4" x 11-7/8" x 22-1/2"

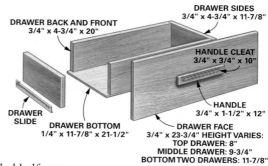

DRAWER BACK AND FRONT
3/4" x 4-3/4" x 20"

DRAWER SIDES
3/4" x 4-3/4" x 11-7/8"

HANDLE CLEAT
3/4" x 3/4" x 10"

DRAWER
SLIDE

DRAWER BOTTOM
1/4" x 11-7/8" x 21-1/2"

HANDLE
3/4" x 1-1/2" x 12"

DRAWER FACE
3/4" x 23-3/4" HEIGHT VARIES:
TOP DRAWER: 8"
MIDDLE DRAWER: 9-3/4"
BOTTOM TWO DRAWERS: 11-7/8"

1 Rip 24-in.-wide shelves and 23-in.-wide aprons from each 3/4-in. sheet of plywood. Use a factory edge as a straight-edge guide.

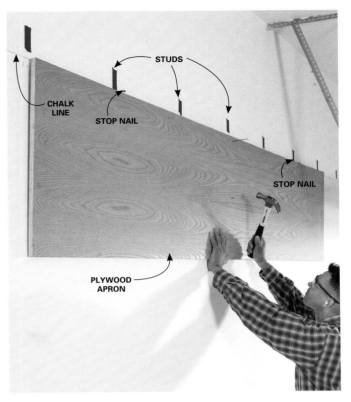

2 Snap a chalk line to mark the top of the apron and then mark the stud locations. Hold the plywood apron even with the line and nail the apron with 16d finish nails, four to each stud.

and then mark all of the studs with masking tape. Take your time with this step; it's important that the apron nails anchor into solid framing since they support the entire weight of the shelf. To be sure, poke nails through the drywall (just below the line, where holes will be hidden) to find the centers of studs. Start the first apron somewhere in the middle of the wall, making sure that both ends fall on the centers of the studs. Then work toward the corners where the freehand crosscut ends will be hidden. If you're working alone, partially drive a couple of "stop" nails at the chalk line to help align the apron (Photo 2). That'll eliminate any guesswork. Prestart a couple of nails at stud locations before hoisting the apron into place so you can tack it to the wall while supporting it with one hand.

Cut and mount the braces

Cut the triangular braces from 20-in. squares (Photo 3). You can cut the diagonal freehand because the trim will hide minor cutting flaws. Use two 1-3/8-in.-wide spacers to center and support the brace while you're screwing the 1x4 brace cleat to the back side (Photo 4). Drill 1/8-in. pilot holes into both pieces and countersink holes in the cleats to prevent splitting. Use three 2-1/2-in. screws, one about 2 in. in from each end and one more centered. Run the wood grain the same direction on each brace.

Drill four pilot holes in the cleats, two 1-1/2 in. from the

Planning your shelves

There are no magic heights or widths for your shelves; you'll want to customize them for your garage and needs. The best strategy is to build a 3-ft.-long mockup of the shelf shown and hold it against the walls in various positions to test the fit. It just takes a little effort and may help prevent headaches later. Then you can decide what height and size the shelves need to be to clear obstacles.

Some rules of thumb for sizing and positioning:
- Choose shelf heights that'll allow enough space between the ceiling and the shelf for the tall items you plan to store.
- Make sure that shelves and braces will clear obstructions like garage doors, garage door tracks and service doors.
- In foot traffic areas (near car doors, for example), keep braces above head level and back from doorways, so you don't bump into them.
- If you have an SUV or a pickup truck, make sure the braces won't obstruct the doors.
- If you need to build narrower shelves, just shrink the plywood braces and shelves by the same amount.

3 Rip 20-in.-wide lengths of plywood and cut them into 20-in. squares. Draw a diagonal line and cut the triangular braces. Use a sharp blade to minimize splintering.

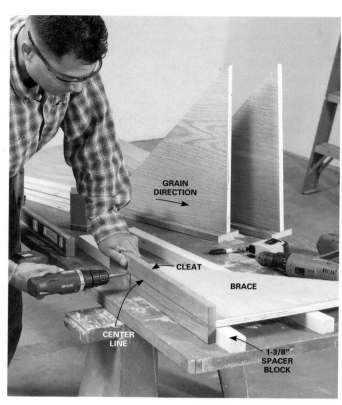

GRAIN DIRECTION

CLEAT

BRACE

CENTER LINE

1-3/8" SPACER BLOCK

4 Rest the braces on 1-3/8-in.-thick spacer blocks, then mark the center of each 1x4 cleat. Predrill 1/8-in. holes and screw the cleat onto the brace with three 2-1/2-in. screws.

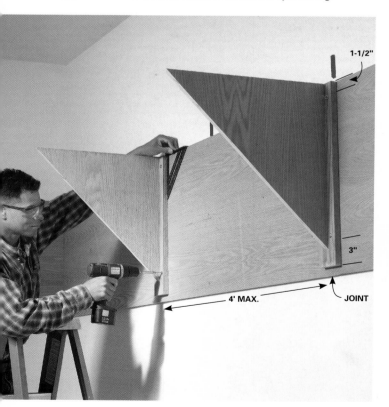

1-1/2"

3"

4' MAX.

JOINT

5 Fasten each brace to the apron, flush with the top, with four 1-5/8-in. screws. Space the braces at the ends and middle of each full sheet.

JOINT

BRACE

6 Nail the shelves to the apron and to the braces with 2-in. nails spaced every 8 in. Make sure joints meet at the center of the 3/4-in. braces.

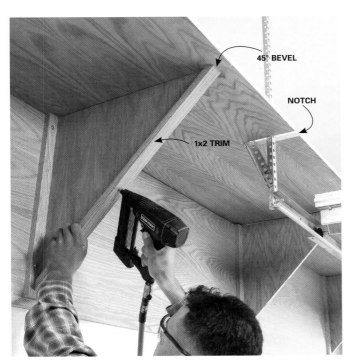

45° BEVEL

NOTCH

1x2 TRIM

7 Cut the 1x2 brace trim pieces to fit with opposite 45-degree bevels at each end. Glue and nail them to the braces with 2-in. brads.

1x2 EDGE TRIM

8 Cut the 1x2 edge trim to length, then glue and nail it to the front edge of the shelf with 2-in. brads.

top and two 3 in. up from the bottom. Then screw each brace assembly to the apron (Photo 5). Use finish washers under the screws for a polished look. Position a brace directly over each apron seam, and place one more in the center so no shelf span is more than 4 ft. Make sure they're flush and square with the top of the apron. When shelving turns a corner, center a brace exactly 24 in. from one wall (Figure B). This brace will support the front edge of the shelf on the adjoining wall as well as a shelf end.

Nail on the shelves and add the trim

Lay the shelves in place so joints fall over the braces and nail them to the braces and the apron with 2-in. brads spaced every 8 in. As with the apron, start somewhere in the center of each wall so you'll have factory edges abutting each other at joints and the saw cuts will be hidden at the ends. Angle the nails slightly at joints so they hit the center of the braces.

Add trim to the raw plywood edges for a nice finished look. Trim also strengthens the assembly and stiffens the shelves. Cut the brace trim to fit with opposing 45-degree bevels at each end. Then glue and nail them to each brace with 2-in. brads (Photo 7).

Starting at one end of each wall and working toward the other wall, cut the shelf edging to fit (Photo 8). Overlap plywood joints by at least 2 ft. for better support. The plywood will be a little wavy, but it'll straighten out as you nail on the trim.

Customize shelving

You can easily customize this shelving to fit special items like golf clubs, hanging clothes or anything else that's best stored in a cabinet or on open shelving. Just assemble a cabinet box like the one shown

CLEATS

here so that the sides fall over the wall studs. Go as narrow as 16 in. or as wide as 4 ft., but make sure you can attach the cleats directly to wall studs. Attach those cleats to the back of the cabinet with 2-in. screws placed every foot just as you did with the braces, and then screw the assembly to the wall. The cabinet sides replace the 45-degree braces and support the shelf. A simple unit like this one takes no more skill than the shelves required. If you're interested in drawers or fancier cabinetry work, you're only limited by your cabinet-making skills.

Simple utility cabinets

These sturdy cabinets are designed for simple assembly. Just glue and screw plywood together to make the basic box, then add a premade door, actually an inexpensive bifold door panel. Since bifolds are readily available in several styles, including louvered and paneled, it's easy to make a wide range of practical yet handsome cabinets without the time and hassle of making the doors.

Make the cabinets big and deep to store clothing and sports gear; shallow and tall for shovels, rakes, skis or fishing rods; or shallow and short to mount on walls for tools, paint cans and other small items. Or mount them on wheels and roll the tools right to the job. The only limitation is the size of standard bifold doors.

Here you'll learn how to build one of the smaller hanging wall cabinets. Use the same techniques and the Cutting lists on p. 152 to build others.

Advanced skills or special tools are not needed to build this entire set of cabinets. However, it does require cutting a lot of plywood accurately. A table saw helps here, but a circular saw with a guide works fine too. Add a drill or two, a couple of clamps and some careful advance planning, and start building!

tip

Most lumberyards and home centers have a large saw (called a panel saw) for cutting sheets of plywood. For a nominal fee, they will rip all of the plywood to proper widths. (Cut the pieces to length later.) It requires planning the cabinet depths in advance, but it's quicker than ripping the plywood at home and makes hauling it a lot easier.

Buying the bifolds and plywood

When planning the cabinets, begin by choosing the bifold door and build the rest of the cabinet to match its dimensions. Standard bifolds are 79 in. high and available in 24-in., 30-in., 32-in. and 36-in. widths. Keep in mind that it takes two doors for each of these widths, each approximately 12, 15, 16 or 18 in. wide. The cabinet can be any of the single-door widths or any of the double-door widths. Or cut the doors down to make shorter cabinets, as demonstrated here. Make them any depth desired.

Bifolds come in several styles and wood species. This project shows louvered pine doors ($60 for 30 in. wide) and birch plywood ($40 per sheet) for a handsome, natural look. All the materials for the ventilated wall cabinet shown at top, p. 149, including hardware, cost about $70. The five cabinets

Figure A:
Ventilated wall cabinet

Cutting list

KEY	PCS.	SIZE & DESCRIPTION
A	2	14-3/4" x 43-3/4" doors (30" bifold)*
B	2	3/4" x 11-1/4" x 43-3/4" sides
C	2	3/4" x 11-1/4" x 28-1/8" top and bottom
D	3	3/4" x 11-1/4" x 28-1/8" shelves
E	2	3/4" x 3" x 28-1/8" hanging cleats
F	1	1/4" x 29-5/8" x 43-3/4" back

*Exact door sizes vary. Measure the doors before deciding exact cabinet dimensions.

TOP **(C)**

DOOR (BIFOLD CUT OFF) **(A)**

6"

HANGING CLEAT **(E)**

11-1/4"

HINGE

MAGNETIC LATCH

FIXED SHELF **(D)**

CATCH PLATE

SIDE **(B)**

KNOB

ADJUSTABLE SHELVES **(D)**

DOOR (BIFOLD CUT OFF) **(A)**

43-3/4"

HANGING CLEAT **(E)**

BACK **(F)**

BOTTOM **(C)**

HINGE

6"

29-5/8"

Other cabinet options (Cutting lists and dimensions on p. 152)

Storage locker

Compact storage for long items like skis, fishing rods, long-handled tools; either on the floor or wall-hung; 12-in.- wide door and one fixed shelf.

Closet on wheels

Large storage capacity (about 32 in. wide and 22-1/2 in. deep); fixed shelf; closet rod; 3-in. swivel casters.

Paneled wall cabinet

Shorter version of cabinet above; made from the paneled portion of partial louvered doors; one adjustable shelf.

Narrow floor or wall cabinet

Shelf version of storage locker (left); top and bottom shelves fixed; intermediate shelves mounted on adjustable shelf standards.

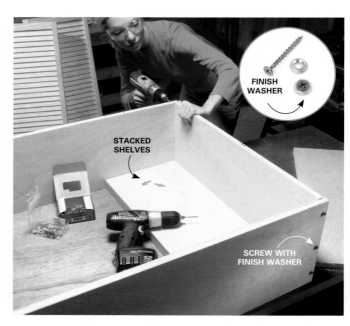

1 Mark the door length and clamp a straightedge to the door to guide the saw. Cut the other cabinet pieces using the straightedge as well.

2 Predrill screw holes through the sides 3/8 in. from the ends. Drive 1-5/8-in. screws with finish washers through the sides into the top and bottom. Stack extra shelves in the corners to keep the box square.

cost $320. Cut that cost considerably by using less expensive plywood, bifolds and hinges.

Also save by using plywood efficiently. Decide on the door sizes, then lay out all the cabinet pieces on a scale drawing of a 4 x 8-ft. sheet of plywood (graph paper helps). Feel free to adjust the cabinet depths a bit to achieve best use. The five cabinets shown were built from four sheets of 3/4-in. plywood and two sheets of 1/4-in. plywood for the backs.

The "partial wraparound" hinges may not be available at home centers or hardware stores. However, woodworking stores carry them; see photo at right. If exposed hinges are OK, simply use bifold hinges, which cost less than $1 each at home centers.

Cut out all the parts

Begin by cutting the bifold doors to size (Photo 1). This will determine the exact cabinet height. Be sure to use a guide and a sharp blade for a straight, crisp cut. Center the cut on the dividing rail. Be prepared for the saw to bump up and down slightly as it crosses each stile (Photo 1). Then trim each newly created door so that the top and bottom rails are the same width.

Some bifold door manufacturers use only a single dowel to attach each rail to the stile. If that's the case, one of the rails (after being cut in half) is no longer attached to the door.

Partial wraparound hinges

The hinges shown are available at woodworking stores such as Rockler Woodworking and Hardware; rockler.com; No. 31456; Less expensive styles are also available.

Don't panic. Dab a little glue on each rail and stile and clamp them back together. After 20 minutes or so, they'll be ready.

Then cut the plywood to size using a guide to keep all the cuts straight and square. If the plywood splinters a bit, score the cutting line first with a utility knife.

Assemble the box

Assemble the box face down on a flat surface. The garage floor works well for this step.

Mark and predrill screw holes through the sides for the top and bottom pieces (Photo 2).

This project uses finish washers for a more decorative look.

Attach the fixed shelf next to stiffen and strengthen the box (Photo 3). Use the extra shelves as guides to help position and square the shelf. Predrill and drive three screws through each side into the fixed shelf.

Attach cleats at the top and bottom of the cabinet to use for screwing the cabinet to a wall (Photo 4). Use three or four screws across the top and bottom. Clamp the cleat into place until the screws are driven. Because the screws won't be visible on the top and bottom, skip the finish washers. Make sure the cleat sits flush with the side (Photo 4).

The 1/4-in. plywood back stiffens the frame and keeps it square, which is essential for the doors to fit accurately. Spread glue along the cabinet edges, including the fixed shelf and the hanging cleats (Photo 5). Carefully set the back onto the cabinet, keeping the top flush with the cabinet top. Nail in

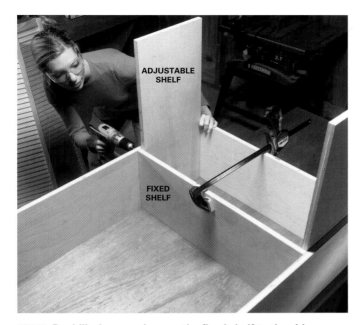

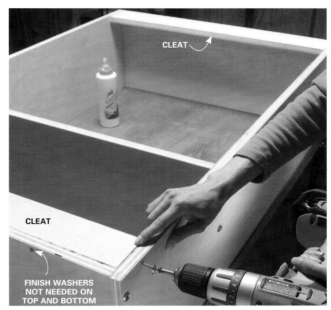

3 Predrill, clamp and screw the fixed shelf to the sides. Use adjustable shelves as a guide to space it and keep it square.

4 Glue and clamp hanging cleats to the top and bottom. Predrill and drive screws through the top, bottom and sides into the cleats.

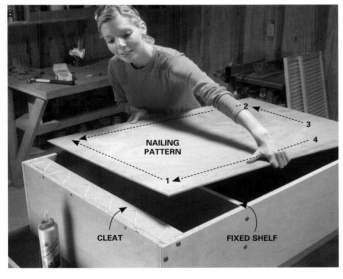

5 Spread a bead of glue on all back edges. Then align the plywood back with the top and nail with 1-in. brads. Align the other sides and nail in the order shown.

6 Mark shelf pin locations on both front and back sides of a pegboard template. Mark one side of the cabinet, then slide (not flip) the pegboard to the opposite side and mark matching holes. Drill the 1/4-in. pin holes.

the order and direction shown in Photo 5. Align the edges carefully before nailing each side to keep the cabinet perfectly square.

Shelves, hinges and other hardware

Use a scrap of pegboard to help lay out the holes evenly for the adjustable shelf support pins. Mark each hole clearly (red circles; Photo 6) on the front and back of the pegboard. Mark each hole position on one side of the cabinet, then slide the pegboard across to the other side for marking. Don't flip the pegboard over; it can throw the

MASKING TAPE DEPTH GAUGE

pattern off and the shelves will rock rather than lie flat.

Most shelf support pins require a 1/4-in. hole, but check the pins to be sure. In addition, measure how far the pins are supposed to go into the cabinet sides. Wrap a piece of masking tape around the drill bit at this depth. This ensures that the bit won't go completely through the side of the cabinet. Check the bit after every few holes to make sure the tape hasn't slipped.

Install the door hinges 6 in. from the top and bottom of the doors (add a third hinge on taller doors). The

7 Screw the hinges to the cabinet doors. Align the door edges with the cabinet top and bottom. Then predrill and screw the hinges to the cabinet sides.

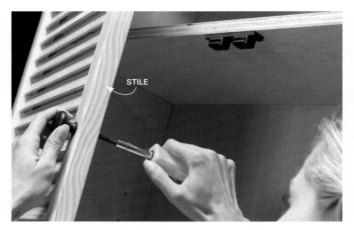

8 Attach cabinet knobs to the doors and install a pair of magnetic latches to hold the doors closed. For full-length doors, install latches at both the top and the bottom.

best type is a "partial wraparound" hinge (Photo 7). Its hinge leaves are hidden when the door is closed, and the design avoids driving screws into the weak plywood edge grain.

Begin by installing the hinges on the door (Photo 7). Keep them perfectly square to the door edge and predrill screw holes as precisely as possible. An extra set of hands will be helpful when attaching the doors to the cabinet. Have one person align the door exactly with the top or bottom of the cabinet while the second person marks, predrills and screws the hinges to the cabinet side. Repeat for the other door. Ideally the doors will meet evenly in the center with about a 1/8-in. gap between. If not, "tweak" the hinge positions slightly with paper shims, or plane the doors a bit to make them perfect.

Choose any type of knob and magnetic latch. However, bifold door stiles (the vertical edges) are narrow, so make sure the neighboring door will clear the knob when opened (Photo 8). If there's a rail (the horizontal door frame member), mount the knobs there.

Another potential problem: Bifold stiles are usually 1 to 1-1/8 in. thick and most knobs are designed for 3/4-in. doors. Look for longer knob screws at a local hardware store. Or try

this trick: With a 3/8-in. bit, drill a 1/4-in.-deep hole on the back side of the stile to recess the screw head.

To mount a magnetic latch, first mount the magnet to the underside of the fixed shelf (Photo 8). Stick the catch plate to the magnet with the "mounting points" facing out (photo, right). Close the door and press it tightly against the latch. The points on the catch plate will indent the door slightly and indicate where to mount the plate.

Finishing

That's about it. These cabinets are finished inside and out with two coats of clear water-based satin polyurethane. It dries quickly (one-half hour), has little or no odor, and cleans up with soap and water. The first coat raises the wood grain a bit, so sand it lightly with fine sandpaper (150 grit or finer). Whether using a clear finish, paint or stain, it's generally faster to remove the doors and hardware first.

Cutting lists

Storage locker

ITEM	QTY.	SIZE & DESCRIPTION
Door	1	11-3/4" x 79" (half of a 24" bifold)*
Sides	2	3/4" x 11-1/4" x 79"
Top, bottom, shelf	3	3/4" x 11-1/4" x 10-1/4"
Cleats	2	3/4" x 3" x 10-1/4"
Front cleat	1	3/4" x 3" x 10-1/4"
Back	1	1/4" x 11-3/4" x 79"

Closet on wheels

ITEM	QTY.	SIZE & DESCRIPTION
Doors	2	15-3/4" x 79" (32" bifold)*
Sides	2	3/4" x 22-1/2" x 79"
Top, bottom, shelf	3	3/4" x 22-1/2" x 30-1/8"
Cleats	3	3/4" x 3" x 30-1/8"
Back	1	1/4" x 31-5/8" x 79"
Casters	4	3"

Paneled wall cabinet

ITEM	QTY.	SIZE & DESCRIPTION
Doors	2	14-3/4" x 32-1/4" (30" bifold)*
Sides	2	3/4" x 11-1/4" x 32-1/4"
Top, bottom, shelves	4	3/4" x 11-1/4" x 28-1/8"
Cleats	2	3/4" x 3" x 28-1/8"
Back	1	1/4" x 29-5/8" x 32-1/4"

Narrow floor cabinet

ITEM	QTY.	SIZE & DESCRIPTION
Door	1	11-3/4" x 79" (half of a 24" bifold)*
Sides	2	3/4" x 11-1/4" x 79"
Top, bottom, shelves	9	3/4" x 11-1/4" x 10-1/4"
Cleats	2	3/4" x 3" x 10-1/4"
Back	1	1/4" x 11-3/4" x 79"

*Exact door sizes vary. Measure doors before deciding cabinet dimensions.

Car care cabinet

Simple shelves, plus a handy worktable

It's a whole lot easier to be a gearhead when all your gear is in one place. Here's an easy-to-build organizer you can complete in one morning, even if you're a beginning DIYer. If you build it from construction-grade pine boards and plywood, the materials will cost you about $40. If you use maple boards and birch plywood as shown here, it will cost about $70. The only must-have power tools for this project are a drill and a circular saw, although a table saw and a miter saw make the job much faster and easier.

To get started, cut the sides to length, lay them back to back and mark the shelf locations (Photo 1). Then mark and drill 3/16-in. pilot holes for the screws that fasten the shelves. Measure 1 in. and 2-3/4 in. from the back edges of

Figure A:
Car care cabinet
Overall dimensions: 34" tall x 24" wide x 5-3/4" deep

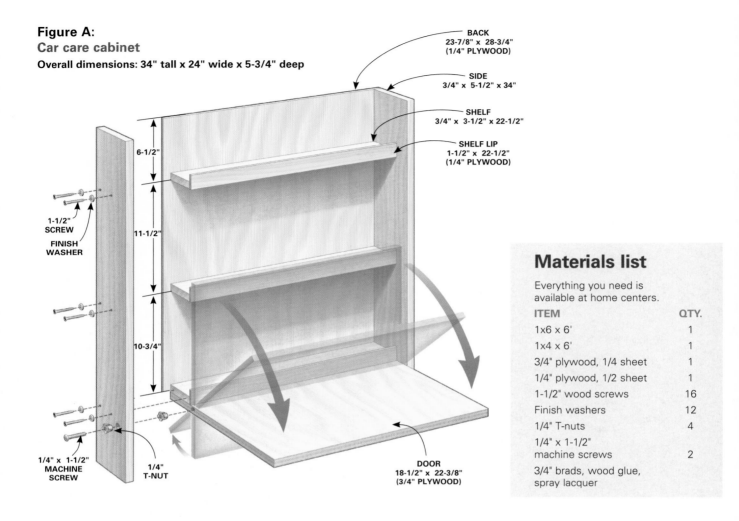

BACK
23-7/8" x 28-3/4"
(1/4" PLYWOOD)

SIDE
3/4" x 5-1/2" x 34"

SHELF
3/4" x 3-1/2" x 22-1/2"

SHELF LIP
1-1/2" x 22-1/2"
(1/4" PLYWOOD)

6-1/2"

1-1/2"
SCREW

FINISH
WASHER

11-1/2"

10-3/4"

1/4" x 1-1/2"
MACHINE
SCREW

1/4"
T-NUT

DOOR
18-1/2" x 22-3/8"
(3/4" PLYWOOD)

Materials list

Everything you need is
available at home centers.

ITEM	QTY.
1x6 x 6'	1
1x4 x 6'	1
3/4" plywood, 1/4 sheet	1
1/4" plywood, 1/2 sheet	1
1-1/2" wood screws	16
Finish washers	12
1/4" T-nuts	4
1/4" x 1-1/2" machine screws	2
3/4" brads, wood glue, spray lacquer	

the sides when you locate these holes. Set the 1x4 shelves between the sides and drill pilot holes into the shelf ends using the holes in the sides as guides. Drilling these pilot holes and screwing the shelves into place is easier if you clamp the whole cabinet together first (Photo 2). But you can hand-hold the shelves against the sides if you don't have long clamps. After the shelves are screwed into place, rip 1/4-in. plywood into 1-1/2-in.-wide strips for the front lips on the shelves. Glue the lips to the shelves, using 3/4-in. brads or clamps to hold the lips in place while the glue sets.

To complete the cabinet box, lay it face down and make sure it's square by taking diagonal measurements. Then run light beads of wood glue on the sides and shelves and tack on the plywood back with 3/4-in. brads spaced about 8 in. apart. The back is slightly narrower than the cabinet, so you don't have to line up the edges perfectly.

Flip the cabinet onto its back and clamp the door into place with the back edge of the door resting flat on your workbench. Using a square, mark the location of the door on the outer sides of the cabinet. Then drill 5/16-in. holes 1-3/8 in. from the front edges of the cabinet sides. Drill through

tip

The worktable is also a door that encloses the bottom shelf. Flip it up and you've got a mounting surface for a towel holder and other accessories. You can mount a fold-up door on special hinges, but a faster method that requires just a couple of bucks' worth of hardware is shown in Photos 3 and 4.

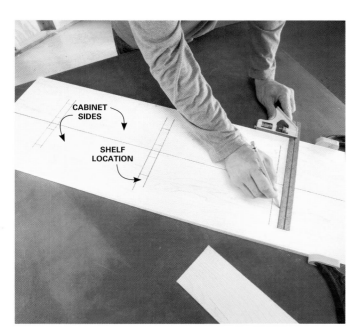

1 Prevent mistakes by marking shelf locations on both cabinet sides at once. Then mark the screw locations and drill pilot holes.

2 Clamp the shelves between the sides and screw the cabinet together. Give the exposed screw heads a neater look with finish washers.

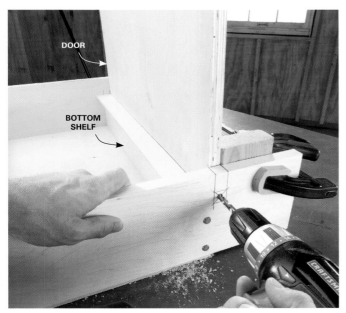

3 Drill the T-nut holes with the door locked tight against the bottom shelf. Drill as straight as you can through the sides and into the door.

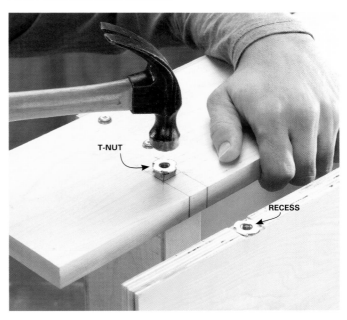

4 Drive the T-nuts into the holes. File the recesses so the T-nuts sit flush with the edges of the door. Attach the door with machine screws.

the sides and into the door, stopping at a depth of about 1-1/2 in. (Photo 3). Cut shallow recesses in the door for the T-nuts using a coarse file or wood rasp. Position the door and drive in the machine screws that act as pivot points for the door. Make sure the door opens and closes freely. If not, sand down the edges that bind with a belt sander or an orbital sander. If the fit is a bit sloppy, remove one of the screws and place a washer over the T-nut.

To put a quick finish on the cabinet, remove the door.

Sand away any pencil marks and smooth sharp edges. Take the cabinet to a well-ventilated area and apply a couple of light coats of aerosol spray lacquer. The lacquer will harden in just a few minutes. Then lightly sand with a fine sanding sponge and spray on a final coat. Wait about an hour to reattach the door. To mount the cabinet, drive four 1-1/2-in. screws through the back and into studs. Add a dry-erase board and paper towel holder if you like and load those shelves!

Hang-it-all storage wall

The wall space in your garage is way too valuable just to hang rakes, bikes and garden hoses at random on nails, hooks or shelves. To make every square inch of that wall space work for you, build this wall storage system.

This system is made entirely from plywood and standard hardware. It's easy to build and easy to customize to suit your needs. You can install it to fill any size wall or cover only part of a wall. You can hang shelves, bins or hooks and arrange them to make efficient use of wall space. With special store-bought hangers, you can hang hard-to-hold items like bikes or wheelbarrows. Best of all, everything hangs from sturdy rails, so you can rearrange the wall in minutes without any

tools. Some store-bought systems provide the same versatility, but they can cost two or even three times as much as this homemade system.

The only power tools you'll need are a circular saw and a drill. Other tools—a table saw, router, miter saw and brad nailer—will save you time, but they aren't necessary. All the materials you'll need are available at home centers (see p. 162). The total materials bill for this 8 x 20-ft. wall system and accessories was about $400. If you don't expect to hang anything from the lower half of the wall, you can cut time and expenses by covering only the upper half. If you completely cover a large wall as shown, expect to spend a weekend building the system and another finishing it and assembling shelves and hooks.

Hooks and shelves slip onto plywood rails, so you can move them anywhere instantly.

Cover the wall with plywood

You could nail and glue the rails directly to bare studs or drywall, but we chose to cover our wall with 1/4-in. plywood, for three reasons: First, the birch plywood matches the rails and gives the whole system a rich, finished appearance. Second, plywood won't scratch, gouge or dent as easily as drywall; and third, you can quickly clean it with a damp cloth.

The sheets of plywood should meet at studs, so start by locating studs with a stud finder. Chances are, you'll have to cut the first sheet

STUD LOCATION

1 Cover the wall with 1/4-in. plywood. Spread construction adhesive on each sheet, then nail them to studs. Mark stud locations with masking tape.

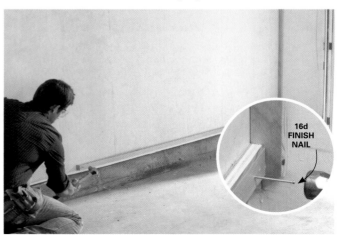

16d FINISH NAIL

2 Frame the wall with 1-1/2-in.-wide strips of 3/4-in. plywood. At corners, nail the strips flat against adjoining walls. Then run strips across the top and bottom.

3 Position your ripping guide using a spacer block and clamp it into place. Then cut the 3-1/2-in.-wide plywood rails. Cut two sheets at once to speed up the job.

4 Cut three 45-degree chamfers 1/8 in. deep on each rail using a router and chamfer bit.

5 Glue 2-1/2-in.-wide strips of 1/4-in. plywood to the back of each rail, even with the non-chamfered edge. Tack the strip into place with a pair of 3/4-in. brads every 12 in.

lengthwise so the edge aligns with a stud's center. Then you can use full sheets until you reach the end of the wall and cut the final sheet to fit. Your cuts don't have to be perfect and the sheets don't have to fit tightly into corners because you'll cover the edges with trim later (see Photo 2).

If you're installing the plywood over drywall as shown, run a bead of construction adhesive around the edges of each sheet and cover the middle with a zigzag pattern (Photo 1). Use at least half a tube of adhesive per sheet. If you're fastening plywood to bare studs, apply a heavy bead of adhesive to each stud. Nail the sheet to studs with 1-5/8-in. paneling

nails to secure the plywood until the adhesive dries.

Frame the plywood-covered wall with strips of 3/4-in. ply-wood (Photo 2). Make the strips using the same techniques used to make the rails (see Photos 3 and 4). Rip 3/4-in. plywood into 1-1/2-in.-wide strips, chamfer one edge with a router and nail them into place with 16d finish nails.

Combine thick and thin plywood to make rails

Begin rail construction by cutting strips of 1/4-in. and 3/4-in. plywood. If you don't have a table saw, make a simple ripping guide to ensure straight cuts. Cut a 3-5/8-in. spacer block to position the ripping guide (Photo 3). Tip: If you make the guide from 1/2-in. plywood, you can rip two sheets of 3/4-in. plywood at once. Cut a 2-5/8-in. block to position the guide when cutting the 1/4-in. plywood strips. You'll get 13 rails from a sheet of 3/4-in. plywood; 18 strips from a sheet of 1/4-in. plywood. Shown are twenty-three 8-ft.-long rails for this 8 x 20-ft. wall.

The chamfers on the rails are optional (Photo 4). The two on the face of the rail are purely decorative. The one on the back lets the aluminum cleats slip over the rail more easily. Instead of chamfering the edge, you can simply round it slightly with sandpaper. For appearance, the shelves and hook mounting plates here are also chamfered. A carbide chamfer bit costs $20.

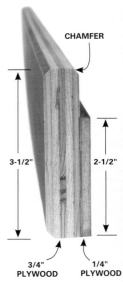

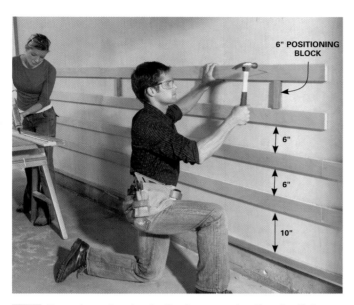

6" POSITIONING BLOCK

6"

6"

10"

6 Spread two beads of adhesive on each rail and nail them to studs with 16d finish nails. Start at the bottom and work up.

HANGER STRIP

MOUNTING PLATE

ALUMINUM CLEAT

RAIL

Fasten 1/4-in. plywood strips to each rail (Photo 5). To save time, finish the rails before you install them. Water-based polyurethane was used here. But don't coat the back side; construction adhesive will grip bare wood better than sealed wood.

Use glue and nails for rock-solid rails

Attach rails with two beads of construction adhesive and a 16d finish nail driven at each stud (Photo 6). Cut rails so that the ends meet at stud centers. For better appearance and strength, avoid putting rail joints at plywood seams.

Use a level to make sure the lowest course of rails is straight and level. Then use a pair of spacer blocks to position the rest of the rails. You can space the rails however you like. The closer you position them, the more flexibility you'll have when hanging shelves or hooks. This wall was constructed with a 10-in. space between the bottom strip of trim and the lowest rail, then the rest of the rails were spaced 6 in. apart. When all the rails are in place, finish the entire wall with a coat of polyurethane.

7 Cut aluminum angle and flat stock into 4-in.-long sections. Round off the razor-sharp edges of each cut with a file or sandpaper.

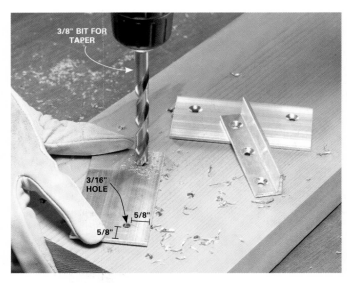

8 Drill three 3/16-in. screw holes in angled cleats and two in flat cleats. Then drill a shallow screw head recess with a 3/8-in. bit.

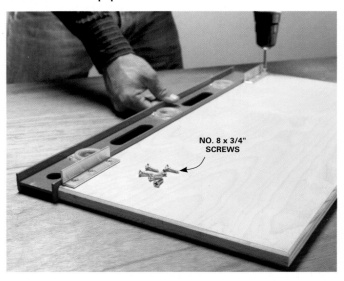

9 Screw cleats to the shelf about 1/4 in. from the ends. Use a straightedge to position the cleats flush and parallel with the back edge of the shelf.

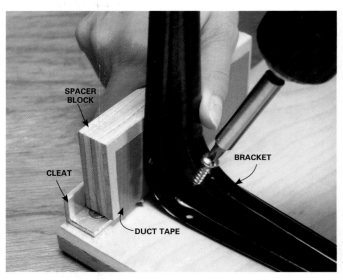

10 Position shelf brackets with a 3/4-in. plywood spacer block. Add a strip of duct tape to slightly widen the space so the cleat slips easily onto rails.

Mass-produce hanger cleats from aluminum stock

The cleats that hook onto the rails are made from 1/8-in.-thick aluminum stock that's available in 2- to 8-ft. lengths. Use 3/4-in. x 3/4-in. angle for shelves and 2-in.-wide flat stock for mounting plates (see Photos 9 and 11). Cutting and drilling aluminum is fast and easy. Cut the aluminum with a metal-cutting blade ($10; Photo 7). These cleats were cut 4 in. long, but you can vary the length to suit your needs. Drill 3/16-in. screw holes and 3/8-in. recesses with standard drill bits (Photo 8). Wear eye protection when cutting and drilling aluminum.

Plywood mounting plates let you hang just about anything

Mounting plates are just pieces of plywood that hold hooks, bins, drawers or anything else that you'd want to mount on a wall. Cut 4-1/2 x 4-1/2-in. plates for small hooks. Glue and nail a 1-1/2-in.-wide plywood hanger strip across the back of each plate. Coat the plates with polyurethane. When the finish is dry, position the aluminum cleats about 1/4 in. from the upper edge of the hanger strip and fasten it with 1-1/4-in. drywall screws (Photo 11). Finally, screw hooks to the plates (Photo 12). Larger mounting plates were made for bins, drawer units and a bicycle holder.

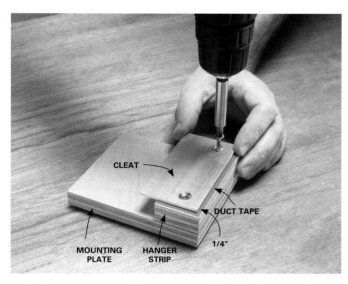

CLEAT

MOUNTING PLATE

HANGER STRIP

DUCT TAPE

1/4"

11 Glue a hanger strip to the mounting plate. Then add a strip of duct tape and screw on the cleat 1/4 in. from the top edge.

12 Predrill and screw hooks near the top of the plate where they can penetrate two layers of plywood.

Don't hang plates or shelves on the rails until the polyurethane has dried for at least 24 hours. Otherwise, the fresh polyurethane can "glue" parts together. Put your deepest shelves near the ceiling where they'll be out of the way. That out-of-reach space is the best place for stuff you don't use often and a good spot for child hazards like lawn chemicals.

Hanging options

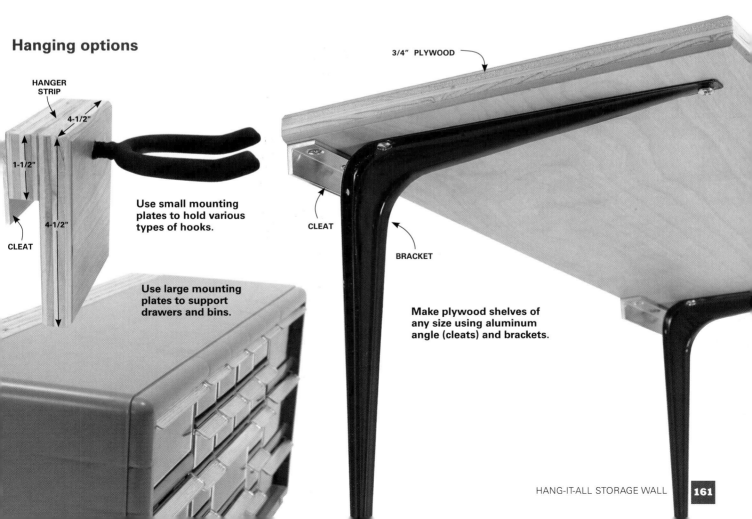

HANGER STRIP

4-1/2"

1-1/2"

4-1/2"

CLEAT

Use small mounting plates to hold various types of hooks.

Use large mounting plates to support drawers and bins.

3/4" PLYWOOD

CLEAT

BRACKET

Make plywood shelves of any size using aluminum angle (cleats) and brackets.

13 Slip the cleats over the rails and push down to anchor the shelves and mounting plates.

14 Use plywood scraps and your imagination to build custom racks for hard-to-store items.

Make a dozen sturdy shelves in an hour

The shelves are made from aluminum angle cleats, 3/4-in. plywood and brackets that are available in a range of sizes. These shelves are 6, 12 and 15 in. deep and 24 in. long. You could make yours longer than that, but remember that long shelves are less versatile than short ones. To keep shelves from sagging, place brackets no more than 30 in. apart. You can chamfer three sides of each shelf with a router and coat them with water-based polyurethane before adding cleats and brackets (Photos 9 and 10), as shown here.

tips

- One of the best features of this storage system is its adaptability. With a little ingenuity, you can make special holders for all those oddball items that don't fit conveniently on shelves or store-bought hooks (Photo 14). But before you make a custom holder, visit a home center so you don't spend a couple of hours building a bike rack only to find a better one for $7 at the store.

- Don't waste time on the storage system by making too few mounting plates for hooks. Assembling five or six extras takes just a few minutes. If you make too few, you'll have to drag out your tools and run through the whole process a second time.

- Like most garages, the one shown had too few electrical outlets. Before building this storage wall, hack holes in the drywall to easily run new electrical lines. No need to patch up the wall, since it will soon be covered with plywood anyway!

Materials list

All the tools and materials for this project are available at home centers. Here's what it took to build the 8 x 20-ft. wall system shown here, including 12 shelves and 16 mounting plates. The various brackets and hooks aren't included—choose those to suit your needs.

ITEM	QTY.
4' x 8' 1/4" plywood (wall covering, rails)	7
4' x 8' 3/4" plywood (rails, shelves, mounting plates)	4
Tubes of construction adhesive (fastening 1/4" plywood and rails)	6
Wood glue (assembling rails, mounting plates)	12 ozs.
3/4" aluminum angle, 1/8" thick (shelf cleats)	8'
2" aluminum flat stock, 1/8" thick (mounting plate cleats)	8'
1-5/8" paneling nails (fastening 1/4" plywood)	1 lb.
3/4" brad nails (assembling rails)	4 ozs.
16d finish nails (fastening rails to studs)	1 lb.
No. 8 x 3/4" taper-head screws (fastening cleats to shelves)	100
1-1/4" drywall screws (fastening cleats to mounting plates)	1 lb.
No. 8 x 3/4" pan-head screws (fastening shelf brackets)	100
Water-based polyurethane (coating wall, rails, shelves and mounting plates)	1 gal.

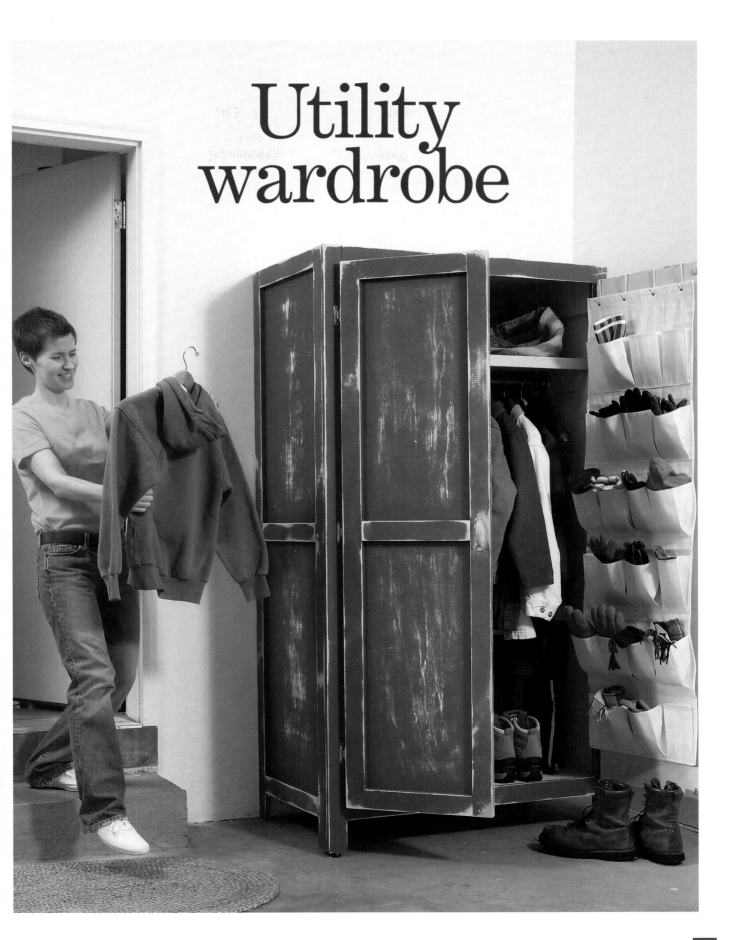

Utility wardrobe

This simple wardrobe is the perfect spot to store those heavy jackets, boots, hats and gloves in the summer and beach balls, swim fins and the bocce ball set in the winter. Or you could add shelves and make it the permanent storage cabinet for backpacks, tents, life preservers or any other seasonal items that stack up in your garage.

Here you'll learn to build this practical, sturdy cabinet out of low-cost materials. You'll make simple, strong joints using a pocket screw jig. A miter saw, a table saw and an air compressor with a brad gun will make the job a lot easier, but you can get by without them. Allow about a day to build the cabinet, plus a half day for painting.

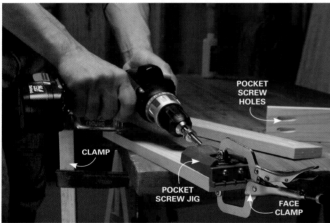

1 Cut the 1x3 rails and stiles to size for all the frames, following the Cutting list on p.165. Drill pairs of pocket screw holes in each end of the rails.

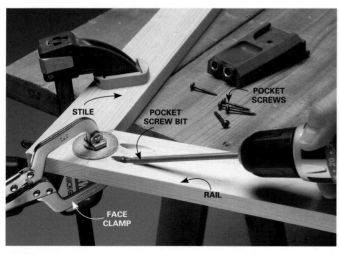

2 Spread glue on the rail ends and fasten them to the stiles with pocket screws. Clamp the boards as you fasten them to hold the board edges even.

3 Spread glue on the leading edge of the side frames and clamp them to the front frame so the top and sides are flush. Nail the frames together with 1-1/2-in. brads.

Figure A:
Utility wardrobe

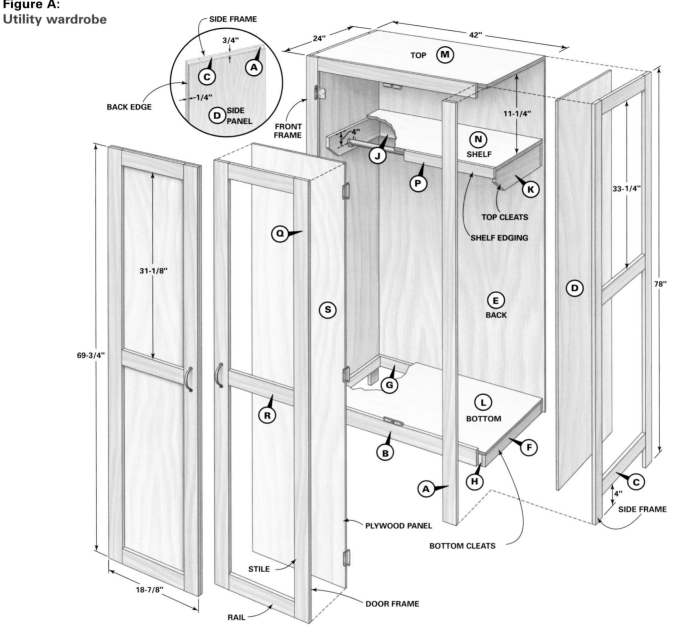

Cutting list

KEY	PCS.	SIZE & DESCRIPTION
A	6	3/4" x 2-1/2" x 78" poplar stiles
B	2	3/4" x 2-1/2" x 37" poplar front rails
C	6	3/4" x 2-1/2" x 18-1/4" poplar side rails
D	2	1/2" x 23" x 73-1/4" plywood side panels
E	1	1/4" x 40-1/2" x 73-1/4" plywood back panel
F	2	3/4" x 1-1/2" x 22-1/4" poplar bottom cleats (side)
G	1	3/4" x 1-1/2" x 39-1/2" poplar bottom cleat (back)
H	1	3/4" x 1-1/2" x 38" poplar bottom cleat (front)
J	1	3/4" x 5-1/2" x 39-1/2" poplar top cleat (back)

KEY	PCS.	SIZE & DESCRIPTION
K	2	3/4" x 5-1/2" x 19-1/4" poplar top cleats (side)
L	1	3/4" x 23" x 39-1/2" plywood floor
M	1	3/4" x 23-1/4" x 40-1/2" plywood top
N	2	3/4" x 20" x 39-1/2" plywood shelf
P	1	3/4" x 1-1/2" x 39-1/2" shelf nosing
Q	4	3/4" x 2-1/2" x 69-3/4" poplar door stiles
R	6	3/4" x 2-1/2" x 13-7/8" poplar door rails
S	2	1/2" x 18-7/8" x 69-3/4" plywood door panels

4 Cut the side panels to size. Apply glue to the inside face of the frame, set the side panels in place, clamp them, then nail them with 1-in. brads.

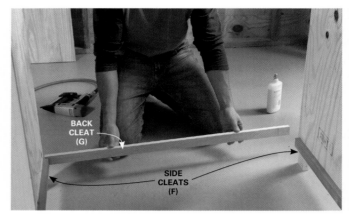

5 Cut the bottom 1x2 cleats to length. Glue and nail the side cleats first. Then glue and nail the front and back cleats.

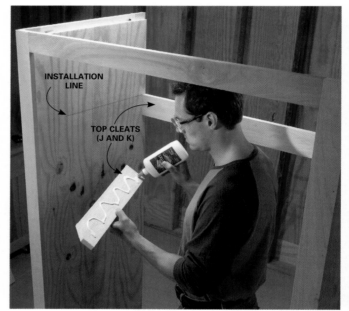

6 Cut the top cleats to length. Nail the back cleat into place. Then glue and nail the side cleats.

7 Lay the wardrobe face down. Spread glue and nail the back panel (E) into place with 1-in. brads spaced every 8 to 10 in.

Materials and costs

To keep costs low (about $250, including hardware), make the wardrobe from BC-grade plywood and knot-free 1x3s. If you want to make the cabinet even more utilitarian, you can use lower grades of wood and cut the cost in half. However, the doors might twist a bit and not shut evenly. BC plywood has a smooth, sanded face that's nice for painting. The knot-free poplar 1x3s (available from a local home center) are stable and easy to cut and join. Be sure to choose straight ones!

Build the frame

Start by cutting the 1x3 rails and stiles for the frames to length (A, B and C), following the Cutting list. Then use a pocket screw jig and the "step bit" that comes with it to drill two holes at both ends of each rail (Photo 1). You'll cover

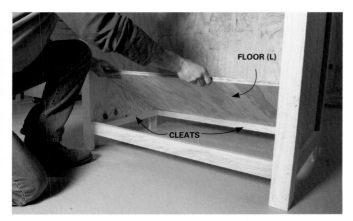

8 Cut the floor, top and shelf to size. Glue the top and nail it into place. Stand the wardrobe upright, then glue and nail the floor and shelf to the cleats.

9 Position the closet pole brackets 4 in. below the shelf and 10-3/4 in. from the back cleat. Screw them into place. Measure and cut the closet pole to length.

10 Cut the door panels to size, then glue and nail them to the door frames. All edges should be flush.

these holes with plywood later, so begin your holes on the less attractive side. The jig used here fastened to the end of the rail with a face clamp, although other types are available (see Buyer's guide, p. 169).

To create solid, smooth joints, apply a bead of wood glue along the end of a rail (B), then butt it against the top of a stile (A) so the top edges are flush (Photo 2). With the joint overhanging your work surface, clamp the rail and stile together with a "face" clamp (part of the pocket screw kit) to keep them aligned. Also clamp your stile to the work surface. The key is to make sure the edges and the faces of the two boards are flush before you drive the screws. Then, using the special pocket screw drive bit, fasten the joint with 1-1/2-in. pocket screws. If you're a pocket screw "rookie," practice on scrap wood first to get the hang of it.

Assemble the two side frames, the front and the two door frames in this manner, using Figure A as a guide. If your end cuts are perfectly square, your frame should also be square, but check them with a framing square anyway.

With the frames built, apply glue along the edge of a side frame, clamp it to the front frame so the edges are flush (make sure the pocket screw holes face inside), then fasten them with 1-1/2-in. nails (Photo 3). Do the same for the other side frame. Wipe away any glue that oozes out. The glue provides the primary holding power. The nails simply hold everything in place until the glue dries.

Add the sides and back

Add 1/2-in. plywood to the side frames for stability. Hold it 3/4 in. short of the top and 1/4 in. from the back to provide

11 Lay the wardrobe on its back. Screw the hinges to the doors, then center the doors over the opening. Insert a 1/8-in. spacer between the doors.

Materials list

ITEM	QTY.
3/4" x 4' x 8' BC-grade plywood	1
1/2" x 4' x 8' BC-grade plywood	2
1/4" x 4' x 8' BC-grade plywood	1
1x6 x 8' poplar	1
1x3 x 8' poplar	12
1x2 x 8' poplar	2
1x2 x 6' poplar	1
6' chrome closet pole	1
Closet pole brackets	2
Self-closing flush door hinges	6
Door handles	2
Threaded metal base glides	4
Magnetic catches	4
1-1/2" brad nails	1 box
1" brad nails	1 box
1-1/2" pocket screws	1 bag

Now cut the 1x2 bottom cleats and 1x6 top (shelf) cleats to length (see the Cutting list, p. 165). Glue and nail the 1x2 side cleats first (F). Align them with the bottom of the plywood panels, and butt them against the front frame. Clamp them before nailing them. Glue and install the front and back cleats as well (G and H; Photo 5).

Measure down 12 in. from the top of the side panels and install the 1x6 top back cleat (J) so the back is aligned with the edge of the plywood side panels (toenail the cleat into the plywood). Then glue and install the top side cleats (K; Photo 6). Drive 1-1/2-in. nails through the cleats into the stiles and drive 1-in. nails through the plywood panels into the cleats from the outside.

Now place the wardrobe face down on the floor. Apply glue along the back edges of the side panels and cleats. Install the back panel (E) and tack it into place with 1-in. brads (Photo 7).

Install the top, bottom and shelf

Use 3/4-in. plywood for the floor, ceiling and shelf to add stiffness and strength. Cut the floor, top and shelf (L, M and N) to size. With the wardrobe still on its face, apply glue along the top of the side and back panels. Fasten the top into place using 1-1/2-in. brads.

Then stand the wardrobe back up and install the floor (Photo 8). Cut the 1x2 nosing (P) to length. Glue and nail it along the front of the shelf, then install the shelf. The nosing will stiffen the shelf and keep it from bowing.

Mark the side cleats under the shelf 10-3/4 in. from the back cleat (the halfway point inside the wardrobe) and install closet pole brackets. Fasten the brackets into place with screws (Photo 9).

Cut the closet pole to length and install it. It's best to use

convenient grooves for inserting and nailing the top and back panels (Figure A).

Cut the side and back panels (D and E) accurately. If they're not square, the cabinet won't be square. Building a support spacer with two 2x4s and 1/2-in. plywood simplifies the side panel installation (Photo 4). Set the spacer under the bottom rail on a side frame. Apply a generous bead of glue to the side frame, then set the side panel in place (the good side facing out), resting it on the spacer. Butt the panel against the front frame. The frame may not be exactly square, so flex the frame if necessary to align it with the panel.

Clamp the panel to the framing. Use several clamps to keep the panel tight against the rails and stiles. Nails won't close any gaps between the plywood and the framing—that's the clamps' job. Anchor the panel with 1-in. nails. Install the panel on the other side the same way.

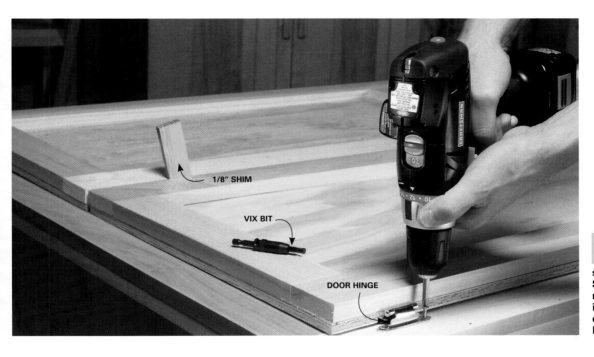

1/8" SHIM

VIX BIT

DOOR HINGE

12 Predrill holes in the front stiles and screw on the hinges. Stand the wardrobe upright, then install the magnetic catches and door handles.

a chrome pole rather than wood, since chrome can hold a heavier load without sagging.

Paint the wardrobe, and build and attach the doors

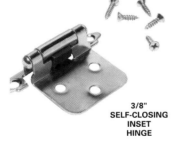

3/8" SELF-CLOSING INSET HINGE

Follow the Cutting list to cut the door panels (S) to size. Apply glue to the back of a door frame, set a panel over it, aligning it with the top and sides of the frame, then tack it into place (Photo 10). Do the same for the second door.

It isn't shown here, but it's easiest to prime and paint the wardrobe and doors at this point. Shown on p. 164 is an exterior latex paint, since this wardrobe will be kept in a garage. For a smoother finish, lightly sand the first coat with 120-grit paper before applying the second coat. Once the paint is dry, fasten the door hinges. You have some flexibility where you place the hinges, but keep the location the same on both doors. These were installed 2 in. from the top and bottom, and at the middle.

Installing the doors can be tricky. You want the doors to open and close without banging together, yet you want the gap between them kept to a minimum. To do this, place the wardrobe on its back and make a tiny mark on the rails at the midpoint of the door opening. Center the doors over the opening, overhanging the sides, top and bottom by 3/8 in. Insert a shim between the doors at the top and bottom to create a 1/8-in. gap (Photo 11). Use the midpoint marks to keep the doors centered.

Predrill the hinge holes on the stiles using a 3/32-in. bit. Shown is a special Vix bit (Photo 12), which precisely centers the holes. Standard drill bits may shift slightly, offsetting the hole. Even this slight movement may keep the doors from closing properly.

Stand the wardrobe upright to attach the remaining hardware. Installing metal magnetic catches at the top and bottom of the doors will hold them firmly closed and help keep them from warping.

The wardrobe is designed for function, but you can still have fun with its appearance. The wardrobe shown here was given three coats of "red pepper" latex paint, then spot-sanded for a weathered, rustic look. To complete the theme, galvanized pipe was used for the closet pole instead of chrome, as were complementary hinges and door handles.

Buyer's guide

Kreg Tool Co. offers several pocket hole jig kits. For more information, visit kregtool.com.

tip

Since most garages and some basement floors are not level, install inexpensive adjustable "feet." Drill a 1/4-in. hole in the bottom of the stiles, stick in the inserts, then place the glides inside the inserts. When you move the wardrobe to the garage or basement, adjust the glides until level. If you live in a hot, humid climate, consider adding two 4-in. round vents to the top to allow for better air circulation.

INSERT

THREADED METAL SLIDE

Super-size cabinets

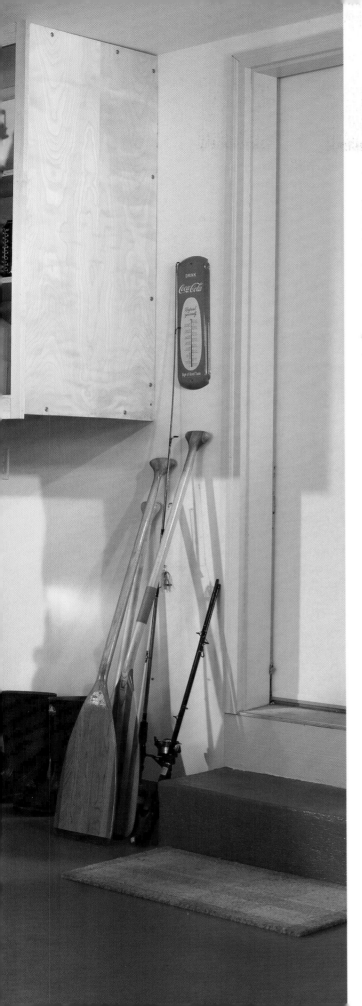

Everyone needs "deep" storage, that is, a place for camping gear, holiday decorations and seasonal toys and clothes. Not to mention all the other stuff you want to tuck away for a few months and keep clean. This cabinet system fits the bill. It's spacious, inexpensive and easy to build. You can also easily customize its size to suit just about any open wall space and your storage needs. The cabinet shown was tucked up against the ceiling to fill the little-used space over the car hoods.

The cabinet is divided into 32-in.-wide compartments because they hang from every other garage stud. Sliding cabinet doors keep out the dust while allowing wide open, instant access to your stuff.

You can build this project in four simple steps! Uncomplicated 2x2 and plywood construction makes assembly a snap. In fact, two people can build the cabinets you see here in about three hours. If you have a circular saw, a jigsaw, a screw gun and a little ambition, you can build these cabinets in an afternoon.

1 Rip one 8-ft.-long, 24-in.-wide length of 3/4-in. plywood for the end panels and 22-1/2-in. widths for each divider panel. Cut the panels to 4-ft. lengths.

4'
22-1/2" DIVIDER PANELS
4'
24" END PANELS

FIRST STUD FROM CORNER
WALL END PANEL

2 Press one end panel against the ceiling and the rear wall and screw it to the corner and first wall stud. Angle the back screws slightly to catch the corner stud.

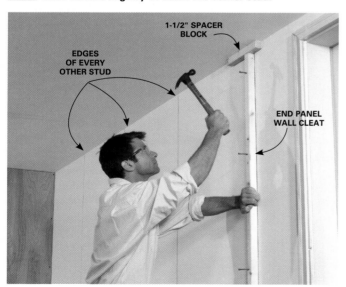

1-1/2" SPACER BLOCK
EDGES OF EVERY OTHER STUD
END PANEL WALL CLEAT

3 Locate the studs. Mark one edge with a 4-ft. level, then nail the end panel wall cleat into the last stud, spacing it 1-1/2 in. from the ceiling.

Planning your cabinets

Like most overhead wall cabinets, these are hung from wall studs. They're built in place using the ceiling and wall surfaces for the backs and top. This simplifies construction and saves on materials. If you don't have a finished wall behind the cabinets, begin the project by screwing 1/2-in. plywood or drywall over the wall studs. If your ceiling is open, add drywall or plywood there as well to keep out dust.

Most garage walls have studs spaced every 16 in., so size individual bays to fit over two stud spaces, or 32 in. If you have studs that are spaced every 24 in., make the compartments that wide.

These cabinets were sized to use 4x8 plywood sheets efficiently. When planning your cabinet dimensions, consider:

Height: In most garages, a 4-ft. cabinet against the ceiling leaves about 5 ft. between cabinet bottoms and the garage floor. If you park long vehicles in the garage or have a shallow garage, you may need to use the space under the cabinets for the fronts of vehicles. If so, when choosing cabinet heights, measure the height of the hood to make sure you'll have clearance. Also consider the heights of items you may want to store beneath the cabinets. Motorcycles, bikes, storage cabinets and wheeled tools are ideal candidates for that space. Two other heights that efficiently use plywood are 32 in. (six panels per sheet) and 24 in. (eight panels per sheet). Keep in mind that protruding cabinets invite head bumps. So make sure walking patterns don't pass too close to corners.

Depth: If you need to walk in front of the cabinets to access car doors, reduce the cabinet depth. Park your car in the garage to determine the maximum depth that still leaves plenty of room for foot traffic, and size accordingly. Depths of 16 or 12 in. will allow for six or eight panels per

1-1/2" SPACE
WALL CLEAT
1-1/2" SPACE

4 Press the end panel against the ceiling and wall, then screw it to the outside edge of the wall cleat with 2-in. screws.

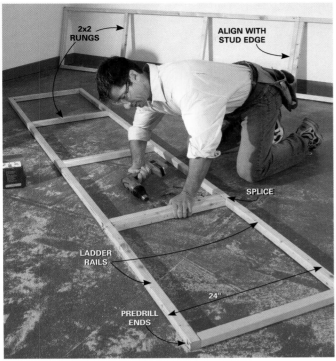

Width: The cabinets don't have to start against a wall as shown, but they do have to begin and end on a stud. So locate and mark all studs before deciding on how many compartments fit on the wall. There's a good chance you'll have an odd 16-in.-wide compartment at one end. You can use those compartments for open shelving or build oversized sliding doors to cover a standard opening plus the oddball. Be sure to consider access to service doors near the cabinets. Too close and it might be difficult to negotiate around cars to get into the house or backyard.

Lay out the cabinet footprint on the floor with masking tape and park the cars in the garage before you start building the cabinets. Walk around the garage and test access to the cars and service doors to make sure your cabinet layout is garage user–friendly.

5 Cut the ladder rails to fit between the end panels. Then carefully lay out the 2x2 rung locations using the wall studs as a guide for spacing. Nail the ladders together. Screw splices together with 3-in. screws.

Figure A:
Assembly

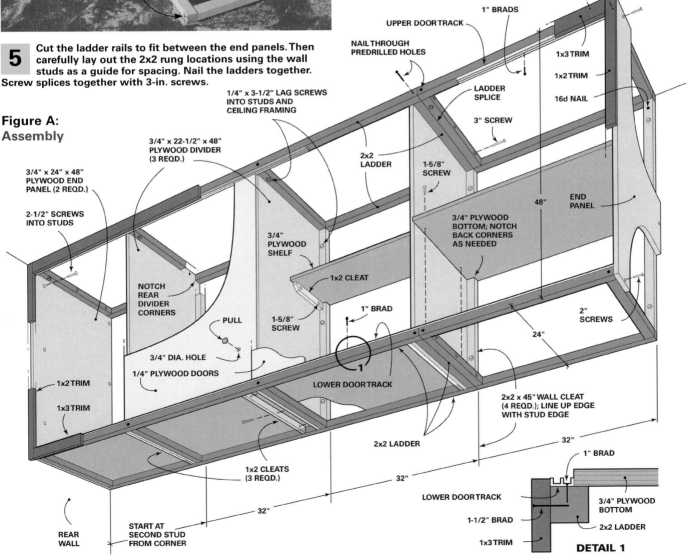

ALIGN EDGES WITH STUD EDGES

TEMPORARY CLEAT

6 Tack a temporary cleat 1-3/4 in. below the ceiling, rest the top ladder on it, and lift it into place. Screw it to the end panels and then fasten it to any available ceiling framing and to the wall with lag screws.

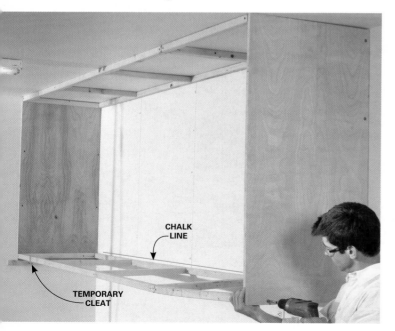

CHALK LINE

TEMPORARY CLEAT

7 Snap a chalk line 1-1/2 in. above the bottom of the end panels, add another temporary cleat and screw the bottom ladder to the end panels. Align the 2x2 rail to the chalk line and nail it to the wall studs.

Selecting the materials

Just about any type of sheet material will work for your cabinets. For the handsome, natural wood look shown, use 3/4-in. birch plywood for the end and divider panels and 1/4-in. birch plywood for the sliding doors. You can reduce the cost by using MDF (medium-density fiberboard) for painted cabinets or even construction-grade plywood for down-and-dirty utility cabinets.

The sliding doors glide on plastic track (see Buyer's guide, p. 177) that'll handle any 1/4-in.-thick material. You can even choose 1/4-in. hardboard or pegboard for ventilated cabinets. If you select plywood, plan to seal all the surfaces and edges of the doors to prevent warping.

Four-step cabinet building

These cabinets are incredibly easy and quick to build, because you only have to snap lines and freehand most of the cuts with a circular saw or jigsaw (Photo 1).

1. Attach the end panels and mount the wall cleats

Begin the cabinet assembly by attaching the first end panel to the end wall (Photo 2). To make it easier, start screws in the panel and then hold it against the wall, especially if you're short on help. Angle the screws slightly at the corner to hit the corner stud and add more screws into the first stud near the corner. Attach the end panel at the opposite end by securing it to a 2x2 cleat that's nailed and then lag-screwed to the stud. Cut all the cleats 3 in. shorter than the end panels to leave a 1-1/2-in. space at the top and bottom of the panels for the ladders (Photo 4). It's easiest to nail the cleats to the wall first and then install the lag screws in the center of the studs. Remember that they support nearly all of the weight of the cabinet and contents.

2. Build and install the ladders

You'll be nailing the ladder parts together before holding them up and fastening them to the end panels and wall. It's easy to split 2x2s, so predrill ends before nailing. Don't assume the ladders will be the same size, because walls and end panels can be out of plumb. Measure and assemble the top and bottom ladders independently rather than making carbon copies. Make sure the rung edges line up with the stud edges so the framing will be aligned for the panels. Since 2x2s are generally only sold in 8-ft. lengths, cut the rails to break at a wall cleat, and splice the sections together by doubling the 2x2 rungs at that point. They'll be wobbly, but as soon as they're fastened, they'll be plenty sturdy.

Sight along the outside of the bottom ladder or string lines along the outside edge to make sure the ladder is straight before fastening the divider panel bottom (Photo 11). Otherwise the sliding doors might slip out of the tracks or bind.

3. Install the dividers, bottoms and shelves

You'll need to cut 1-1/2-in. corner notches at the top and bottom of the back of the divider panels to clear the ladder

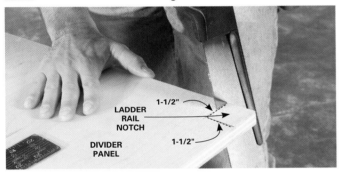

8 Nail the divider wall cleats to the studs, then predrill three evenly spaced 3/16-in. pilot holes and bolt the cleats to the studs with 3-1/2-in. lag screws.

9 Cut notches in the divider panels to clear the back upper and lower ladder rails. (The divider panels stop just short of the front ladder rails; see Photo 10.)

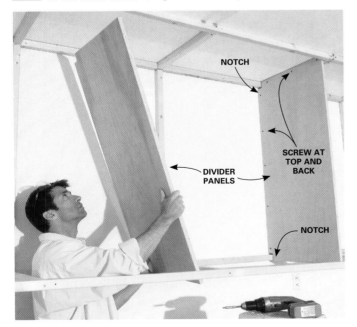

10 Lift the divider panels into position. Using 2-in. screws, attach them to the wall cleats and top ladder rungs only.

11 String a line along the bottom corner of the front rail. Straighten the rail to the line, clamp it, then screw the panels to the rungs.

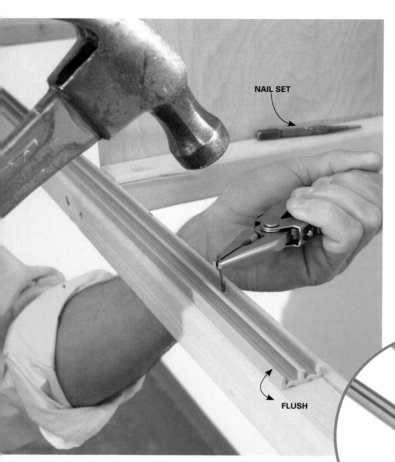

NAIL SET

FLUSH

framing (Photos 9 and 10). Cut them a little on the big side so you won't have to struggle with wedging the divider panels into place. Place one on each side of the cleats. You'll have to add another cleat on the bottom of the plywood side to support the cabinet bottom (Photo 13). Then you're ready to install the sliding door track (Photo 12). Cut the cabinet bottoms to fit against the door track and notch the corners wherever necessary to clear framing. Decide on shelving depths and heights, then cut 1x2 cleats to match the depths.

4. Install the sliding doors and finish

Cut the 1/4-in. door panels to width so they overlap the end and/or divider panels on both sides of the opening. Cut the panels to length so they clear the bottom track by about 1/8 in. when you slip them into the top track first. If you're using plywood for the doors, cut them from the back side to avoid splintering on the "show side."

For a finish detail, you can cover the exposed end panel edges and the exposed 2x2 ladder edges with maple (Photo 17). Use any wood type you'd like, but select 1x3s for the ladder trim and 1x2s for the end panels.

Finish the cabinets with latex paint or polyurethane. If you're using plywood for the door panels, coat the back side first, then flip them over and immediately seal the front side to prevent the doors from warping.

TOP TRACK

BOTTOM TRACK

12 Cut the tracks to length, then tack the bottom track to the bottom rail with 1-in. brads. Punch the brads to the bottom of the grooves with a nail set. Spread polyurethane glue on the top track and tack it into place.

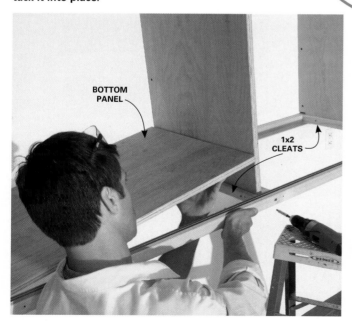

BOTTOM PANEL

1x2 CLEATS

13 Cut 1x2 cleats and screw them to the bottom of the divider panels to support the bottom panels. Cut the bottom panels to butt against the door track. Screw them into place.

CUT WITH BACK SIDE FACING UP

STRAIGHT EDGE

14 Measure the distance from the top of the bottom track to the inside of the top track and subtract 1/8 in. to determine door height. Cut the door from 1/4-in. plywood.

Buyer's guide

1/4-in. x 6-ft. track. Catalog No. KV2417 60, Woodworker's Hardware, wwhardware.com.

Cutting list

Lumber: For every four 32-in. bays, you'll need:

End and divider panels, bottoms: Two 4x8 sheets of 3/4-in. plywood

Shelving: One 4x8 sheet of 3/4-in. plywood

Sliding door panels: Two 4x8 sheets of 1/4-in. plywood

Framing: Eight 8-ft. 2x2s

Shelving cleats: approx. 4 ft. of 1x2 per 24-in. shelf

Hardware:

Lag screws: Sixteen 1/4 x 3-1/2 in.

Framing fasteners: 1 lb. of 16d nails

Panel fasteners: 1 lb. of 2-in. screws

Shelving cleats and cabinet bottom fasteners: 1 lb. of 1-5/8-in. screws

Track and trim fasteners: Small box of 1-in. brads

Door track: One 4-ft., one 8-ft. (see Buyer's guide).

Finger pulls: Four 3/4-in. diameter

15 Test-fit all the doors and slide them to the closed position. Mark the best finger pull placement. Then drill 3/4-in. holes and press in the finger pulls. (A dab of polyurethane glue will keep them from popping out.)

16 Lay out shelf sizes and spacing as desired, then cut and screw 1x2 cleats to the inside of the cabinets and cut the 3/4-in. shelves to fit.

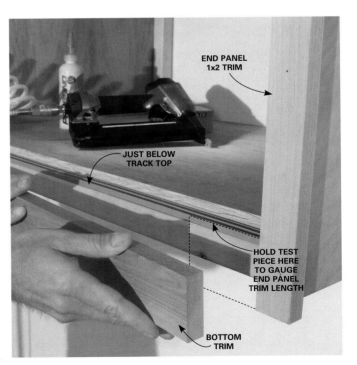

17 Cut 1x2 end panel trim to extend about 3/4 in. below the end panel. Nail into place. Cut and nail 1x3 trim for the top and bottom rails.

Multipurpose storage towers

This versatile storage system is the ultimate all-purpose odds and ends organizer for your garage. It's composed of tall, shallow towers that hold a wide variety of adjustable shelves and bins. By installing the towers along the same wall, you can add a range of special storage features between them—notched shelves for skis and fishing rods, pairs of dowels to corral balls, brackets for the trolling motor, and more (photo below). The tower shelves can be crafted into bins, tote boxes or almost any other accessory you can imagine (Photos 8–10). Here' you'll learn how to build the basic tower framework and a few custom accessories. You can devise variations to fit your storage needs.

The materials for the three towers cost just short of $200. The towers and shelves go together relatively quickly—you can easily build three in a day. Allow an additional day for 10 or so bins, depending on how detailed you choose to make them. They're well worth the extra effort.

The cabinets are constructed of 3/4-in. birch plywood. The cleats and back are made of 1/2-in. MDF (medium-density fiberboard).

Assembly details

Start by cutting the plywood for the cabinet, following the dimensions shown in Figure A, p. 181. Use a circular saw and a straightedge for accuracy (Photo 1). Then cut the tops and bottoms of the cabinet 1/2 in. narrower than the sides (Figure A). Because of the cutting waste, you can only cut four 11-7/8-in.-wide pieces from a 4-ft.-wide sheet of plywood. One 4 x 8-ft. sheet will make two tower frames with sawdust left over.

Next cut a sheet of 1/2-in. MDF (Figure A) to make the back, cleats and shelves. After cutting the cleats and back, you'll have enough stock remaining for four shelves from each sheet. Cut your shelves to length after you've assembled the cabinet. Then double-check your measurements and cut the shelves to fit a little loose so they'll slide easily.

Make the jig shown in Photo 2 to cut the cleats fast and accurately. Screw a 24-in. 2x4 perfectly perpendicular to the edge of a scrap of plywood. (Check it with a framing square.) Then screw a 1/4-in. stop block to the 2x4 so the cutoff distance is 5-3/8 inches.

1 Cut the plywood sides, tops and bottoms according to the dimensions in Figure A. Clamp a straightedge to the plywood as a saw guide to ensure straight, accurate cuts.

CIRCULAR SAW

STRAIGHTEDGE

CLEAT BOARD

JIG

STOP BLOCK

2 Rip two 11-3/8-in. x 8-ft. pieces from the MDF and cut cleats plus one shelf from each. Assemble a simple jig from a 2x4 and an MDF shelf (or plywood scrap) to ensure square cuts and speed up the job. Cut the back and shelves from the remaining piece of MDF.

tip

MDF (medium-density fiberboard) definitely has its pros and cons. First the pros. It's more stable than plywood, so it stays flat. It cuts and machines incredibly easily with little chipping or splintering. Because it's also kind of slippery, it works great for the smooth sliding bins and shelves in this project. And it's cheaper than plywood. But MDF has a couple of drawbacks. It doesn't tolerate moisture. If the cabinets get rain soaked or you live in an extremely humid area, you should seal the MDF (and entire cabinet) with polyurethane.

MDF works great, but if you're a die-hard plywood fan, go ahead and use that instead.

Caution: Don't use a stop block thicker than 1/4 in. or the cleat might pinch the saw blade, making the saw kick back.

Cut 12 cleats from each 11-3/8-in. x 8-ft. length of MDF, leaving about 30 in. for a shelf. Screw the cleats to the plywood sides (Photo 3), positioning your first cleat 3/4 in. up from the bottom edge to allow space for the plywood bottom. Recess the drywall screw heads in the MDF so the bins won't get hung up on them. MDF is so hard that the screws will snap if you try to drive them flush. Create the recess with a counterbore bit (Photo 3 inset), which you can buy at any hardware store. Position the top cleat down 3/4 in. from the top of each side panel to leave room for the plywood top.

To simplify attaching the cleats to the second side, clamp both sides back to back and flush top and bottom (Photo 3). Use a spacer long enough to bridge both sides. This ensures that all your shelves and bins will line up.

Tip: Before you remove the clamps, label both sides so you don't confuse them with another pair.

The tedious part is over. Now assemble the cabinet sides, top, bottom and back (Photo 4), working on a flat floor where you have plenty of space. In addition, drive a couple of screws through the back into the cleats near the middle to keep the sides from bowing. Predrill the screw holes with a 1/8-in. bit so you don't split the narrow 1/2-in. cleats.

Figure A:
Tower details

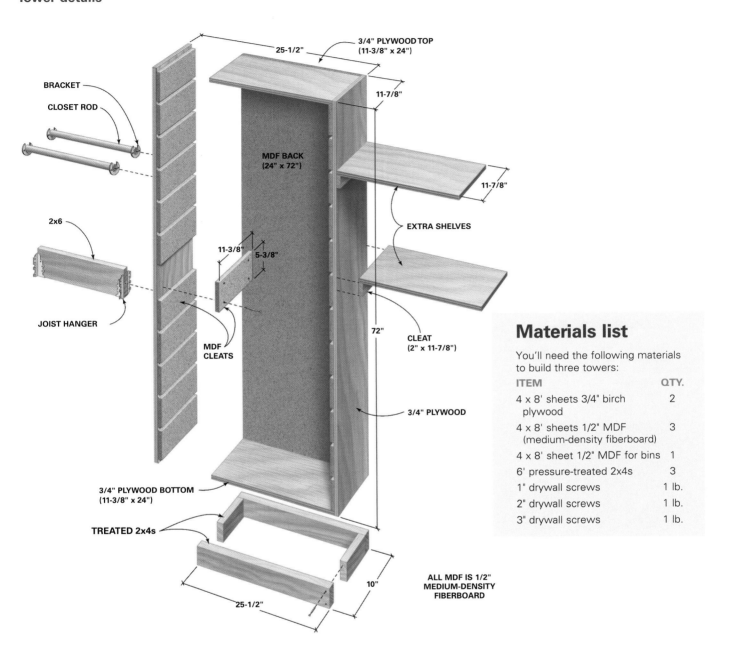

BRACKET

CLOSET ROD

3/4" PLYWOOD TOP
(11-3/8" x 24")

25-1/2"

11-7/8"

2x6

MDF BACK
(24" x 72")

11-7/8"

EXTRA SHELVES

JOIST HANGER

11-3/8"

5-3/8"

**MDF
CLEATS**

72"

CLEAT
(2" x 11-7/8")

3/4" PLYWOOD

3/4" PLYWOOD BOTTOM
(11-3/8" x 24")

TREATED 2x4s

25-1/2"

10"

ALL MDF IS 1/2"
MEDIUM-DENSITY
FIBERBOARD

Materials list

You'll need the following materials
to build three towers:

ITEM	QTY.
4 x 8' sheets 3/4" birch plywood	2
4 x 8' sheets 1/2" MDF (medium-density fiberboard)	3
4 x 8' sheet 1/2" MDF for bins	1
6' pressure-treated 2x4s	3
1" drywall screws	1 lb.
2" drywall screws	1 lb.
3" drywall screws	1 lb.

Install the towers

If you rest the plywood tower directly on a concrete floor, it'll absorb moisture and the plywood will swell. Instead, set the cabinet on a pressure-treated 2x4 frame (Photo 5). Make the frame the same width as the tower (25-1/2 in.) but narrower in depth (about 10 in.) to provide a recessed toe-kick, as in a kitchen cabinet. Either nail or screw the frame pieces together with 3-in. fasteners.

Finally, mount the tower on the frame (Photo 5) and check it for plumb. **Caution:** Screw the tower through the back into the wall studs so it doesn't tip over.

Customize for special uses

The space between towers is just as useful as the room inside them. Install a pair of closet poles 6 to 8 in. apart between two cabinets to hold soccer balls, basketballs or footballs (Photo 6). Hang a 2x8 on edge with a couple of joist hangers to hold a boat or trolling motor. Or simply cut 3/4-in. plywood shelves to various sizes and shapes for other special items.

Then build bins for the smaller stuff (Photo 7). Photos 8–10 and Figures B, C and D, p. 183, show handy, easy-to-build bin styles. Cut in a few handholds and you can carry the

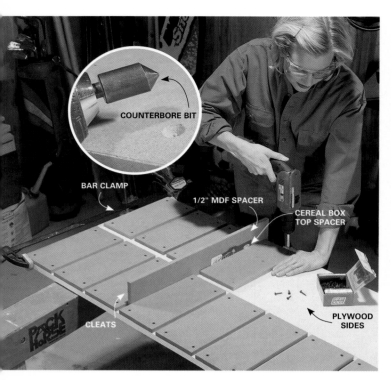

COUNTERBORE BIT

BAR CLAMP

1/2" MDF SPACER

CEREAL BOX
TOP SPACER

CLEATS

PLYWOOD
SIDES

BOTTOM

3 Screw the cleats to the plywood sides with four 1-in. dry-wall screws. Hold the cleat flush to the front edge of the cabinet. Use a scrap piece of shelf material plus a cereal box top as spacers. Use a counterbore bit to provide a recess for the drywall screws (inset photo).

4 Assemble the towers by driving three 2-in. drywall screws through the sides and into each edge of the top and bottom. Then screw on the back to square up and stiffen the cabinet (Figure A).

WALL
STUDS

2x4 PRESSURE-
TREATED FRAME

SHIMS

LEVEL

CLOSET
POLES

2x8 JOIST
HANGERS

1x2 CLEAT

3/4" PLYWOOD
SHELF

5 Cut and nail together a 2x4 frame for each tower. Position the frames, level them using shims and screw them to the wall with 3-in. screws. Then tip each tower onto a frame. Fasten each tower to wall studs with at least four 2-in. drywall screws.

6 Space additional towers at least 2 ft. apart. Then screw cleats, closet rod hangers and other types of supports to the outside faces of the sides to support more shelves and other storage devices.

7 Slide in the shelves. Build and insert the bins between the cleats according to our photos and plans (Figures B, C and D).

stuff right to where you're working (Photo 8). Insert a dowel through the side of a bin and you have a tote you can carry with one hand (Photo 9). Set dividers through the bin and for the first time in 35 years you'll have nails and screws that actually have a place they can call home (Photo 10). Combine this with a cutout for a handle and you've made them a mobile home.

The secret to assembling bins is to begin with a shelf with 1 in. cut off the long side. This shelf is the bottom. Then cut the ends, fronts and backs and screw and glue them to the bottom (Photos 8–10 and Figures B, C and D). Place dividers and handholds wherever they work best. Be sure to predrill all your screw holes, staying at least an inch away from the ends so you won't split the 1/2-in. MDF pieces.

If you have a router table and finish nailer as well as some spare time, you can really go design crazy. Setting the dividers into routed grooves adds strength. Use your imagination and you'll come up with all kinds of other ideas for customizing this system.

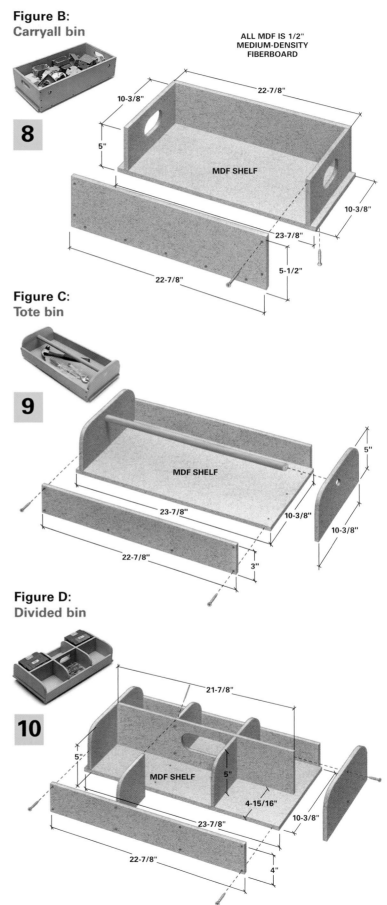

Figure B:
Carryall bin

Figure C:
Tote bin

Figure D:
Divided bin

Giant garage cabinet

At 7 ft. tall, 2 ft. deep and 16 ft. long, this cabinet not only holds a ton of stuff, but also handles bulky items that other cabinets can't: camping gear, benchtop tools, outdoor toys. You can even hang off-season clothes inside on hooks. The big sliding doors keep it all neatly hidden and provide instant, easy access.

With birch doors and trim and AC plywood on the partitions, the project cost $1,015. Simply substituting oak or lauan doors and replacing the AC plywood with oriented strand board (OSB), you could trim the cost to $750.

How fast is this project? If you stick to it, you could complete most of it in a day. Plan a second day to complete the details and get started on the finishing. In addition to standard hand tools like a tape measure, level, framing square and Speed Square, you'll need a circular saw and drill. A power miter saw and pneumatic trim nailer would simplify the trim work but aren't necessary.

This cabinet was designed to accommodate six doors and fit against the right wall, but you can easily modify it to suit your needs. You can make the cabinet wider or narrower by changing the number or size of the doors. Reverse the plan if you want to mount it against the left wall instead. You could also build the cabinet tight to the ceiling, but you'll have to reverse the order of construction. To do that, start by fastening the ceiling frame to the studs and to the ceiling. Then mount the uprights to the walls. And finally build the

It's just a big box with closet doors

Don't let the size of this project fool you. It may be big, but you can build it in a weekend. The cabinet is just a basic box: nothing more than simple framing covered with plywood. Installing the doors is exactly like installing sliding closet doors. You only need inexpensive hollow-core doors and sliding door hardware.

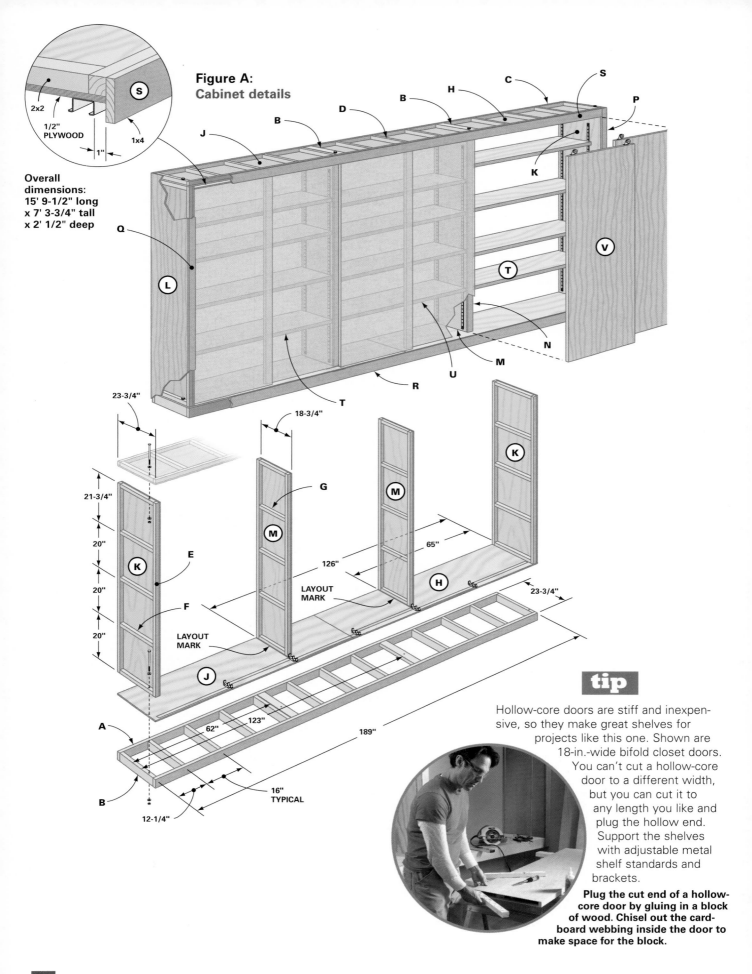

Figure A:
Cabinet details

S
2x2
1/2" PLYWOOD
1x4
1"

Overall dimensions:
15' 9-1/2" long
x 7' 3-3/4" tall
x 2' 1/2" deep

D
B
B
H
C
S
P
J
K
Q
L
T
V
N
M
U
R
T

23-3/4"
18-3/4"
21-3/4"
20"
20"
20"
G
M
M
K
K
E
F
65"
126"
LAYOUT MARK
H
LAYOUT MARK
J
23-3/4"
A
62"
123"
189"
B
16" TYPICAL
12-1/4"

tip

Hollow-core doors are stiff and inexpensive, so they make great shelves for projects like this one. Shown are 18-in.-wide bifold closet doors. You can't cut a hollow-core door to a different width, but you can cut it to any length you like and plug the hollow end. Support the shelves with adjustable metal shelf standards and brackets.

Plug the cut end of a hollow-core door by gluing in a block of wood. Chisel out the cardboard webbing inside the door to make space for the block.

Cutting list

KEY	PCS.	SIZE & DESCRIPTION
A	2	2x4 x 189" bottom frame
B	16	2x4 x 20-3/4" crosspieces
C	2	2x2 x 189" top frame
D	12	2x2 x 20-3/4" crosspieces
E	8	2x2 x 81-3/4" upright frame
F	10	2x2 x 20-3/4" upright crosspieces
G	10	2x2 x 15-3/4" upright crosspieces
H	2	1/2" x 23-3/4" x 96" top and bottom plywood
J	2	1/2" x 23-3/4" x 93" top and bottom plywood
K	3	1/2" x 23-3/4" x 81-3/4" upright plywood
L	1	1/2" x 23-3/4" x 87-3/4" outside upright plywood

KEY	PCS.	SIZE & DESCRIPTION
M	4	1/2" x 18-3/4" x 81-3/4" upright plywood
N	2	3/4" x 2-1/2" x 81-3/4" upright trim
P	1	3/4" x 3-1/2" x 87-3/4" upright trim (trim width to fit)
Q	1	3/4" x 2-1/2" x 87-3/4" upright trim
R	1	3/4" x 4" x 185" horizontal trim (trim length to fit)
S	1	3/4" x 3-1/2" x 185" horizontal trim (trim length to fit)
T	8	1-3/8" x 18" x 60" shelves (cut bifold doors)
U	4	1-3/8" x 18" x 58" shelves (cut bifold doors)
V	6	1-3/8" x 32" x 80" doors

base, including the plywood floor, and bolt it to the uprights and the wall.

If you have block or concrete walls in your garage, attach the base, uprights and top frame with lag shield anchors and lag screws or expanding concrete anchors. If you build the cabinet against open studs, you'll have to install horizontal blocking between the studs in areas where the uprights don't align with an existing stud.

Build the base

The most critical part of the project is getting the base square, level and straight before you screw it to the wall. If your wall is bowed (like most), you'll have to shim behind the frame before bolting it to the wall.

Start by snapping a level chalk line on the wall to indicate the top of the lower frame. This cabinet was positioned about 24 in. above the floor. Next, use a stud finder to locate and mark the studs. Cut temporary 2x4 legs that rest on the floor and extend to 3-1/2 in. below the chalk line, and then screw them to the wall. Make another set of legs about 1/4 in. shorter than the first set to support the front edge and add a cleat to each one (Photo 1). Assemble the base (Figure A) with nails or screws and rest it on the legs. Attach the front legs through the cleat with screws and attach the base to the wall with a temporary screw at each end.

Using a level, adjust the height of

1 Support the base frame with temporary legs and screw it to wall studs. Use a string line and shims to make sure the front edge is perfectly straight.

2 Fasten the uprights to the wall with screw-in drywall anchors. Make sure each upright is plumb and squared with the base.

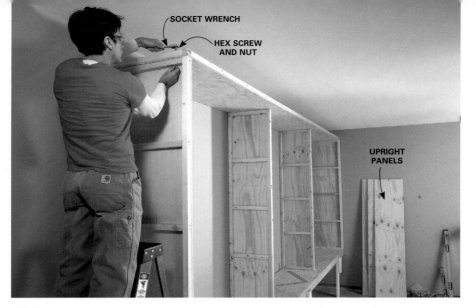

3 Set the top on the uprights and bolt it to them. Also bolt the uprights to the base. Then nail plywood panels to the uprights to enclose the framing.

4 Dress up the front edges of the base and uprights by nailing on trim boards. The top trim overhangs the top to hide the door track.

the front legs by shimming under them until the frame is level from front to back on both ends. Next, nail small blocks of 1/2-in. plywood to both ends of the base and stretch a string or chalk line between them. Use a third block of 1/2-in. plywood to check the distance between the front 2x4 and the string (Photo 1). Add shims between the wall and the frame as needed to create a consistent 1/2-in. space between the string and the front 2x4. If your wall is straight, you won't have to add any shims. Lag-screw the frame to the studs (Photo 1). Finish the base by nailing on the plywood.

Bolt on the uprights

Cut the 2x2s to length and screw them together to form the frames for the uprights. To provide maximum rigidity, spread a bead of construction adhesive on the face of the 2x2s before nailing plywood to one side of each frame. To ensure the frames are square, be careful to cut the plywood square and line it up with the frame before nailing. Use the measurements in Figure A to locate the partitions, and make square layout lines on the plywood base with a framing square. Use a 4-ft. level to extend the layout lines up the wall.

Where uprights don't align with wall studs, use screw-in drywall anchors to secure them (Photo 2). These anchors aren't supporting the cabinet. They simply hold the uprights in position

Materials list

ITEM	QTY.	ITEM	QTY.	ITEM	QTY.
2x4 x 16' spf (spruce, pine, fir) lumber	2	1-3/8" x 32" x 80" hollow-core doors	6	5/16" hex head nuts	8
2x2 x 16' spf lumber	2	1/4" x 4" lag screws	24	5/16" washers	16
2x4 x 8' spf lumber	4	1/4" washers	24	Construction adhesive	2 tubes
2x2 x 8' spf lumber	15	3" deck screws	200	6' shelf standards	12
4' x 8' x 1/2" plywood	6	1-1/2" finish nails	1 lb.	Shelf clips	36
1x3 x 8' trim board	3	2" finish nails	1 lb.	Johnson 2200-096 96" track*	2
1x4 x 8' trim board (trim to fit)	1	Hollow wall anchors	16	Johnson 2216 single wheel hanger*	6
1x4 x 16' trim board	1	6" x 5/16" hex head machine screws	2	Johnson 2238 single wheel hanger*	6
1x6 x 16' trim board (rip to 4" width)	1	4" x 5/16" hex head machine screws	6	Johnson 2135 bypass door guide*	5
36" hollow-core bifold doors	6			*Order these parts online directly from Johnson Hardware at johnsonhardware.com.	

until the top is installed.

Since the uprights hold up the base, they have to be securely bolted to the base. With a spade bit, drill a 3/8-in. hole through the bottom 2x2, base plywood and 2x4 frame. Connect the outside uprights to the base with 6-in. hex-head machine screws, washers and nuts, and the center uprights to the base with 4-in. versions. You'll repeat this process at the top after installing the top frame (Photo 3).

Install the top

The top frame has the same dimensions and layout as the base frame but is made from 2x2s instead of 2x4s. As you cover the frame with plywood, use the plywood edges as a guide to make it straight and square.

Locate and mark the studs along the line where the top will be. Then lift the top onto the uprights (plywood side down), align the ends and lag-screw the frame to the wall. If your situation is like most, with just a narrow 6-in. space (Photo 3) between the cabinet top and the ceiling, this part is no fun! But it's crucial that the top be securely fastened to studs. Add shims between the wall and the frame if there are gaps. Then bolt the top to the uprights and nail the second side of the plywood to all the uprights (Photo 3). Shown here is birch plywood on the exposed left side to match the doors. This outside plywood piece is 6 in. longer than the interior plywood to cover the top and bottom framing.

Install the trim and hang the doors

Start by cutting trim boards to cover the uprights and nail them on with 2-in. finish nails (Photo 4). Trim a 3-1/2-in.-wide board to fit tight against the wall. Complete the trim by cutting and installing the top and bottom (horizontal) boards to fit between the ends.

Mount the door track 1 in. from the back side of the top trim (Photo 5). This cabinet has two 8-ft. tracks. The

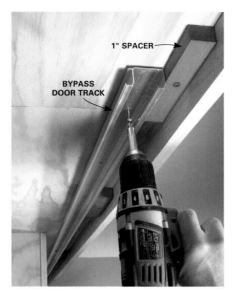

5 Screw the door tracks to the top, using spacers to position them. Make sure the sections of track align perfectly where they meet so the doors slide smoothly.

6 Screw two rollers to the back of each door. Later, you can loosen the screws to raise or lower the door for a perfect fit.

7 Tilt the doors to hook the rollers onto the track. Hang three doors on the inner track and three on the outer. Install door guides at each upright and halfway between them.

ends were cut so there would only be one joint in the center of the track. Mount the hangers. Then tilt the doors and hook the wheels onto the track to install them (Photo 7). If you're having trouble installing the front doors, loosen the adjusting screws on the wheels and extend them to maximum height. After installing the doors, crawl inside the cabinet and readjust

the wheels so the doors hang level and are even with each other. Finish the door installation by installing the door guides. Locate them where the doors overlap, centered 2-5/8 in. back from the front edge of the trim.

With the shelves in, all that's left to do is brush on two coats of polyurethane, load up your new storage space, and say goodbye to that mess in your garage.

Pet-food dispenser

Build this bin and you can fill the dog dish with the flick of a finger and do away with that crumpled bag of dog food lying on the garage floor. It easily holds two 20-lb. bags of food and allows you to dispense it right into the dish. This bin even holds two types of food so the cat won't get jealous.

You can put it together in a half day with basic power and hand tools. The materials cost $90, and most of them can be bought from a home center or lumberyard. Shown here is 3/4-in. clear aspen, selected because it's straight, soft and easy to work with. You can save about $20 by building it out of No. 2 pine boards. If possible, buy the 18 x 24-in. acrylic sheet already cut to size. To cut it without chipping it, you'll need a fine-tooth blade and a table saw.

Cutting list

PCS. SIZE & DESCRIPTION

2	1x8 x 18-1/4" (bin bottom and shelf)
2	1x8 x 40-3/4" (outer sides) **Note:** Cut a 45-degree angle on one end set in 2" from the edge.
3	1x6 x 29" (inner sides and divider) **Note:** Cut a 45-degree angle on one end set in 1" from the edge.
1	1x12 x 21-1/4" (lid and top) **Note:** Rip it to 22-1/2 degrees set 2" in from the edge. 2" is the narrow side.
1	1/4" x 29" x 18-1/4" (hardboard back)
1	1x6 x 18-1/4"(mounting cleat) **Note:** Rip in half at 45 degrees.
1	1x2 x 18-1/4" (back brace)
2	1x1 x 8" (front cleats)

SPEED SQUARE
STRAIGHTEDGE
LID
22-1/2° BEVEL

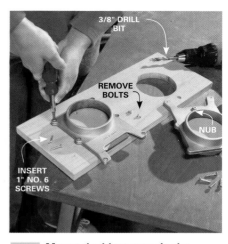

5/8" SPADE BIT
BLAST GATE
STARTER HOLE
COMPASS

3/8" DRILL BIT
REMOVE BOLTS
NUB
INSERT 1" NO. 6 SCREWS

1 Set your saw to an angle and rip the lid (22-1/2 degrees) and mounting cleat (45 degrees). Clamp or screw the boards to your workbench and use a straight guide for these cuts. Cut the other parts to length (see Cutting list, p.190, and Figure A) using a Speed Square as a guide to keep the cuts square.

2 Lay out the bays on the bin bottom using Figure A as a guide. Find the center of each bay and draw the circular cutout for the blast gates with a compass. Drill a 5/8-in. starter hole and cut out the openings with a jigsaw.

3 Mount the blast gates in the openings. Replace the bolts that hold the two sides of the blast gate together with four 1-in. No. 6 wood screws. Don't overtighten or you'll pinch the gate closed. (Note: A 3/8-in. hole was drilled to recess a little nub and bolt in the top of the blast gate shown.)

Figure A:
Dispenser details

TOP AND LID
(1x12 x 21-1/4")
2" WIDTH
PIANO HINGE
22-1/2° ANGLE

WALL-MOUNTING CLEATS (CUT AT 45°)
2"
1"
45° ANGLES
1/4" BACK
DIVIDER
INNER SIDE

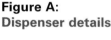 **tip**

The height of the cleat shown is perfect for a 6-ft.-tall person to operate the gate. Lower or raise to fit your height.

SHELF MOLDING
ACRYLIC SHEET
1x1 CLEAT
BACK BRACE
40-3/4"
BLAST GATE
BIN BOTTOM
SHELF
OUTER SIDE
19-3/4"
7-1/2"

Materials list

ITEM	QTY.
10' length of 1x8 aspen	1
9' length of 1x6 aspen	1
2' length of 1x12 aspen	1
2' length of 1x2 aspen	1
2' length of 1x1 aspen	1
1-3/4" x 8' quarter round or shelf molding	
1-1/4" x 2' x 4' tempered hardboard	
18" x 24" x .093" acrylic sheet	1
24" piano hinge	1
4"-diameter blast gates	2
2-1/4" trim head screws	1 lb.
1-1/4" screws	1 lb.
1" No. 6 flat head wood screws	8
2-1/2" screws	4
3d finish nails	16

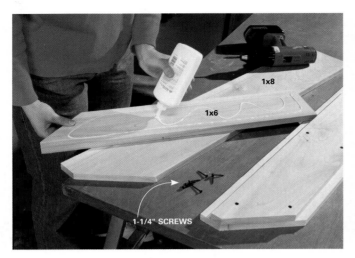

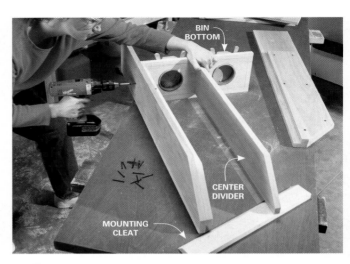

4 Glue and screw the two-piece sides together (Figure A). Use 1-1/4-in. screws and predrill with a 1/8-in. bit to avoid splitting the wood.

1x8
1x6
1-1/4" SCREWS

5 Predrill and screw the center divider to the bin bottom with 2-1/4-in. trim head screws. Then add the sides, bottom, and top. Next attach the back and the top half of the cleat with 1-1/4-in. screws.

BIN BOTTOM
CENTER DIVIDER
MOUNTING CLEAT

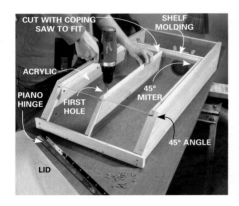

CUT WITH COPING SAW TO FIT
SHELF MOLDING
ACRYLIC
PIANO HINGE
FIRST HOLE
45° MITER
45° ANGLE
LID

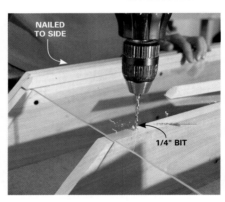

NAILED TO SIDE
1/4" BIT

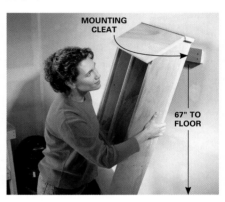

MOUNTING CLEAT
67" TO FLOOR

6 Set acrylic in place, leaving a 1/8-in. gap on all sides for expansion. Cut and fit the moldings (Figure A). Nail the sides and bottom moldings to the bin with 3d finish nails, sandwiching the acrylic in place. Set the center molding and predrill 1/16-in. nail holes through both the molding and the acrylic.

7 Remove the center molding and enlarge the hole in the acrylic with a 1/4-in. bit to provide room for expansion. Press the drill gently so the bit doesn't grab and crack the acrylic. Replace the molding and nail it on. Cut the piano hinge to length and screw it to the top.

8 Level and screw the other half of the mounting cleat to the wall with four 2-1/2-in. screws driven into the wall studs. Hang the cabinet on the interlocking mounting cleats.

"Blast gates" make handy food dispensers. Woodworkers use them for dust collection systems, so they're readily available at woodworking shops or online. Get the metal ones—the plastic ones don't slide as well. (One source is Rockler, part No. 20864, rockler.com).

These gates do have limitations. Medium- to large-sized food works best; they can jam with small stuff like birdseed. If the gate jams, quickly open and slam it shut.

Follow the photo series for step-by-step assembly instructions. The acrylic requires special handling. Leave extra room around it so it can expand and contract freely. Carefully nail the perimeter molding so the nails don't nick the acrylic and crack it (Photo 7).

Most types of hinges will work to secure the lid. Shown here is a short piano hinge. Cut it to fit with a hacksaw. The cabinet hangs on the wall on a cleat cut to 45 degrees (Photo 8).

Stacked recycling tower

Five plastic containers, six 2x2s and screws, and one hour's work are all it takes to put together this space-saving recycling storage rack. The frame fits containers that have a top that measures 14-1/2 in. x 10 in. and are 15 in. tall. The containers are made by Rubbermaid.

If you use different-size containers, adjust the distance between the uprights so the 2x2s will catch the lip of the container. Then adjust the spacing of the horizontal rungs for a snug fit when the container is angled as shown.

Start by cutting the 2x2s to length according to the illustration. Then mark the position of the rungs on the uprights. Drill two 5/32-in. holes through the uprights at each crosspiece position. Drill from the outside to the inside and angle the holes inward slightly to prevent the screws from breaking out the side of the rungs.

Drive 2-1/2-in. screws through the uprights into the rungs. Assemble the front and back frames. Then connect them with the side crosspieces.

Build a space-saving tower for plastic recycling containers with simple 2x2 and screw construction.

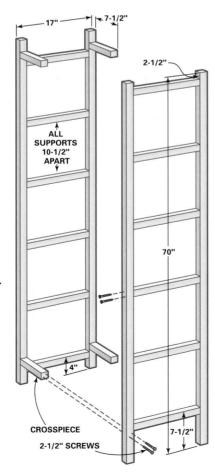

17"   7-1/2"

2-1/2"

ALL SUPPORTS 10-1/2" APART

70"

4"

CROSSPIECE

2-1/2" SCREWS

7-1/2"

Garage storage & organizing

hints & tips

WOOD BLOCK

Save your lawn products

Leave a bag of fertilizer or weed killer open for long and it'll soak up moisture from the air and won't go through a spreader. Even grass seed could use an extra layer of protection from a moisture-wicking concrete floor. Place opened bags of lawn products in large resealable plastic bags ($1 at discount stores). The products will be free of clumps or pests when you need them.

GIANT RESEALABLE PLASTIC BAG

Dustpan caddy

Keep a dustpan handy with an "unbreakable" wall file folder from an office supply store. Attach the file folder to the garbage can with eight 32 x 3/4-in. machine bolts and nuts. Position the screw heads inside the garbage can so the bag doesn't snag on the end of the bolt.

Storage tubes

Cardboard concrete-forming tubes are inexpensive ($7 at any home center) and provide a great place to store baseball bats, long-handled tools and rolls of just about anything. Rest the tubes on a piece of 2x4 to keep them high and dry. Secure each tube to a garage stud with a plumbing strap.

WOOD BLOCK

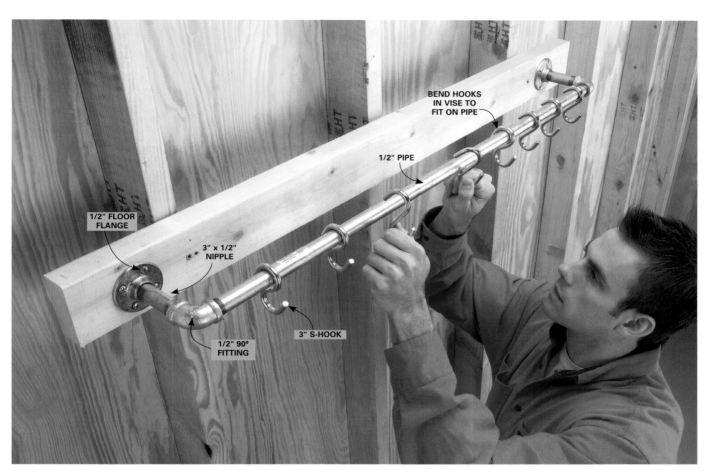

BEND HOOKS IN VISE TO FIT ON PIPE

1/2" PIPE

1/2" FLOOR FLANGE

3" x 1/2" NIPPLE

1/2" 90° FITTING

3" S-HOOK

Sturdy cord and tool hanger

Store a load of cords, air hoses, ropes and tools on this rugged rack. To build one, you'll need:

- One 3- or 4-ft. x 1/2-in. iron pipe threaded on both ends
- Two 3-in. x 1/2-in. pipe nipples
- Two 1/2-in. 90-degree pipe fittings
- Two 1/2-in. floor flanges
- Several 3-in. S-hooks
- Cable Clamps (cableclamp.com or look for them at home centers). Also, you can use leftover strips of plastic-sheathed electrical cable.

Assemble the pipe, elbows, nipples and floor flanges, then screw through the flanges to a horizontal 2x4 set at shoulder height on a shop wall. Attach your S-hooks. If yours don't fit, clamp the hooks in a vise and bend open one end just enough to fit on the pipe after assembly. Now snap Cable Clamps on all your coils and hang them from the S-hooks.

CABLE CLAMPS

Upside-down shelves!

Here's some neat and fast storage for your garage's upper regions. Bolt together a set of inexpensive metal shelves (about $12 at a home center) and attach them upside down to the ceiling joists with lag bolts. The spacing between shelves is completely adjustable. Hang the shelves so they're easy to reach, or set them high so you won't bonk your head. Trim the shelf posts to just the right height with tin snips.

TRIM POSTS TO LENGTH AND ATTACH TO JOISTS

ADJUSTABLE HEIGHT SHELVES

BUILT-IN LIP PREVENTS ITEMS FROM FALLING OFF SHELF!

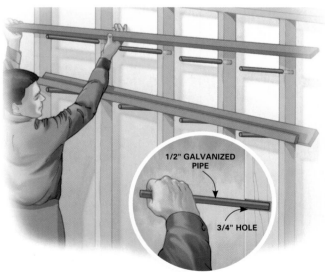

1/2" GALVANIZED PIPE

3/4" HOLE

Simple storage rack

Use this storage rack for lumber and other long stuff. Simply drill a line of 3/4-in. holes about 1-1/2 in. deep in adjacent studs, angling the holes slightly downward. Then insert 15-in.-long sections of 1/2-in. galvanized pipe. Keep the lowest pipes at least 6 ft. above the floor so you won't crack your skull on them.

Double-duty shelf brackets

Shelf brackets designed to support clothes hanger rods aren't just for closets. The rod-holding hook on these brackets comes in handy in the garage and workshop too. You can bend the hook to suit long tools or cords. Closet brackets cost about $3 each at home centers and hardware stores.

Hang-it-all hooks

Those plastic hooks that plumbers use to support pipes make convenient hangers for just about anything. They're strong, cheap (25¢ to $1 each) and come in a range of sizes. Find them in the plumbing aisle at home centers and hardware stores.

Garage ceiling track storage

If you store stuff in big plastic storage bins and you need a place to put them, how about the garage ceiling? Screw 2x2s to the ceiling framing with 3-1/2-in. screws spaced every 2 ft. Use the bins as a guide for spacing the 2x2s. The lips on the bins should just brush against the 2x2s when you're sliding the bins into place. Then center and screw 1x4s to the 2x2s with 2-in. screws. The garage ceiling is a perfect place to store light and medium-weight seasonal items like holiday decorations and camping gear.

Easy lawn chair storage

Here's how to store your lawn and folding chairs so they're out of your way. Take two pieces of 1x4 lumber (any scrap lumber will do) and create some simple, cheap and useful brackets on the wall. Cut each board 7-3/4 in. long with a 30-degree angle on both ends. Fasten pairs of these brackets with three 2-in. screws to the side of the exposed wall studs, directly across from each other, and you've got a perfect place to hang your chairs.

Garage ceiling storage

Organize your garage by tucking light and medium-weight stuff onto shelves suspended from the ceiling. The shelves are designed to fit into that unused space above the garage doors (you need 16 in. of clearance to fit a shelf and standard 12-1/2-in. high plastic bins). However, you can adjust the shelf height and put them anywhere. The only limitation is weight. The 4 x 6-ft. shelf is designed to hold about 160 lbs., a load that typical ceiling framing can safely support. It's best to save the shelf for "deep storage," using labeled bins with lids, because you'll need a stepladder to reach them.

First, find which way the joists run in your garage ceiling, then plan to hang one shelf support from three adjacent joists (Photo 2). The joists in this garage are 24 in. apart; if yours are spaced at 16 in., skip one intermediate joist. This project is built to hold plastic bins, but if you put loose stuff

up there, add 1x4 sides to keep things from falling off. Assemble the 2x4s as shown (Figure A), using 5-in. corner braces ($2 each) and 1/4-in. x 1-in. hex head lag screws (drill pilot holes first).

Now attach the corner braces on both ends of a shelf support to the center of a joist/truss by drilling pilot holes and using 1/4-in. x 2-in. hex head lag screws (Photo 2). The only challenge is finding the center of joists through a drywall ceiling (if your ceiling is finished) to attach the shelf supports. Tap a small nail through the drywall until you locate both edges of the joist. Measure to find the center of the adjacent joists, and measure to keep the three supports in alignment with one another. Finish the shelf unit by attaching a 3/8-in. x 4-ft. x 6-ft. plywood floor (Photo 3).

1 Measure from the ceiling to the top of the raised garage door. Subtract 1 in. to determine the height of the side 2x4s.

2 Build three identical shelf supports, align the side supports, and predrill and lag-screw each into the center of the ceiling trusses/joists.

3 Cut 3/8-in. plywood for shelf base and attach it to 2x4 shelf supports with 1-in. wood screws.

4 Don't overload bins with heavy stuff. Limit the total weight to about 160 lbs.

One shelf holds all this!

Each shelf holds eight containers 16 in. wide x 24 in. long x 12-1/2 in. high.

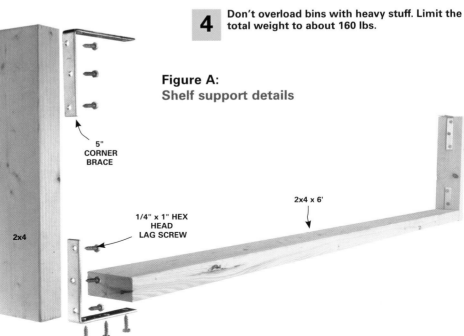

Figure A:
Shelf support details

CEILING TRUSS

2' SHORTER
THAN LADDER

CAUTION
For extra security,
wrap a bungee cord
around the ladder and
one bracket.

STANLEY

Build two identical brackets, then screw them both to ceiling
trusses with 1/4 x 2-in. lag screws. Space the brackets so the
ladder will extend at least 1 ft. beyond the end of each one.

Suspended extension ladder

It's always most convenient to hang an extension ladder on
brackets on a wall. But unfortunately that wipes out all other
storage potential for that wall. To save that valuable wall
space, here's a pair of 2x4 suspended brackets so a ladder
can be stored flat along the ceiling.

Simply slide one end of the ladder into one bracket, then
lift and slide the other end into the other bracket. Most
people will need to stand on something solid to reach the
second bracket. The 2x4 bracket sides are 16 in. long with
5-in. corner braces lag-screwed into the top for attachment
to the ceiling truss (Figure A).

The bracket base is a 1/2-in. x 24-in. threaded steel rod
that extends through 5/8-in. drilled holes on the bracket
sides. It's held in place with flat/lock washers and a nut on
each side of both 2x4 uprights. A 3/4-in. x 18-in.-long piece of
PVC conduit pipe surrounds the rod for smooth rolling action
when you slide the ladder in and out.

Figure A:
Ladder support details

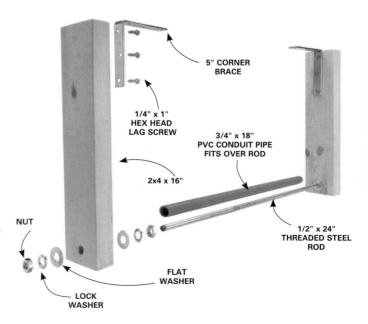

5" CORNER
BRACE

1/4" x 1"
HEX HEAD
LAG SCREW

3/4" x 18"
PVC CONDUIT PIPE
FITS OVER ROD

2x4 x 16"

NUT

1/2" x 24"
THREADED STEEL
ROD

FLAT
WASHER

LOCK
WASHER

SELF-STICK HOOK-AND-LOOP STRIPS

CLOSET POLE AND SHELF BRACKET

Bike rack

Closet pole and shelf brackets can keep your bikes up and out of the way of car doors and bumpers. Just screw the brackets to the wall studs. Line the pole carriage with self-stick hook-and-loop strips so it won't scratch your bike frame.

DRIP TRAYS

SCREW

Stay-put balls

Keep sport balls off the floor and out of the way by resting them in flowerpot drip trays (80¢ at home centers). Screw the trays down to an inexpensive shelving unit. The balls will stay put.

Lawn chair brackets

Don't throw away those old lawn chairs. Cut out all the right angles of the frames and use them as hanging brackets. The reinforced corners are surprisingly strong. Just drill holes for screws, then squeeze closed the ends of the horizontal sections in a vise. Bend these ends up about 1 in. to keep things from falling off the brackets.

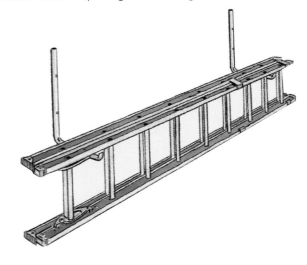

Foldaway workshop

This workshop has loads of storage for all your gear and yet keeps it easily accessible. Best of all, when you're finished for the day, you can put everything away, shut the doors and lock it up. You'll also appreciate its modest profile. With the doors shut, it protrudes a mere 14-1/2 in. from the wall, so if you build it in your garage, you'll still be able to share space with your car!

This workshop is also designed to be easy to build with simple woodworking tools. In fact, all you'll need besides your measuring and marking tools are a circular saw, a jigsaw and a drill. And it doesn't have any tricky wood joints to slow down the building process—just screws and nails. If you have basic carpentry skills, you'll find you can easily work your way through the how-to steps in a single weekend. You'll also like the price; the whole thing will only cost you about $300.

You'll be able to buy everything at a home center except the folding L-brackets. These heavy-duty brackets will support up to 750 lbs. The brackets have four positions: straight up for tabletop work and flat down for storage, as well as two in-between locking positions that transform the work top into a handy drawing board. Check the Buyer's guide on p. 209 for a source.

Besides the fold-down work top, you'll appreciate the adjustable shelves in each door recess that'll hold boxes of nails and screws, paint, glue bottles, spare parts—you name it. And the sturdy piano hinges are strong enough to hold nearly anything you can pack into the shelves. The tried-and-true pegboard is great for organizing your hand tools, and there is space for an overhead fluorescent light and an outlet strip for power tools. There is plenty of room on the bottom shelf for bigger tools like your circular saw, belt sander and router. The foldaway workshop is also great for hobby, craft and even gardening supplies and tools.

1 Rip 2x10 lumber to 9 in. wide to create a flat edge and ensure that all the frame pieces are uniform. Then mark and cut the 1-1/2-in.-deep notches for the rear stretcher pieces (Figure A).

2 Set the rear stretchers (B) into the notches of the sides (A) and screw them into place. Next, screw the top and bottom pieces (C) to the sides and stretchers.

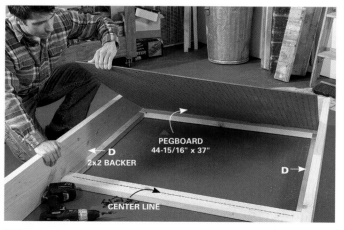

3 Set the rear stretchers (B) into the notches of the sides (A) and screw them into place. Next, screw the top and bottom pieces (C) to the sides and stretchers.

Choose straight lumber

Go to a home center and choose your lumber carefully. The main frame of the project is built with sturdy, dry, construction-grade 2x10s and 2x4s. Buy them as straight as you can find. If they have a twist or bow, they'll throw off the frame and the doors will be difficult to fit. The plywood should be 3/4 in. and flat. You can get by with construction grade, but for nice looking, perfectly flat plywood, use birch. The door sides and shelves should be hardwood for strength. Shown is maple, but you can substitute poplar, oak or birch. Here again, make sure the lumber is straight. Boards that aren't perfectly straight can be cut up for the shorter shelves.

Note: Assemble the project on an even, flat surface. You can end up with some unintentional twists in the main frame and the doors if you build them on an uneven surface. Choose a flat area in your garage or driveway for the assembly work.

Notches in the frame keep it square

Ripping your 2x10s to 9 in. wide gives you a nice, square edge on the face of the frame to mount your piano hinges to later. Once they're ripped, notch the back sides of the frame sides as shown in Photo 1 to accept the horizontal stretchers. Set your saw to a 1-1/2-in. depth of cut and make multiple passes about 1/4 in. apart the width of the 2x4. Break out the notches with a chisel and file the bottom of the notches smooth.

Take care to get the frame square as you screw the stretchers (B) into the notches and screw the top and bottom panels (C) into place. The best way to ensure the frame is square is to measure the diagonals and adjust the frame until they're equal.

Find the right spot

There may be a few snags to look out for if you build this workshop in your garage. If you're installing it near the garage door, make sure it will clear the track. The height of the project is 78 in. Low-clearance overhead doors may have a track in the way. Also keep in mind that it opens to a full 8 ft. You'll find you still have 3-1/2 in. behind the doors when they're open so you can hang rakes and shovels behind it.

Your garage may have a row of concrete block near the floor that sticks out past the wall surface. If so, plan ahead and cut the side pieces longer past the bottom stretcher to accommodate the block and then notch them to fit around it. Also feel free to make the project shorter or a bit taller to suit your needs and adjust the work top to a height that suits you. The workbench shown here sits at a comfortable 36 in. off the floor.

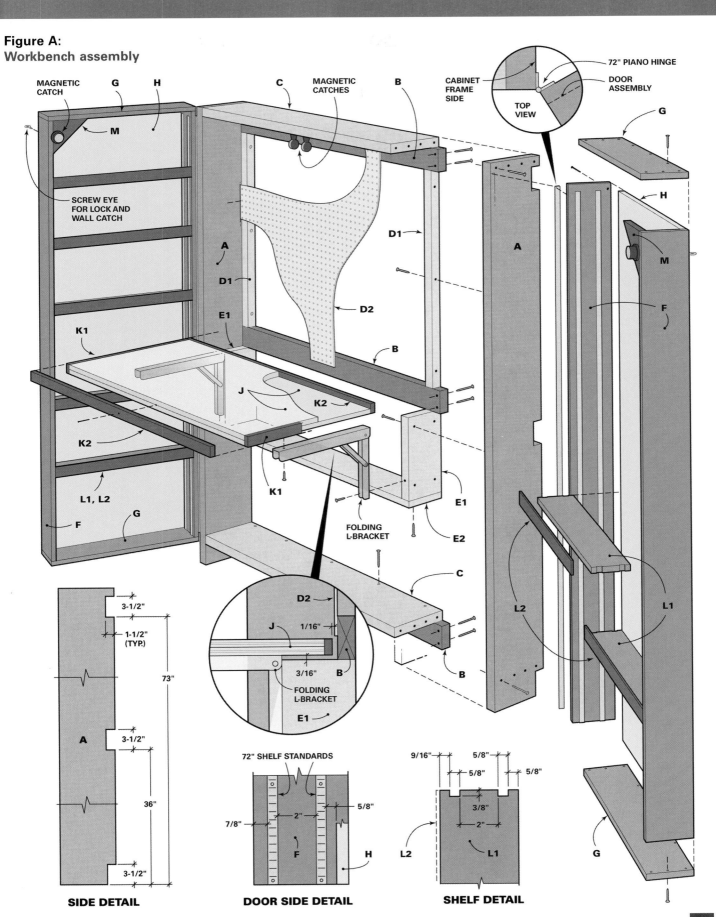

Figure A:
Workbench assembly

MAGNETIC CATCH

G

H

M

SCREW EYE FOR LOCK AND WALL CATCH

K1

K2

L1, L2

F

G

A

D1

E1

C

MAGNETIC CATCHES

B

D1

D2

B

J

K2

K1

FOLDING L-BRACKET

E1

E2

C

B

CABINET FRAME SIDE

72" PIANO HINGE

DOOR ASSEMBLY

TOP VIEW

G

H

A

M

F

L2

L1

D2

J

1/16"

3/16"

B

FOLDING L-BRACKET

E1

SIDE DETAIL

3-1/2"

1-1/2" (TYP.)

73"

A

3-1/2"

36"

3-1/2"

DOOR SIDE DETAIL

72" SHELF STANDARDS

7/8"

2"

5/8"

F

H

SHELF DETAIL

9/16"

5/8"

5/8"

5/8"

3/8"

2"

L2

L1

G

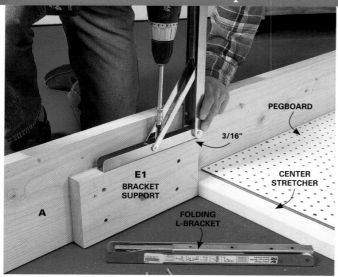

4 Screw the folding L-bracket supports (E1) to the sides. Position the brackets 3/16 in. past the top of the support and flush with the support's inside edge. Screw the brackets into the support with No. 8 x 1-1/4-in. pan head screws.

5 Cut the door frame sides (F) and top and bottom pieces (G) to length from 1x6 boards. Position the 6-ft. shelf standards flush with the bottom edge of each door side (F) and nail them every 6 in.

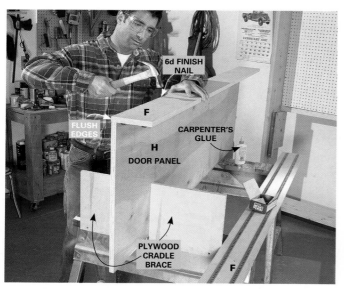

6 Cut the door panels (H) and place them into a cradle brace as shown. Spread glue on the edge of the plywood and predrill and nail the sides (F) to the plywood door panels every 6 in. Once the sides are fastened, predrill and glue and screw the door tops and bottoms (G) to the door panels.

7 Set the door assemblies onto the frame assembly as shown. Fold the top flap of your piano hinge so it's trapped between the door edge and the side of the frame to position it evenly. Screw it to the frame, then open the hinge and screw it to the door.

The pegboard stiffens the frame

Once you've got the basic frame assembled, cut your pegboard and center it onto the top and middle stretchers. You'll know in a hurry if your frame is out of square because the panel should fall into place (Photo 3). Fasten the pegboard every 6 in. to the stretchers and 2x2s with 1-1/4-in. wood screws.

L-brackets make a rock-solid top

Position the brackets carefully as you install them on the bracket supports to make sure they'll open and close once the project is complete. Keep them flush with the inside edge of the supports and make sure they extend 3/16 in. past the top (Photo 4). This little extension gives a bit of room for the folding L-brackets to release properly when it's time to fold them down.

Take the same care later (see Photo 9) when you attach the top to the folding L-brackets. Make sure the top is 1/16 in. from the pegboard and that the tops of the L-brackets are parallel to the sides of the worktop.

8 Cut and glue two pieces of 3/4-in. plywood (J) to make the work surface. To complete the work top, cut 1x2 boards to length and nail them to the sides with 6d finish nails.

9 Center the work top (J) between the sides and leave a 1/16-in. gap from the face of the pegboard. Make sure the folding L-brackets are evenly spaced front-to-back along the edge of the work top. Screw the L-bracket to the underside of the work top with No. 8 x 1-1/4-in. pan head screws.

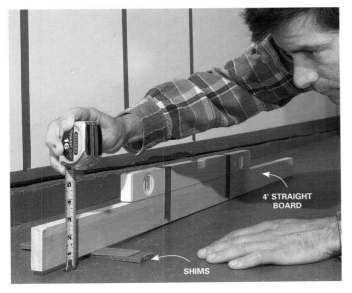

10 Check your floor with a level placed on a 4-ft. board to see how much you may need to shim the cabinet sides. Our garage floor had a 1/2-in. slope in 4 ft. from front to back.

11 Mark the stud locations. Cut and set the shim. Tip the cabinet up slowly with the doors closed. Slide it into position.

Install the shelf standards precisely

The shelf standards support the shelves, and the notches in the shelves hold them in place so they don't fly out when you open the door. Set your combination square to the dimensions shown in Figure A and slide it up along the edge of the door frame sides (F) as you nail the standards into place. Also make sure you flush the standard bottoms to the bottom of the door sides so all the shelves will be level.

Rip your shelves to width and again be precise with the layout of the notches in the ends of the shelf. These are a

bugger to cut, but making multiple passes from each end with a jigsaw works well. You can clean up the cuts with a file.

Cutting your plywood door panels

Use a table saw to first rip the panels for a nice, straight edge. If you don't have a table saw, use a circular saw and a long straightedge guide. Once the panels are cut for width, mark the length using a framing square as a guide. Cut each panel carefully with your circular saw equipped with a sharp 40-tooth blade.

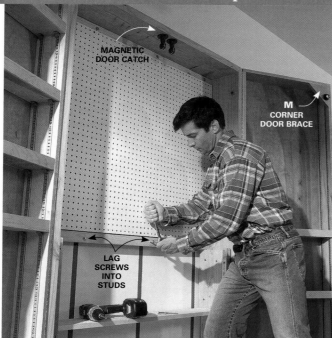

12 Drill 3/16-in. pilot holes through the stretchers into the studs. Insert 1/4-in. x 4-in. lag screws and washers and use a wrench to tighten the cabinet to the wall. Add the magnetic catches and the shelves.

13 Flip the top down, close the doors and secure the padlock until you're ready for your next project.

Attach the door sides, making sure they're flush with the plywood door panel face. If a little glue oozes out, wipe it off with a wet rag right away to keep it from showing through your finish later.

Screw the top and bottom of the door frame (parts G) to the panel (H) instead of nailing them. The 1-5/8-in. screws, along with the glue, bond the door sides and plywood panel together for a rock-solid door. To complete the door frame, cut a pair of triangular pieces of maple (M) 5-1/2 in. on a side and glue and nail them to the top inside corners of the doors to hold the closing plates of the magnetic door catches.

Piano hinges give total door support

Piano hinges can be a pain to install, but you can simplify the process by tucking the top flap between the door and the frame (Photo 7) to hold it in place while you screw the lower exposed flap to the frame side. To predrill perfectly centered holes, use a No. 3 Vix bit in your drill. This nifty bit has a tapered front edge that fits into the hole on the hinge and exactly centers itself. As you push on the bit, the spring-loaded bit pilots itself dead center. Drive the screws as you go to keep the hinge from shifting.

Once the bottom flap of the hinge is secured, lift the door, pivot the top flat out, position the door side even with the frame and secure the hinge to the door frame in exactly the same way.

Use a double layer of plywood for a solid work top

Cut your work top pieces (J) from 3/4-in. plywood and glue them (Photo 8) together with carpenter's glue spread liberally between. Screw the pieces together on the underside with 1-1/4-in. wood screws. Once the glue sets, cut 1x2 maple and nail it around the edges as shown in Figure A.

Position the top carefully onto the folding L-brackets. Hold the top securely, align the brackets parallel to the edge and screw it into place. You'll need a bit extension for your power screwdriver to get inside the bracket mechanism. If you don't have one, you can mark it, predrill it and then use a long-blade screwdriver to drive the screws. At this point, test the mechanism to make sure it folds down. If the bracket binds, loosen the screws and shift the bracket until it works.

Lag-screw the frame to the studs

Every installation situation has its own set of problems, and the one shown here was no exception. The floor was out of level, so one side had to be shimmed to get the project to sit level on the floor. The concrete foundation at the bottom of the wall stuck out 1/2 in., so 1/2-in. strips were added to the back side of the frame to move it out from the wall a bit. Use your ingenuity to get past any problems you might find. You can secure some bolt snaps to the wall (see photo, top, p. 209) with wall anchors and screw eyes to keep the doors

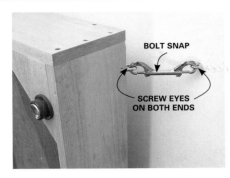

Keep the doors open with a wall anchor and double-ended bolt snap.

BOLT SNAP

SCREW EYES ON BOTH ENDS

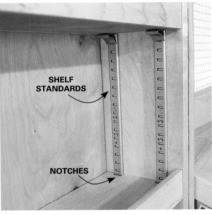

The notches in the shelves keep them secure as you open and close your doors.

SHELF STANDARDS

NOTCHES

Shopping list

ITEM	QTY.
2x10 x 8' spruce, pine or fir	3
2x4 x 14' spruce, pine or fir	1
2x2 x 8' spruce, pine or fir	1
1x6 x 12' hardwood (door sides and shelves)	4
1x8 x 4' pine shelf (under-bracket blocks)	1
37" x 44-15/16" pegboard (1/4" thick)	1
3/4" x 4' x 8' birch plywood	2
1x2 x 12' hardwood work top edging	1
6' piano hinges	2
6' shelf standards and brackets	8
1/4" x 1-3/4" x 10' pine or hardwood lattice (shelf edging)	2
6d nails	1 lb.
3" wood screws	2 lbs.
2-1/2" wood screws	1 lb.
1-5/8" wood screws	1 lb.
1-1/4" wood screws	1 lb.
1/4" x 4" lag screws and washers	6
Folding L-brackets (see Buyer's guide)	1 pr.
Magnetic catches (see Buyer's guide)	2
Wall anchors, bolt snaps, door handles	
Mini-tube fluorescent light	1

Cutting list

KEY	PCS.	SIZE & DESCRIPTION
A	2	1-1/2" x 9" x 78" pine sides
B	3	1-1/2" x 3-1/2" x 48" pine stretchers
C	2	1-1/2" x 9" x 45" pine top and bottom
D1	2	1-1/2" x 1-1/2" x 33-1/2" pine backers for pegboard
D2	1	1/4" x 44-15/16" x 37" pegboard
E1	2	1-1/2" x 6-1/8" x 12-3/4" pine bracket supports
E2	1	3/4" x 6-1/8" x 45" fixed pine shelf
F	4	3/4" x 5-1/2" x 73" maple door sides
G	4	3/4" x 5-1/2" x 23-7/8" maple door tops and bottoms
H	2	3/4" x 22-3/8" x 73" birch plywood door panels
J	2	3/4" x 22-3/8" x 43-3/8" birch plywood work top pieces
K1	2	3/4" x 1-1/2" x 22-3/8" maple
K2	2	3/4" x 1-1/2" x 44-7/8" maple
L1	10	3/4" x 4-7/16" x 22-3/8" maple shelves
L2	10	1/4" x 1-3/4" x 22-1/4" maple shelf stops
M	2	3/4" x 5-1/2" maple triangular braces

open when in use. The screw eyes on the front of the door also double as a place to slip in a padlock to keep out unwanted visitors.

Caution: The doors of this project can fly open when you're moving it into position. Use a strap hinge and brace the bottom of the doors until you get it secured to the wall.

Finishing touches

The magnetic catches for the doors are actually interior door catches (see Buyer's guide, below). Screw the ball section to the top of the frame and the steel plate onto the door. You can buy a mini-tube fluorescent light fixture at a home center and screw it to the underside of the top, and an outlet strip mounted to the side of the frame makes plugging in power tools a snap. You can drill a 1-1/2-in. hole in the frame side to slip the plug end through to the nearest outlet.

Although not completely necessary, two coats of furniture oil or polyurethane will help preserve the project, especially in a garage that gets seasonally damp. Just remove the hardware and apply your finish. Be sure to wait a couple of days for the project to dry before using it.

Buyer's guide

Folding L-brackets and Vix bits: Woodworker's Hardware, wwhardware.com

Magnetic door catches shown on p. 208: improvementscatalog.com

1-day workbench

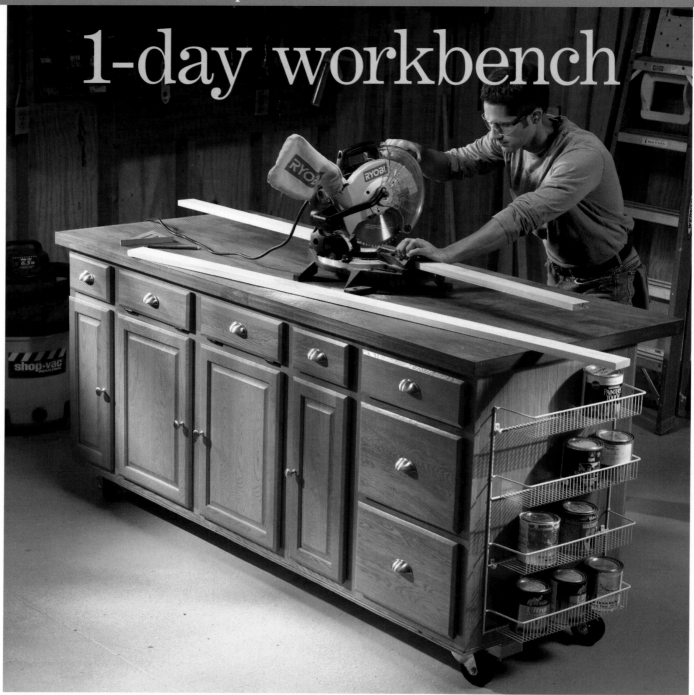

Like a traditional woodworker's bench, this workbench offers a large, rock-solid work surface and plenty of storage space below. But because it's built mostly from ready-made components, constructing this bench doesn't take much time or skill. If you have a little experience with simple hand and power tools, you can complete it in a Saturday afternoon.

You'll find everything you need for this project at home centers. You can use any combination of cabinets that add up to a width of less than 80 in. (the length of the door). Shown is a 60-in. sink base cabinet and an 18-in. drawer

unit. Buy a solid-core door rather than a flimsy hollow-core door for the top. Although these cabinets are oak, a mahogany (lauan) door was used, which provides a smoother work surface than oak. The total materials bill for this cabinet was $600. If you choose unfinished cabinets rather than prefinished cabinets, and construction-grade plywood rather than oak for the back, your cost will be about $400. That's not exactly cheap, but you'd have to spend at least twice as much to buy a workbench of comparable size, storage capacity and durability.

Assemble the base

Set the cabinets on their faces on a drop cloth and cut off the pedestal that forms the toe-kick under the cabinet (Photo 1). Pull off the front toe-kick. Make sure that the cut leaves at least a 3/4-in. space for the 1x4 filler strips that the plywood is attached to so that the weight of the workbench is carried by the sides of the cabinets.

Lay the door on cardboard or a drop cloth and set the two cabinets upside down on top of it so you can join them on a perfectly flat surface. Shim any low spots under the door so it stays flat. Attach the filler strips under the cabinets, predrilling

and screwing up through the base with 1-1/4-in. screws (see Figure A). Align the cabinet stiles, then screw the cabinets together with 2-1/2-in. screws at the top and bottom (Photo 2).

Use a shim and a clamp to hold the cabinet sides parallel (see Photo 2). Cut a 3/4-in. plywood base the same length as the assembled cabinets but 1/2 in. wider. Mount the base flush with the front of the cabinets and overhanging the back by 1/2 in. (This provides a lip for the back to rest on.) Predrill and screw on the casters with lag screws 1 in. back from the edges, placing the locking wheels in front. Glue and screw two 2x4s to the plywood behind the farthest turn of

1 Cut the back and sides of the cabinet to remove the pedestal under the cabinet box. Break off the toe-kick beneath the front of the cabinet.

2 Align the cabinets and screw their face frames together. The door you'll use for the top provides a perfectly flat surface to set the cabinets on.

Off-the-shelf components make it easy

This workbench is made from two store-bought cabinets mounted on casters and topped off with a solid-core door. To build it, all you need are the materials shown here. But don't let the simple construction fool you; this is a heavy-duty workbench that will stand up to decades of use and abuse.

Figure A:

1-day workbench

Shown are 60-in. and 18-in. cabinets. You can use any combination of cabinets as long as their total width is less than 80 in.

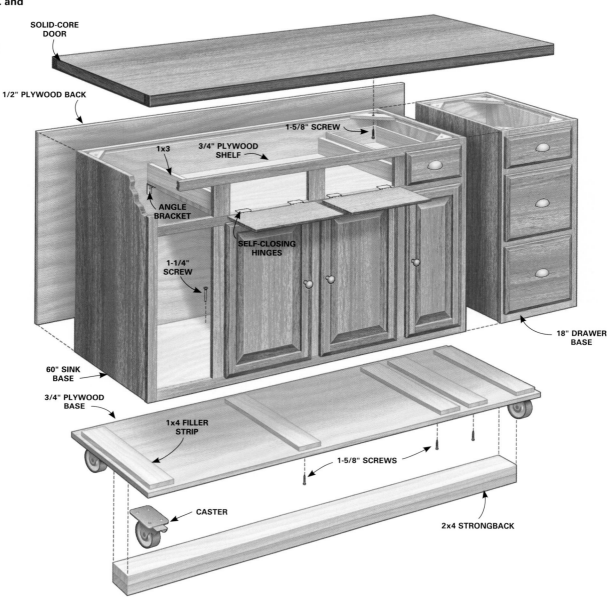

SOLID-CORE DOOR

1/2" PLYWOOD BACK

1-5/8" SCREW

1x3

3/4" PLYWOOD SHELF

ANGLE BRACKET

SELF-CLOSING HINGES

1-1/4" SCREW

18" DRAWER BASE

60" SINK BASE

3/4" PLYWOOD BASE

1x4 FILLER STRIP

1-5/8" SCREWS

CASTER

2x4 STRONGBACK

Materials list

ITEM	QTY.		
60" unfinished oak kitchen sink base	1	200-lb.-capacity locking caster wheels	2
18" unfinished oak drawer base	1	Drawer pulls (optional)	11
2' 8" x 6' 8" solid-core door (work top)	1	1-1/4" screws	1 lb.
4' x 8' x 3/4" plywood for base	1	1-5/8" screws	1 lb.
4' x 8' x 1/2" plywood for back	1	1/4" x 1" lag screws	16
1x4 x 10' for filler strips	1	2-1/2" screws (for joining cabinet stiles)	2
200-lb.-capacity caster wheels (3" wheels for a 36-1/4"-high workbench, 4" for 37-1/4")	2	No. 8 x 3/4" pan head screws	1 box
		Self-closing cabinet hinges	2 sets
		1-1/2" angle brackets	8

STRONGBACK

3 Screw a plywood base to the undersides of the cabinets and add a double 2x4 "strongback" to prevent the workbench from sagging in the middle.

4 Glue and screw a plywood back to the cabinets. The back strengthens the workbench and provides a fastener surface for shelves, hooks or other hardware.

the front wheels to keep the center of the workbench from sagging (Photo 3).

Tip the base upright and lock the wheels. Set the plywood back on the base's lip (Photo 4) and fasten it to the cabinets with 3/4-in. pan head screws from inside (cabinets with thicker backs may require a different size screw). The plywood back strengthens the workbench and provides a base for shelving and hooks.

Add the top

Set the solid-core door blank on top of the base. Center the door blank from side to side, then leave a 1-1/2-in. overhang in front to create an edge for clamping.

Attach the top at the corner braces (Photo 5). Screw on additional angle brackets to the front and back if needed for more strength.

Sand any rough edges on the door, then add shelves to the sides and back. If you need to compensate for an uneven floor, jam shims or wedges under the bench after you roll it into position.

5 Fasten the top with screws only—no glue. After years of wear, you can simply flip the top over to get a flawless new work surface.

Save money with a sink cabinet

A 60-in. sink base cabinet was chosen for this workbench because it cost $100 less than two 30-in. cabinets. The downside of a sink base is that it has false drawer fronts instead of drawers. To make use of that space, install a shelf in the cabinet and mount the drawer fronts on hinges, creating a perfect cubbyhole for bar clamps and other long tools. Mark the drawer front positions with tape before you remove the fronts and attach the hinges.

SHELF

SELF-CLOSING HINGE

Rock-solid workbench

This workbench has all the features of a professional woodworker's bench. It features a 3-1/4-in.-thick rock-solid flat top, plenty of storage and robust vises that'll hold your work for any woodworking task. And it's mounted on casters, so you can wheel it away from the wall and get the sawdust flying in minutes. Best of all, you don't need the skills of a woodworker to build it. Even though the workbench looks like a fine piece of furniture, simple joinery and cut-to-fit trim make this project fairly easy even if you've done only rudimentary cabinet building, like a simple bookcase.

Here you'll learn the key construction techniques, including a unique, low-tech way to glue up the thick top. Figure A on p. 217 shows all the details. You won't need any exotic tools, only a table saw, a miter saw, a heavy-duty belt sander and at least four 4-ft.-long bar clamps. Beyond those, a circular saw and a screw gun are the only tools you'll absolutely need. While not critical, an 18-gauge brad nailer (Photo 2) with several clips of 1-1/2-in. brads will really speed up assembling the cabinet and nailing on the trim. Allow at least three days for this project: two days for the cabinet, trim and drawers and a third for gluing up and flattening the top.

Expect to pay about $600 for your bench materials, including the cost of the vises and "bench dogs" (pins that work with a vise). That may seem spendy, but consider that a comparable bench bought from a woodworker's store would cost at least $1,200.

Bench design

The heart of this bench is the heavy, thick top, which is made from glued-up 2x4s (Photos 12–16). The super-strong base is made from three identical 3/4-in. plywood boxes screwed to a

1 Cut all of the 3/4-in. AC plywood pieces and 2x4 platform parts (Figure A). Screw the platform framing together and then screw on the plywood base.

3" SCREWS

BASE PLATFORM

2 Glue and pin the box sides together with 1-1/2-in. brads, then predrill and anchor them with three 1-5/8-in. screws along each edge.

CABINET BOX

COUNTERSINK BIT

18-GAUGE NAILER

1-5/8" SCREWS

2x4 platform (Photo 1). The base is dressed up with veneered plywood, the bench is trimmed with hardwood, and there are heavy-duty drawers and sliding shelves for storing tools and supplies.

This workbench is finished with oak plywood and solid oak trim. However, you can save about $100 if you build it from construction-grade plywood and use pine for the trim.

This bench is a true heavyweight, weighing in at about 400 lbs. (without tools). That's intentional, to give it the strength and stability for first-class work. It rests on heavy-duty casters, so you can tuck it out of the way when it's not in use and roll it out when you're ready to create those family heirlooms.

Buying the materials

Use special care and select straight 2x4s for the base platform (Photo 1). In addition, choose boards that have small, tight knots (or no knots) on one edge for the laminated work top. Buy 14-ft. 2x4s and cut them to 7-ft. lengths, because longer boards are generally of higher quality than shorter, stud-length boards. If you have trouble getting the long boards home, have the lumberyard cut them in half for you.

It's best to use 3/4-in. AC plywood for the basic cabinet structure, the drawer and sliding shelf bottoms, and any shelves. When you're selecting this plywood, don't worry about surface defects. Flaws will never be seen. Just make sure the sheets are flat. Use the 3/4-in.-thick veneer oak plywood to clad the cabinet assembly and to make the doors and drawer fronts and drawer sides. If you choose another plywood type, buy matching (or contrasting) trim.

Select side-mount, full-extension drawer slides (Photos 8 and 9) that are rated to handle 90-lb. loads for sturdy, smoothly operating drawers. This beast will weigh upward of 600 lbs. fully loaded, so buy swivel casters that are rated for at least 100 lbs. Use six: two in the center and one at each corner to fully support the bench and to make it roll smoothly on uneven floors (Photo 4). When you roll out the bench, add four shims (tap one under each of the four corners) to keep the bench stable while you work.

To get the most from your bench, plan on buying two vises. Buy a 7-in. "tail" vise that's mounted at one end of the bench to use with the bench dogs for clamping bench-top work. Pick a 9-in. "face" vise for clamping work at the bench front. Plan on spending at least $70 for the tail vise and $100 for the face vise to get high-quality, smoothly operating vises. Make sure they have quick-release mechanisms so you can quickly slide the vises open and closed. You'll have to add the hardwood "cheeks" yourself.

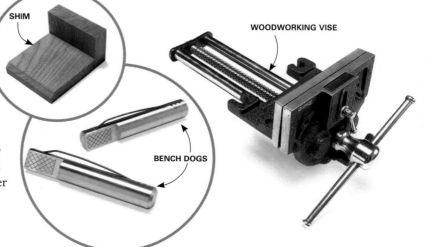

SHIM

WOODWORKING VISE

BENCH DOGS

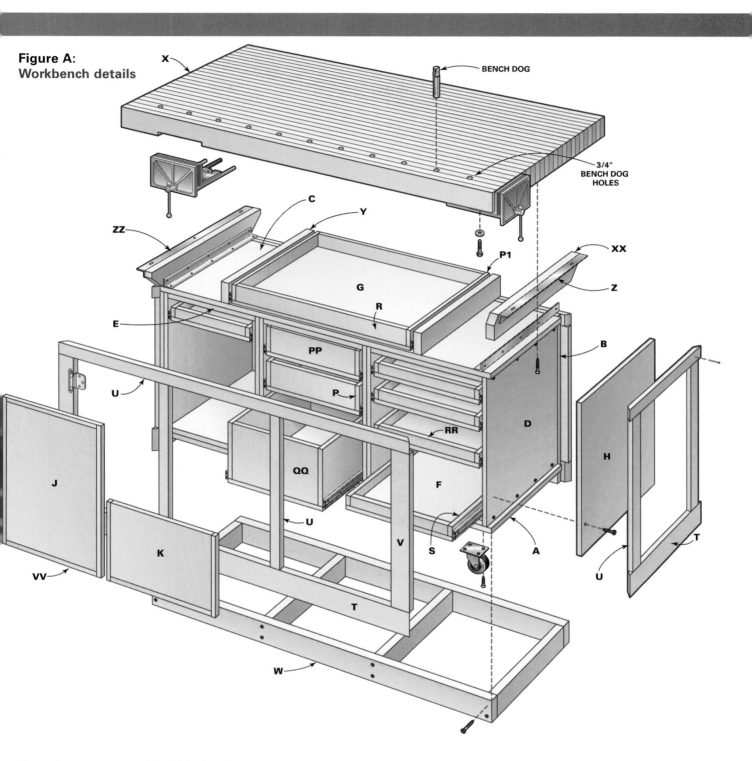

Figure A:
Workbench details

BENCH DOG

3/4"
BENCH DOG
HOLES

X

ZZ

C

Y

P1

XX

Z

E

G

R

B

PP

U

P

D

H

RR

J

QQ

F

V

S

A

U

VV

K

U

T

T

W

Cut the parts and build the base

Start by cutting all of the AC plywood pieces following the cutting diagrams (Figure C, p. 222). To save on materials, cut a few of the pieces from leftover oak plywood. Mark each piece with its letter to save confusion later. Assemble the base platform and then the boxes (Photos 1 and 2). Finish the back cabinet structure by centering the triple box assembly on the base, screwing it down and screwing on the top sheet of plywood (Photo 3). When you mount the wheels (Photo 4), make

sure they pivot freely and won't bind against the frame.

After the structure is together, finishing the outside of the cabinet is straightforward. Simply cover the sides and back with the oak plywood cut to fit (Photo 5). Nail each piece around the perimeter with 1-1/2-in. brads spaced every 4 in. Then add 1-5/8-in. screws to the back panels for more strength (they'll be covered by trim later). Trim out the cabinet by cutting boards to fit as shown in Figure A and Photo 6, starting with the horizontal bands at the base and top. It's

3 Screw the three boxes together, then center the box assembly on the base (3/4 in. from each end) and screw it down. Then screw on the plywood top.

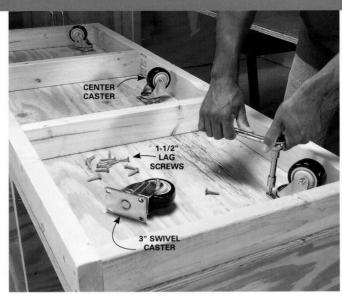

4 Flip the bench upside down and screw the wheels to the underside with 1-1/2 x 5/16-in. lag screws. Position two in the cabinet center.

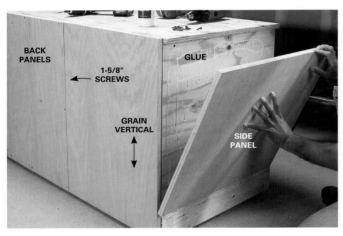

5 Glue the plywood end and back panels onto the boxes and nail them with 1-1/2-in. brads. Screw the perimeter of the three back panels to the boxes with 1-5/8-in. screws.

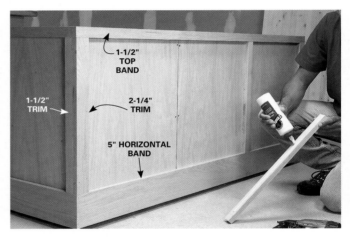

6 Miter, then glue and nail on the bottom and top horizontal trim pieces. Then cut, glue and nail the vertical trim in place (Figure A).

a little extra work, but the bench will look more polished if you miter the top and bottom horizontal trim at the corners. Finally, cut and nail on the vertical trim boards. Be sure to cut or plane the vertical trim boards flush with the box openings at the front. Otherwise, the drawer slides will be too narrow at the front and won't operate smoothly.

Build the drawers

The measurements given here for the drawer fronts and backs assume that you cut and assembled your cabinet boxes perfectly. It's best to measure the box widths at this point and cut the front and back of the drawers exactly 1 in. shorter than the openings. Double-check those pieces before assembling the drawers. If they're any larger or smaller, the slides won't work.

Photos 8 and 9 show how to use plywood spacers to mount the drawer slides accurately. (See the Cutting list, p. 222, for spacer sizes.) Slightly angle in the spacers and rest the drawer on them so the drawer projects a few inches beyond the cabinet front. Pull out both drawer slides until they're flush with the drawer front and drive the first screws through the slots (Photo 8). Slide out the drawer until the next screw holes are showing and install the next two screws and then slide it out farther to access the last ones. Rip the spacer and mount the second drawer the same way. Use a 1/4-in. spacer for the bottom sliding shelf, bottom drawer and utility drawer (Photo 10).

Cut and edge the drawer and door fronts

Cut three identical panels of oak plywood (Figure A) for the doors and drawers. Cover the edges with strips of matching hardwood for a neat, durable edge treatment. Rip your own

7 Glue and nail the drawer sides to the fronts and backs. Square up each drawer with the bottom panel and glue and nail it into place.

DRAWER FRONT

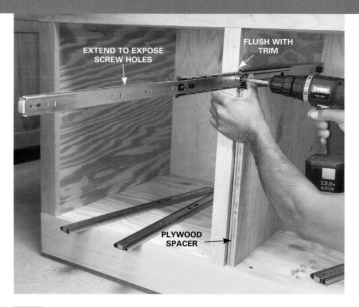

EXTEND TO EXPOSE SCREW HOLES

FLUSH WITH TRIM

PLYWOOD SPACER

8 Rest the top-drawer slides on a spacer flush with the front trim, then extend them and screw them to the sides of the cabinet boxes.

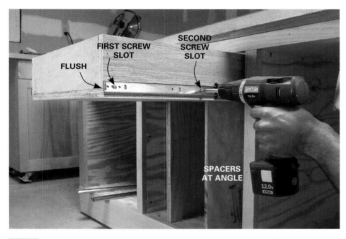

FIRST SCREW SLOT

SECOND SCREW SLOT

FLUSH

SPACERS AT ANGLE

9 Rest the drawers on the spacers. Screw the slides onto the drawer at the front first, slide the drawer out and drive the second pair, then repeat for the third.

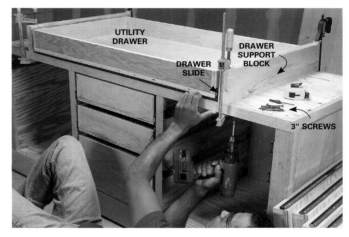

UTILITY DRAWER

DRAWER SUPPORT BLOCK

DRAWER SLIDE

3" SCREWS

10 Mount the drawer slides to the utility drawer blocks using 1/4-in. spacers and then mount the drawer. Center and clamp the drawer blocks to the cabinet base and fasten them with 3-in. screws.

Figure B:
Drawer details

SIDE

FRONT

P

F

PP

GLUE

1-1/2" BRADS

strips or buy 1/2 x 3/4-in. "parting stop" at the lumberyard. Glue and pin on the edging with 1-in. brads and slightly ease the edges with sandpaper to prevent splinters. Then cut the drawer fronts from one of the panels on the table saw. When the drawer fronts are mounted, the spaces between the drawers will be the thickness of the saw kerf (use 16d nails as spacers), so the top and bottom will remain aligned with the doors. Mount the fronts as shown in Photo 17. Tack strips of wood spaced 1/2 in. from the openings on the bottom and one side to align the bottom drawer fronts. Screw the hinges on the cabinet doors (3 in. from the top and bottom) first and then center the doors and screw the hinges to the cabinet.

Glue up the bench top
Gluing up and flattening your bench top will take most of a

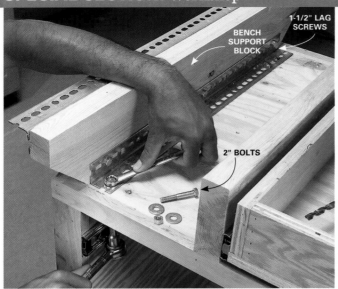

11 Lag-screw the angle iron to the bench-top support boards with 1-1/2-in. x 5/16-in. lag screws. Then bolt them to the base with 2-in. x 5/16-in. nuts and bolts.

12 Rip twenty-four 7-ft.-long 2x4s to 3-1/4-in. widths. Lay three pipe clamps on a flat surface. Roll a thin layer of glue over the two mating faces of the 2x4s.

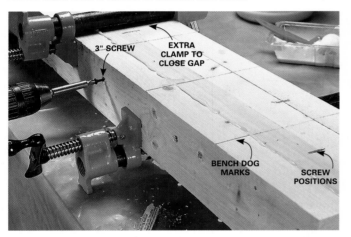

13 Clamp each board and screw it to the others with 3-in. screws spaced every 6 in. Add another clamp and more screws as needed to close large gaps.

14 Mark the bench at 6 ft. long, then cut off both ends with a guide and circular saw. Cut from both sides.

day. You can get by with four pipe clamps, but if you have any buddies with pipe clamps, borrow them too; they'll speed up the process and ensure gap-free glue joints.

Begin your top by cutting twelve 14-ft. long 2x4s in half. Choose the best edge of each piece: the one with the fewest, smallest knots and without any corner defects. Rip each 2x4 to 3-1/4 in. wide, trimming the best edge square. Cluster together the first five boards, find the center of the group and mark lines every 6 in. (Photo 13). Later, avoid these locations when you're driving screws so you can drill clean holes for the bench dogs.

It's important to glue and clamp the top on a flat surface. Lay out three pipe clamps and glue and screw the 2x4s one by one (Photos 12 and 13). A mini paint roller speeds up the glue spreading considerably. Keep the board tops as flush as possible to minimize sanding later. And mark the screws on the bench top as you go to avoid hitting them with the next row of screws.

You can tell if the joint is tight by looking for an even glue "squeeze-out." Where you don't see oozing glue, add the fourth clamp to pull together the 2x4s before running in a screw. Predrill 1/8-in. holes through the first 2x4 for each screw to help draw the boards together.

After gluing a few boards, scrape off the glue squeeze-out (top and bottom) with a chisel and wipe off the joints with a damp rag (top only). Otherwise the glue will clog up your sandpaper during the flattening process later. You can really beat yourself up striving for a perfectly gap-free top. If that's your goal, use at least eight clamps and carefully cull any twisted 2x4s. The truth is, a few narrow gaps in your top won't hurt anything but your pride.

Cut the top to length and sand it flat

Mark a square cutoff line on the right side of the bench 6 in.

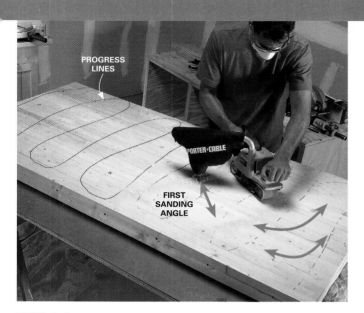

15 Belt-sand the top flat diagonally first one way, then the other until the "progress" lines disappear. Then finish sanding with a random orbital sander.

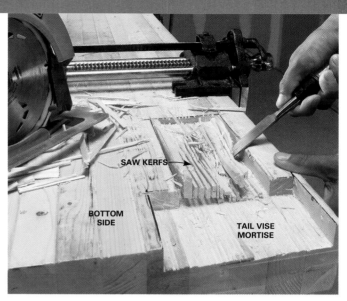

16 Set the top on the bench and mark the 1/4-in. pilot holes for the angle iron. Flip the bench over and drill the holes. Cut and chisel mortises for the vises and mount them. Screw down the top.

away from one of the bench-dog layout marks and another 6 ft. away on the other end.

Your circular saw will cut about halfway through, so flip over the top and transfer the cutting lines to the bottom and cut the other side (Photo 14). If you're using a cutting jig as shown, remove it and follow the saw kerf freehand to finish the cut. Be careful: If your cuts are misaligned, you'll be facing lots of sanding to flatten the ends!

Draw pencil "progress" lines over the surface while you're belt sanding (Photo 15). As the lines disappear, you'll be able to keep track of which areas have been sanded and where more work is needed.

Belt-sand the top with coarse paper in a diagonal direction first one way, then the other, until the top is flat (Photo 15). You'll have to repeat this process several times to achieve a flat surface. Then, belt-sand parallel with the grain to remove sanding marks with coarse-, then medium-, then fine-grit belts. Finish up the sanding with a random orbital sander using 100-grit paper.

Set the top and mount the vises

Cut the slotted angle iron to length with a hacksaw and screw the pieces to the support blocks with 1-1/2 x 5/16-in. lag screws. Place the blocks on the cabinet, mark the angle iron holes, then drill and through-bolt the blocks to the cabinet with 5/16 x 2-in. bolts with nuts (Photo 11).

Center the bench top on the cabinet and mark the center and outside angle iron holes on its underside. Hold the vises in place and scribe their footprints on the underside. You may have to clip one block end to get the vise to clear (Figure A, part XX). Flip over the top and drill 1/4-in. pilot holes for

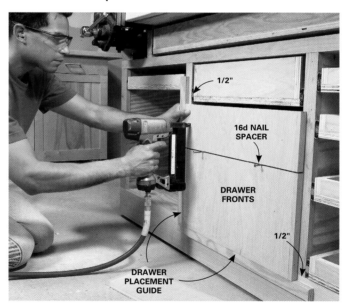

17 Tack guide boards 1/2 in. from the bottom and side of the center box. Pin the drawer fronts into place. Then screw the fronts on from the back side with four 1-1/4-in. screws. Mount the doors.

the angle iron lag screws, and then cut out mortises so the tops of the vises will be flush with the bench top (Photo 16). (It will save time if you first make several passes with a circular saw set at the right depth.) Then bolt the vises in place, flip over the bench top and lag-screw it to the angle irons.

Draw a light pencil line centered on the tail vise dog and parallel to the side to center the 3/4-in. bench dog holes. Then drill the holes spaced every 6 in. along the line. Apply three coats of polyurethane to the top and two coats to the cabinet, sanding between coats with 120-grit paper.

Buyer's guide

Full-extension 24" drawer slides, and swivel-plate 3" industrial casters
Woodworker's Hardware: (800) 383-0130 wwhardware.com

Bench dogs, pair; 9" quick-release vise, and 7" quick-release vise
Highland Woodworking: tools-for-woodworking.com

Drawer and sliding shelf spacer sizes*

Top shelves: 18-1/2"
Second shelf: 14"
Third shelf: 8"
Bottom shelf: Space it from cabinet bottom 1/4"
Top drawer: 17"
Second drawer: 11"
Bottom drawer: Space it from cabinet bottom 1/4"

*See Photos 8 and 9

Figure C:
Cutting diagrams

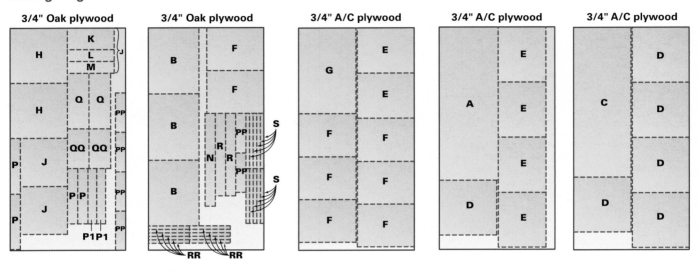

Cutting list

KEY	PCS.	SIZE & DESCRIPTION
A	1	23-3/4" x 64-1/2" 3/4" AC plywood (base)
B	3	21" x 28-3/4" 3/4" oak (back)
C	1	23-3/4" x 64-1/2" 3/4" AC plywood (top)
D	6	23-3/4" x 23-3/8" 3/4" AC plywood (box sides)
E	6	19-1/2" x 23-3/4" 3/4" AC plywood (box tops and bottoms)
F	8	18-1/2" x 23-3/4" 3/4" AC plywood (drawer and sliding shelf bottoms)
G	1	39" x 23-3/4" 3/4" AC plywood (utility drawer bottom)
H	2	24-1/2" x 23-3/4" 3/4" oak plywood (cabinet end panels)
J	3	19-1/2" x 22-1/4" 3/4" oak plywood (drawer and door fronts). Plywood cut sizes only. Add banding (U) for final sizes.
K	1	20-1/2" x 11" 3/4" oak plywood (bottom drawer face). Cut sizes after banding is installed.
L	1	20-1/2" x 6" 3/4" oak plywood (middle drawer face). Cut sizes after banding is installed.
M	1	20-1/2" x 6" 3/4" oak plywood (top drawer face). Cut sizes after banding is installed.
N	1	43" x 4-1/4" 3/4" oak plywood (utility drawer face). Cut size before banding.
P	4	4-1/4" x 23-3/4" 3/4" oak plywood (drawer sides). Top and middle drawers only.
P1	2	3-1/4" x 23-3/4" 3/4" oak plywood (utility drawer side)
PP	4	4-1/4" x 17" 3/4" oak plywood (drawer fronts and backs). Top and middle drawers only.
Q	2	9" x 23-3/4" 3/4" oak plywood (bottom drawer sides)

KEY	PCS.	SIZE & DESCRIPTION
QQ	2	9" x 17" 3/4" oak plywood (bottom drawer front and back)
R	2	3-1/4" x 37-1/2" 3/4" oak plywood (utility drawer front and back)
RR	10	1-1/2" x 17" 3/4" oak plywood (sliding shelf front and backs)
S	10	1-1/2" x 23-3/4" 3/4" oak plywood (sliding shelf sides)
T	2	5" x 8' 3/4" oak hardwood (base molding). Cut to fit for lengths.
U	4	1-1/2" x 8' oak hardwood (trim). Cut to fit for lengths.
V	1	2-1/4" x 8' oak hardwood (vertical trim). Cut to fit for lengths.
VV	24'	1/2" x 3/4" oak hardwood (door and drawer edge banding). Cut to fit for lengths.
W	4	1-1/2" x 3-1/2" x 6' framing lumber (base platform). Cut and assemble to fit part A.
X	12	1-1/2" x 3-1/2" x 14' framing lumber (work top)
XX	2	5" x 30" framing lumber (top supports; one is 27" long)
Y	2	5" x 25-1/4" framing lumber (utility drawer supports)
Z	3	23-1/2" angle iron (top hold-down)
ZZ	1	30" angle iron (top hold-down)
	6 sets	2" x 5/16" nuts, bolts and washers (angle iron to cabinet base)
	30	1-1/2" x 5/16" lag screws (wheels to cabinet base, angle iron to supports)
	6	2" x 5/16" lag screws (angle iron to work top)
	1 lb.	1-5/8" screws (base to platform framing)
	1 lb.	1-1/2" screws (all plywood-to-plywood connections)
	1/2 lb.	3" screws (utility drawer supports to cabinet base)
	9 pairs	24" drawer slides

Top (10) tips
for a tidy workshop

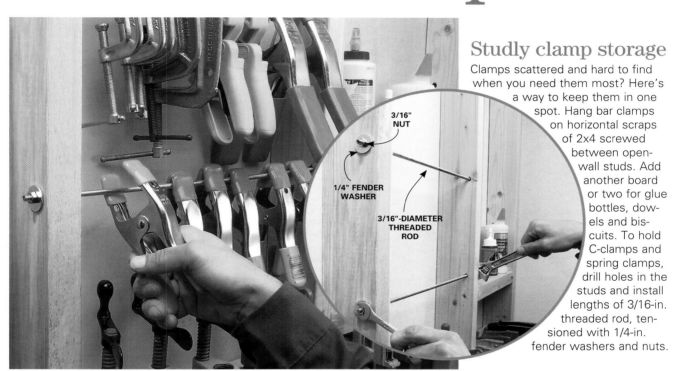

Studly clamp storage

Clamps scattered and hard to find when you need them most? Here's a way to keep them in one spot. Hang bar clamps on horizontal scraps of 2x4 screwed between open-wall studs. Add another board or two for glue bottles, dowels and biscuits. To hold C-clamps and spring clamps, drill holes in the studs and install lengths of 3/16-in. threaded rod, tensioned with 1/4-in. fender washers and nuts.

3/16" NUT

1/4" FENDER WASHER

3/16"-DIAMETER THREADED ROD

Band saw blade hangers

If you've ever suffered the indignity—and possible danger to eyes and face—of a band saw blade uncoiling as you've pulled it off the peg you hung it on, you'll love this tip. Nest the coiled blades into binder clips and store them on your pegboard, and they'll never spring out at you again. Apply labels to the clip so you can simplify size selection and storage.

Wrenches bound in the round

You need a 5/8-in. wrench but can't find it in the drawer without rummaging around and eyeballing all the other scattered wrenches. Instead, store your end wrenches on a 3-1/2-in.-diameter loose-leaf ring ($1 at a hardware store). It only takes a second to snap the ring open and pull off the one you need. And you can throw them back into the toolbox knowing they'll stay together next time.

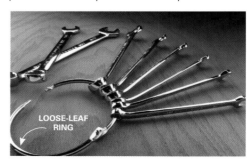

LOOSE-LEAF RING

Glue-go-round

Here are three good reasons to build this glue caddy for your shop. First, no more hunting for the right type of glue; they'll all be right at your fingertips. Second, you can store the containers upside down. That keeps the glue near the spout—no more shaking down half-filled bottles. Third, upside-down storage helps polyurethane glues last longer without hardening because it keeps the air out.

Here's how to make yours:

First, arrange all your glue bottles in a circle with 1-in. spacing between the bottles. Add 2 in. to the circle diameter and cut out two 3/4-in. plywood discs. Drill 7/8-in. holes in the center of each one. Measure the various bottle diameters and drill storage holes around the top disc a smidgen larger than the bottles. Glue the discs on a 12-in.-long, 7/8-in. dowel, with a 5-in. space between the discs.

Add a knob of your choice, load up your glue, and you've got an instant grip on every type of sticky problem that comes your way.

See-through junk drawer in a bag

Store extra fasteners in a clear plastic bag instead of a coffee can or junk drawer. Searching for the correct nut, bolt or whatever is as easy as looking "through" the bag, reaching in and plucking it from the mix.

Tidier tool trays

A piece of short-pile carpet in the bottom of each tray in your tool chest will keep tools from shifting and knocking about. So, the next time you open the tray, the tools will still be laid out nice and neat the way you left them. Another benefit: less noise.

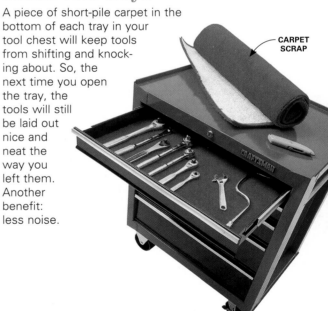

CARPET SCRAP

File by grit

Organize sandpaper by grit in a handy plastic file box ($9) available at office supply stores. Just list the grits on the tabs and you can instantly find the right one. The box is also a good place to store those partially used pieces that often find their way into the trash can prematurely.

PROBLEM

SOLUTION

GRIT NUMBERS

HALF OF AN EXTENSION LADDER

Store sheet goods on a ladder

Got a decade's worth of leftover pieces of plywood, drywall and plastic laminate and spare boards? Here's how to round them up and protect them from moisture, dirt and dings. If you have an old extension ladder lying around, take the sections apart and lay one on the floor near a wall to use as a sheet goods rack. The rail will keep stuff from sliding off. It'll hold everything high and dry off the floor and ready to sort when that next project comes along.

Super-duty steel stud shelf brackets

Build two super-strong shelf brackets with a steel-framing track. Use tin snips to cut two 41-in. lengths. Then cut V-notches 1 ft. in from both ends as shown. Screw one end of the track to the wall studs with a 10-in. 1x4 and then fold the track at the notches, bringing the ends together. Reinforce all the corners with steel framing screws. Set a shelf board on top. **Caution:** Steel stud track has sharp edges. Wear gloves to protect your hands.

10" 1x4

5-gallon bucket spacer

It's nice to keep some empty 5-gallon buckets around, but the only way to efficiently store them is to stack them. The problem is, they can get stuck so tight it feels like they're glued together. Put a short chunk of 2x4 between the buckets when you stack them. It'll be a cinch to pull them apart.

Outdoor

Pine garden hutch

Wouldn't it be nice to have all your gardening tools and supplies in one handy location? This pine hutch holds long-handled tools like shovels, rakes and hoes on one side, and smaller tools and supplies on shelves on the other side. The lumber and copper sheet cost about $300.

Start by building the face frame

Build the face frame (Photo 3) first and use it as a guide for assembling the doors and cutting the curve on the back panel.

A full sheet of 3/4-in. MDF (medium density fiberboard) or particleboard set on sawhorses makes a good workbench for this project. Set up for marking the arcs (for the curved pieces) by drawing a center line parallel to the long edge of the sheet. Center a 4-ft. length of 1x12 on the line. Line up the top edge

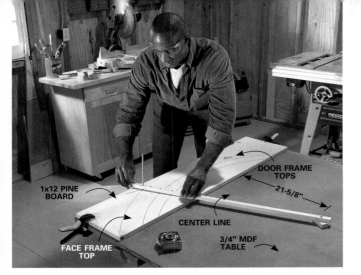

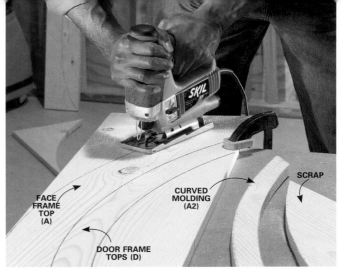

1 Build a large compass by drilling holes in a 36-in.-long stick using Figure B as a guide. Draw arcs for the face frame top (A1) and door frame tops (D) on a 4-ft. 1x12. On a second 4-ft. 1x12, draw arcs for the curved molding (A2) under the front roof (Figure B, p. 230).

2 Saw out the curved pieces with a jigsaw. Use the pattern on p. 230 to draw the curve on the face frame bottom (C1) and saw it out.

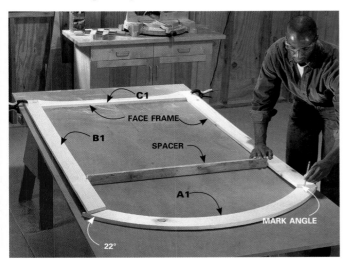

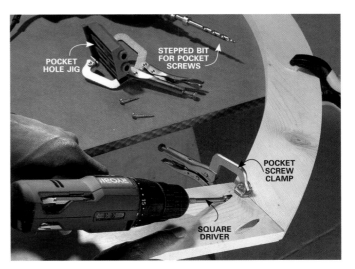

3 Cut the side pieces (B1) to length with 22-degree angles on the tops. Snug the face frame sides to the bottom (C1) and to a 39-in.-long spacer and clamp them to the table. Scribe lines on the curved top (A1) and cut off the ends.

4 Drill pocket holes on the back side of the face frame pieces with a pocket hole jig. Glue the joints and connect them with pocket screws.

with the edge of the workbench and clamp it. Screw the point of the homemade compass in the center line 21-5/8 in. below the bottom edge of the 1x12 (Photo 1). Draw three arcs for the face frame top and door top pieces (Figure B, p. 230). Then replace the 1x12 with another 48-in. 1x12 and relocate the screw point (see Figure B). Draw two arcs to outline the 1-1/2 in.-wide curved roof trim molding. Cut out the curves (Photo 2).

Even with careful jigsaw work, sand the curves for a smooth arch. Use 80-grit sandpaper on a sanding block to even out the curve and remove saw marks. Then sand again with 100- and 120-grit paper. For the best-looking finish, sand all the boards before assembly. Use a random orbital sander or hand-sand with the grain of the wood.

After cutting and sanding the curved pieces, rip the remaining face frame and door trim pieces to width and cut them to length according to Figure A and the Cutting list, both on p. 230. Use the pattern on p. 230 to cut the curve on

the 39-in.-long 1x6 bottom frame piece (C1). Cut the same curve on the 44-in.-long x 5-in.-wide piece (C2). Use this for the bottom cleat (Photo 5). Assemble the face frames and door frames and the back frame with pocket screws. Photos 3 and 6 show how to mark for the angle cuts where the curved pieces join the straight ones.

Use a miter box to cut angles on the ends of the curved pieces, and steady them by supporting them with one of the scrap concave corners cut from the 1x12. Place the straight edge of the concave scrap against the fence and nestle the curves. Then sight along the blade and adjust the angle to cut along the line. Use this same technique for cutting the angles on the ends of the curved door frame tops (D) as shown in Photo 6.

After assembling the face frame, flip it over and screw on the cleats (B2 and C2; Photo 5). The cleats overlap the joints to add strength and serve as a nailing surface for the floorboards and side panels.

Figure A:
Garden hutch

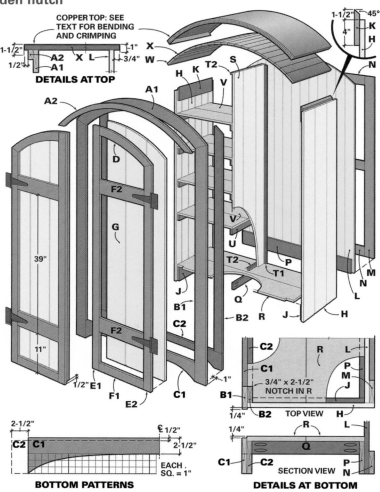

DETAILS AT TOP

COPPER TOP: SEE TEXT FOR BENDING AND CRIMPING

1-1/2" · A2 · X · L · 1" · 3/4" · 1/2" · A1 · W · X

1-1/2" · 45° · 4" · K · H · N

A2 · A1 · H · K · T2 · S · V

D · F2 · G · V · U · T2 · T1 · P · M · N · L · H

39" · 11" · 1/2" E1 · F1 · E2 · J · B1 · C2 · B2 · R · J · H · C1

BOTTOM PATTERNS

2-1/2" · C2 · C1 · 1/2" · 2-1/2" · EACH SQ. = 1"

TOP VIEW

C2 · C1 · R · L · P · M · J · 3/4" x 2-1/2" NOTCH IN R · B1 · 1/4" · B2 · H

SECTION VIEW / **DETAILS AT BOTTOM**

1/4" · R · L · C1 · C2 · Q · P · N

Figure B:
Arc patterns

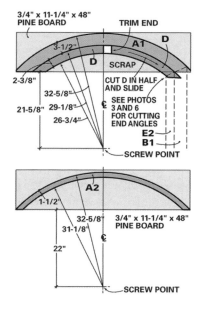

3/4" x 11-1/4" x 48" PINE BOARD · TRIM END · A1 · D · D · SCRAP · 3-1/2" · 2-3/8" · CUT D IN HALF AND SLIDE · 32-5/8" · 29-1/8" · 21-5/8" · 26-3/4" · SEE PHOTOS 3 AND 6 FOR CUTTING END ANGLES · E2 · B1 · SCREW POINT

A2 · 1-1/2" · 32-5/8" · 31-1/8" · 22" · 3/4" x 11-1/4" x 48" PINE BOARD · SCREW POINT

Cutting list

KEY	PCS.	SIZE & DESCRIPTION
Face frame		
A1, D1		48" x 3/4" x 11-1/4" (curved frame and door tops)
A2	1	48" x 3/4" x 11-1/4" (curved molding; cut curve and ends)
B1	2	68" x 3/4" x 3-1/2" (sides)*
B2	2	66" x 3/4" x 2-1/2" (side cleats)*
C1	1	39" x 3/4" x 5-1/2" (bottom; cut curve to pattern)
C2	1	44" x 3/4" x 5" (bottom cleat; cut curve to pattern)
Doors		
D	2	Curved tops (cut from "door top" above)
E1	2	68-5/8" x 3/4" x 2-1/4" (door sides)*
E2	2	61" x 3/4" x 2-1/4" (door sides)*
F1	2	14-13/16" x 3/4" x 2-1/4" (door bottom rail); see Figure B
F2	4	14-13/16" x 3/4" x 4" (intermediate rails)
G	6	72" t&g 1x8 (door panels); cut to fit
Sides		
H	6	68-1/4" t&g 1x8 (19-1/2" x 68-1/4" side panels)
J	2	5" x 3/4" x 17-1/4" (bottom cleats)
K	2	5-1/2" x 3/4" x 17-1/4" (top cleats; bevel top to 45 degrees)
Back		
L	7	78" t&g 1x8 (44" x 78" back panel; cut top curve)
M	2	3-1/2" x 3/4" x 68" (frame sides)
N	3	3-1/2" x 3/4" x 37" (frame crosspiece)
P	1	5" x 3/4" x 42-1/2" (bottom cleat)
Interior Parts		
Q	1	2" x 3/4" x 16-1/2" (floor crosspiece)
R	2	9" x 3/4" x 44" (floorboards)
S	3	72" t&g 1x8 (17-1/4" x 72" center panel)
T1	1	3/4" x 3/4" x 72" (center panel cleats)
T2	2	3/4" x 3/4" x 17-1/4" (center panel cleats)
U	8	1-1/2" x 3/4" x 17-1/4" (shelf cleats)
V	8	8-5/8" x 3/4" x 21-5/8" (shelf boards)
W	3	3-1/2" x 3/4" x 21-1/2" (roof boards)
X	18	2-1/2" x 3/4" x 21-1/2" (roof boards)

* Cut top angles at 22 degrees

Shopping list

ITEM	QTY.
1x2 x 8' pine	3
1x3 x 8' pine	9
1x4 x 6' pine	4
1x4 x 8' pine	3
1x6 x 6' pine	4
1x10 x 8' pine	3
1x12 x 8' pine	1
1x8 x 6' t&g pine	15
1x8 x 8' t&g pine	7
8" gate hinges	4
Latch	1
Tubes of construction adhesive	2
Magnetic catches	4
Water-resistant wood glue	
1-1/4" finish nails	
Copper or brass weatherstrip nails	
Pocket screws and jig	
2' x 5' 16-oz. copper sheet	

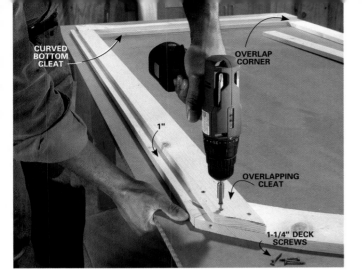

5 Cut backing cleats (B2 and C2) that overlap the face frame joints (Figure A, parts A1, B1 and C1). Predrill and screw them to the back of the face frame.

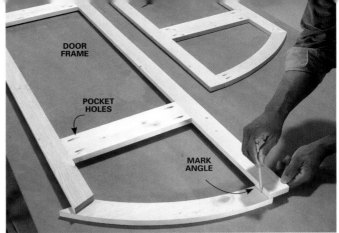

6 Assemble the door frame with pocket screws as shown. Then cut the curved top (D) in half and cut angles on the ends to fit. Attach them with pocket screws as well. Place the assembled door frames in the face frame to check the fit. Plane and sand as needed to allow a 1/8-in. space around and between the door frames.

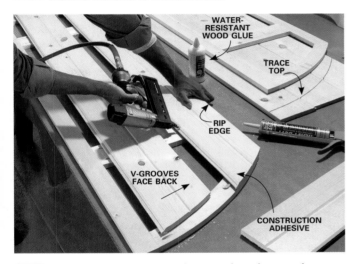

7 Temporarily assemble the door panels and center the frames over them. Mark the bottom, sides and top. Rip the sides and cut the top curve. Cut the bottoms 1/4 in. shorter than marked. Then glue and nail the boards together with wood glue and fasten them to the frame with construction adhesive.

8 Assemble the back frame (M and N) with pocket screws. Glue and nail tongue-and-groove boards to it to form the cabinet back. Rip the first and last boards to fit.

Take time building the doors

Use the completed face frame as a guide to check the fit of the doors as they're built. The goal is to end up with a 1/8-in. space between the doors and the face frame and between the two doors. Sand or plane them as needed to create an even gap. Build and fit the door frames first. Then use them as a guide to cut out the tongue-and-groove boards that make up the door panels (Photo 7). Rip the groove off the first board in each door panel and then rip the last board to fit. Glue and nail the boards to the frames and then sand the edges flush. A belt sander works great for this task.

Build the side and back panels

The panels for the sides and back are constructed just like the door panels. Rip the tongues and grooves from the outermost boards after figuring out how wide they should be (Photo 8). The exact ripping widths will probably vary between projects, based on the boards that are used. The easiest approach is to

temporarily assemble the tongue-and-groove boards, using clamps if needed to draw them tight together. Then mark the panel widths on them, making sure to measure over the panel to remove an equal amount from the outside boards. Rip the outside boards to width. Then assemble the panels. Run a small bead of water-resistant wood glue along the tongue of each board before sliding it into the groove. Clean up any squeezed-out glue right away with a damp cloth. When the glue hardens, the panels will be rigid and strengthen the cabinet. Use construction adhesive to glue the panels to the frames and/or cleats.

Here are a few special considerations for building the panels. First, use a framing square to make sure the panels are perfectly square before the glue dries. Cut the curve on the back panel after it's constructed (Photo 9). The beveled top cleat (K) on the side panels (H) is a little tricky. Study Photos 10 and 13 and Figure A to see its location and orientation.

9 Center the face frame over the back panel and line up the bottoms. Mark the top curve. Saw it out with a jigsaw.

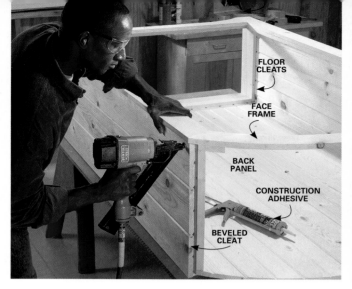

10 Assemble the side panels (Figure A). Then glue and nail the side panels to the back panel and the face frame.

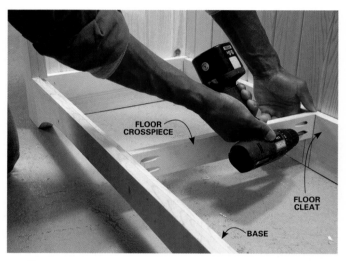

11 Screw in the crosspiece (Q) with pocket screws to support the floorboards. Notch the first floorboard (R) to fit around the face frame and glue and nail it down. Cut the back floorboard to fit and nail it in.

12 Glue and nail together the center divider and attach it to the bottom and back with cleats (T1 and T2) and screws. Attach the top to the ceiling boards after they're installed (Photo 13).

Assemble the cabinet, then mount the doors

Glue and nail the completed panels and face frame together (Photo 10). Then add the floorboards and center panel (Photo 12). Center the curved molding (A2) and nail it to the top of the face frame. Finally, glue and nail the roof boards along the curve (Photo 13). Start with 1x4s aligned with the ends of the curved molding. Then complete the roof with 1x3s, working from both sides to the center. To make sure everything is square, temporarily tack the 1x4 in place. Then set four of the 1x3s on the roof with their ends perfectly aligned and measure the front overhang to make sure it's consistent. If the overhang is getting larger or smaller, move the back end of the 1x4 down or up, respectively, to correct the problem.

When the cabinet is complete, tip it on its back to install the doors (Photo 14). Use any strong, gate-type hinge. Just make sure to leave an even space around the perimeter of the doors and between them. Use a belt sander to trim tight spots.

Crimping tool simplifies curve of the metal roof

Start with a 24-in. x 60-in. piece of 16-oz. copper sheeting. Screw down a 2x4 frame on the bench top to provide clearance for bending down the edges. Start by snipping the corners of the copper with tin snips (Photo 15). Then hand-bend the edges of the sheet down over the 2x4s. The last step is to crimp the edges with the crimping tool (see Buyer's guide, at right) to curve the sheet (Photo 16). Keep the crimps parallel by aligning one of the crimping blades in the previously made crimp before squeezing it. Crimp about 12 in. on the front. Then crimp 24 in. on the back to even up the curve. Continue alternating until the end. Adjust the arch for an exact fit once the copper is back on top of the cabinet. Hold off, on nailing the copper in place (Photo 17) until after a finish has been applied to the hutch.

Since the hutch is pine and will rot quickly if left unprotected

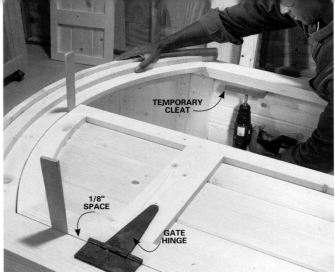

13 Nail the curved molding (A2) to the face frame. Then glue and nail the ceiling boards to the top of the cabinet. Start by overhanging the 1x4s as shown and work from both sides to the center with the 1x3 boards. Cut the last piece to fit.

14 Screw temporary cleats to the back of the face frame to support the doors. Set the doors in place and trim them if necessary to allow 1/8-in. clearance all around. Predrill for hinge screws and screw on the door hinges and hardware.

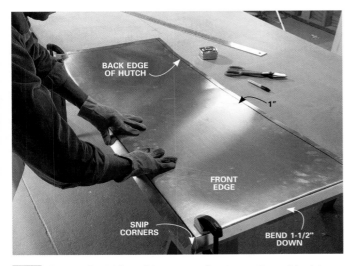

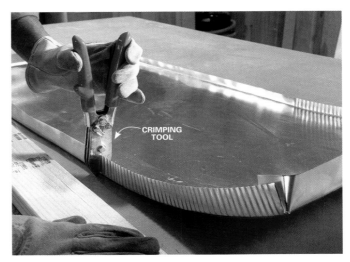

15 Center the 24-in.-wide copper sheet over the cabinet top with a 1-1/2-in. overhang in front. Mark along the back, front and ends with a permanent marker. Add 1-1/2 in. to the ends and cut the copper sheet to length with tin snips. Snip the corners as shown. Bend the front, back and ends down over the 2x4 frame.

16 Crimp the front and back edges to form the curved top using a special sheet metal crimping tool. Alternate between the front and the back until you reach the end.

outdoors, apply a durable finish. This hutch has an oil stain and three coats of spar varnish. Be sure to seal the bottom edges thoroughly. If putting the hutch in a wet location, install metal or plastic feet on all four corners to elevate it slightly. Setting the hutch on an uneven surface can cause the doors to bind or fit poorly. Shim under the cabinet to level it, if needed.

Buyer's guide

Malco C4, 5 blade downspout crimper is available online from amazon.com, or Seven Corners Hardware, 7corners.com.

The Kreg jig and the #KHC-Premium Face Clamp 3-in. reach are available at kregtool.com.

The primitive latch (02006027) is available from Van Dyke's Restorers, vandykes.com.

The 16-oz. copper sheet is available from Sheridan Sheet Metal Co., sheridansheetmetal.com.

17 Drill 1/16-in. pilot holes (through the copper only) about every 12 in. along the edges. Drive small copper or brass weather strip nails through the copper into the wood slats to hold the copper roofing in place.

Storage bench

At first glance, this bench may look like a complex project. But take a closer look and you'll see that the structure couldn't be more basic. It's just a box made from four frames with legs that wrap around the corners. The panels that fill the frames are plywood with waterproof outdoor fabric stapled over them. Covering the plywood seat with foam and fabric is something even an upholstery novice can manage. This bench is easy to customize, too: You can change the dimensions, choose fabric to complement other patio furniture, and stain the wood to match your deck or paint it to match your house.

Build it from 1x4s and plywood

The wood and hardware for our bench cost about $120. Upholstery supplies can cost $50 to $150, depending on what you select (see "Choosing Upholstery," p. 238).

This bench is built from pine 1x4s. Using a rot-resistant wood like cedar, redwood or teak will more than double the lumber cost. Top-grade pine is expensive too. Shown is lower-grade pine instead—buy extra material and "harvest" the knot-free sections for the visible bench parts. Use some of the leftovers for the slats (G) that form the floor inside the bench. The upholstered seat and panels are all cut from a

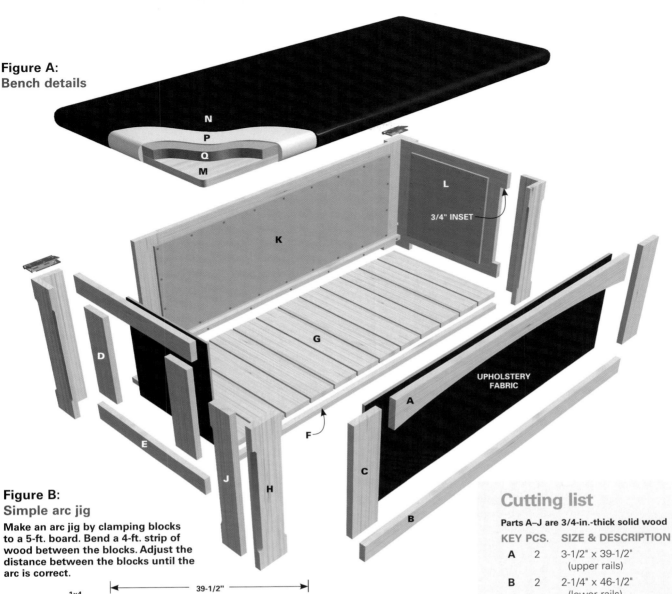

Figure A:
Bench details

N

P

Q

M

L

3/4" INSET

K

D

G

UPHOLSTERY
FABRIC

A

E

J

H

C

F

B

Figure B:
Simple arc jig

Make an arc jig by clamping blocks
to a 5-ft. board. Bend a 4-ft. strip of
wood between the blocks. Adjust the
distance between the blocks until the
arc is correct.

1x4
39-1/2"
2-1/2"
3-1/2"

Cutting list

Parts A–J are 3/4-in.-thick solid wood

KEY	PCS.	SIZE & DESCRIPTION
A	2	3-1/2" x 39-1/2" (upper rails)
B	2	2-1/4" x 46-1/2" (lower rails)
C	4	3-1/2" x 14" (front/back stiles)
D	4	3-1/2" x 11-3/4" (side stiles)
E	4	2-1/4" x 19-1/2" (side rails)
F	2	3/4" x 46-1/4" (cleats)
G	13	3-1/2" x 17-7/8" (slats)
H	4	3-1/2" x 18" 1x4 pine (leg fronts)
J	4	2-3/4" x 18" (leg sides)
K	2	13-1/2" x 41-1/2" 3/8" BC plywood (front/back panels)
L	2	13-1/2" x 13-1/2" 3/8" BC plywood (side panels)
M	2	22-1/2" x 51" BC plywood (seat)
N	1	29" x 57" upholstery fabric
P	1	24-1/2" x 53" batting
Q	1	23-1/2" x 52" foam (1" thick)

Materials list

Available at home centers:

- 70' of 1x4 pine (this is a minimum amount; we bought 100' and selected sections)
- 4' x 8' of 3/8" BC-grade plywood
- 1-5/8" galvanized drywall screws
- 1-1/4" galvanized drywall screws
- No. 8 x 1" pan head screws
- 1-1/4" galvanized nails
- 5/16" staples
- 3-1/2" zinc-plated hinges (Stanley No. 819051)

- Exterior wood glue (such as Titebond II or Titebond III)
- Lid support (Stanley No. 80-1535)
- Spray adhesive (such as 3M Super 77)
- Weather stripping (adhesive-backed foam or rubber)
- Plastic or rubber foot pads

Shown is the Kreg R2 pocket hole jig. Other versions cost from $25 to $145. To find a dealer, go to kregtool.com. To find online retailers, search for "Kreg jig."

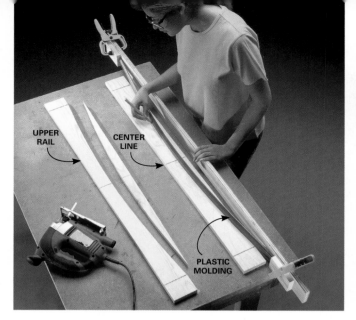

1 Mark a curve on upper rails using the arc jig. Cut the curve with a jigsaw. Don't cut the rails to their final length until you've sanded the curve.

UPPER RAIL

CENTER LINE

PLASTIC MOLDING

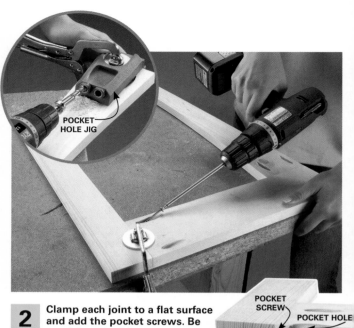

2 Clamp each joint to a flat surface and add the pocket screws. Be careful not to drive screws too deep in soft wood.

POCKET HOLE JIG

POCKET SCREW

POCKET HOLE

3 Glue and nail bottom cleats to the front and back frames. Then predrill and fasten the four frames together with 1-5/8-in. screws.

CLEAT

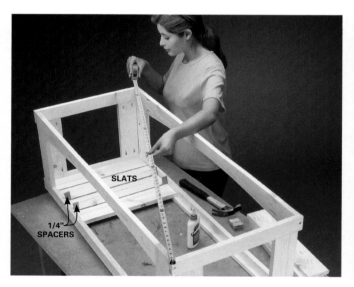

4 Glue and nail the slats in place, using 1/4-in. spacers to position them. Take diagonal measurements to make sure the box is square.

SLATS

1/4" SPACERS

single sheet of 3/8-in. BC-grade plywood.

You'll need a table saw, a jigsaw, a sander and a drill to complete this project. A router and chamfer bit are optional (see Photo 5). You'll also need a pocket hole jig (Photo 2) or a biscuit joiner to assemble the frames.

Cut curved rails

Each of the four frames that form the box is made from four parts: The vertical frame parts, or "stiles" (C, D), are simply pieces of 1x4 cut to length. The horizontal frame parts, or "rails" (B, E), are ripped to the correct width on a table saw. The Cutting list on p. 235 provides all the dimensions.

Don't cut the curved rails (A) to their final length until the curves are cut and sanded. Instead, start with boards at least 41 in. long. Mark them as shown in Figure B and Photo 1. Plastic doorstop molding ($3 at home centers) works great in an arc jig, but any thin, knot-free strip of wood will do.

Take your time as you cut the arc with a jigsaw. Don't worry if the cut is a bit wavy. You can smooth it out with a random-orbital or finishing sander and 100-grit sandpaper. If you move the sander back and forth across the entire arc using even speed and pressure, minor waves will gradually even out.

Assemble frames with pocket screws

You could assemble the frames using biscuits or dowels, but

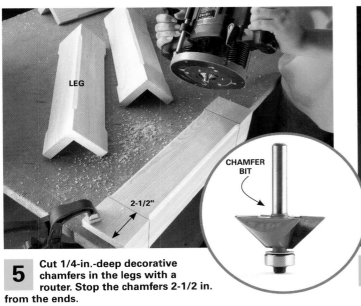

5 Cut 1/4-in.-deep decorative chamfers in the legs with a router. Stop the chamfers 2-1/2 in. from the ends.

LEG

2-1/2"

CHAMFER BIT

6 Glue and screw the legs to the corners of the box from the inside. Predrill 1/8-in. clearance holes so the screws can draw the legs tight against the frames.

CLEARANCE HOLES

TEMPORARY 2x4s

7 Glue two layers of 3/8-in. plywood together to make the seat. Drive screws every 6 in. through both layers into straight 2x4s and remove the screws after the glue sets.

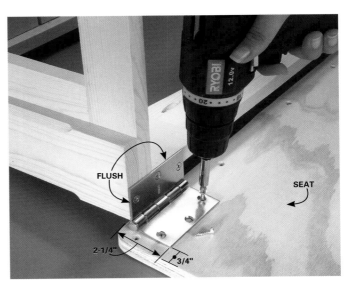

FLUSH

SEAT

2-1/4"   3/4"

8 Fasten the hinges to the box first. Then lay the seat on the floor and position each hinge as shown. Remove the seat to upholster it.

for this bench pocket screws were chosen because they're fast, easy to master and nearly foolproof. Here's how they work: A stepped drill bit—guided by a jig—bores into the wood at a steep angle to create a pocket (Photo 2 inset). Then you simply place a screw in the pocket and drive it into the adjoining piece (Photo 2).

In addition to pocket screws, use an exterior wood glue such as Titebond II or Titebond III to strengthen joints. When you assemble the side frames, be sure to position the stiles (D) 3/4 in. from the outer ends of the rails (E). Allow the glue to set for a couple of hours, then sand each frame with an orbital sander.

Join the frames and add slats to complete the box

Before you join the frames to form the box, fasten cleats (F) to the lower front and back rails (B). The frames that form the box are fastened together only with 1-5/8-in. screws at the corners (Photo 3), so the box isn't very strong until you add the legs later (Photo 6). Handle the box carefully if you need to move it.

The slats (G) not only form the floor of the box but also hold it square. Take diagonal measurements as you install the slats—equal measurements mean the box is square (Photo 4). You have only about five minutes before the glue begins to set, so it's best to have a helper hold the box square as you work. You'll have to rip the final slat on your table saw to fit.

Choosing upholstery

Craft and fabric stores may carry some outdoor upholstery, but for the best selection and advice, start with an upholstery store. Outdoor fabric costs about $6 to $30 per yard. With batting and foam added, expect your total bill to be at least $45. The standard width of upholstery fabric is 54 in. You'll need a piece at least 90 in. long and an equal amount of batting. Shown is 1-in.-thick, medium-density foam. Many suppliers will cut the foam to size for you (29 x 57 in.) Here are three things to keep in mind while choosing fabric:

- Most outdoor fabrics are vinyl, but a few other materials are available. Make sure the fabric you choose is waterproof and easy to clean.
- Tell the salesperson how and where your bench will be used. Some vinyl can crack in cold weather or degrade in direct sunlight.
- Solid colors or subtle patterns are easiest to work with. Stripes are the most difficult.

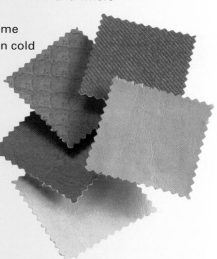

9 Staple batting to the panels. Then attach the fabric with staples around the perimeter. Trim off the excess batting and fabric with a utility knife.

10 Screw the panels inside the frames with 1-in. pan head screws spaced every 6 in.

Add the legs

Each leg is made from two parts (H and J) glued together. The final length of the legs is 18 in., but start with pieces that are at least 1/2 in. longer. That way, you don't have to perfectly align the ends when you glue and clamp them together. Scrape away excess glue and let the glue set for at least an hour before removing the clamps. Sand the legs and cut them to length. For a decorative option, chamfer the three edges of each leg (Photo 5). Use eight 1-1/4-in. screws (four on each side) and glue to fasten each leg to the box (Photo 6).

Make the seat from two layers of plywood

You could cut the seat (M) from a single piece of 3/4-in. plywood, but for this bench, two layers were glued together (Photo 7) for two reasons: First, this trick allows you to buy

only a single sheet of 3/8-in. plywood. Second, it creates a flatter seat. Single plywood sheets are often bowed. By gluing two sheets together (with both bows facing in or out) the bows cancel each other and you end up with a flat sheet. Start with sheets cut about an inch oversize and then cut the seat to final size after gluing. Drill eight 1/2-in. holes in the seat so air can escape from under the upholstery when someone sits on it. Using your jigsaw, round the corners of the seat to about the radius as a nickel. To protect against moisture, paint both the plywood seat and the panels before upholstering them.

Fastening hinges to the seat is a lot easier before the seat is upholstered (Photo 8). Remove the hinges to upholster the seat and finish the bench. With the screw holes established, remounting the hinges later is foolproof.

Upholster the seat

Here's the best thing about simple upholstery work: Most mistakes are no big deal. All you have to do to correct them is pry out the staples and try again.

Cut the fabric, batting and foam to size (see Cutting list, p. 235) and lay them on your workbench. The foam is easy to cut with scissors or a utility knife. Take the seat outside and coat one side with spray adhesive. Position the seat carefully as you set it on the foam; it will bond immediately and you won't be able to reposition it. Photos 9 – 12 show the upholstery process. Here are some pointers:

- Start by tacking the fabric at the middle of all four sides (Photo 11). If your fabric has a pattern, flip the seat over to make sure the pattern is properly aligned.
- Work outward from the middle of one side, then go to the other side and stretch the fabric as you work outward. Tug gently—the fabric doesn't have to be stretched super-tight.
- Stop occasionally and flip the seat over to see if you're creating ripples in the fabric. Usually you can make ripples disappear by prying out a few staples and stretching the fabric more or less.
- Stop stapling about 3 in. from each corner and deal with the corners only after all four sides are done.
- Cut out "V" sections of fabric at corners to avoid creating a thick lump of excess fabric (Photo 12). Start by cutting out a small "V" and enlarge it if necessary.
- If your fabric is a stiff vinyl that won't conform well at corners, heat it with a hair dryer to soften it.

Final touches

With the bench stained and the panels covered, screw the panels inside the frames (Photo 10). To keep the legs off the wet patio or deck, screw on 3/4-in. plastic feet. Even with the seat closed, a little rainwater can seep into the box. To minimize this seepage, run weather stripping around the upper edge (photo right). It's also a good idea to add a lid support to hold the seat open.

If you store furniture cushions in the bench, you'll create a paradise for mice. To keep them out, staple 1/4-in. galvanized hardware cloth to the underside of the slats. The most important thing you can do to preserve your bench is to maintain the finish. Since the panels and seat are removable, adding a fresh coat of paint or stain is easy. Finally, and most critical of all, if you have children around, don't store yard chemicals inside the bench.

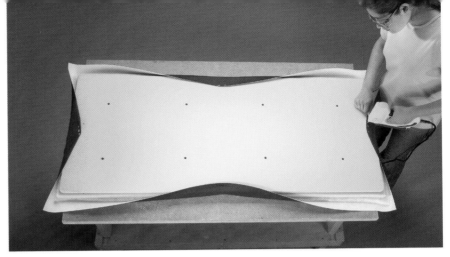

11 Lay out the fabric, batting and foam. Lightly coat the plywood seat with spray adhesive and center it on the foam. Staple the fabric to the plywood, starting at the middle of each side and working toward the corners.

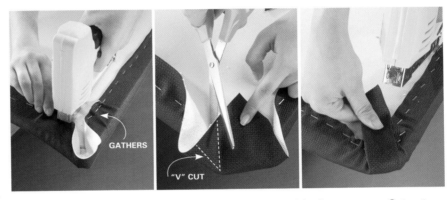

GATHERS

"V" CUT

12 Create small gathers in the fabric, starting about 3 in. from corners. Cut out "V" sections on both sides of the corner. Then fold the fabric inward, pull the corner back and staple.

LID SUPPORT

WEATHER STRIPPING

Backyard storage locker

A clear roof lets in the sunshine

These clear plastic roof panels let in sunlight so you can easily see inside. They're lightweight, faster to install than asphalt shingles and don't need sheathing underneath. You can cut them with a carbide blade in a circular saw. And best of all, they won't peel or tear like shingles, and they last for decades. The downside is they're not in stock at most home centers. You may have to special-order them.

Lawn and garden tools present a paradox: You can never find the right tool when you need it, then when you aren't looking for it, it's in your way. This simple-to-build locker solves both problems. It stores tools so they're easy to find, and it does so in a convenient location in your yard so they're not cluttering your garage.

The locker's 4 x 8-ft. footprint provides ample room to store space-hogging items like walk-behind lawn mowers and snowblowers. Long- and short-handled garden tools, lawn treatments and potting materials also fit nicely inside.

Here you'll learn how to build this attractive storage locker using easy construction techniques. It's a great project for beginners looking to expand their building skills.

Time, tools and money

You can build and paint this locker in a weekend, although you might need another half day to give the pressure-treated trim a second coat of paint. The straightforward construction requires only basic power tools—a circular saw with a standard carbide blade and a drill. An air compressor and nail gun aren't necessary but will make the framing and trim work easier (and faster!).

Shown are fiber cement panels for siding because they resist rot and hold paint well (the panels come primed). If you substitute plywood panels, be aware that they'll eventually rot along the bottoms where they're in ground contact. Corrugated plastic panels were chosen for the roof because they let

in light and are easy to install. Materials for this locker cost about $500.

Preconstruction planning

A flat or nearly flat site (less than a 6-in. slope over 6 ft.) is ideal for this storage locker. You can add gravel or stack up several sleepers on one side if your site has a steeper slope, but the doors need 3 ft. of space to open. If the locker faces a steep slope, you'll have to dig away the ground in front of the doors so they can fully open.

You can find all the materials except perhaps the roof panels at most home centers. Shown are Sequentia panels from Crane Composites (kemlite.com), which are available in

1 Lay sleepers over gravel to create a flat foundation fast. Add or remove gravel until the sleepers are level.

PEA GRAVEL

SLEEPER

2 Screw the floor framing to the sleepers at each corner. Then double-check the floor for level.

SLEEPER

3 Build the walls and screw them to the floor. Attach temporary bracing to hold the walls plumb.

BRACE

Materials list

ITEM	QTY.
2x4 x 8' treated pine (floor joists)	6
1/2" x 4' x 8' treated plywood (floor)	1
2x4 x 8' pine (studs, plates, supports, trimmers, rafters, purlins)	16
2x4 x 8' treated pine (plates)	2
2x6 x 8' pine (header, sleepers)	3
2x10 x 8' pine (shelves)	2
5/16" x 4' x 8' fiber cement (siding)	6
5/8" x 1" x 8' plugs	3
5/8" x 5/8" x 100" supports (quarter round)	1
27" x 9' roof panels	3
1x4 x 10' pine (fascia)	3
1x3 x 10' pine (fascia)	3
1x4 x 10' treated pine (corner boards and door top, bottom and center trim	8
1x4 x 8' treated pine (door trim)	4
2x4 x 12' treated pine (door casing)	1
1-5/16" x 2-1/4" x 8' pine molding (astragal)	1
Fence brackets	10
1-1/2" hex head panel screws	1 box
4d galvanized nails	1 lb.
6d galvanized nails	5 lbs.
8d galvanized nails	5 lbs.
3" exterior screws	1 lb.
16d galvanized nails	5 lbs.
4" T-hinge	4
Gate pull	1
Gate latch slide bolt	1
Pea gravel (50-lb. bags)	10

several colors and clear.

Buy treated trim material a few weeks before you build and let it dry. Otherwise, the wet wood will shrink and won't hold paint. Make sure to use galvanized nails or exterior screws because they won't corrode.

Lay the floor on sleepers

Start by digging parallel trenches 10 in. wide by 6 in. deep and centered 3 ft. 6 in. apart. If the ground is slightly sloped

Figure A:
Storage locker details

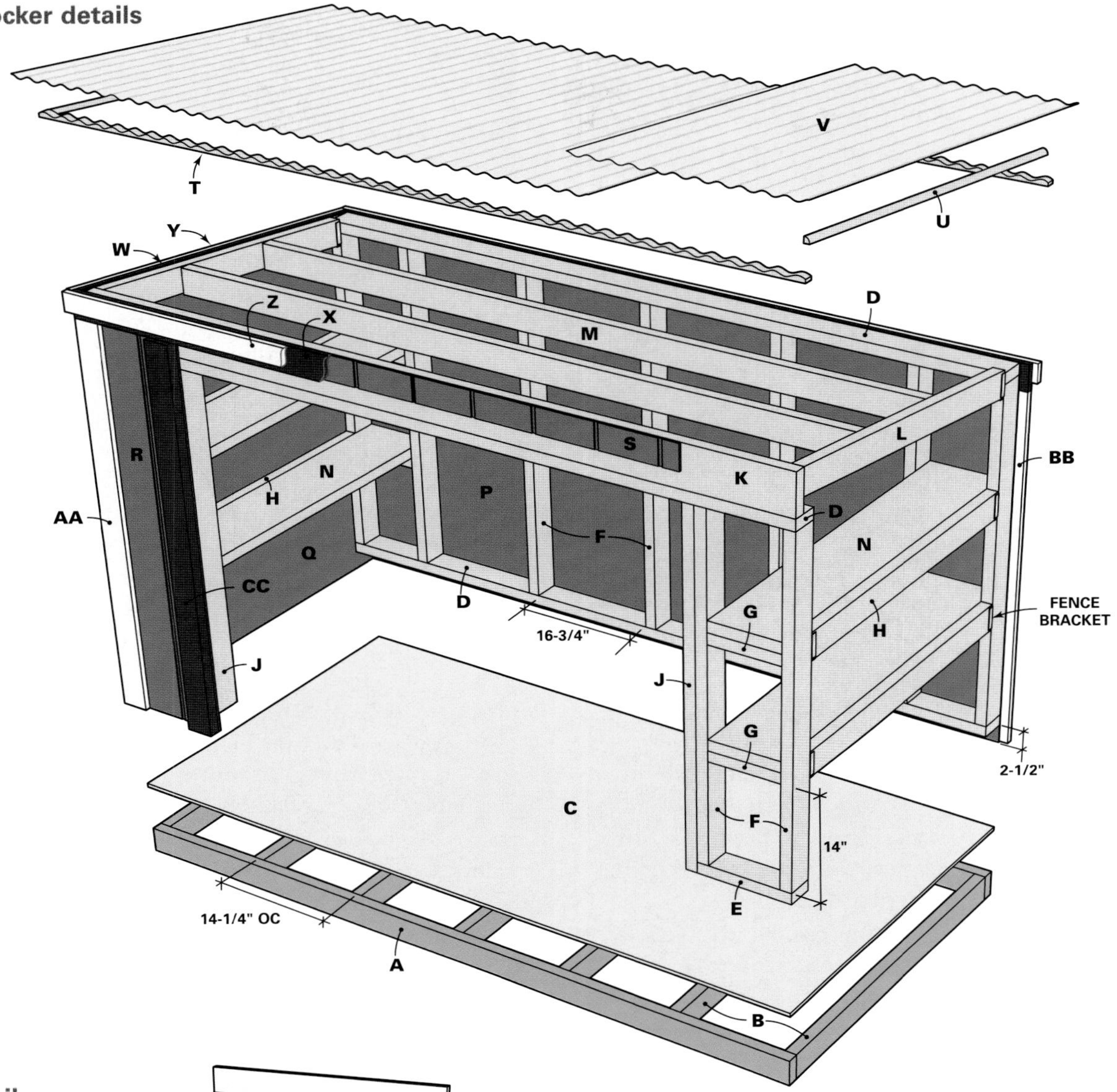

V

T

U

W
Y
D
Z
X
M
BB
R
L
N
S
H
P
K
AA
D
F
N
Q
H
D
G
FENCE
BRACKET
16-3/4"
J
J
H
G
2-1/2"
C
G
F
14"
14-1/4" OC
E
A
B

Figure B:
Door detail

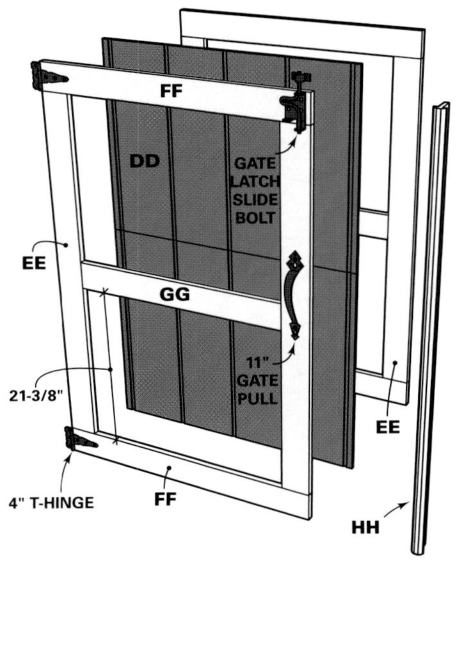

FF
DD
GATE
LATCH
SLIDE
BOLT
EE
GG
11"
GATE
PULL
21-3/8"
EE
4" T-HINGE
FF
HH

Overall dimensions:
4' x 8' x 56-15/16" (front height)

4 Install the purlins. Inexpensive fence brackets make fastening the purlins easy.

5 Nail the rafters to the header and align them with the top of the back wall to create a flat plane for the roof.

(like the site shown), dig out any high areas between the trenches so you can (later) place a level across the sleepers.

Fill the trenches with pea gravel so they're roughly level. Then cut treated 2x6 sleepers to size and set them over the gravel so the outside edges are 4 ft. apart. Place a 4-ft. level over one of the sleepers. Level it, then adjust the second sleeper until it's level with the first (Photo 1).

Frame the floor on your driveway or other flat surface with treated lumber using 16d nails or 3-in. screws, follow-

ing Figure A on p. 243. Lay a full sheet of 1/2-in. 4 x 8-ft. treated plywood over the floor frame. Adjust the floor frame so the corners are aligned with the edges of the plywood, then fasten the plywood using 8d nails or 1-1/2-in. screws. Snap chalk lines at the floor joist locations to make them easy to find. Drive fasteners every 6 to 8 in. along the edges and every 12 in. in the field.

Place the floor over the sleepers, align the corners, then drive 3-in. screws at an angle into the sleepers (Photo 2).

Cutting list

KEY	PCS.	SIZE & DESCRIPTION
A	2	2x4 x 96" treated (rim joists)
B	7	2x4 x 45" treated (joists)
C	1	1/2" x 48" x 96" treated (floor)
D	3	2x4 x 96" (plates); one treated
E	2	2x4 x 12-1/4" treated (bottom plates)
F	11	2x4 x 45-3/4" (studs)
G	8	2x4 x 9-1/4" (shelf supports)
H	4	2x4 x 40-7/8" (purlins)
J	2	2x4 x 47-1/4" (trimmers)
K	1	2x6 x 96" (header)
L	2	2x4 x 44" (rafters)*
M	2	2x4 x 93" (mid-beams)
N	4	2x10 x 48" (shelves)
P	2	5/16" x 48" x 51-1/4" (siding)
Q	2	5/16" x 48" x 57" (siding)*
R	2	5/16" x 13-3/4" x 56-3/4" (siding)

KEY	PCS.	SIZE & DESCRIPTION
S	2	5/16" x 34-1/4" x 3-5/16" (siding)
T	2	5/8" x 1" x 99-5/8" (plugs)
U	2	5/8" x 5/8" x 50" (supports)*
V	5	27" x 54" (roof panels)
W	2	1x4 x 50" (fascia)*
X	2	1x4 x 98-1/8" (fascia)
Y	2	1x3 x 52" (fascia)*
Z	2	1x3 x 99-5/8" (fascia)
AA	4	1x4 x 53-7/16" treated (corner boards)
BB	4	1x4 x 48-1/8" (corner boards)*
CC	2	2x4 x 53-7/16" treated (casings)
DD	4	5/16" x 33-15/16" x 26-5/8" (panels)
EE	8	1x4 x 46-1/4" treated (trim)
FF	8	1x4 x 33-15/16" treated (trim)
GG	4	1x4 x 26-15/16" treated (trim)
HH	1	1-5/16" x 2-1/4" x 53-1/4" (astragal)

*Cut to fit

6 Nail on the siding. Support the heavy siding panels with temporary nails placed 1-1/2 in. from the bottom of the floor framing.

FASCIA

CORNER BOARD

7 Trim the storage locker, starting with the fascia. Then add the corner boards.

Frame the walls and roof

Build the front and back walls following Figure A. Use treated lumber for the bottom plates and the door trimmers. Attach the assembled walls to the floor with 16d nails or 3-in. screws. Drive the fasteners near the outside edge to ensure they go into the underlying framing, not just into the plywood.

Have a helper place a level on a stud near one end of a wall. When the wall is plumb, fasten temporary bracing between the wall and the floor (Photo 3).

If you're not an experienced builder, toenailing the purlins into place can be tricky since it's hard to drive nails and keep the purlins at their marks. Avoid this frustration by using fence brackets. Nail them to the outside studs on the front and back walls with 8d nails, keeping the tops 1-1/2 in. above the top of the shelf supports. This keeps the tops of the purlins and the shelves (installed next) aligned for a flat surface.

Cut the purlins to size, set them into the brackets and drive 4d nails through the bracket holes (Photo 4). Cut the shelves to size and fasten them with 8d nails. It's important to install the shelves now since they won't fit after the siding is on.

Set the header in place, flush with the outside of the front wall. Drive 16d nails or 3-in. screws through the underside of the top plate into the header every 6 to 8 in.

To mark the angled end of the rafters, hold them in place alongside the header and the back wall. Mark the rafters and cut them to size. Use the fence brackets to hold the rafters in place on the back wall. Nail the brackets so the top is slightly above the top of the wall.

Nail the rafters in the brackets. Hold the opposite end

flush with the top and side of the header, then face-nail it with two 16d nails or 3-in. screws.

To frame the roof, install the rafters (Photo 5). Cut two mid-beams at 93 in. Mark the rafters at the one-third and two-thirds distances between the walls. Place the mid-beams at the marks and attach them with 16d nails or 3-in. screws.

Side with fiber cement

Use a carbide saw blade for cutting the fiber cement siding panels with a circular saw—and be sure to wear a mask. Cutting cement siding is extremely dusty. And be prepared—the 4 x 8-ft. panels are heavy.

We kept the siding 1-1/2 in. from the bottom of the locker to avoid direct contact with the ground.

Cut panels for the back and front walls following Figure A. Install the front panels, starting at a corner. Then install the back panels so they butt together over the middle stud on the wall. Don't worry that the panels don't fully cover the corners. You'll cover them later with trim.

Nail the panels with 8d nails. Drive the nails snug with a smooth-face hammer so you won't mar the siding. Drive nails straight, not at an angle. Keep nails 3/8 in. from panel edges and 2 in. from corners. Hold the side panels in place (don't nail them yet) and mark them along the top of the rafters. Cut them to size and nail them into place (Photo 6).

Add the trim

Painting along the roof panels is a pain, so it's best to paint the trim now. If you're using two colors, paint everything—you won't have to cut in with paint later.

8 Lay a heavy bead of caulk over the plug strip before screwing on the roof panel.

9 Hold the doors in perfect position with shims. Then screw on the hinges.

Install 1x4 fascia along the top of the locker. Start with the back, then add the sides, then the front. Hold each piece in place to mark the angle and cut it to size, then attach it with 8d nails before moving on to the next piece. Then cut and install 1x3 fascia over the 1x4 fascia.

Use treated lumber for the corner boards since they're in ground contact. Cut the corner boards to size and nail them into place with 8d nails. Nail the boards on the sides first, then install the boards on the back and front walls, overlapping the side boards (Photo 7).

Cut and nail treated 2x4 door supports flush with the door opening, butted against the fascia. Use 16d nails. The door supports stick out a little proud of the fascia, but the extra thickness is needed to support the doors.

Install a clear roof

Before installing the roof, place wooden panel plugs flush with the outside of the fascia along the front and the back walls. Drill pilot holes through the peaks and nail the plugs into place with 4d nails. The plugs conform to the shape of the roof panels, sealing the openings to keep out the birds and the bees. For roof support along the sides, install supports (quarter round).

Cut the 9-ft.-long roof panels in half with a circular saw. Run a generous bead of silicone caulk along both plugs for 27 in., then set the panels in place so there's an equal overhang on the front and back and about 2 in. on the side.

Drill 1/8-in. pilot holes through every third peak at the plugs and the mid-beams, then insert 1-1/2-in. hexhead panel screws.

Caulk along the edge of the installed roof panel and the panel plugs (Photo 8). Then install the next roof panel. Overlap the panels by 3 in. When you get to the end, cut the last panel to size.

Paint 'er up!

Build the doors using treated lumber and following Figure B. Use scrap siding panels for the door panels since the middle 1x4 hides the gap. Assemble the doors with 6d nails driven at a slight angle so they don't poke through the opposite side. Make sure the seams in the top and bottom scrap pieces are aligned before nailing them into place.

If you haven't painted the locker yet, now is a good time. Install the doors. Start by nailing a scrap piece of wood in front of the opening so the top is 1-1/2 in. from the bottom of the locker. Drill pilot holes and attach heavy-duty door hinges to the top and bottom of both doors. Set both doors in place over the scrap lumber. Insert shims so the doors don't pinch at the top and side, then attach the hinges to the door supports with screws (Photo 9). Add handles and a lock as desired.

Garden tool cabinet

Imagine this: You drive home with a carload of new plants and flowers. You open your new outdoor garden tool cabinet and grab your shovel, bulb planter, trimmer or whatever you need—and it's all there in plain view! This scenario doesn't have to be a dream. You can build our cabinet in one weekend and paint and organize it the next.

This cabinet is compact, but it can store all of your garden hand tools and still have room for boots, fertilizers and accessories. Most gardeners set aside a tiny spot in their garage for their tools, which often end up tangled in a corner. Now your garden tools can have a home of their own, outside the garage. The design is flexible, so you can customize the interior to suit your needs and add a lock if you wish.

Here you'll learn how to assemble the cabinet in your

garage and then wheel it out and mount it on your garage wall. And you don't have to be a crackerjack carpenter or own special tools to build it.

Besides being good looking, this project is designed to last. The shingled roof will keep the rain out. And if moisture does get in, the slatted bottom and 4-in.-diameter vents near the top allow enough air circulation to dry everything out. The storage cabinet shown is mounted on the outside of a garage, but you can easily mount it to the back of your house or to a shed.

The 4-ft. by nearly 8-ft. cabinet is made from exterior plywood with pine trim. All the materials are available at home centers and lumberyards. You can find a huge variety of tool mounting clips and retainers at hardware stores for hanging rakes, shovels, clippers and everything else. Just let your imagination solve the need. Figure on spending about $250 on the materials, not including hardware or paint.

1 Cut the plywood sides and 2x10 shelf, prop up the shelf with 2x4 blocks and fasten the sides into the shelf with 2-in. deck screws.

2 Turn the assembly over and screw the back to the sides and center shelf. Use a level or straightedge to mark the shelf location on the back side of the plywood.

3 Cut the subrails (D) and the roof supports (H), then screw them into place. Use 2-in. screws for the subrails and 3-in. screws for the roof supports.

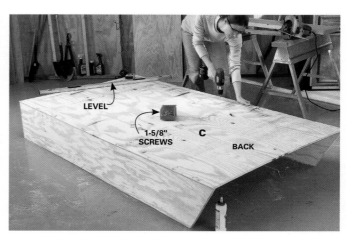

4 Glue and nail the 1x2 cleats (E and F) to the sides, back and subrail (D) and then screw the 1x4 floor slats (G) to the cleats. Start with the center slat and leave 7/16-in. gaps.

Figure A:
Garden tool cabinet

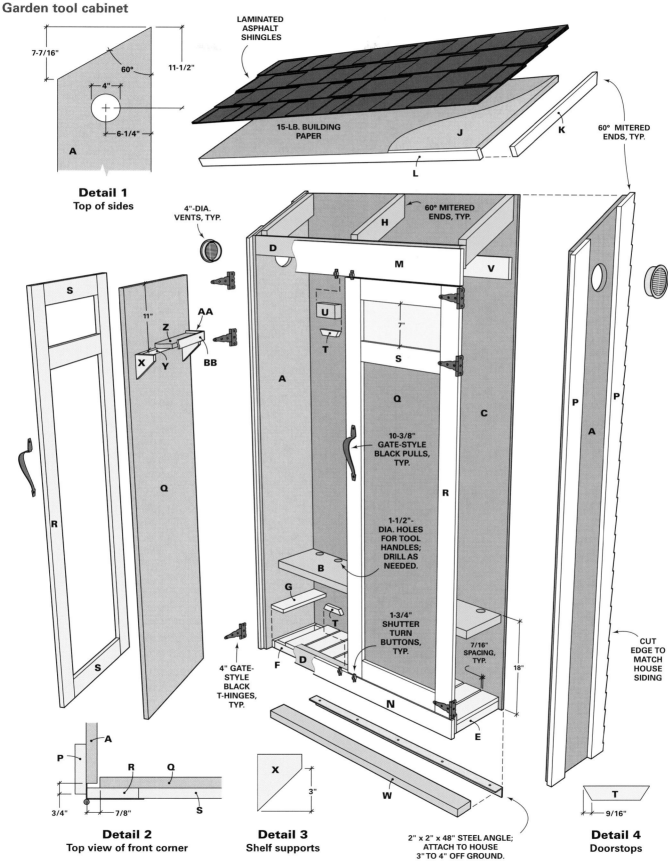

Detail 1
Top of sides

7-7/16"
60°
11-1/2"
4"
6-1/4"
A

LAMINATED ASPHALT SHINGLES

15-LB. BUILDING PAPER

J

K

L

60° MITERED ENDS, TYP.

4"-DIA. VENTS, TYP.

60° MITERED ENDS, TYP.

D
H
M
V
S
Z
AA
X Y BB
11"
U
T
S
A
Q
C
Q
R
7"
10-3/8" GATE-STYLE BLACK PULLS, TYP.
1-1/2"- DIA. HOLES FOR TOOL HANDLES; DRILL AS NEEDED.
R
B
G
T
F D
4" GATE-STYLE BLACK T-HINGES, TYP.
1-3/4" SHUTTER TURN BUTTONS, TYP.
7/16" SPACING, TYP.
18"
N
E
P A P
CUT EDGE TO MATCH HOUSE SIDING

S

R

Detail 2
Top view of front corner

A
P
R Q
S
3/4" 7/8"

Detail 3
Shelf supports

X
3"

W
2" x 2" x 48" STEEL ANGLE; ATTACH TO HOUSE 3" TO 4" OFF GROUND.

Detail 4
Doorstops

T
9/16"

5 Mount the 1x2 roof trim to the 3/4-in. plywood roof, then center it and mark the position. Then temporarily screw it to the roof supports with a pair of 2-in. screws on each side.

6 Glue and screw the 1x4 side trim to the plywood sides, keeping the trim pieces 3/4 in. proud at the front. Cut the 4-in.-diameter side vents.

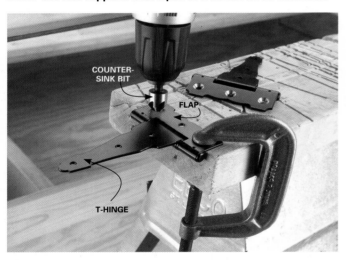

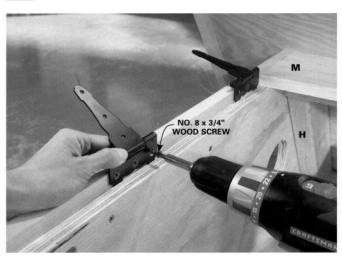

7 Countersink the holes in the inside of the hinge flaps to accept the tapered heads of the mounting screws.

8 Position the flaps of the hinges against the plywood sides at the centers of the door rail locations. Drill pilot holes and drive the screws into the side trim to secure the hinges.

Assemble the main box

Exterior-grade plywood is the basic building material for this project. Unfortunately, you'll never find *absolutely* flat pieces of plywood at a home center or lumberyard, but the flatter you can find them, the better this project will turn out. Choose a BC grade of plywood. This will ensure you have one good side "B" that'll look good on the outside, and the "C" side can go inside.

Once you get the plywood home, keep it out of the sun to reduce the chance of warping. It's best to cut the pieces in the shade or in your garage. A long straightedge cutting guide for your circular saw will help you get nice straight cuts if you don't have a full-size table saw. Look at the Cutting list on p. 253 and cut all the parts to size except the door stiles, rails and trim pieces, which are best cut to fit once you've constructed the main plywood box.

Choose the flattest sheet of 3/4-in. plywood for the door cores. As you lay out all the pieces, choose the best-looking side of the plywood for the painted parts. The sides of the cabinet form a 30-degree slope for the roof. Use a Speed Square (see Photo 1) to mark the angled roof supports (H) and ends of the trim pieces that follow the roofline. It's easier to cut accurate slopes on the larger side pieces (A) by first measuring each side, marking a diagonal line from point to point and then cutting along the mark. Assemble the main box of the cabinet as shown in Figure A and Photos 1–5. Drill pilot holes for all screws with a No. 8 combination countersink and pilot bit. Use 2-in. galvanized deck screws to fasten the sides to the shelf and 1-5/8-in. screws to fasten the back to the sides.

Note: Cut a piece of 1/4-in. hardware cloth to fit under

7/8"
OVERHANG
ON SIDE

9 Glue and nail the door rail and stile trim to the 3/4-in. plywood core. Overhang the stile on the hinge side of each door 7/8 in. See Figure A for the exact placement.

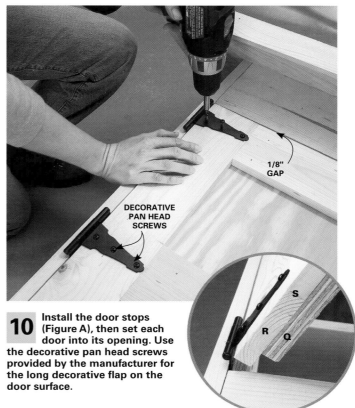

1/8"
GAP

DECORATIVE
PAN HEAD
SCREWS

10 Install the door stops (Figure A), then set each door into its opening. Use the decorative pan head screws provided by the manufacturer for the long decorative flap on the door surface.

the floor slats of the cabinet. This wire mesh will keep furry critters from making your tool cabinet into a cozy winter home!

Cut the roof panel (J) and trim pieces (K and L), then glue and nail the trim to the front and side edges of the roof panel. Center the panel (Photo 5) and temporarily screw it to the roof supports so you can install the side trim (P) and the upper rail (M).

Note: You'll need to remove the roof and the doors after assembly to make the project light enough to move to your site.

Add trim and assemble the doors

Make sure to extend the front edge of each side. Set the trim (P) 3/4 in. beyond the front edge of the plywood side (Photo 6). Next cut and nail the front upper rail (M) and the lower rail (N) to the subrails. Both ends should butt tightly to the side trim.

Even though the doors are made mainly from plywood, the rail and stile trim boards glued and screwed to the front side give the doors a handsome frame-and-panel look. Be sure to lay the doors out on a flat surface and then glue and nail the rails (short vertical pieces) and stiles (long horizontal pieces) to the plywood surface. The stile on each hinge side must hang 3/4 in. past the plywood (see Photo 10 inset).

You'll need to alter the factory T-hinge for the inset design of the doors. The hinge flap is screwed to the side trim (P) as shown in Photo 8. If you were to use the factory-supplied

pan head screws, the door would bind on the screw heads. To solve this problem, taper the edges of the existing holes with a countersink bit. Remove just enough steel (Photo 7) so the head of the tapered No. 8 x 3/4-in. screw fits flush with the hinge flap surface.

Cut the small doorstops with a handsaw and then glue and nail them to the edges of the subrails. With the doorstops in place, set the doors into the opening. Make sure you leave a 1/8-in. gap at the top and bottom and a 3/16-in. gap between the doors. You may need to plane or belt-sand the door edges to get a good fit.

Note: Because the flaps of the hinge that fasten to the side trim are about 7/8 in. wide instead of 3/4 in., your doors will sit about 1/8 in. proud of the side trim.

Mount the cabinet to the wall

Fasten a 4-ft. 2x4 to the top flange of a 4-ft.-long piece of steel angle (Figure A). At a hardware store, you can usually find steel angle that measures 1-1/2 in. x 1-1/2 in. with holes drilled every 3 in., but any steel angle that's 1/8 in. thick or larger will do.

Locate the exact position of your cabinet on the wall at least 3 in. above grade and then fasten the angle to the wall with 1/4-in. galvanized lag screws. It must be level. You may need to cut a course or two of siding to get the angle to lie flat. At the site shown, the garage slab was several inches off the ground, so holes were drilled into the side of the slab, lag shields were installed and steel angle was installed. If your

11 Fasten a steel angle to the foundation with a 2x4 attached to its top (Figure A). Lift the cabinet into place and stabilize it with an 8-ft. 2x4 brace against the ground, forcing the cabinet back against the wall.

2x4 x 8' BRACE

2x4 x 4' MOUNTING BOARD

2" x 2" STEEL ANGLE

slab is too close to the ground, you can fasten the angle farther up into the wood studs of the garage. The weight of your cabinet rests entirely on this wall cleat. It's not necessary to fasten the bottom of the cabinet to it.

Measure the locations of the wall studs and transfer these to the cabinet back. Locate three 1/4-in.-diameter pilot holes in the hang rail (V) and another three holes 4 in. up from the bottom at the stud locations.

Now, strap your cabinet to a furniture dolly (with the doors and roof removed to reduce the weight) and wheel it over to the wall cleat. Set the bottom of the cabinet onto the

If you have vinyl, aluminum or steel siding, here's how to prevent the siding from deforming as you tighten the cabinet to the wall. Instead of tightening the lag screws one at a time, gently tighten them alternately to even out the pressure as you go.

cleat, center it and temporarily brace it against the wall. Drill 5/32-in.-diameter pilot holes into the wall studs using the existing pilot holes as a guide. Drive the 3-in. lag screws (including washers) and snug the cabinet to the wall.

Finishing touches

Lay the side trim (P) against the siding. You may need to trim it with your jigsaw to conform (Photo 12). Screw the roof panel to the cabinet. Staple a layer of 15-lb. building paper to the roof panel and shingle the panel using 7/8-in. roofing nails. Avoid driving shingle nails through the overhangs

where the points might show. When you get to the last course, trim the shingles to fit and run a bead of matching caulk at the siding to seal the edge.

Rehang the doors and then mount the door handles and the catches at the top and bottom of the door. Wait to add your vents until you've finished painting. You can spray-paint the vents to match the color of the sides.

Take a trip to the hardware store and shop for a variety of fasteners, from angle screws to rake and broom holders. Once you finish organizing the cabinet, prime it and then paint it to match your garage, home or shed.

12 Scribe the 1x4 side trim to fit the siding. Cut the notches with a jigsaw. Nail it to the cabinet side. Screw on the roof panel and shingle it.

Cutting list

KEY	PCS.	SIZE & DESCRIPTION
A	2	3/4" x 12-7/8" x 90" plywood sides
B	1	1-1/2" x 9-1/4" x 46-1/2" pine shelf
C	1	1/2" x 48" x 90" plywood back
D	2	1-1/2" x 3-1/2" x 46-1/2" pine subrails
E	2	3/4" x 1-1/2" x 11-3/8" pine bottom cleats
F	2	3/4" x 1-1/2" x 45" pine bottom cleats
G	12	3/4" x 3-1/2" x 11-3/8" pine bottom slat
H	3	1-1/2" x 3-1/2" x 15-1/8" pine roof supports
J	1	3/4" x 21-7/8" x 60" plywood roof
K	2	3/4" x 1-1/2" x 21-7/8" pine roof trim
L	1	3/4" x 1-1/2" x 61-1/2" pine roof trim
M	1	3/4" x 5-1/2" x 48" pine upper rail
N	1	3/4" x 3-1/2" x 48" pine lower rail
P	4	3/4" x 3-1/2" x 91" pine side trim
Q	2	3/4" x 23" x 72-3/4" plywood doors
R	4	3/4" x 3-1/2" x 72-3/4" pine door stile
S	6	3/4" x 3-1/2" x 16-7/8" pine door rail trim
T	2	3/4" x 1" x 4-1/2" pine doorstop
U	1	1-1/2" x 2-7/16" x 4-1/2" pine doorstop support
V	1	3/4" x 3-1/2" x 46-1/2" pine hang rail
W	1	1-1/2" x 3-1/2" x 48" treated mounting board
X	1	3/4" x 3" x 4" pine shelf supports
Y	1	3/4" x 3/4" x 16-1/2" pine shelf-mounting cleat
Z	1	3/4" x 3" x 20" pine shelf
AA	2	1/4" x 1-1/2" x 3" pine shelf edging
BB	1	1/4" x 1-1/2" x 20-1/2" pine shelf edging

Materials list

ITEM	QTY.
3/4" x 4' x 8' BC plywood	2
1/2" x 4' x 8' BC plywood	1
2x10 x 4' pine	1
2x4 x 8' pine	2
1x6 x 8' pine	1
1x4 x 8' pine	12
1x2 x 8' pine	3
2x4 x 8' treated wood	1
12" x 48" hardware cloth (1/4" grid)	1
bundle of asphalt shingles	1
3' x 5' strip of 15-lb. building paper	1
1-5/8" galv. screws	2 lbs.
2" galv. screws	2 lbs.
3" galv. screws	1 lbs.
4" T-hinges	6
Shutter turn buttons	4
4" round vents	2
1-1/4" finish nails	1 lb.
1/4" x 3" galv. lag screws and washers	9
2" x 2" steel angle	1
7/8" shingle nails	1 lb.

Compact storage shed

If you need a home for all your garden tools and supplies but have limited yard space, this small shed is a perfect storage solution. With its 6 x 6-ft. footprint and classic Georgian styling, it fits into tight spots and adds charm to any backyard. The "front room" (53 x 65 in.) provides plenty of space for shelves and even a small potting bench, while the double door on the back of the shed creates a spacious easy-access tool locker. For easy care, choose low-maintenance siding and trim materials that hold paint and resist rot better than wood.

Tools, time and money

This shed was engineered for easy, modular construction; you can build the major parts in your driveway and assemble them on site. While this isn't a complex project, it does require basic building skills. Here you'll learn how to assemble the frame, but not all the finish details like how to hang doors or shingle the roof.

You'll need a drill, a circular saw, a miter saw and a router. Although not absolutely essential, a table saw will make the project go much easier and faster. A compressor is recommended and an air-powered brad nailer makes for faster, better trim installation. Plan to spend two weekends building the shed and another day or two painting. The total materials bill for this shed was about $1,300. If you opt for a blank wall on the back of the shed rather than a double door and a tool locker, you'll save about $200.

Preconstruction planning

Call your city building department to find out whether you need a permit to build this 36-sq.-ft. shed. Also ask about any restrictions on where you can place the shed. If you plan to build near the edge of your lot, for example, you may have to hire a surveyor to locate your property lines. You can build this shed on a site that slopes as much as 6 in. over 6 ft. But if your site is steeper, consider building a low retaining wall to create a level site. To find some of the shed materials—especially the fiber cement panels and composite trim boards—you'll probably have to call local lumberyards or special-order through a home center. Special orders can take six weeks to arrive, so choose your materials long before you plan to build.

Frame the whole shed on your driveway

Framing the floor and walls is the fastest part of this project. Before you get started, select your prehung front

1 Frame the walls and floor following Figures A and B. Cover the floor with 3/4-in. plywood, the walls with cement panels and the divider wall with pegboard.

2 Cut the truss parts and assemble them with 1/2-in. plywood gussets and 1-1/4-in. screws. Screw 1/2-in. spacers to the bottom chord on the main truss.

door so you know the dimensions of the rough opening needed in the front wall. Shown is a 36-in. door that required a 38 x 82-1/2-in. rough opening. Your door may require slightly different dimensions. The big opening at the back of the shed will easily accept two 30-in.-wide prehung doors.

Frame the 6 x 6-ft. floor from pressure-treated 2x6s as shown in Figure A. Whenever you fasten treated lumber,

be sure to use nails or screws that are rated to withstand the corrosive chemicals in the lumber (check the fastener packaging). Use pressure-treated 2x4s for the bottom plates of the walls. Cut the plates to the dimensions shown in Figure B. Then cut 20 wall studs to 94 in. and assemble the four walls. Also frame the small header wall (14 in. x 65 in.) that fits above the back doors.

Before you sheathe the floor and

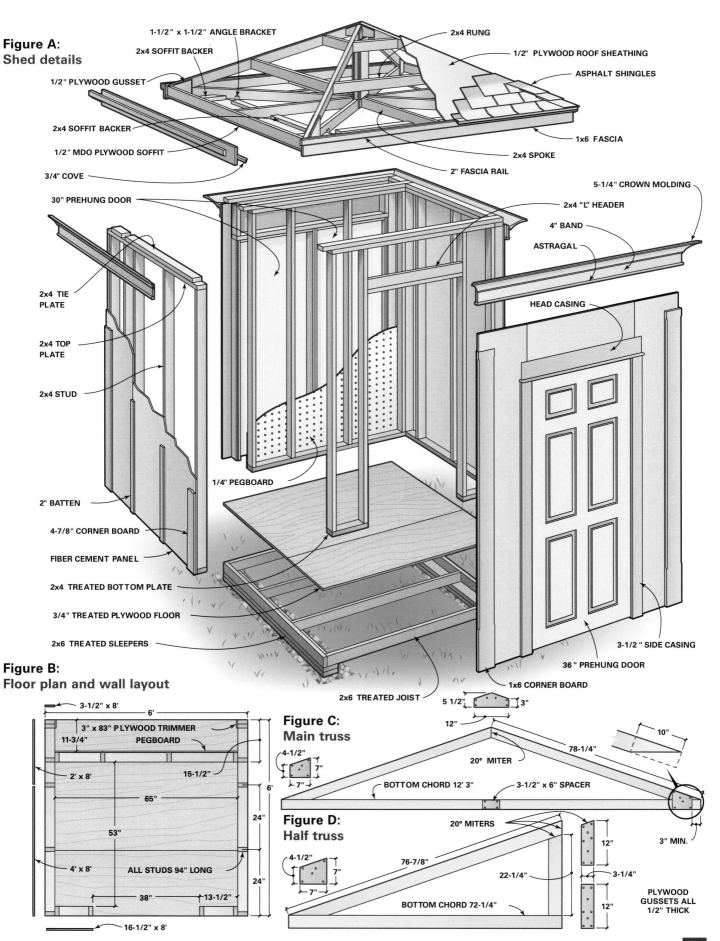

Figure A:
Shed details

1-1/2" x 1-1/2" ANGLE BRACKET

2x4 SOFFIT BACKER

1/2" PLYWOOD GUSSET

2x4 SOFFIT BACKER

1/2" MDO PLYWOOD SOFFIT

3/4" COVE

30" PREHUNG DOOR

2x4 TIE PLATE

2x4 TOP PLATE

2x4 STUD

2" BATTEN

4-7/8" CORNER BOARD

FIBER CEMENT PANEL

2x4 TREATED BOTTOM PLATE

3/4" TREATED PLYWOOD FLOOR

2x6 TREATED SLEEPERS

2x4 RUNG

1/2" PLYWOOD ROOF SHEATHING

ASPHALT SHINGLES

1x6 FASCIA

2x4 SPOKE

2" FASCIA RAIL

5-1/4" CROWN MOLDING

2x4 "L" HEADER

4" BAND

ASTRAGAL

HEAD CASING

1/4" PEGBOARD

3-1/2" SIDE CASING

36" PREHUNG DOOR

1x6 CORNER BOARD

2x6 TREATED JOIST

Figure B:
Floor plan and wall layout

3-1/2" x 8'

6'

3" x 83" PLYWOOD TRIMMER

11-3/4" PEGBOARD

2' x 8'   15-1/2"

65"

53"

4' x 8'   ALL STUDS 94" LONG

38"   13-1/2"

16-1/2" x 8'

6'

24"

24"

Figure C:
Main truss

5 1/2"   3"

12"

4-1/2"
7"
7"

20° MITER

78-1/4"

10"

BOTTOM CHORD 12' 3"   3-1/2" x 6" SPACER

3" MIN.

Figure D:
Half truss

4-1/2"
7"
7"

20° MITERS

76-7/8"

22-1/4"

12"

3-1/4"

12"

BOTTOM CHORD 72-1/4"

PLYWOOD GUSSETS ALL 1/2" THICK

wall frames, take corner-to-corner diagonal measurements to make sure each frame is square. Fasten 3/4-in. treated plywood to the floor frame with 1-5/8-in. screws. Also screw pegboard to the interior pegboard wall. Nail cement panels to the front and sidewalls (Photo 1). Position the cement panels flush with the bottom plate, not the top plate (the wall frames are 1 in. taller than the cement panels). The two sidewalls have identical framing, but be sure to attach the sheathing so the right and left sides mirror each other. The cement panels on the front wall overhang the framing by 3 in.

A complex roof made simple

A typical pyramid roof requires lots of compound angle cuts and endless trips up a ladder to test-fit all the tricky parts. Not this one. There are no compound angles or complex calculations at all. And ground-level construction means faster progress with less strain.

Build the main truss and two half trusses first (Photo 2). Choose the straightest 2x4s you can find for these parts. Figures C and D show the dimensions and angles. Your angle cuts don't have to be perfect; the gussets will make the trusses plenty strong even if the parts don't fit tightly.

Join the three trusses with two hub gussets (Photo 3) made from plywood left over from the floor. The "rungs" that fit between the trusses have 45-degree bevel cuts on both ends. You can tilt the shoe of your circular saw to cut bevels or use a miter saw. In order to create a square roof frame, all four lower rungs must be the same length. Cut them to 103-1/8 in., set them all in place to check the fit and then trim them all by the same amount until they fit identically between the trusses.

With the lower rungs in place, insert the spokes (Photo 4). One end

3 Screw half trusses to the main truss and tie them together with 9 x 21-in. hub gussets and 2-1/2-in. screws. Trim the main truss to form a pyramid.

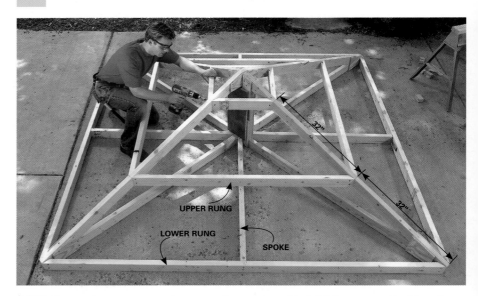

4 Fasten the upper rungs between the trusses with 2-1/2-in. screws. Position the outer edge of the rungs flush with the tops of the trusses.

5 Dig two trenches 6 in. deep and fill them with pea gravel. Then level treated 2x6 sleepers over the gravel and set the floor on the sleepers.

6 Anchor the walls to the floor with 3-in. screws. Start with a sidewall, then add the front wall, followed by the pegboard wall and the other sidewall.

PLYWOOD TRIMMER

REAR HEADER

TIE PLATE

7 Set the rear header on 1/2-in. plywood trimmers and screw it into place from inside. Nail on overlapping tie plates to lock the walls together.

SOFFIT BACKERS

8 Screw 16-ft. 2x4s to the shed to form a ramp. Position your stepladders before you slide the roof frame up the ramp and onto the shed. Center the roof frame and fasten the trusses at each corner with a pair of angle brackets. Install 2x4s to provide nailing backers for the soffit.

of each spoke has a double bevel cut; make a 45-degree bevel from one side, then flip the 2x4 over and cut from the other side. This forms a 90-degree point that fits into the corner where the main truss and half truss meet. To complete the roof frame, install the upper rungs (Photo 4).

Assemble the shed on site

The shed floor rests on a simple foundation: 2x6 pressure-treated "sleepers" laid on a bed of pea gravel. Dig two parallel trenches about 10 in. wide, 6 in. deep and centered 6 ft. apart. The trenches can run parallel to the sidewalls or the front and back walls of the shed. Fill the trenches with pea gravel. Lay the 6-ft.-long sleepers on the gravel. Using a level, determine which sleeper is higher (Photo 5). Level the higher sleeper along its length by adding or removing small amounts of gravel. Then add a little gravel under the other sleeper to make it level with the first. On a sloped site, one end of a sleeper may sit below grade while the other rests above the surrounding soil. You can also screw extra layers of 2x6 over the sleepers to compensate for a sloped site. For the shed shown, two extra layers were added to both sleepers. That raised the shed and allows you to slope the surrounding soil away from the shed. Set the floor on the sleepers so that the joists span the space between the sleepers. At each corner, drive a 3-in. screw at an angle through the floor frame into the sleepers.

Stand the walls and set the roof

You'll need a helper to carry and stand up the walls. Set one of the sidewalls in place and screw it to the floor every 2 ft. Position the bottom plate (not the cement sheathing) flush with the outer edge of the floor. Use a level to make sure the rear end of the wall is plumb and brace it with a 2x4 (Photo

6). Position the front wall and screw it to the floor. Then drive 1-5/8-in. screws through the overhanging front sheathing to tie the front and sidewalls together. Add the pegboard wall next, followed by the other sidewall and finally the rear header wall. Make sure all the walls are plumb, and nail tie plates over the walls (Photo 7).

To safely set the 160-lb. roof frame into place, you'll need two helpers, two stepladders and a ramp made from a pair of 16-ft.-long 2x4s. Secure each 2x4 with three 3-in. screws and brace them near the middle with a horizontal 2x4. Then simply slide the roof frame up the ramp and onto the shed (Photo 8). Center the roof frame so that all four lower rungs are the same distance (16-1/2 in.) from and parallel to the walls. Fasten the roof frame with metal angle brackets and install soffit backers (Photo 8) before you sheathe the roof with 1/2-in. plywood (Photo 9).

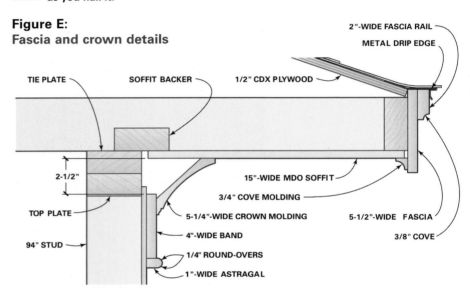

9 Sheathe the roof with 1/2-in. plywood. Cut each piece 3 in. extra long, nail it in place and cut off the excess. Temporary support blocks help position the plywood as you nail it.

Figure E:
Fascia and crown details

TIE PLATE
SOFFIT BACKER
1/2" CDX PLYWOOD
2"-WIDE FASCIA RAIL
METAL DRIP EDGE
2-1/2"
TOP PLATE
94" STUD
15"-WIDE MDO SOFFIT
3/4" COVE MOLDING
5-1/4"-WIDE CROWN MOLDING
4"-WIDE BAND
1/4" ROUND-OVERS
1"-WIDE ASTRAGAL
5-1/2"-WIDE FASCIA
3/8" COVE

tip

"Fiber cement" siding is basically cement reinforced with cellulose fibers. It was used for this shed because it's durable, affordable and rot-proof, but especially because it holds paint longer than most other exterior materials. Exactly how much longer depends on a variety of factors, but builders have told of cases where paint on fiber cement lasted twice as long as paint on nearby wood.

Fiber cement is most common in a plank form that's used for lap siding. But it's also available in 4 x 8-ft. sheets (3/16 in. thick) with textured or smooth surfaces (this one used the smooth). Some home centers and lumberyards stock the sheet material; others have to special-order it (about $30 per sheet).

Working with fiber cement is a lot like using other sheet materials. Pick up a brochure where you buy the panels or go to the manufacturer's Web site for specific instructions. You have to leave 1/8-in. spaces between sheets, for example. When nailing, place nails at least 3/8 in. from edges and 2 in. from corners. Although pros use special blades to cut fiber cement, you can cut it with a standard carbide circular saw blade. Cutting whips up a thick cloud of nasty dust, so a dust mask is mandatory.

Two suppliers of fiber cement siding are jameshardie.com and certainteed.com.

Figure F:
Corner boards

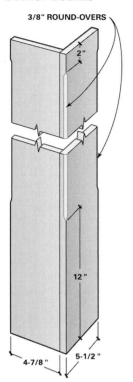

3/8" ROUND-OVERS

2"

12"

4-7/8"

5-1/2"

CORNER BOARD

10 Nail and glue the corner boards in place. Install the narrower side first, making sure it's flush with the corner. Then add the full-width piece.

Figure G:
Door trim

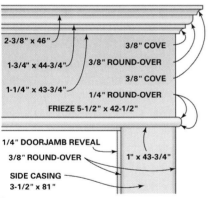

2-3/8" x 46"

3/8" COVE

1-3/4" x 44-3/4"

3/8" ROUND-OVER

3/8" COVE

1-1/4" x 43-3/4"

1/4" ROUND-OVER

FRIEZE 5-1/2" x 42-1/2"

1/4" DOORJAMB REVEAL

3/8" ROUND-OVER

1" x 43-3/4"

SIDE CASING
3-1/2" x 81"

(The lengths of your trim components may differ)

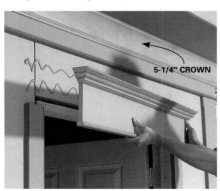

5-1/4" CROWN

FRIEZE

11 Nail and glue the moldings to the frieze board one at a time. Then fasten the head casing above the door with construction adhesive and brad nails.

Elegant trim from plain boards

Most of the trim on our shed is made from a "composite" material that stands up to Mother Nature better than wood (see Tip, p. 260). Shown are pine wood moldings only where they're sheltered from sun and rain. The composite boards shown here are 5/8 in. thick and come in the same widths as standard wood boards. In a few cases these boards were used "as is." But for most of the trim parts a router was used. The router work adds only a couple of hours to the project and creates a much more elegant look. You'll need three router bits to shape the trim boards: a 1/4-in. round-over, a 3/8-in. round-over and a 3/8-in. cove bit. Figures E and F provide the specifics. Here are some other details:

■ Install the fascia and fascia rails first (Figure E). Then shingle the roof. Shown are asphalt shingles. Be sure to install metal drip edge over the fascia.

■ Composite trim must be butted at corners, not mitered, since miter joints often open over time.

■ For soffit material, 1/2-in. MDO (medium density overlay), which is plywood with a tough resin coating, was used. MDO is available at some home centers and lumberyards ($45 per 4 x 8-ft. sheet). You could also use plywood or fiber cement soffit board.

■ For the crown molding under the soffits, a large (5-1/4-in.) cove profile (Figure E) was used. To get molding that wide, you may have to visit a lumberyard or special-order from a home center.

■ Corner boards hide nail heads and the edges of the cement panels (Photo 10). To hide the cement panel joints and other nails, nail and glue two 2-in.-wide battens over the studs on each sidewall.

Composite trim looks better after it's installed and keeps its good looks longer than wood. Every board is straight and free of imperfections like knots or splits. It doesn't chip or splinter when you cut or rout it. It holds paint longer than wood and resists rot better than most "rot-resistant" woods. As a bonus, composite costs less than good-quality wood boards.

Composites aren't perfect; they're heavy and floppy, so they're more difficult to install solo. Cutting or routing churns up a thick, powdery dust cloud, so always wear a dust mask and do your cutting outdoors. The material is harder than wood and difficult to nail by hand. Manufacturers recommend using a framing nailer or predrilling and hand nailing. Predrilling is slow and framing nails leave big, ugly nail heads to cover up. So I use a brad nailer along with plenty of exterior-grade construction adhesive. Brads alone don't have enough holding power, but they hold the trim in place until the adhesive sets.

Composite trim is available at lumberyards and some home centers.

Materials list

ITEM	QTY.
2x6 x 12' treated	4
2x4 x 8' (2 treated, 28 untreated)	30
2x4 x 10'	6
2x4 x 12'	4
2x4 x 14'	1
2x4 x 16'	2
3/4" treated plywood	2
1/2" CDX plywood	5
MDO plywood	2
1x6 x 16' composite trim	14
4 x 8'' fiber cement panels	5
10' metal drip edge	4
30" doors	2
36" door	1
Doorknobs	3
1 square of shingles	
30' of ridge shingles	
Construction adhesive	4 tubes
Acrylic caulk	2 tubes
L-brackets	8
3" exterior screws	1 lb.
2-1/2" exterior screws	1 lb.
1-5/8" exterior screws	1 lb.
1-1/4" exterior screws	1 lb.
8d galvanized nails	5 lbs.
16d galvanized nails	5 lbs.
1" roofing nails	5 lbs.
1-1/4" brads	
1-3/4" brads	
Pea gravel (50-lb. bags)	10

The 22-in.-tall copper roof finial plus many others are available at weathervanesofmaine.com.

Doors and casing

For this shed, a classic six-panel door was chosen for the front of the shed and it was trimmed with elaborate casing. To make the side casings, just rip your trim material to 3-1/2 in. wide and rout both edges with a round-over bit. Install the side casings so they project 1/4 in. above the doorjamb opening. Your side casings may be slightly longer or shorter than the length listed in Figure G.

Photo 11 shows how to assemble the head casing that fits over the side casings. The five parts that make up the head casing may also be longer or shorter than the lengths listed in Figure G. To determine the correct lengths, measure across the side casings from the outer edge on one to the outer edge of the other. For this shed, that measurement was 42-1/2 in. If your measurement is more or less, just add or subtract from the length measurements given in Figure G.

Two simple prehung 30-in. steel doors: a left-hand swing and a right (about $100 each) were purchased for the tool locker on the back of the shed. The factory-installed trim was pulled off the doors and the jambs were screwed together to form a double door. To stiffen the assembly, screw a 4-in.-wide strip of 1/2-in. plywood across the top of the jambs. Then install the double door backward, so it swings out rather than inward (see p. 255).

The corner boards on the back side of the shed act as the door casing, so you can't install them until the doors are in place. Don't round over the edges of these back corner boards. To complete the back-door casing, install a composite 1x6 above the doors.

Primer and caulk for a lasting paint job

Prime the wood and fiber cement with high-quality acrylic primer. The composite trim is factory-primed, but you'll have to prime any exposed cut ends and all the routed profiles. Be sure to prime the bottom ends of the corner boards and battens so they don't absorb moisture. The primer will raise wood fibers in the exposed composite, leaving a rough surface. Remove these "whiskers" by lightly sanding with 100-grit sandpaper.

Careful, thorough caulking is essential for a lasting paint job because it prevents moisture from penetrating the cement panels and trim. Fill all the nail holes and seal any gaps between and along the trim parts with acrylic caulk. Also caulk the two short cement panel joints above the door. After the caulk cures, apply two coats of high-quality acrylic paint.

Outdoor storage & organizing

hints & tips

Overhead storage for garden tools

Rakes, shovels, brooms and other long-handled tools seem to be in the way no matter how they're stored in the garage. Here's a rack that works: Cut two pieces of plywood about 12 in. x 48 in. and drill matching 2-in. holes in each, spaced about 6 in. apart. Mount the racks on crossties below your garage roof rafters.

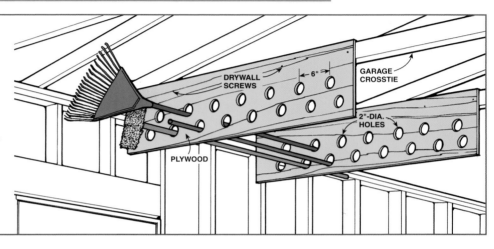

DRYWALL SCREWS

6"

GARAGE CROSSTIE

2"-DIA. HOLES

PLYWOOD

Long-handled tool

Cut an old hose into 7-in. pieces, slit them, and nail them to the wall to make good holders for handled tools in the garage.

2-minute tool rack

One way to get rid of clutter in your storage shed or garage is to screw 16-in. scrap 2x4s at a slight upward angle to each side of a wall stud. They will hold a wide variety of yard tools.

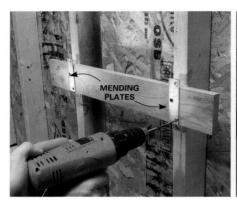

Wheelbarrow rack

Hang your wheelbarrow on the garage wall to free up floor space. Center a 2-ft. 1x4 across two studs, 2 ft. above the floor. Tack it into place, then drive 3-in. screws through metal mending plates and the 1x4, into the studs. Leave about 3/4 in. of the plate sticking above the 1x4 to catch the rim. Rest the wheelbarrow on the 1x4 as shown, and mark the studs 1 in. above the wheelbarrow bucket. Drill pilot holes and screw ceiling hooks into the studs. Twist the hooks so they catch on the wheelbarrow lip and hold it in place.

Yard tool organizer

Create a simple long-handled tool hanger out of two 1x4s. On the first one, drill a series of 2-in. holes along the edge of the board. The trick is to center each hole about 1 in. from the edge. That leaves a 1-1/2-in. slot in the front that you can slip the handles through. Space the holes to accommodate whatever it is you're hanging. Screw that board to another 1x4 for the back and add 45-degree brackets to keep it from sagging. If you wish, pound nails into the vertical board to hang even more stuff. No more tripping over the shovels to get to the rakes!

Lawn tool carrier

An old golf bag with a cart makes a perfect holder for garden tools. The large wheels make it easy to haul the tools over long distances and rough terrain.

Propane tank carrier

When you take your 20-lb. propane tank to be filled, does it always roll around in the trunk of your car? To solve the problem, stick it in an old milk crate. The crate's wide, flat base keeps the tank stable.

Bulb storage

Tender bulbs that must be overwintered indoors are hard to keep organized. These include canna lilies, freesias, caladiums, gladioluses, dahlias and tuberous begonias. Keep track of who's who by storing them in egg cartons, with each bulb identified on the top of the carton. The cartons even have ventilation holes that help prevent rot and mildew.

Garden tool hideaway

A mailbox near your garden provides a convenient home for tools. A small mailbox like this one costs less than $10 at hardware stores and home centers. King-size models cost about $25.

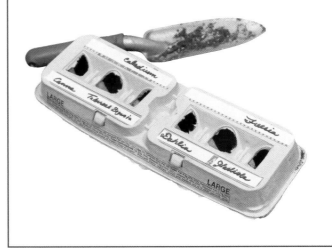

Hose caddy

Here's an easy way to store unwieldy garden hoses without strangling yourself. Coil them up in a round laundry basket or plastic bucket. Then hang the basket or bucket on the garage wall or slide it into an obscure corner.

Milk jug tarp weights

Use milk jugs partially filled with water or sand to weight the edges of a tarp. It looks weird, but for awkwardly shaped stuff it works better than trying to tie the tarp down.

Lid leash

Tired of losing your garbage can lid because the wind blew it away, or because it skittered away when you tried to knock it off when your hands were full of trash? Drill a small hole just below the rim of the can, and another near the center of the lid. Then thread a 24-in. length of rope through the holes, and knot the ends as shown. The lid will always be right there when you go to put it back.

No-tip garbage cans

There really is a simple way to keep those garbage cans from getting blown or knocked over. For each garbage can, all you need are two 3/4-in. screw eyes and a 30-in. hook-end elastic cord from the hardware store.

Storing your lawn mower for the winter

Gasoline left in your mower during storage can deteriorate and leave gum deposits that clog the fuel system. There are two storage methods: completely draining the system or leaving it completely filled with fresh, stabilized gasoline.

Most manufacturers of newer mowers recommend draining the gas completely. Do this by opening the drain valve or drain bolt on the carburetor bowl and draining the gas into a container. If your carburetor doesn't have a drain valve, check with the manufacturer or lawn mower repair center for instructions.

Older lawn mowers with a foam filter and carburetor that's screwed to the top of the gas tank should be filled with stabilized fuel for the winter. Purchase a container of fuel stabilizer, available at hardware stores, home centers, gas stations or lawn mower service centers, and mix as recommended with fresh gas. Fill the empty lawn mower tank with the stabilized gas and run the mower for about 10 minutes. Then top off the fuel tank with stabilized gas and shut the fuel valve. Check your owner's manual for storage instructions.

Simple spiral hose storage

Here's a handy tip for storing your spiral hoses next winter so you won't end up with a tangled mess in the spring. Just wrap them around the handle of a rake or shovel you won't be using during the winter. Your long-handled tool will do double duty by keeping your hoses tangle-free.

Storage hooks

Get ladders, tree pruners, kids' bikes and other unwieldy items off your garage floor with these inexpensive PVC hooks. For heavy items you could even make them out of iron pipe.

Handy bench and tool bucket

A 5-gallon bucket comes in handy out in the garden—and not just for collecting weeds. You can load it up with all your gardening tools and carry them easily from place to place. If it starts to rain, protect the tools with the lid. But here's the best part—it doubles as a portable stool when you need to rest or do some pruning. The only problem is that the lid can be hard to pry off. Solve that by cutting off all but two of the plastic tabs. The lid will go on and off in a snap.

Simple shelves

Stud-space cabinet

When you can't find a convenient nook for a set of shelves, you can often create one by recessing the shelves into the wall itself. Choose the location before you build the project to make sure it will fit. Start by looking for a space with no obvious obstructions. Locate the studs with a stud finder. Some stud finders can also locate electrical wires and plumbing pipes inside walls. When you've found a promising spot, cut a 6-in.-square inspection hole between the studs. Use a flashlight and a small mirror to inspect the stud cavity for obstructions. You can often modify the size of the cabinet to avoid obstructions.

When you find a good space, mark the perimeter of the opening and use a drywall keyhole saw to cut it out. Measure the opening and subtract 1/4 in. from the height and width to determine the outer dimensions of your cabinet.

For standard 2x4 stud walls with 1/2-in.-thick drywall, build the cabinet frame from 1x4s that measure 3-1/2 in. wide (see illustration). If your walls are different, adjust the depth of the frame accordingly. Then add a 1/4-in. back. Screw 1/4-in. pegboard to the back so you can hang stuff from pegboard hooks.

Add casing that matches the trim in your house. Drill holes into the sides to accept shelf supports. Shelf supports fit in 3mm, 5mm or 1/4-in. holes depending on the style.

Install the cabinet by slipping it into the opening, leveling it and nailing through the trim into the studs on each side. Use 6d finish nails placed every 12 in. along both sides.

1/4" PEGBOARD

14"

1x4 (3/4" x 3-1/2")

2" SCREWS

CASING

81"

HOLES FOR SHELF SUPPORTS

3-1/2"

4d FINISH NAIL

Bonus storage space! Take a few hours and remove the drywall from between two studs, then construct a shallow cabinet to fit the space.

Between studs shelving

Store smaller containers—spray paint, putty cans, glue bottles—right in the wall! Screw shelf brackets to the studs, then install shelves, cut from standard 1x4 boards, on adjustable clips. The boards fit perfectly; there's no need to saw them to width.

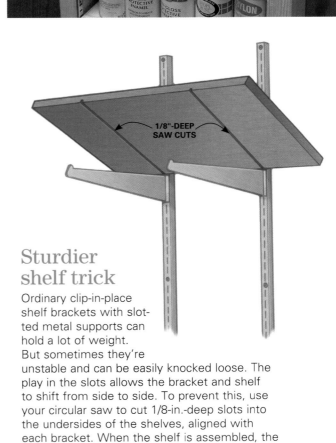

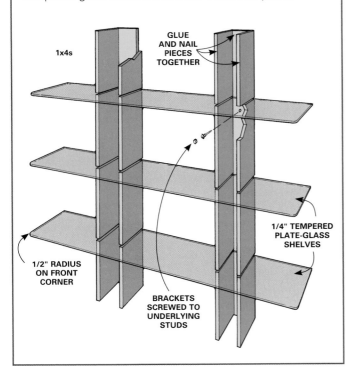

SNAP-IN CLIPS

STUD

INEXPENSIVE SHELF BRACKETS

Display shelving

Assemble this simple shelf from 1x4s and tempered glass. Fasten the side boards to the 4-ft. back sections with wood glue and 6d finish nails. Paint the brackets and screw them to wall studs. Buy round-cornered tempered glass shelves and slide them into place.

1x4s

GLUE AND NAIL PIECES TOGETHER

1/4" TEMPERED PLATE-GLASS SHELVES

1/2" RADIUS ON FRONT CORNER

BRACKETS SCREWED TO UNDERLYING STUDS

1/8"-DEEP SAW CUTS

Sturdier shelf trick

Ordinary clip-in-place shelf brackets with slotted metal supports can hold a lot of weight. But sometimes they're unstable and can be easily knocked loose. The play in the slots allows the bracket and shelf to shift from side to side. To prevent this, use your circular saw to cut 1/8-in.-deep slots into the undersides of the shelves, aligned with each bracket. When the shelf is assembled, the brackets fit into the slots, eliminating the sway.

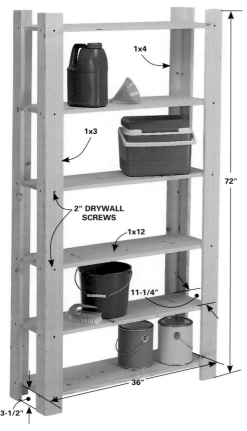

1x4

1x3

2" DRYWALL
SCREWS

1x12

72"

11-1/4"

36"

3-1/2"

Utility shelves

This sturdy, freestanding shelf unit can be made from any inexpensive 1-by lumber (3/4 in. thick) for the legs, and plywood or particleboard for the shelves. Glue and nail the four L-shaped legs together with 6d finish nails. Clamp the shelves in place, getting them evenly spaced and level, then secure each shelf with eight 2-in. screws through the legs.

Sliding bookends

To corral shelf-dwelling books or CDs that like to wander, cut 3/4-in.-thick hardwood pieces into 6-in. squares. Use a band saw or jigsaw to cut a slot along one edge (with the grain) that's a smidgen wider than the shelf thickness. Stop the notch 3/4 in. from the other edge. Finish the bookend and slide it on the shelf.

PVC
FENCE POST

Stadium-seating bookshelf

Cut a hollow PVC fence post to the length of your bookshelf and push it to the back of the shelf. This creates a second tier for paperback storage, doubling the number of books you can put on display.

Petite shelves

Turn a single 3-ft.-long, 1x12 hardwood board into some small shelves to organize a desktop or counter. Cut off a 21-in.-long board for the shelves, rip it in the middle to make two shelves, and cut 45-degree bevels on the two long front edges with a router or table saw. Bevel the ends of the other board, then cut dadoes (grooves cut into the wood) with a router or a table saw with a dado blade (cut a dado on scrap and test-fit the shelves first!). Rip it into four narrower boards, two at 1-3/8 in. wide and two at 4 in. Finish, then assemble with brass screws and finish washers.

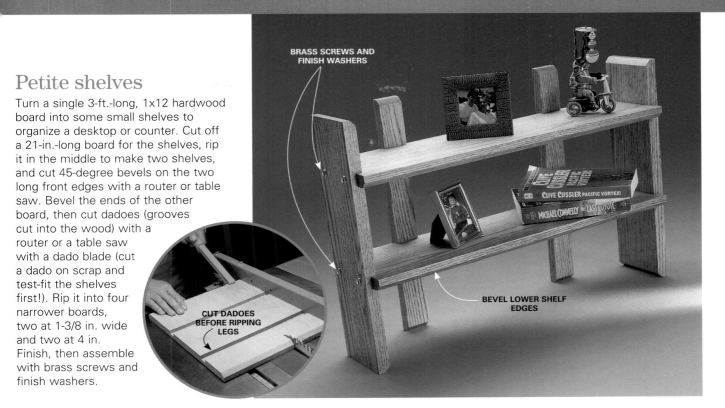

BRASS SCREWS AND FINISH WASHERS

CUT DADOES BEFORE RIPPING LEGS

BEVEL LOWER SHELF EDGES

Portable bookshelf

Here's a cool knock-down shelf for a dorm room or den. You just slide the shelves between the dowels, and they pinch the shelves to stiffen the bookshelf. It works great if you're careful about two things:

- Make the space between the dowel holes exactly 1/16 in. wider than the thickness of the shelf board.

- Be sure the shelf thickness is the same from end to end and side to side.

After test-fitting a dowel in a trial hole (you want a tight fit), drill holes in a jig board so the space between the holes is your shelf thickness plus 1/16 in. Clamp the jig board on the ends of the risers and drill the holes. Cut the dowels 1-3/4 in. longer than the shelf width, then dry assemble (no glue). Mark the angled ends of the risers parallel to the shelves and cut off the tips to make the risers sit flat. Disassemble and glue the dowels in the riser holes. When the glue dries, slide the shelves in and load them up.

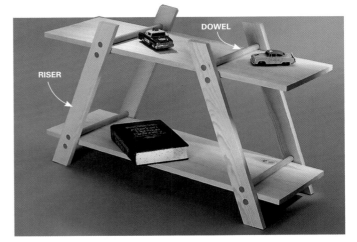

DOWEL

RISER

Cutting list

2 shelves: 11-1/4 in. wide x 3 ft. long, perfectly flat 1x12 lumber or plywood

4 risers: 2-1/4 in. wide x 24 in. long

8 dowels: 3/4 in. dia. x 13 in. long

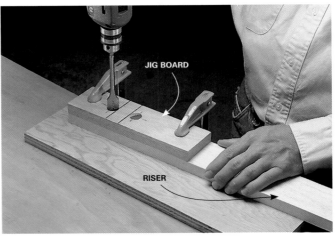

JIG BOARD

RISER

Build sturdy, simple shelves, custom sized to hold boxes or other storage containers.

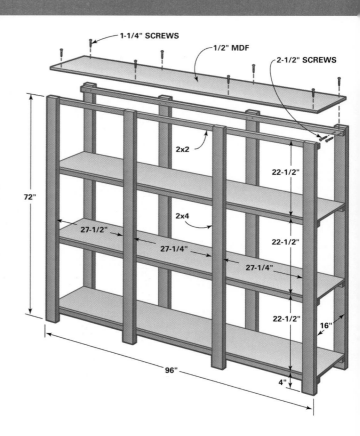

Sturdy storage shelves

Store-bought shelving units are either hard to assemble, flimsy or awfully expensive. Here's a better solution. These shelves are strong, easy to build and cost about $70. The sturdy shelf unit is sized to hold standard bankers' boxes. If you want deeper storage, build the shelves 24 in. deep and buy 24-in.-deep boxes. If you prefer to use plastic storage bins, measure the size of the containers and modify the shelf and upright spacing to fit.

Refer to the dimensions above to mark the location of the horizontal 2x2 on the back of four 2x4s. Also mark the position of the 2x4 uprights on the 2x2s. Then simply line up the marks and screw the 2x2s to the 2x4s with pairs of 2-1/2-in. wood screws. Be sure to keep the 2x2s and 2x4s at right angles. Rip a 4 x 8-ft. sheet of 1/2-in. MDF, plywood or OSB into 16-in.-wide strips and screw it to the 2x2s to connect the two frames and form the shelving unit.

You can modify the study storage shelves above and create a great-looking storage center.

The only modifications to the project shown above are the addition of one shelf, the 22-1/2-in. measurement was changed to 14 in., and the 4-in. measurement was changed to 6 in.

Overall dimensions:
62-1/2" tall x 96" wide x 19" deep

Paint used on shelves:
Behr Premium Plus Eggshell Castlestone 360E-2

Behind-the-door shelves

The space behind a door is a storage spot that's often overlooked. Build a set of shallow shelves and mount it to the wall. The materials cost about $40 and you'll be finished in just a couple of hours. Measure the distance between the door hinge and the wall and subtract an inch. This is the maximum depth of the shelves. Use 1x4s for the sides, top and shelves. Screw the sides to the top. Then screw three 1x2 hanging strips to the sides: one top and bottom and one centered. Nail metal shelf standards to the sides. Complete the shelves by nailing a 1x2 trim piece to the sides and top. The 1x2 dresses up the shelf unit and keeps the shelves from falling off the shelf clips.

Locate the studs. Drill clearance holes and screw the shelves to the studs with 2-1/2-in. wood screws. Put a rubber bumper on the frame to protect the door.

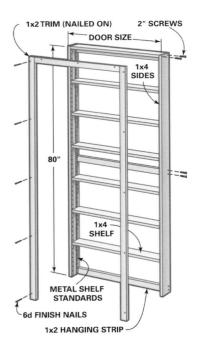

- 1x2 TRIM (NAILED ON)
- 2" SCREWS
- DOOR SIZE
- 1x4 SIDES
- 80"
- 1x4 SHELF
- METAL SHELF STANDARDS
- 6d FINISH NAILS
- 1x2 HANGING STRIP

Build shallow shelves to fit behind the door in your laundry room, utility room or pantry.

---

tip

Stud-space shelves

Open wall framing in a basement or garage makes ideal storage space for narrow items like cleaning supplies or small boxes of nails and screws. Simply cut 2x4s to fit between the studs and toe-screw them in to form shelves.

Traditional bookcase

This is one of those rare woodworking projects that has it all: high style at a low cost, and fast, easy construction that delivers sturdy, lasting results. This bookcase design is versatile, too. You can easily make it shorter or taller, wider or deeper. With a little know-how, you can even adapt the building methods to other projects; the fireplace mantel shown here was built using similar techniques.

You could save a few hours of work by building just one bookcase, but there's a financial incentive to build two. By mostly using the plywood left over from the first bookcase, you can get a second one for half price!

You'll need a table saw and a miter saw for this project. A pneumatic brad nailer will make the job faster and easier. All the materials are at home centers. You may not find the solid wood panel shown here for the bookshelf top (made from glued-together boards). You could use oak stair tread material or glue boards together. Also, the home center may not carry the board widths listed on p. 276, but you can easily rip wider boards to width.

A plywood box, dressed up with simple trim

This was the challenge given to a team of professional woodworkers: Build a classic Craftsman-style bookcase using construction methods that any intermediate builder could handle. The result is a screw-together plywood shelf trimmed with strips of solid wood. There's no fancy joinery—no dadoes, biscuits or dowels. And that simplicity also makes this a quick project. You can easily build a pair of bookcases in one weekend and apply the finish the following weekend.

Cut the plywood parts

To get started, rip the plywood parts to width on a table saw. If cutting full sheets is difficult in your small shop, cut the parts slightly oversized with a circular saw and then trim them on the table saw. Rip two 9-in.-wide planks of 3/4-in. plywood (for the shelves) and two from the 1/2-in. plywood (for the sides). Then cut them to length. To make the cross-cuts with a miter saw, use a stop block (Photo 1).

Next, drill the screw holes in the sides using a 3/32-in. bit (Photo 2). Measuring from the bottom, mark the screw holes at 3-3/8, 16-1/8, 26-7/8, 37-5/8, 48-3/8 and 58-1/8 in.

Position the holes 1 in. from the edges so the screw heads will be covered by the stiles later.

Sand all the plywood parts before assembly to avoid awkward inside-corner sanding later. Plywood usually requires only a light sanding with 150-grit paper. But watch for shallow dents or scratches that need a little extra sanding. And be careful not to sand through the micro-thin veneer along the edges.

Assemble the case

When you screw the sides to the shelves, use plywood spacers to eliminate measuring errors and out-of-square shelves

Figure A:
Traditional bookcase

With this simple design, you can easily alter the dimensions to suit your needs. This bookcase is 60 in. tall, 11 in. deep and 33-1/2 in. wide.

Materials list

ITEM	QTY.
3/4" x 4' x 8' plywood (shelves)	1
1/2" x 4' x 8' plywood (sides)	1
1/4" x 4' x 8' plywood (back)	1*
1x2 x 6' solid wood (shelf rails, front and side stiles)	7*
1x3 x 6' solid wood (arched rails, rear side stiles)	3*
1x12 x 3' glued panel (top)	1*

Wood glue, No. 8 x 2" screws, No. 6 x 3/4" screws, 1-3/4" finish nails

*To build two bookcases, double these quantities.

Solid wood thicknesses and widths given are nominal. Actual thickness is 3/4 in. Actual widths are 1/2 in. less.

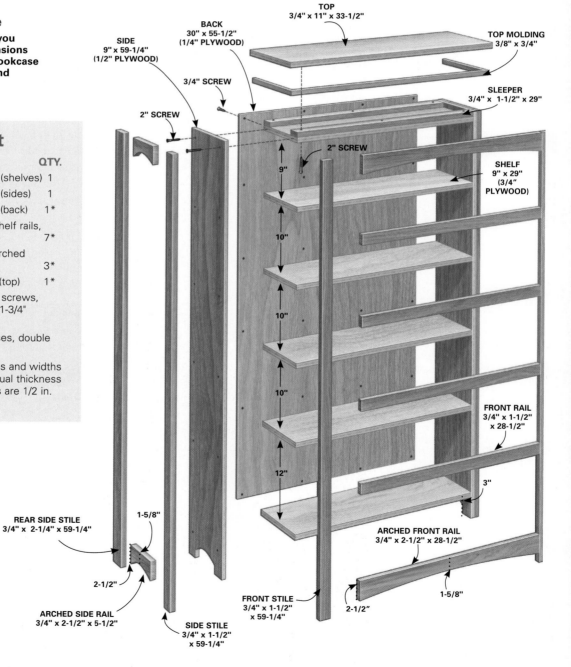

1 Crosscut the parts quickly and accurately using a stop block. The parts are too wide to cut in one pass, so flip the plank over after the first cut and make a second cut.

FIRST CUT

STOP BLOCK

2 Stack up the sides, mark the screw locations and drill through both sides at once. This cuts measuring and marking time, especially if you're building two bookcases.

(Photo 3). Before you cut the spacers, measure the thickness of the shelves. Although they're cut from 3/4-in. plywood, you'll probably find that they're actually a hair thinner than 3/4 in. To compensate, simply cut your spacers a bit longer (your 12-in. spacer may actually be 12-1/16 in. long, for example).

Inspect the sides before assembly and orient them so the best-looking veneer faces the outside of the case. Drill 3/32-in. pilot holes in the shelves using the side holes you drilled earlier as a guide. Also drill countersinks for the screw heads. Pilot bits drill a pilot hole and countersink in one step. Screw all the shelves to one side, then add the other side. Don't use glue. The screws alone are plenty strong, and any squeezed-out glue would prevent the plywood from absorbing stain later.

With all the shelves screwed into place, add the back. Measure the case from corner to corner in both directions; equal diagonal measurements means the case is square. Set the back in position and use a straightedge to mark the locations of the shelves. Fasten the back with screws rather than nails. That way, you can remove the back later to make finishing much easier.

Cut arched rails

Although straight rails would look good, for this bookcase, arches were cut in the top and bottom rails for a more elegant look. If you want curved rails, cut the top and bottom rails 28-5/8 in. long (you'll trim them to final length later). To mark the curves on the front arches, screw two blocks to a long scrap 35-7/8 in. apart. Bend a 36-in. metal straightedge between the blocks. Align the straightedge with the corners of the rail

(Photo 4). To mark the side rails, use the bottom of a 5-gallon bucket (or any circle that's about 10 in. in diameter).

If you end up with a small hump or two, smooth them with sandpaper. For a perfect arc, use the cutout as a sanding block (Photo 5). Cut 80-grit sandpaper into 1-in.-wide strips and apply a light coat of spray adhesive to their backs.

Next, cut the stiles to length, but don't cut the rails to length just yet. Before you attach any rails or stiles to the case, position the arched bottom rails on the case sides and use them to mark arcs. Cut these arcs with a jigsaw.

Add the trim and top

Fasten the rails and stiles following this sequence: Attach both of the side stiles along the front of the case. Align your nails with the shelves so they don't poke into the case. Then add one front stile. Set one front rail in place. Set the other front stile in place to check the length of the rail. If the length is right, cut the other rails to identical length. Attach the front rails and the second front stile. Don't worry if the rails and stiles aren't quite flush; you can sand them flush later. Next, add the side rails and the rear side stiles (Photo 6).

Two to four nails should be adequate for each part, although you may need more if the rail or stile is badly bowed. The glue will provide plenty of strength regardless of how many nails you use.

Allow the glue to set for an hour before you sand all the rails and stiles using a random orbital sander. Start with a 100-grit disc to sand flush uneven joints and remove any

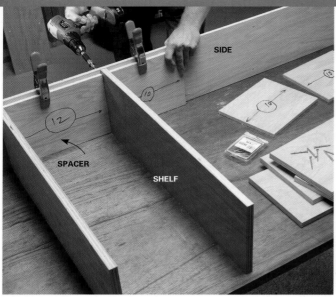

3 Screw the sides to the shelves using plywood spacers to hold the shelves in precise position.

4 Mark arches on the front rails using a simple arc jig made from wood scraps and a metal straightedge. Cut the arches with a jigsaw.

5 Sand out bumps or waves in the arches using the cutout. Stick sandpaper to the cutout with spray adhesive.

6 Glue and nail the trim to the plywood case. Use as few nails as possible—just enough to hold the parts in place while the glue sets.

shallow scratches. Then switch to a 150-grit disc.

To attach the top, glue 3/4-in. plywood sleepers to the top shelf as shown in Figure A. Then predrill and screw the top in place. The top molding is simply 3/8-in.-thick strips cut from leftover scraps. Miter the corners and glue the strips in place, again using as few nails as possible.

Finish the bookcase

Unscrew the bookcase's back for easier finishing. This bookcase was finished with stain and three coats of polyurethane.

With all the surfaces sanded to 150-grit, apply one coat of Minwax Red Oak stain. Shown here is a satin sheen for the clear finish. But because three coats of satin can look like a cloudy sheet of plastic over the wood, begin with two coats of gloss, sanding lightly with a 320-grit sanding sponge between coats. Fill nail holes with color-matched wood putty after the first coat. After the second coat, add a coat of satin polyurethane. After setting the bookcase in place, drive one 2-1/2-in. screw through the back and into a wall stud to prevent the bookcase from tipping forward.

Versatile box shelves

Not only do these storage boxes look nice, but they're easy to build—just fasten together four sides and put on the back. This is one of those rare wood-working projects that combines high style, low cost and super-simple construction.

Built from standard oak or birch plywood, these 12 x 12-in. boxes are very inexpensive to build. If you use standard ply-wood, you'll have to patch voids in the edges with wood filler or cover the edges with edge banding. To avoid that extra work, you can use Baltic birch plywood, which has better-looking, void-free edges. However, Baltic birch costs more than oak or birch. If your home center doesn't stock Baltic birch, look for it at a hardwood specialty store (search online for "hardwood suppliers" to find a source). Use standard 1/4-in. plywood for the backs even if you use Baltic birch for the sides.

Time and tools
You can build a dozen or more boxes in a few hours. Spend Saturday assembling the boxes and applying the finish, then hang them or fasten them together on Sunday. To complete the project, you'll need a table saw to rip the plywood sheets and a circular saw to crosscut the top, back and sides. A brad nailer will make nailing the boxes together a lot easier, but you could also use a hammer.

Elegant or practical

The boxes work equally well in a formal setting and a utilitarian room, like the laundry or garage. They offer an unlimited number of uses and arrangements.

Figure A:
Versatile box shelves

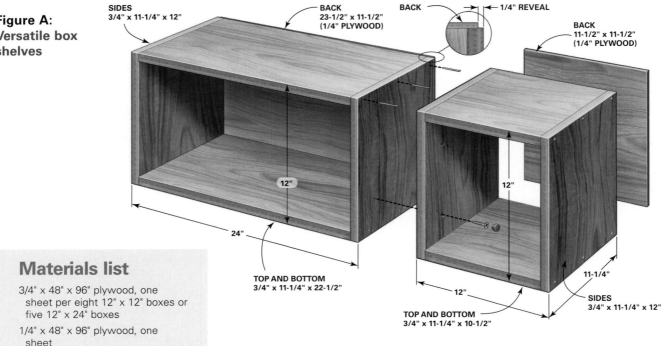

SIDES
3/4" x 11-1/4" x 12"

BACK
23-1/2" x 11-1/2"
(1/4" PLYWOOD)

BACK

1/4" REVEAL

BACK
11-1/2" x 11-1/2"
(1/4" PLYWOOD)

12"

12"

24"

TOP AND BOTTOM
3/4" x 11-1/4" x 22-1/2"

12"

11-1/4"

SIDES
3/4" x 11-1/4" x 12"

TOP AND BOTTOM
3/4" x 11-1/4" x 10-1/2"

Materials list

3/4" x 48" x 96" plywood, one
sheet per eight 12" x 12" boxes or
five 12" x 24" boxes

1/4" x 48" x 96" plywood, one
sheet

Cut the pieces to size

Get started by ripping the 3/4-in. plywood sheets into 11-1/4-in.-wide strips on a table saw. Cut out any dents and dings along the edges. It's important that these pieces be exactly the same width so the boxes will be aligned when they're stacked together. Also rip the 1/4-in. plywood sheet into 11-1/2-in.-wide strips.

Crosscut the box tops, bottoms, sides and back panels to length following Figure A, above. Make the crosscuts with a circular saw and a guide (Photo 1).

Assemble the boxes

Placing adjacent sides in a carpenter's square ensures crisp 90-degree angles when you fasten the corners together. Set the square over wood blocks and clamp it to your work surface. Set one side and the top or bottom in the square, apply wood glue along the edge, and nail the corner together with 1-1/2-in. brad nails (Photo 2).

Fasten the remaining corners the same way. Leave the box in the carpenter's square to keep the corners square, then add the back panel (Photo 3). The back panels are 1/2 in. smaller than the overall box size to leave a 1/4-in. reveal along each edge. This makes the edges less conspicuous when the boxes are installed.

Apply a finish

Once your boxes are fully assembled, it's time to apply a finish. Sand the boxes with 120-grit sandpaper to smooth out any rough spots, then wipe away the dust with a clean cloth.

1 Cut the box parts straight and square with a homemade crosscut guide. Stack two layers of plywood strips to cut perfectly matching parts fast.

If you want to paint the boxes, first prime them with a latex primer. Foam rollers work great for applying smooth coats of primer and paint. Brush on the primer in the corners, then roll the rest. Let the primer dry, lightly sand the boxes with 120-grit sandpaper, then apply the paint.

These stained shelves have two coats of stain—Minwax Golden Oak followed by Minwax Ebony—and two coats of a water-based polyurethane.

2 Build perfectly square boxes by assembling them against a carpenter's square. Drive three nails per corner to hold them together until the glue dries.

3 Center the back panel over the box, leaving a small gap along each side. Glue and nail the panel into place. The back panel keeps the box square.

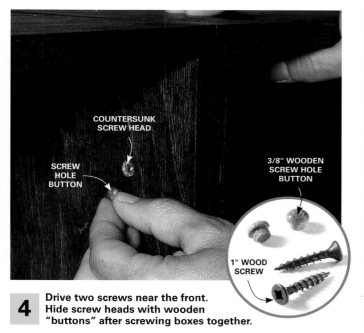

4 Drive two screws near the front. Hide screw heads with wooden "buttons" after screwing boxes together.

5 Arrange the boxes any way you like. Spaces between boxes can form compartments too.

Hang the boxes

Once the finish is dry, you can screw the boxes together or hang them on a wall. Be sure to hang the boxes with the side pieces overlapping the top and bottom, as shown in Figure A. This keeps the corner nails horizontal and makes the box stronger. Still, the boxes are not designed to hold a lot of weight. Countersinking the screw head and filling the hole with a 3/8-in. screw hole button hides the fastener. Screw hole buttons are available at home centers.

To fasten boxes together, first clamp them so they're perfectly flush. Then drill a 3/8-in.-diameter, 3/16-in.-deep countersink hole with a brad point drill bit ($3). The brad point won't tear or chip the veneer. Then drill 1/8-in. pilot holes in the countersink holes using a standard bit.

Drive a 1-in. wood screw into the pilot hole, countersinking the head. Dab paint or stain on the screw hole button and plug the hole (Photo 4).

To hang a box where there's a stud, drill two 1/8-in. pilot holes. Then spray-paint the heads of 2-1/2-in. screws and drive them into the stud at the pilot holes (there's no alternative to leaving the heads exposed). If there's not a stud available, use self-drilling anchors, such as E-Z Ancors. Drill pilot holes through the box into the wall, remove the box and drive the anchors into the wall at the marks. Then fasten the box to the wall using the screws included with the anchors.

Leaning tower of shelves

This shelf unit may look lightweight and easy to topple. But don't be fooled. It's a real workhorse. The 33-1/2-in. x 82-3/4-in. tower features five unique, tray-like shelves of different depths to hold a wide variety of items up to 13-1/4 in. tall. Despite its 10-degree lean, the unit is surprisingly sturdy, and its open design won't overpower a room.

Whether you choose to make this piece more functional, as in this office setting, or place it in a family room to showcase treasures, the basic construction is the same. Select the type of wood and stain or paint to dress it up or down to fit the look of any room.

All the materials can be purchased at home centers or lumberyards. The only special tools you'll need are a power miter saw for crisp angle cuts and a brad nailer for quick assembly and almost invisible joints. And you'll have to rustle up an old clothes iron for applying oak edge banding. Once you've gathered all the material, you can build the shelf unit in one afternoon.

Buying the wood

This unit was built with red oak and oak veneer plywood and finished with two coats of red oak stain. The beauty of this project is that any wood species will work.

Figure A:
Tower of shelves

Figure B:
Top of upright

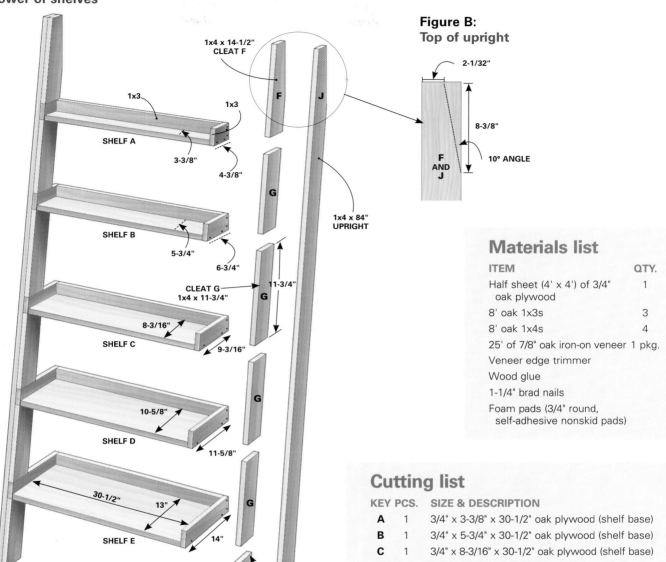

1x4 x 14-1/2"
CLEAT F

1x3

1x3

SHELF A

3-3/8"

4-3/8"

SHELF B

5-3/4"

6-3/4"

CLEAT G
1x4 x 11-3/4"

11-3/4"

8-3/16"

SHELF C

9-3/16"

10-5/8"

SHELF D

11-5/8"

30-1/2"   13"

SHELF E   14"

CLEAT H
1x4 x 10"

CUT CLEAT
ENDS
AT 10°

F   J

G

G

G

G

H

1x4 x 84"
UPRIGHT

2-1/32"

8-3/8"

F
AND
J   10° ANGLE

Materials list

ITEM	QTY.
Half sheet (4' x 4') of 3/4" oak plywood	1
8' oak 1x3s	3
8' oak 1x4s	4
25' of 7/8" oak iron-on veneer	1 pkg.
Veneer edge trimmer	
Wood glue	
1-1/4" brad nails	
Foam pads (3/4" round, self-adhesive nonskid pads)	

Cutting list

KEY	PCS.	SIZE & DESCRIPTION
A	1	3/4" x 3-3/8" x 30-1/2" oak plywood (shelf base)
B	1	3/4" x 5-3/4" x 30-1/2" oak plywood (shelf base)
C	1	3/4" x 8-3/16" x 30-1/2" oak plywood (shelf base)
D	1	3/4" x 10-5/8" x 30-1/2" oak plywood (shelf base)
E	1	3/4" x 13" x 30-1/2" oak plywood (shelf base)
A	2	3/4" x 2-1/2" x 4-3/8" oak (shelf A sides)*
B	2	3/4" x 2-1/2" x 6-3/4" oak (shelf B sides)*
C	2	3/4" x 2-1/2" x 9-3/16" oak (shelf C sides)*
D	2	3/4" x 2-1/2" x 11-5/8" oak (shelf D sides)*
E	2	3/4" x 2-1/2" x 14" oak (shelf E sides)*
A–E	5	3/4" x 2-1/2" x 30-1/2" oak (shelf backs)
F	2	3/4" x 3-1/2" x 14-1/2" oak shelf cleats (cut with 10-degree angles)
G	8	3/4" x 3-1/2" x 11-3/4" oak shelf cleats G (cut with 10-degree angles)
H	2	3/4" x 3-1/2" x 10" oak shelf cleats (cut with 10-degree angles)
J	2	3/4" x 3-1/2" x 84" oak uprights (cut with 10-degree angles)

*Front part of side cut at 10 degrees

If you plan to paint it, select alder or aspen for the solid parts and birch for the plywood.

One note when buying boards: Use a tape measure to check the "standard" dimensions of 1x3s and 1x4s. They sometimes vary in width and thickness. Also check the two full-length 1x4s you plan to use as the uprights to be sure they're straight, without warps or twists. And always examine the ends, edges and surface for blemishes or rough areas that won't easily sand out.

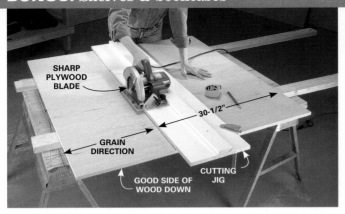

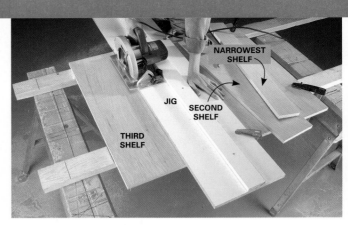

1 Cut 3/4-in. shelf plywood to width first, using a circular saw and a homemade jig for exact cuts. Use a sharp plywood blade and cut with the best side of the wood facing down to minimize splintering.

2 Cut the individual shelves, beginning with the narrowest, using the jig for perfectly straight cuts.

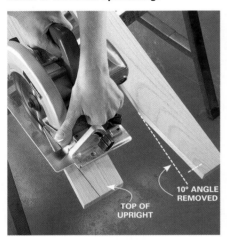

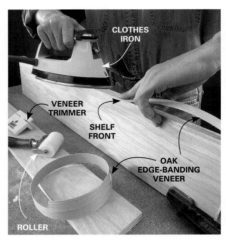

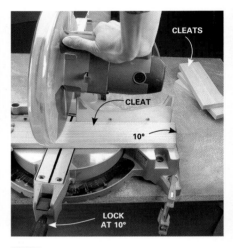

3 Cut both shelf uprights to length with a miter saw. Clamp to sawhorses. Mark the 10-degree angle at the top (dimensions in Figure B), then cut with a circular saw.

4 Iron edge-banding veneer to the front edge of all five shelves. Roll the entire surface to ensure a solid bond, and trim the edges.

5 To maintain accuracy, lock the miter box at 10 degrees, then cut all angled pieces—uprights, cleats and one end of shelf sides—without changing the table.

Cut plywood shelves first

Lay a couple of 2x4s across sawhorses (Photo 1) to cut the half sheet of 3/4-in. plywood cleanly and without pinching the saw blade. Since all five shelves are 30-1/2 in. wide, cut this width first, making sure the grain will run the long way across the shelves. Remember to wear safety glasses, earplugs and a dust mask. Make a homemade jig to fit your circular saw and clamp it to the plywood.

Next, cut all five shelf depths, starting with the smallest shelf (3-3/8 in.) first. Cut smallest to largest so you'll have enough wood to clamp the jig. **Important:** Make sure you account for the width of your saw blade when you cut each shelf.

Now mark and cut the top of all four 1x4 uprights (the end that rests against the wall), according to Photo 3 and the two dimensions provided in Figure B. Use a sharp blade in your circular saw to prevent splintering.

Select the best front of each plywood shelf, clamp it to the

bench on edge and sand it smooth with 150-grit paper on a sanding block. Then preheat a clothes iron to the "cotton" setting and run it over the top of the edge-banding veneer, making sure the veneer extends beyond all edges (Photo 4). Roll it smooth immediately after heating. Let each shelf edge cool for a couple of minutes before trimming and sanding the edges.

Cut the uprights and shelf frame next

Now enter the miter saw, which you use to make all the 90-degree straight cuts first (five shelf backs and 10 shelf sides; see Cutting list). **Important:** Remember that one end of each shelf side has a 10-degree cut, so first cut them square at their exact length, then cut the angle carefully so the long edge of each piece remains the same.

Next, rotate the miter saw table to the 10-degree mark and cut all the angle pieces. First cut the bottom of both uprights so each upright rests flat against the floor and wall (see Figure A). Then trim the top of the upright to match the bottom,

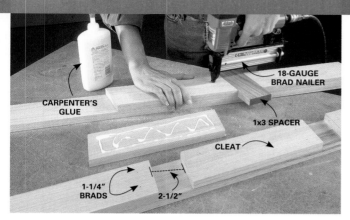

CARPENTER'S GLUE

18-GAUGE BRAD NAILER

1x3 SPACER

CLEAT

1-1/4" BRADS

2-1/2"

6 Glue and nail the shelf cleats to the uprights using a 1x3 spacer. Hold each cleat tight to the spacer.

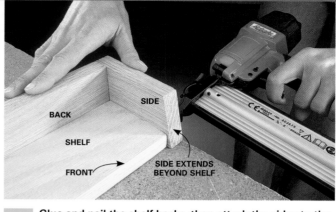

BACK

SIDE

SHELF

FRONT

SIDE EXTENDS BEYOND SHELF

7 Glue and nail the shelf backs, then attach the sides to the plywood shelves. Position the sides to overlap the shelf base as shown.

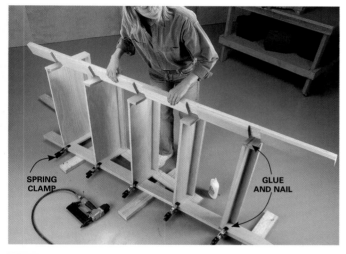

SPRING CLAMP

GLUE AND NAIL

8 Clamp the shelves into one upright. Spread glue in the shelf notches of the other upright, position it flush with the front of the shelves and nail. Flip the unit over and attach the other upright.

BAR CLAMP

1/2" GAP

9 Set the shelf unit against a straight wall, check for squareness and apply three bar clamps until the glue dries.

being careful to maintain the 84-in. total length. Next, cut the cleats based on the Cutting list dimensions, which are measured edge to edge (Photo 5 and Figure A). Leave the top cleats long and cut them to exact fit during assembly. Then, to speed finishing, use an orbital sander with 150-grit sandpaper to smooth all pieces before assembly.

Assemble uprights first, then the shelves

To begin assembly, lay out both uprights and all cleats to ensure that the angles are correct so the shelves will be level when the unit is against the wall. Then glue and nail the first cleat flush with the base of each upright (using five or six 1-1/4-in. brads) on each cleat. Work your way upward using 1x3 spacers (Photo 6). Make sure the spacer is the exact same width as the shelf sides! Set these aside to dry.

For shelf assembly, first glue and nail on the shelf backs. Next, apply the sides with glue and nails (Photo 7).

For final assembly, lay one upright on 2x4s, then clamp

on the shelves as shown in Photo 8. Apply the glue, position the second upright on top flush with the front edge of the shelves, then sink four 1-1/4-in. brads into each shelf from the upright side. Carefully turn the unit over and repeat the process to attach the second upright. Work quickly so the glue doesn't set. Lift the ladder shelf and place it upright against a straight wall. Check it with a framing square and flex it if necessary to square it up and to make sure that the uprights rest flat against the floor and wall (assuming your floor is level). Attach three bar clamps as shown in Photo 9 while the glue dries.

The shelf is highly stable as designed, but once you've stained or painted it, you can add self-adhesive foam gripping pads to the bottom of the uprights. And if you don't feel secure having it on a slippery floor, the unit's width is perfect for screwing the top of the uprights into wall studs.

NONSKID FOAM PAD

Index

Acknowledgments

For The Family Handyman

Editor in Chief	Ken Collier
Senior Editors	Travis Larson
	Gary Wentz
Associate Editors	Elisa Bernick
	Mary Flanagan
	Jeff Gorton
Senior Copy Editor	Donna Bierbach
Art Directors	Vern Johnson
	Becky Pfluger
	Marcia Roepke
Photographer	Tom Fenenga
Production Artist	Mary Schwender
Office Administrative Manager	Alice Garrett
Financial Assistant	Steven Charbonneau
Admin. Editorial Assistant	Roxie Filipkowski
Production Manager	Judy Rodriguez

Contributing Editors

Spike Carlsen	Dave Munkittrick
Tom Dvorak	Rick Muscoplat
Duane Johnson	David Radtke
Brett Martin	Jeff Timm

Contributing Art Directors

Roberta Peters	Bob Ungar
David Simpson	

Contributing Photographers

Tate Carlson	Ramon Moreno
Mike Krivit,	Shawn Nielsen
Krivit Photography	Bill Zuehlke

Illustrators

Steve Björkman	Don Mannes
Gabe De Matteis	Paul Perreault
Mario Ferro	Frank Rohrbach III
John Hartman	

Other Consultants

Charles Avoles, plumbing
Al Hildenbrand, electrical
Joe Jensen, Jon Jensen, carpentry
Dave MacDonald, structural engineer
William Nunn, painting
Dean Sorem, tile
Costas Stavrou, appliance repair
John Williamson, electrical
Les Zell, plumbing

For information about advertising in
The Family Handyman magazine, call (646) 293-6150

To subscribe to *The Family Handyman* magazine:
- By phone: (800) 285-4961
- By Internet: FHMservice@rd.com
- By mail: The Family Handyman
             Subscriber Service Dept.
             P.O. Box 6099
             Harlan, IA 51593-1599

Hundreds of articles published in *The Family Handyman* are available at familyhandyman.com.

Photocopies of articles are available for $3.00 each. Call (800) 285-4961 from 8 a.m. to 5 p.m. Central, Monday through Friday or send an e-mail to FHMservice@rd.com. Visa, MasterCard and Discover accepted.

We welcome your ideas and opinions.
Write: The Editor, *The Family Handyman*
2915 Commers Drive, Suite 700
Eagan, MN 55121
Fax: (651) 994-2250
E-mail: editors@thefamilyhandyman.com